To the Criminal Justice Fraternity

CRIMINAL JUSTICE IN THE AGE OF ALGORITHMS

PREDICTION, PUNISHMENT, AND THE LIMITS OF DELEGATED JUDGMENT

ADV. ISHAAN D. JOSHI

Made with ♥ on the Notion Press Platform
www.notionpress.com

Contents

Contents

Contents

Contents

Foreword

"The life of the law has not been logic; it has been experience."
Oliver Wendell Holmes Jr. (*The Common Law*, 1881.)

The authority that the law has always protected closely- to look into the person's eye, weigh the whole of their circumstance, and decide what is owed to them. That authority has never been purely rational. It is compounded of evidence, inference, experience, and something less easily named—a faculty for moral judgment that resists full articulation even by the judges who exercise it. The present work 'Criminal Justice in the Age of Algorithms' takes the above as subject, asking a question the profession has been slow to ask with the seriousness it deserves: what happens to that authority when a portion of the inference is outsourced to a machine?

Adv. Ishaan D. Joshi does not arrive at this question as a technologist enchanted by new tools, nor as a critic determined to resist them on principle. He arrives as a lawyer who understands that the criminal process is a moral and constitutional undertaking before it is an administrative one. Much of the existing literature on predictive justice treats the algorithm as a technical artifact to be audited for bias and folded into the machinery of the court as one more instrument among many. This book refuses that framing, insisting that the question is not only whether these systems work, but what becomes of judicial reasoning, evidentiary discipline, and human responsibility once they work alongside us.

The four principles that anchor the manuscript—Authority, Explainability, Contestability, and Harm—are not offered as a checklist for compliance. They function as something closer to a constitutional grammar: a way of asking, in any instance of algorithmic deployment, whether the institution has preserved what it cannot afford to lose. Authority insists that a human being remains answerable for the judgment rendered, however it was informed. Explainability insists that a person whose liberty is at stake be given reasons, not merely outputs. Contestability insists that no instrument of state power be placed beyond the reach of adversarial challenge. Harm insists that the consequences of error be reckoned honestly, not absorbed silently into aggregate statistics. Together these principles do not resolve the tension between efficiency and legitimacy; they make it visible, and refuse to let it be resolved by default.

What distinguishes this manuscript, in my reading, is its refusal of the false choice that structures public debate on this subject—between unreflective embrace of predictive tools and reflexive rejection of them. The book takes seriously the possibility that algorithmic systems may, under the right conditions, improve consistency and reduce the arbitrariness that has long afflicted criminal adjudication. But it takes equally seriously the danger that statistical characterizations of risk, however accurate at the population level, cannot substitute for the individualized moral reckoning legitimate punishment requires. The chapters on responsibility and moral agency are, to my mind, among the most important in the book, because they name a cost easy to overlook amid debates about accuracy and bias: the risk that defendants come to be seen, by the institutions meant to judge them as persons, primarily as instances of a category.

The manuscript's engagement with evidentiary epistemology deserves particular attention from practitioners. Conflating statistical prediction with legal proof is not a marginal error but a structural temptation built into the appearance of numerical certainty. A risk score expressed to two decimal places carries a rhetorical authority that testimony rarely commands. Courts untrained to interrogate base rates, calibration, and the difference between correlation and causation are poorly equipped to subject such evidence to the scrutiny the Constitution demands—a failure the book's attention to procurement and judicial statistical literacy addresses with welcome seriousness.

I have spent enough years in proximity to the criminal process and law to know that its legitimacy depends on something more fragile than correct outcomes: the felt experience, by the accused and the public, that someone has attended to the particulars of the case—that punishment has been reasoned toward, not merely arrived at. Algorithmic systems, deployed without the safeguards this book describes, threaten to substitute the appearance of rigor for the substance of reasoned judgment. Deployed with those safeguards, they may yet help courts grow more consistent without becoming less human, and which future arrives will be decided not by the technology itself but by institutional choices made in the years ahead. This book offers no comfort to those who wish predictive technology would disappear, nor to those who wish its adoption could proceed without friction; it offers a disciplined framework for thinking clearly about a transformation already underway. That clarity is its principal achievement. The present work 'Criminal Justice in the Age of Algorithms' belongs on the desk of every judge, legislator, and scholar who senses that something important is changing in the architecture of judicial authority, and who wants the vocabulary to say precisely what that something is.

Dr. Ashwani Pant

Program Director, MIT-WPU School of Law

About The Author

Adv. Ishaan D. Joshi

Adv. Ishaan D. Joshi is an interdisciplinary criminal-law, forensic-intelligence and behavioural-sciences scholar-practitioner working at the convergence of law, policing, forensics, criminal psychology, medico-legal analysis, cybercrime, national security, offender rehabilitation and institutional ethics. His work is centred on the study of crime as a legal, behavioural, evidentiary, technological, psychological and state-response phenomenon.

His professional and academic trajectory has been built around one central concern: how crime is conceived, committed, investigated, evidenced, interpreted, prosecuted, prevented and responded to by institutions of justice and security. Joshi works across criminal law, criminology, forensic psychology, cyberpsychology, predictive policing, police legitimacy, investigative intelligence, trauma, coercion, offender rehabilitation, medico-legal reasoning, digital conflict, counterterrorism ethics, wildlife crime, ecological criminality, handwriting-based behavioural observation and the ethical use of state power.

Adv. Ishaan D. Joshi currently serves as Founder and Director of the Centre for Crime Sciences and Forensic Intelligence, where he leads independent doctrinal and interdisciplinary research, mentors scholars, and develops serious work in crime sciences, forensic intelligence, criminal psychology and law. Alongside this, he holds academic roles involving teaching, curriculum development, centre advisory work, crime scene investigation, criminal psychology, logical reasoning, cybersecurity, forensics and criminal law. He is also engaged in forensic and criminal intelligence consultation, medico-legal and forensic psychology advisory work, legal practice as an advocate, international civil/commercial mediation, negotiation training, graphology, and expert peer review for international journals and scientific bodies across policing, psychiatry, military health, pharmacology, psychology and multidisciplinary research.

His publications, lectures and research examine the deep structures of criminal behaviour and justice: forensic psychology, cyberpsychology, predictive policing, AI ethics, prison rehabilitation, restorative justice, trauma, fear, police legitimacy, coercion, interrogation, criminal profiling, legal education, child protection, financial crime, counterterrorism ethics, digital evidence, wildlife crime and the relationship between power, vulnerability and evidence. Across books, articles, lectures, workshops, reviewing roles, forensic consultation and institutional work, Joshi seeks to build a rigorous Indian interdisciplinary framework for understanding crime not merely as an offence, but as a convergence of mind, method, evidence, technology, institution and consequence.

His long-term work is directed toward strengthening the intellectual and operational capacity of India's justice, policing, forensic, legal and security systems through serious scholarship, forensic intelligence, behavioural analysis, ethical reasoning, professional training, mediation, negotiation, and institution-building.

Preface

I wrote this book because something quiet has been happening in courtrooms, and quiet changes are the ones that later become irreversible. The judge still sits where the judge has always sat, the forms still move, the orders still come out, the rituals of legitimacy still play their part. Yet the decision—what it is, how it is formed, what counts as a "reason," and who can truly challenge it—is increasingly being pre-shaped by instruments that speak in numbers, categories, and recommendations. Risk scores. Sentencing recommender systems. Pretrial "public safety" matrices. Predictive analytics marketed as consistency, neutrality, and evidence-based governance. This is not merely an upgrade of efficiency. It is a renovation of authority.

If you are reading me as a lawyer, you will recognise the doctrinal questions immediately: due process, disclosure, the right to contest, standards of review, the meaning of reasons, the reach of equality, the integrity of evidence, and the constitutional limits on coercion. If you are reading me as a psychologist, you will see the behavioural problems beneath the doctrine: how human beings anchor on numbers, defer to machine outputs, rationalise deference as "objectivity," and then misremember abdication as prudence. If you are reading me as an investigator, you will feel the missing discipline: where is the validation before authority, the chain of custody for outputs, the known error, the conditions of use, the contamination pathways, the incentives of procurement, the pressure of caseload, the feedback loops that quietly turn prediction into destiny?

My work has always lived at the intersections—criminal law with behavioural reality, courtroom literacy with forensic method, ethical theory with operational constraints. I have served alongside judicial office, worked with institutions and practitioners, trained students in crime scene discipline, and lived in a monastery long enough to understand that "reasoning" is not a vocabulary list. It is a moral craft under conditions of uncertainty, temptation, fear, and power. The courtroom is precisely such a place: it is where the state's power becomes intimate, where liberty can be taken in the name of the public, and where the system must be able to answer for itself.

This book is therefore structured as a disciplined journey, and each Part is deliberately named to reflect the level at which the problem must be confronted.

Part I — First Principles: What "Drawing The Line" Even Means

This part begins with first principles. Before we debate tools, we must be precise about what courts are for, what punishment claims to be, and what legitimacy actually is. Here I examine judicial authority in an age of automation, the temptation to confuse administrative efficiency with moral justification, the pressure algorithmic systems place on retributive and utilitarian theories, the behavioural basis of legitimacy, and the framework that will guide the entire text: authority, explainability, contestability, and harm.

Part II — The Courtroom AI Stack: Tools, Claims, and Failure Modes

This part dissects what is actually being adopted. Courts are not adopting one monolithic "AI"; they are adopting layers—risk assessment instruments, guideline calculators, optimisation tools, and predictive models at the point of bail and sentencing. This Part asks the hard question marketing avoids: what exactly is being predicted? What ontology is hidden inside a risk score? What happens when optimisation logic seeps into moral judgment? How do feedback loops and model drift convert assistance into structural bias?

Part III — Evidence, Proof, and The Epistemology Of Prediction

This is where the forensic discipline becomes uncompromising. Probability is not proof. Calibration is not causation. A statistical output is not a fact in the way a witnessed act is a fact. Courts have always dealt with uncertainty, but through evidentiary safeguards—admissibility thresholds, standards of proof, adversarial testing, and reasoned justification. This Part examines base rates, priors, thresholds, error rates, and the epistemic gap between correlation and culpability, and defends the principle that liberty cannot be curtailed without meaningful capacity to challenge the instrument influencing that decision.

Part IV — Fairness: Competing Definitions and Legal Consequences

This part confronts fairness without slogans. Fairness metrics often conflict; they cannot all be satisfied simultaneously. Disparate impact is not merely statistical variance but a constitutional and moral question. The equality paradox—group justice versus individual justice—becomes acute at scale. Procedural justice, dignity, and intelligibility are treated here not as soft ideals but as behavioural infrastructure for legitimacy.

Part V — Responsibility, Agency, and The Psychology of Blame

This part turns to the anthropology of criminal law. If courts forecast risk, how does that alter our conception of agency? If persons are presented as probabilities, how does that reshape culpability and mercy? Criminal law claims to punish agents, not data clusters. This Part interrogates the psychological and philosophical consequences of institutionalising prediction within a system that professes to respect personhood.

Part VI — Legitimacy, Trust, and Public Consent

This is where we shall study the twin pathologies that accompany technological authority. One rejects the machine the moment it errs; the other treats it as neutral truth even when contestable. Neither posture sustains a constitutional democracy. The task is to construct institutions that deserve trust—through transparency, contestability, and accountable design.

Part VII — Due Process, Rights, and The Rule of Law

Here, I address transparency as a legal right, explainability as an operational necessity, the debated right to a human decision-maker, equality of arms when systems are proprietary, and standards of judicial review when algorithmic tools influence adjudication. Here the language of constitutionalism meets the architecture of code.

Part VIII — Institutions, Incentives, and Governance

This is where the book moves beyond theory to institutional reality. It examines procurement incentives, vendor opacity, accountability gaps, comparative governance models, and the urgent need for statistical literacy and cognitive bias training among judicial actors. Many failures in this domain are not mathematical; they are governance failures.

Part IX — Experimental And Empirical Pathways

This part outlines courtroom experiments, human–AI collaboration studies, legitimacy measurement frameworks, counterfactual simulations, and the ethics of field trials in coercive environments. Responsible deployment demands empirical humility.

Part X — The Line Itself: A Normative Blueprint For Limits

The book concludes with a principled framework. It articulates a typology of permissible uses—assist, inform, recommend, decide—draws red lines where automation must not replace human judgment, proposes institutional safeguards for humane prediction, and sketches a constitutional theory of algorithmic punishment. The aim is not prohibition for its own sake, but clarity about where authority must remain unmistakably human.

A word about method. I refuse two temptations. The first is the vendor's temptation to reduce liberty to workflow efficiency. The second is the moralist's temptation to treat every technological instrument as illegitimate. The real danger is corruption of reasoning—where outputs become de facto reasons, where "human in the loop" becomes ceremonial, and where responsibility diffuses until no one owns the decision and yet someone suffers its consequence. This book is written for judges, lawyers, investigators, criminologists, psychologists, policymakers, and students who are serious about the integrity of criminal justice. I am not asking you to become engineers. I am asking you to become disciplined custodians of authority. No authority without validation. No deprivation of liberty without meaningful contestability. No borrowed moral certainty from a number.

Courts have never promised perfection. They have promised reasons that can be tested. If we allow models to influence punishment, we must demand at least the same standard from the instrument and from the institution that deploys it. Pressure of caseload is real. Resource constraints are real. The political demand for consistency is real. But pressure is never a moral defence when liberty is at stake. A court cannot become less accountable because it is busy. A justice system cannot become less humane because the spreadsheet is persuasive.

If you read this book patiently, you will see courtroom AI not as a futuristic novelty but as a familiar constitutional struggle in new clothing: the state's temptation to automate coercion, the human tendency to defer to authoritative outputs, and the enduring obligation to remain answerable in human language to the human beings we judge. That is the standard I have written toward. Not because I am romantic about courts, but because I am realistic about power.

Adv. Ishaan D. Joshi

(Pune, India, 30th June 2026)

Part I — First Principles: What "Drawing the Line" Even Means

CHAPTER I

From Discretion to Delegation: The New Architecture of Judicial Decision-Making

The Quiet Renovation of the Courtroom

If you walk into a courtroom today with the eyes of a forensic examiner rather than the ears of a litigator, you will notice something subtle: the centre of gravity is shifting. The judge still sits where the judge has always sat, the parties still rise, the record still opens, and the ritual still performs legitimacy in public. Yet behind the familiar theatre, the decision itself increasingly arrives pre-shaped by instruments—risk scores, guideline calculators, pretrial "public safety" matrices, sentencing recommender systems, triage tools for case management, and predictive analytics that promise consistency where human discretion has historically produced variance (Monahan and Skeem, 2016; Starr, 2014; Wenzelburger, 2025). The transition is often presented as a technical upgrade, as if courts are simply adopting a faster abacus. But it is not an upgrade of arithmetic; it is a renovation of authority. Discretion is being reconfigured into delegation—sometimes openly, often by stealth, and frequently through the respectable language of "support," "assistance," and "evidence-based decision-making" (Kinchin, 2024; Winter, 2022). The first task of serious scholarship is to name the architecture accurately before one can judge it.

Discretion Was Never a Blank Space

You will sometimes hear that discretion is "subjective" and therefore inferior to algorithmic prediction. That is a shallow reading of what discretion is. Judicial discretion, at its best, is not mood; it is structured moral reasoning under constraints: proportionality, individualisation, reasons-giving, and the capacity of the system to publicly justify coercion (Duff, 2001; von Hirsch, 1976). Even when judges disagree, they are not merely disagreeing; they are choosing between rival moral emphases—desert versus prevention, rehabilitation versus incapacitation, mercy versus deterrence—while staying within legal limits and evidentiary standards (Hart, 1968; Duff, 2001). The point of discretion is not that it is free. The point is that it allows the court to treat a defendant as a person with agency rather than a file with a score. When you replace discretion with delegation, the question is not simply whether predictions get better; the question is whether the system is still making a decision that can be owned, explained, contested, and reviewed in a way that preserves the moral grammar of criminal law (Kinchin, 2024; Fischman-Afori, 2025).

Delegation Changes What "A Reason" Means

Courts run on reasons. Not feelings, not outputs—reasons. A reason is a claim that can be examined, challenged, and either sustained or rejected by a higher court or by the public conscience. Delegation changes the nature of reasons by inserting a new kind of object into the record: not testimony, not expert opinion in the classical sense, but statistical inference packaged as a recommendation. Here the forensic analogy becomes useful. In forensic science, a tool is not admissible merely because it is "accurate on average." The tool must be validated in the conditions of use, its error rates must be understood, its limitations must be stated, and its outputs must be interpretable in a way that does not mislead the trier of fact (Mnookin et al., 2011). Risk and sentencing algorithms are increasingly treated as if they are neutral instruments, but in truth they are socio-technical systems: they reflect choices about outcomes, trade-offs between false positives and false negatives, definitions of "risk," and the institutional incentives of those who build and procure them (Barocas, Hardt and Narayanan, 2023; Greene, 2022). The moment an algorithmic output becomes a reason rather than merely a datum, the legal system is importing a whole epistemology—often without admitting that it has done so.

The Forensic Lens: Validation Before Authority

A forensic mindset demands a strict sequence: define the proposition, define the method, test the method, disclose limitations, and then—only then—assign weight. Algorithmic decision aids in court routinely invert this order. They are adopted because they are administratively attractive, then justified after the fact by references to "objectivity" or "consistency," and only later scrutinised for bias, drift, and contestability (Starr, 2014;

Winter, 2022). Yet the forensic question is simple: what is the instrument's known performance when used on the population before this court, in this jurisdictional ecology, under these data conditions, with these feedback loops? Work on predictive inconsistency shows that equally defensible modelling choices can produce materially different risk scores for the same individual, meaning the "fact" of risk is often underdetermined by the same data (Greene, 2022). Other empirical work illustrates that algorithmic predictions can be no more accurate than lay predictions in certain settings, challenging the comforting belief that the machine is inherently superior (Dressel and Farid, 2018; Lin, 2020). If the system is going to use an instrument to justify depriving liberty, the burden should not be on the accused to prove the instrument is flawed; the burden should be on the state to show the instrument is forensically fit for purpose, with transparent performance characteristics and a clear account of what it is and is not measuring (Monahan and Skeem, 2016; Barocas, Hardt and Narayanan, 2023).

The "Average Accuracy" Trap and the Individual Before the Court

A courtroom is not a laboratory. Most claims made for algorithmic tools rely on population-level performance. But sentencing and bail are individual-level acts of coercion. This is where the moral injury can occur: the state may treat an individual as the bearer of a group-based probability rather than as a person whose culpability and circumstances demand individualised judgement (Starr, 2014; Ugwudike, 2025). The trade-off is not abstract. A false positive in a risk context can mean unnecessary detention, harsher supervision, or a longer sentence for someone who would not have reoffended; a false negative can mean preventable harm to a future victim. Different legal cultures resolve this tension differently, but every legal culture must resolve it openly, because it is a choice about who bears the cost of error (Greene, 2022; Berk, 2024). A purely technocratic posture—"the model is calibrated"—is morally insufficient because calibration does not tell you whether the decision is legitimate in the eyes of those subjected to it, nor does it tell you whether the system has preserved the normative commitments embedded in criminal responsibility (Tyler, 2006; Fine et al., 2025).

Behavioural Reality: Judges Do Not Use Tools as Designers Imagine

The most dangerous myth in courtroom AI is the fantasy of "decision support" that remains politely in the background. Human beings do not consult advice the way manuals assume they do. Behavioural research repeatedly shows that people anchor on numbers, defer to authoritative-seeming outputs, and adjust insufficiently even when warned about limitations (Kahneman, 2011; Grgić-Hlača et al., 2019). In judicial settings, the psychological risk is twofold: automation bias (overreliance) and abdication bias (shifting responsibility onto the tool), both of which corrupt the reasons-giving function of adjudication (Grgić-Hlača et al., 2019; Winter, 2022). Even when a judge believes they are "using it cautiously," the mere presence of an output can structure attention: it frames the defendant as "high risk," primes interpretations of ambiguous facts, and quietly narrows the moral imagination available for mercy, rehabilitation, or contextualised proportionality (Kahneman, 2011; Kinchin, 2024). The forensic point is not sentimental. It is operational: if a tool predictably biases the human decision-maker's cognition, then the tool is part of the causal chain of the outcome and must be evaluated as such (Grgić-Hlača et al., 2019; Portela et al., 2025).

Procedural Justice: Why People Accept Decisions They Dislike

Courts survive not by force alone but by consent—consent shaped by legitimacy. The strongest finding in procedural justice research is that people's willingness to accept outcomes is driven less by whether they win and more by whether the process feels fair, dignified, and voice-respecting (Tyler, 2006; Tyler, 2025). This matters because delegation threatens a core element of procedural justice: the sense that a person was heard by another person who had the authority—and the humanity—to weigh their story. Algorithmic systems, especially opaque ones, risk creating what has been called a procedural gap: they may optimise distributive outcomes while eroding "voice," contestability, and intelligible reasons (Kinchin, 2024; Fischman-Afori, 2025). Experimental work on public perceptions of judges using AI tools suggests legitimacy is contingent and fragile: acceptance varies with perceived transparency, perceived fairness, and whether the tool seems to replace rather than assist the judge (Fine et al., 2025). If you care about compliance, desistance, and social trust in the justice system, you cannot treat legitimacy as a public relations garnish. It is behavioural infrastructure.

The Case Law as a Symptom: When the Court Accepts the Black Box

One of the clearest symptoms of the new architecture is how courts have approached proprietary risk instruments. In State v Loomis the use of a risk assessment tool at sentencing was upheld with cautionary limitations and warnings, even as concerns about proprietary opacity and the ability of the defence to meaningfully challenge the instrument persisted in scholarly debate (Harvard Law Review, 2017; Engel, 2021). The jurisprudential significance is not confined to one jurisdiction. The broader pattern is what should interest you: courts are being invited to accept algorithmic products as if they were neutral expertise while simultaneously tolerating constraints that would be intolerable if the "expert" were a human witness refusing disclosure of methodology. A forensic discipline would call this a mismatch of standards: we demand disclosure and cross-examination for fragile human testimony, yet we are tempted to relax those demands for systems that can scale influence across thousands of cases (Mnookin et al., 2011; Kinchin, 2024). That temptation is precisely the point at which delegation becomes a constitutional problem rather than a managerial one.

Global Governance is Moving, But It Does Not Solve the Courtroom Problem

The regulatory and human-rights conversation has accelerated rapidly. The European Union's risk-based governance approach and the Council of Europe's legally binding convention both treat certain justice-related uses of AI as high stakes for rights, oversight, accountability, and non-discrimination (Cancela-Outeda, 2024; Council of Europe AI Convention analysis, 2025). These instruments matter because they signal an emerging global consensus: criminal justice is not a low-risk domain for experimentation. Yet no regulation can substitute for the internal discipline of adjudication itself. A statute can require transparency, but it cannot by itself teach a judge how not to anchor on a number. A treaty can affirm dignity and autonomy, but it cannot guarantee that the accused experiences voice if the courtroom's practical culture treats the tool as the "real" decider. Governance frameworks are necessary, but the line-drawing work ultimately lives inside legal reasoning: in what counts as evidence, what counts as a reason, and what standards of contestability a court insists upon before allowing an algorithmic output to influence liberty (Kinchin, 2024; Fischman-Afori, 2025).

Delegation Rewrites Responsibility: Who is Morally Accountable?

If you want to see the moral stakes clearly, ask a simple question: when an algorithmic recommendation contributes to an unjust outcome, who carries the moral burden? The vendor will say it is only a tool. The procurement authority will say it complied with the relevant guidelines. The judge may say they merely considered it among many factors. The diffusion of responsibility is not a side effect; it is a structural risk of delegation (Winter, 2022; He, 2025). Criminal law, however, is built on attribution: who did what, with what mental state, under what circumstances. It is intellectually incoherent to operate an institutional system that punishes individuals on strict theories of responsibility while permitting itself to evade responsibility through bureaucratic diffusion when its own instruments cause harm. The moral asymmetry is corrosive. It undermines the legitimacy of punishment itself, because the state begins to look like a machine that can act but cannot answer (Duff, 2001; Tyler, 2006).

The Behavioural Anatomy of "Risk" and the Myth of Stable Disposition

Risk is not merely a number; it is a story about a person. Many risk instruments function by mapping prior contact with the system—arrests, convictions, compliance histories—onto a forecast of future behaviour. But criminology and behavioural science remind us that such data are not pure reflections of "criminality." They are also reflections of policing patterns, surveillance intensity, socio-economic exposure, and structural inequality (Starr, 2014; Hung, 2023). When risk models treat system-contact variables as proxies for individual propensity, they can reify disadvantage as dangerousness and convert social history into personal fate (Barocas, Hardt and Narayanan, 2023; Berk, 2024). From a behavioural analysis standpoint, this is a category error: the model may be detecting institutional pathways rather than moral traits. A system that cannot distinguish propensity from exposure is not merely imperfect; it is conceptually misaligned with criminal law's claim to judge persons for culpable acts rather than for socially produced probabilities (Duff, 2001; Starr, 2014). The danger is not simply bias in the colloquial sense. The danger is moral misclassification.

"Evidence-Based" Cannot Mean "Morally Unexamined"

The phrase "evidence-based sentencing" has enormous rhetorical power, but it can also be an intellectual trap. Evidence-based is admirable only when the evidence pertains to the right question. If the question is "how do we reduce reoffending?" risk tools and targeted interventions may contribute something of value, particularly if they are used to divert low-risk individuals away from incarceration and toward support (Monahan and Skeem, 2016). But if the question is "what punishment does this person deserve for this offence?" then importing risk as a determinant threatens proportionality and desert, because it shifts the centre of punishment from the completed act to predicted future acts (Starr, 2014; Taylor, 2023). Legal systems differ in how they balance desert and prevention, but the philosophical point is stable: punishment justified by prediction must confront the moral difference between blameworthiness and dangerousness. The more a system collapses that distinction, the more it risks becoming preventive detention in formal clothing (Hart, 1968; von Hirsch, 1976).

Human–Machine Collaboration: The Real Problem Is Not Replacement, It Is Corruption

Many institutional actors will reassure you: "The algorithm does not decide; the judge decides." But the serious question is not formal. It is functional. If the algorithm predictably shapes outcomes in a direction the judge would not have chosen independently, then the tool has causal power in adjudication. Studies of machine advice in legal decision contexts show modest but meaningful shifts in human judgement, and they also show that warnings do not reliably neutralise the influence (Grgić-Hlača et al., 2019; Engel, 2021). This is where the court must think like an investigator. In forensic reconstruction, you do not ask what an actor claims influenced them; you ask what actually influenced the outcome given the environment, cues, and pressures. Courts operate under heavy caseloads, time pressure, and institutional risk aversion, all of which make them more likely to accept a tool that offers a defensible-looking rationale (Wenzelburger, 2025; Winter, 2022). Delegation thrives in precisely those conditions. If the justice system wants AI assistance without moral corrosion, it must design the collaboration deliberately: insist on contestability, require intelligible reasons, prevent proprietary opacity from blocking cross-examination, and train decision-makers in statistical reasoning and cognitive bias so they can resist the seductive certainty of a number (Kahneman, 2011; Barocas, Hardt and Narayanan, 2023).

The Line Begins with a Forensic Rule: No Output Without a Chain of Custody

A forensic scientist would not accept a sample without a chain of custody, because provenance matters. Algorithmic outputs also require provenance: what data were used, how were they cleaned, what variables were included, what definitions were chosen, what population the model was trained on, what time period, what known error rates, what drift monitoring, what auditing, and what documentation of limitations. Without that, the "score" is not evidence; it is an assertion with institutional authority but without forensic accountability (Mnookin et al., 2011; Barocas, Hardt and Narayanan, 2023). This is not an academic preference. It is the minimum standard for a system that uses outputs to constrain liberty. If a court cannot require such provenance because the vendor claims secrecy, then the court has already conceded the architecture of delegation: it has accepted that commercial confidentiality can override the accused's meaningful ability to challenge the state's basis for coercion (Harvard Law Review, 2017; Kinchin, 2024). That concession should trouble any legal culture that takes due process seriously.

The Second Line: Preserve Voice as a Structural Feature, Not a Courtesy

The next line is behavioural and moral: preserve voice. Procedural justice is not satisfied by a polite hearing if the decisive weight has already been assigned by an opaque instrument. A future-fit court must build "voice" into the lifecycle of algorithmic use—through disclosure, meaningful explanation, opportunity to contest inputs and assumptions, and the capacity for the defendant's narrative to be integrated as more than noise (Kinchin, 2024; Fischman-Afori, 2025). The idea of "due process by design" is useful precisely because it refuses to treat procedural fairness as an afterthought bolted onto a predictive system; it treats fairness as architecture (Fischman-Afori, 2025). If you want rehabilitation to be credible, and if you want the punished person to accept the legitimacy of the sanction, the person must be able to understand the reason for the decision in human terms, not merely hear that "the model recommended it" (Tyler, 2006; Fine et al., 2025).

The Third Line: Keep Moral Judgement Human, Even When Prediction Is Machine

There is a place for prediction in justice, but prediction must not become moral judgement. Prediction can assist in logistical and preventive domains—allocation of support services, identifying who might benefit from intervention, informing supervision intensity—provided safeguards prevent discriminatory feedback loops and the system remains contestable (Monahan and Skeem, 2016; Berk, 2024). But the moral core of sentencing—proportionality, culpability, and the public meaning of punishment—cannot be offloaded to a model without transforming the justice system into a technocratic risk manager (Duff, 2001; Taylor, 2023). If you accept that transformation, say so openly: admit that the system no longer primarily punishes for wrongdoing but manages for predicted harm. Many systems will not want to admit it because the admission reveals the constitutional and moral costs. That is why delegation often proceeds quietly.

A Reader's Test: If You Cannot Cross-Examine It, Should It Restrict Liberty?

Let me leave you with a working test that is both forensic and moral. Imagine a defendant asks, "Why am I being detained?" If the answer is "because this model predicts you are high risk," the defendant's next question is predictable: "How does it know?" If the system cannot provide an intelligible answer that can be challenged—inputs, method, limitations, and relevance to the individual—then the system has shifted from adjudication to administration. The state may still call it justice, but it has lost a key feature of justice: answerability. Delegation becomes most dangerous when it is normalised as common sense. Your task, as a serious reader of law and behaviour, is to refuse that normalisation. Treat algorithmic tools the way you would treat any powerful forensic instrument: validate, disclose, contextualise, and constrain. Then—and only then—allow them to assist, never to substitute, the human act of judging a human being.

References

- Barocas, S., Hardt, M. and Narayanan, A. (2023) Fairness and Machine Learning: Limitations and Opportunities. Cambridge, MA: MIT Press.
- Berk, R.A. (2024) 'Improving fairness in criminal justice algorithmic risk assessments', Sociological Methods & Research.
- Cancela-Outeda, C. (2024) 'The EU's AI Act: A framework for collaborative governance', Computer Law & Security Review.
- Council of Europe (2025) 'Council of Europe Framework Convention on Artificial Intelligence and human rights, democracy and the rule of law'.
- 'Criminal Law—Sentencing Guidelines—Wisconsin Supreme Court Requires Warning before Use of Algorithmic Risk Assessments in Sentencing' (2017) Harvard Law Review, 130, pp. 1530–.
- Dressel, J. and Farid, H. (2018) 'The accuracy, fairness, and limits of predicting recidivism', Science Advances, 4(1).
- Duff, R.A. (2001) Punishment, Communication, and Community. Oxford: Oxford University Press.
- Engel, C. (2021) 'Machine advice with a warning about machine limitations', Journal of Legal Analysis, 13(1), pp. 284–.
- Fine, A. et al. (2025) 'Public perceptions of judges' use of AI tools in courtroom decision-making'.
- Fischman-Afori, O. (2025) 'Due process by design: Enhancing fairness and trust in AI decision-making through procedural justice theory'.
- Greene, T. (2022) 'Predictive inconsistency in criminal justice algorithmic risk prediction tools', Journal of the Royal Statistical Society: Series A, 185(S2), pp. S692–.

- Grgić-Hlača, N. et al. (2019) 'Human decision making with machine advice'.
- Hart, H.L.A. (1968) Punishment and Responsibility: Essays in the Philosophy of Law. Oxford: Oxford University Press.
- He, J. (2025) 'Algorithm power and legal boundaries: rights conflicts in AI governance', Laws, 14(4), 54.
- Hung, T.W. (2023) 'Predictive policing and algorithmic fairness', Synthese.
- Kahneman, D. (2011) Thinking, Fast and Slow. New York: Farrar, Straus and Giroux.
- Kinchin, N. (2024) '"Voiceless": the procedural gap in algorithmic justice', International Journal of Law and Information Technology.
- Kleinberg, J. et al. (2018) 'Human decisions and machine predictions', The Quarterly Journal of Economics, 133(1), pp. 237–293.
- Lin, Z.J. et al. (2020) 'The limits of human predictions of recidivism', Science Advances.
- Martínez-Garay, L. (2023) 'Evidence-based sentencing and scientific evidence'.
- Mnookin, J.L. et al. (2011) 'The need for a research culture in the forensic sciences', UCLA Law Review, 58, pp. 725–779.
- Monahan, J. and Skeem, J.L. (2016) 'Risk assessment in criminal sentencing', Annual Review of Clinical Psychology, 12, pp. 489–513.
- Okidegbe, N. (2022) 'The democratizing potential of algorithms?'.
- Portela, M. et al. (2025) 'A comparative user study of human predictions in algorithm-based risk assessment', Applied Psychology: An International Review.
- Scaria, A.G. et al. (2024) 'Algorithms and recidivism: a multidisciplinary systematic review', AAAI/AI Ethics Proceedings, pp. –.
- Starr, S.B. (2014) 'Evidence-based sentencing and the scientific rationalization of discrimination', Stanford Law Review, 66(4), pp. 803–871.
- State v Loomis (2016) 881 N.W.2d 749 (Wisconsin Supreme Court); cert denied (2017) 137 S Ct 2290.
- Taylor, I. (2023) 'Justice by algorithm: the limits of AI in criminal sentencing'.
- Tyler, T.R. (2006) Why People Obey the Law. 2nd edn. Princeton, NJ: Princeton University Press.

- Tyler, T.R. (2025) 'Legitimacy-based policing', Criminology & Public Policy.
- Ugwudike, P. (2025) 'Sentencing and risk assessment algorithms', in De Gruyter Handbook of Digital Criminology. Berlin: De Gruyter.
- Wang, X. (2024) 'Algorithmic discrimination: examining its types and regulatory approaches'.
- Wenzelburger, G. (2025) 'Smart justice? Making sense of the rise of algorithm-based criminal justice'.
- Winter, C.K. (2022) 'The challenges of artificial judicial decision-making for liberal democracy', in Springer.

CHAPTER II

Justice Beyond Efficiency: Why Accuracy Is Not a Moral Theory

The Seduction of the Clean Answer

You will be told—sometimes politely, sometimes with the confidence of a consultant—that the courtroom's future lies in "better decisions," and that "better" can be read straight off a spreadsheet: higher accuracy, lower error, faster throughput, fewer inconsistencies. It sounds humane, because it sounds competent. It sounds modern, because it sounds measurable. Yet the first duty of a serious reader is to notice what has been smuggled in with that single word "better." Accuracy is a property of predictions; justice is a property of institutions. Accuracy describes how often an output matches an outcome; justice describes whether the institution is entitled to use coercion in the way it does, for the reasons it gives, under procedures that treat persons as persons rather than as variables. This is not a poetic objection. It is a forensic one. In any forensic discipline, a highly accurate instrument can still be misused if it answers the wrong question, or if its use corrupts the decision process, or if its output is treated as authority rather than as evidence that must be weighed and challenged (Robertson, Vignaux and Berger, 2016; Cooper, 2019). Courts are now importing predictive systems—risk scores, sentencing recommendations, triage engines—because they promise efficiency and consistency, but the moral error is subtle: the system begins to speak as though correctness of forecast is the same thing as legitimacy of punishment (Starr, 2014; Kinchin, 2024).

Why the Courtroom Is Not a Laboratory

A laboratory seeks truth under controlled conditions; a courtroom seeks justified conclusions under contested conditions. The distinction matters because predictive tools are usually validated, if at all, on population-level aggregates, while judicial decisions are individual acts of public coercion—detention, punishment, restriction of movement, stigma, sometimes lifelong consequences. An algorithm can be "accurate on average" while being systematically harsh on the margins where law is supposed to protect the vulnerable, and it can be "fair by one metric" while violating fairness as experienced by those subjected to it (Barocas, Hardt and Narayanan, 2023). This is why debates that remain trapped in performance metrics tend to miss the institutional fact that legitimacy is behavioural: people comply, desist, cooperate, and accept adverse outcomes when they believe they were treated with dignity, had voice, and received reasons they could understand and contest (Tyler, 2006; Fischman-Afori, 2025). If you increase accuracy but erode legitimacy, you may gain a short-term administrative win and lose the long-term behavioural infrastructure that makes criminal justice function without permanent violence (Tyler, 2006; Fine et al., 2025).

Accuracy Answers "What Will Happen," Not "What Ought to Be Done"

The deepest confusion in algorithmic justice is the collapse of two questions that law has spent centuries keeping apart. Prediction asks, "What is likely to happen?" Moral judgement asks, "What ought we to do, given what has been done?" Criminal law, in its classical structure, ties state coercion to culpable acts—what was done, with what mental state, in what circumstances—and it limits punishment through proportionality and desert even when prevention would be tempted to go further (Hart, 1968; von Hirsch, 1976). When risk scores enter sentencing or bail, they introduce a second logic: management of future harm. That logic is not always illegitimate; public protection is a real concern. But the moment a system treats forecast as moral permission, it risks punishing persons for predicted futures rather than proved acts, and it risks converting the human being into a "risk container" whose liberty is priced by probability (Starr, 2014). No amount of statistical accuracy dissolves the moral distinction between "you did" and "you might." That distinction is part of what makes a punishment intelligible as punishment rather than as preventive confinement (Duff, 2001; Hart, 1968).

The Forensic Analogy: A Tool Can Be Sound and Still Be Unsafe

In forensic science, courts have learned—often after miscarriages of justice—that technical capability does not guarantee lawful or ethical use. A method can show strong performance in ideal conditions and still fail when the chain of custody is broken, when contextual bias distorts interpretation, or when the output is presented in a way that invites the trier of fact to over-weight it (Robertson, Vignaux and Berger, 2016; Cooper, 2019). The same is true of algorithmic systems in court. An algorithm's output is not a reason. It is an item of evidence at best, and a potentially misleading artefact at worst. To treat it forensically is to demand: what proposition does the output bear on, what assumptions does it embed, what is its known error under conditions of use, what are the limits of interpretability, and what is the risk of cognitive capture—anchoring, deference, and responsibility-shifting—by the human decision-maker who receives it (Kahneman, 2011; Kazim and Tomlinson, 2023). The behavioural science is not optional here. Evidence on automation bias demonstrates that "human oversight" is not a magical safeguard; humans routinely over-rely on automated outputs, particularly under time pressure and when the output is framed as authoritative (Kazim and Tomlinson, 2023; Ruschemeier and Hondrich, 2024). If your safeguard depends on a human being resisting a neat number that looks objective, your safeguard is fragile by design.

The Psychology of Legitimacy: Voice Is Not a Courtesy, It Is a Condition

When an accused person stands before the state, the moral demand is not merely that the outcome be correct, but that the process be recognisably fair. Procedural justice research shows that voice, respectful treatment, neutrality, and trustworthy motives are central to perceptions of fairness and compliance (Tyler, 2006). Algorithmic systems threaten this not only because they can be opaque, but because they can become functionally decisive while remaining conversationally invisible: the judge still speaks, yet the decision has already been architected by a score. That is what creates a procedural gap—where a person experiences the process as a performance rather than as a hearing (Kinchin, 2024). Recent work that explicitly connects procedural justice theory to AI governance argues that due process must be embedded into the design of AI decision systems, not appended after deployment; otherwise, legitimacy becomes an afterthought that the affected person can sense immediately (Fischman-Afori, 2025).

Empirical studies of public perceptions of judicial AI further suggest that acceptance depends strongly on whether AI is perceived as informational support rather than as a substitute for human judgement, and whether the system's use is transparent and contestable (Fine et al., 2025; Barysė and Sarel, 2024). This is the behavioural spine of the matter: legitimacy is not secured by accuracy; legitimacy is secured by fairness-as-experienced, which is shaped by process, not merely by outcomes.

Bias Is Not Only a Data Problem; It Is a History Problem

You will also hear, with reassuring simplicity, that bias can be fixed with better data. That is partly true and mostly incomplete. Data in criminal justice are not neutral records of "criminality." They are records of contact with institutions: policing intensity, surveillance allocation, prosecution patterns, socio-economic exposure, and historic over-representation of certain groups in enforcement practices. When an algorithm learns from that history, it can stabilise it—turning the past into a prediction and then using the prediction to justify actions that recreate the same patterns, a feedback loop dressed as objectivity (Barocas, Hardt and Narayanan, 2023). The problem here is not merely disparate impact; it is moral misclassification. If the system uses proxy variables—neighbourhood, employment, prior contacts—it may be measuring vulnerability and exposure as if it were propensity, and that is conceptually misaligned with a justice system that claims to punish culpable acts rather than social location (Starr, 2014; Duff, 2001). This is why the fairness debate cannot remain inside metric trade-offs alone; the deeper question is what the model is actually modelling, and whether that object is morally permissible to treat as a basis for coercion (Barocas, Hardt and Narayanan, 2023).

Global Case Signals: When Courts and Societies Push Back on Opaque Scoring

Although the present discussion must remain global in principle, it is intellectually dishonest to ignore the pattern: across jurisdictions, algorithmic scoring systems have been challenged when they operate in secrecy, when affected persons lack meaningful notice and contestability, and when the system shifts power without accountability. In the welfare domain, the litigation around the Dutch SyRI system became a landmark for how secrecy and risk profiling collide with legality and fundamental rights, and scholarly analyses have used it to show how algorithmic systems can fail basic requirements of transparency and protection against arbitrariness (van Bekkum and Zuiderveen Borgesius, 2021; Rachovitsa and Johann, 2022; Wieringa, 2023). In the criminal domain, the debates triggered by the use of proprietary risk tools at sentencing have served as a cautionary template for how outsourcing public power to opaque systems can strain rule-of-law commitments, particularly around contestability and accountability (Liu and Lin, 2019). The point of raising these episodes is not to build a country-specific doctrine; it is to observe a global rule-of-law reflex: when decision systems become influential yet unchallengeable, legitimacy fractures. Even where deployment continues, the controversies reveal where the moral fault lines lie.

The New Governance Moment: Rights-Based Restraint Is Catching Up to Adoption

The last few years have made one thing unmistakable: global governance is converging on the view that AI in justice is high-stakes and must be constrained by human rights, democracy, and the rule of law. The Council of Europe's Framework Convention—opened for signature in September 2024—signals a legally binding turn toward lifecycle governance and rights-consistency for AI systems (Rotenberg, 2025). The EU's risk-based approach has similarly catalysed global debate on how to classify and regulate AI used in justice and law enforcement, with peer-reviewed scholarship analysing accountability structures and the judiciary-specific risks raised by such frameworks (Carnat, 2024; Cascone, 2025; Presno Linera et al., 2025). These developments matter not because they solve the courtroom problem, but because they confirm the diagnosis: "efficiency" cannot be the sovereign value in domains where liberty and dignity are at stake. Yet even the best governance framework cannot repair a court culture that treats algorithmic outputs as de facto authority. That is why the line-drawing must be internal to legal reasoning: what counts as evidence, what disclosure is mandatory, what opportunity to contest must exist, and what kinds of uses are categorically impermissible because they convert prediction into punishment (Kinchin, 2024; Fischman-Afori, 2025).

Behavioural Contamination: When the Number Becomes the Narrative

If you want to understand how accuracy can still produce injustice, look not at the model first but at the human being who receives the model's output. A judge, like any decision-maker, is vulnerable to anchoring: a number offered early shapes the interpretation of everything that follows, and subsequent adjustments tend to be insufficient (Kahneman, 2011). In court, the "risk score" becomes a narrative magnet. It frames the accused as "high risk," it alters how ambiguity is resolved, and it can quietly change the moral temperature of the hearing: caution hardens into severity, and severity starts to feel like prudence. At the same time, responsibility can diffuse: the judge can sincerely believe they are making an independent decision while the institutional reality is that the tool has narrowed the decision-space. This is why scholarship on automation bias and judicial review is so important: it makes explicit that human oversight is itself cognitively fallible, and that legal systems must account for how the human-automation team behaves, not how it is supposed to behave (Kazim and Tomlinson, 2023; Ruschemeier and Hondrich, 2024). Empirical work on how people perceive algorithms in courts further suggests that what matters is not merely whether a tool is used, but which stage is automated: information acquisition may be tolerated, while decision implementation triggers sharper legitimacy concerns (Barysė and Sarel, 2024). In other words, the behavioural science is already drawing a line that performance metrics alone cannot justify.

Trust, Aversion, Worship: The Public Is Not a Spreadsheet Either

There is another behavioural complication that efficiency narratives routinely ignore: the public's relationship with algorithms is not stable. People can be algorithm-averse after seeing errors, penalising machines more harshly than humans for comparable mistakes, even when the machine outperforms (Dietvorst, Simmons and Massey, 2015; Dietvorst, Simmons and Massey, 2018). Yet people can also show algorithm appreciation under certain conditions, particularly when performance is framed as expert and outcomes are favourable (Logg, Minson and Moore, 2019). In a justice system, that volatility matters because legitimacy is a collective belief, and collective beliefs can fracture suddenly after visible failures. If a risk tool contributes to a high-profile wrongful detention, public faith collapses; if it seems to "work," institutions may begin to over-trust it and expand its use beyond its validated scope. Either way, the system is pulled away from the slow discipline of reasons-giving toward the faster emotional economy of scandal and reassurance. That is precisely why accuracy cannot be treated as a moral theory: morality is not only about outcomes, but about whether the institution remains answerable in a way that can survive error without losing its soul.

What Forensic Discipline Teaches the Court: Contestability Is Part of Truth

Forensic science has developed hard lessons about cognition, context, and interpretive error. Systematic reviews show that forensic decisions can be influenced by contextual information and cognitive bias, and that mitigation requires structural safeguards rather than mere appeals to professionalism (Cooper, 2019). Work in forensic pathology demonstrates that even highly trained experts can be affected by bias in decision contexts, strengthening the argument that institutional design must protect decision-making from contamination (Dror et al., 2021). Scholarship on bias cascades further explains how small contextual cues can snowball into downstream conclusions that appear "objective" but are actually the product of a contaminated interpretive path (Dror, 2025). The legal lesson is direct: a system that relies on human beings interpreting outputs—whether forensic traces or algorithmic scores—must build contestability, transparency, and disciplined presentation into the process. Courts should treat algorithmic outputs the way they increasingly aspire to treat forensic evidence: disclose what is necessary to test reliability, communicate uncertainty properly, avoid misleading certainty, and preserve the adversarial capacity to challenge the foundation of the inference (Robertson, Vignaux and Berger, 2016; Williams, 2021). If a model is proprietary such that meaningful challenge is impossible, the court should recognise that it is being asked to accept authority without accountability, which is the opposite of what due process is for.

The Moral Core: Justice Is Communication, Not Calculation

At bottom, criminal punishment is not merely a technique for reducing future harm. It is a public act that communicates condemnation, sets boundaries, and declares the moral terms of membership in a community (Duff, 2001). Even in systems that emphasise deterrence or incapacitation, punishment must remain intelligible as something more than administrative risk management; otherwise, it ceases to be punishment and becomes preventive control. This is why philosophical accounts of responsibility and punishment insist on reasons, proportionality, and the respect due to persons as moral agents (Hart, 1968; von Hirsch, 1976; Duff, 2001). Justice, in this sense, is not the maximisation of a single value like accuracy; it is the disciplined balancing of values that can conflict: public safety, equality, dignity, liberty, mercy, and the integrity of the rule of law. A system that declares "accuracy wins" has not found a moral foundation; it has merely chosen a convenient metric and crowned it sovereign.

Where the Line Begins: The Court Must Refuse Metric Sovereignty

So where should the justice system draw the line, if accuracy is not a moral theory? Begin with a principle that is both behavioural and forensic: no algorithmic output should constrain liberty unless the affected person can meaningfully understand and contest the basis of that output, and unless the court can articulate—in human reasons—why it is relevant to the legal question before it (Kinchin, 2024; Fischman-Afori, 2025). Then add a second principle that is moral: prediction may inform support and supervision in ways that reduce harm, but prediction must not become the moral engine of punishment in a way that collapses culpability into risk and replaces proportionality with optimisation (Starr, 2014; Duff, 2001). Finally add a third principle that is institutional: governance frameworks and laws can guide, but they cannot substitute for courtroom discipline; courts must insist that efficiency serve justice, not rule it. If you keep these distinctions alive—prediction versus judgement, evidence versus authority, accuracy versus legitimacy—you can use technology without becoming a technocracy. If you abandon them, you will still have a courtroom, but it will increasingly function as an interface for decisions made elsewhere.

References

- Barocas, S., Hardt, M. and Narayanan, A. (2023) Fairness and Machine Learning: Limitations and Opportunities. Cambridge, MA: MIT Press.
- Barysė, D. and Sarel, R. (2024) 'Algorithms in the court: does it matter which part of the judicial decision-making is automated?', Artificial Intelligence and Law, 32(1), pp. 117–146.
- Carnat, I. (2024) 'Addressing the risks of generative AI for the judiciary: The accountability framework(s) under the EU AI Act', Computer Law & Security Review, 55, 106067.
- Cascone, G. (2025) 'The use of artificial intelligence in EU criminal justice systems', Open Research Europe, 5, 361.
- Cooper, G.S. et al. (2019) 'Cognitive bias research in forensic science: A systematic review', Forensic Science International, 297, pp. 35–46.
- Dietvorst, B.J., Simmons, J.P. and Massey, C. (2015) 'Algorithm aversion: People erroneously avoid algorithms after seeing them err', Journal of Experimental Psychology: General, 144(1), pp. 114–126.
- Dietvorst, B.J., Simmons, J.P. and Massey, C. (2018) 'Overcoming algorithm aversion: People will use imperfect algorithms if they can (even slightly) modify them', Management Science, 64(3), pp. 1155–1170.
- Dror, I.E. (2025) 'The hidden bias cascade and bias snowball effects', Behavioral Sciences, 15(4), 490.
- Dror, I.E. et al. (2021) 'Cognitive bias in forensic pathology decisions', Journal of Forensic Sciences, 66(5), pp. 1751–1760.
- Duff, R.A. (2001) Punishment, Communication, and Community. Oxford: Oxford University Press.
- Fine, A. et al. (2025) 'Public perceptions of judges' use of AI tools in courtroom decision-making', Psychology, Public Policy, and Law.
- Fischman-Afori, O. (2025) 'Due process by design: Enhancing fairness and trust in AI decision-making', Social Sciences & Humanities Open, 12, 102178.
- Hart, H.L.A. (1968) Punishment and Responsibility: Essays in the Philosophy of Law. Oxford: Oxford University Press.
- Kahneman, D. (2011) Thinking, Fast and Slow. New York: Farrar, Straus and Giroux.

- Kazim, T. and Tomlinson, J. (2023) 'Automation bias and the principles of judicial review', Judicial Review, 28(1), pp. 9–16.
- Kinchin, N. (2024) '"Voiceless": the procedural gap in algorithmic justice', International Journal of Law and Information Technology, 32(4), pp. 1–30.
- Liu, H.-W. and Lin, C.-F. (2019) 'Beyond State v Loomis: artificial intelligence, government algorithmization and accountability', International Journal of Law and Information Technology, 27(2), pp. 122–141.
- Logg, J.M., Minson, J.A. and Moore, D.A. (2019) 'Algorithm appreciation: People prefer algorithmic to human judgment', Organizational Behavior and Human Decision Processes, 151, pp. 90–103.
- Monahan, J. and Skeem, J.L. (2016) 'Risk assessment in criminal sentencing', Annual Review of Clinical Psychology, 12, pp. 489–513.
- Presno Linera, M.Á. et al. (2025) 'Regulating AI from Europe: a joint analysis of the AI Act and the Council of Europe AI Convention', Journal of Cyber Policy, 10(1), pp. 1–25.
- Rachovitsa, A. and Johann, N. (2022) 'The human rights implications of the use of AI in the digital welfare state: lessons learned from the Dutch SyRI case', Human Rights Law Review, 22(2), pp. 1–15.
- Robertson, B., Vignaux, G.A. and Berger, C.E.H. (2016) Interpreting Evidence: Evaluating Forensic Science in the Courtroom. 2nd edn. Chichester: Wiley.
- Rotenberg, M. (2025) 'Framework Convention on Artificial Intelligence and Human Rights, Democracy, and the Rule of Law (Council of Europe)', International Legal Materials, 64(1), pp. 1–25.
- Ruschemeier, H. and Hondrich, L.J. (2024) 'Automation bias in public administration – an interdisciplinary perspective from law and psychology', Government Information Quarterly, 41(3), 101953.
- Starr, S.B. (2014) 'Evidence-based sentencing and the scientific rationalization of discrimination', Stanford Law Review, 66(4), pp. 803–871.
- Tyler, T.R. (2006) Why People Obey the Law. 2nd edn. Princeton, NJ: Princeton University Press.
- van Bekkum, M. and Zuiderveen Borgesius, F. (2021) 'Digital welfare fraud detection and the Dutch SyRI judgment', European Journal of Social Security, 23(3), pp. 1–20.

- von Hirsch, A. (1976) Doing Justice: The Choice of Punishments. New York: Hill and Wang.
- Wieringa, M. (2023) '"Hey SyRI, tell me about algorithmic accountability": Lessons from a landmark case', Data & Policy, 5, e20.
- Williams, G.A. (2021) 'Embracing likelihood ratios and highlighting the principles for evidence interpretation', Forensic Science International: Synergy, 3, 100160.

CHAPTER III

Theories of Punishment Under Algorithmic Pressure: Desert, Prevention, Rehabilitation

The Moment the Courtroom Became a Control Room

You and I grew up inside a legal imagination where punishment was explained in moral sentences: the offender deserves condemnation; society must deter; the dangerous must be restrained; the reformable must be helped; the victim must be acknowledged. This vocabulary was never perfect, but it was at least recognisably human. Now place beside it a new vocabulary that arrives with algorithmic systems: risk stratification, optimisation, harm-minimisation, resource allocation, predictive validity, calibration. It is not that the old words have vanished; it is that the new words increasingly decide what the old words are allowed to mean. When a sentencing tool forecasts recidivism and a court treats that forecast as decisive, desert quietly yields to prevention; when a probation system allocates treatment intensity by a risk score, rehabilitation is reinterpreted as compliance engineering; when institutional actors justify deployment by "improving accuracy," the court begins to behave like a regulator of future harms rather than an adjudicator of past wrongs. This is what algorithmic pressure does: it does not merely add a tool, it reshapes the architecture of justification, and thereby reshapes the moral theory that the institution actually lives by (Feeley and Simon, 1992; Ashworth and Zedner, 2014; Ryberg, 2025a).

What Punishment Theories Really Do, When You Strip the Rhetoric Away

Theories of punishment are not ornaments; they are constraint systems. Retributive ideas of desert, even when contested, aim to limit what the state may do by tying punishment to culpability and proportionality, insisting that penalties answer to the offence rather than to administrative convenience (Hart, 1968; von Hirsch, 1976; Duff, 2001). Preventive rationales, by contrast, naturally pull forward in time: they justify interventions because of anticipated future harm, whether through deterrence, incapacitation, or risk management, and they are perpetually tempted by expansion, because the future can always be made "safer" by doing more (Ashworth and Zedner, 2014). Rehabilitation theories attempt to preserve personhood by treating the offender as capable of change, urging interventions that reduce criminogenic needs and support desistance, but they can degrade into paternalism or surveillance if "treatment" is driven by control imperatives rather than by genuine support (Bonta and Andrews, 2023; Fazel et al., 2024).

Algorithmic systems put pressure on each of these constraint systems in a different way. They make preventive rationales seductive because prediction is their native language. They make desert look "unscientific" because desert cannot be validated against an outcome variable the way prediction can. They make rehabilitation vulnerable because they can convert complex human change into a dashboard of proxies—attendance, compliance, risk category—while ignoring the interior narrative that desistance scholarship repeatedly shows to be crucial (McNeill, 2016; Reich, 2023; de Vel-Palumbo et al., 2023).

Desert Under Pressure: When "Proportionality" Becomes a Prediction Problem

Start with desert, because it is the theory most directly threatened by the logic of algorithms. Desert is not merely vengeance with a vocabulary; at its best, it is a principled refusal to punish beyond what culpability warrants. Yet algorithms enter the sentencing conversation via two doors that retributive thought does not naturally control. First, they offer a number that seems to solve the "how much" question with an empirical sheen: if the person is high risk, severity seems justified; if low risk, leniency seems safe. Second, they promise consistency, and consistency is often mistaken for fairness. But the philosophical point is sharp: desert cannot be derived from predictive accuracy, because desert is about what is owed in response to wrongdoing, not about what is efficient for managing populations. If a model is accurate in predicting reoffending, it still does not tell you what punishment is deserved; it tells you something, at best, about a future that has not yet been chosen by the person (Hart, 1968; Duff, 2001). Under algorithmic pressure, the court risks confusing a forecast with a moral reason.

Recent philosophical work on sentencing algorithms makes this confusion explicit. Ryberg's work presses the practical question of how algorithmic sentencing support should be used in real, ethically non-ideal penal systems, precisely because "just add a model" is not morally neutral; it changes penal practice and can amplify overpunishment if the institutional environment is already severity-biased (Ryberg, 2025a). Taylor argues that sentencing contains an act of condemnation that is valuable in itself, and that algorithmic systems, even in advisory roles, can undermine this condemnatory function unless "meaningful public control" over sentencing is preserved, because the legitimacy of punishment depends on publicly intelligible reasons rather than on opaque optimisation (Taylor, 2023). If you read these arguments as a forensic practitioner would, the red flag is not merely opacity; it is displacement. The moral centre of sentencing shifts from proportional response to managerial risk control.

Now watch what happens in the real courtroom mind. A risk score looks like a fact; it anchors attention; it offers psychological relief under caseload pressure. Behavioural science tells you why this is dangerous: numerical anchors shape judgement even when people intend to resist them, and "advice" from a system framed as objective invites automation bias, especially when the human decision-maker is time-poor and accountability-conscious (Kahneman, 2011; Ruschemeier and Hondrich, 2024). So desert is pressured not only philosophically but cognitively: proportionality is replaced by the felt prudence of acting on "risk."

Prevention Under Pressure: When Risk Management Pretends to Be Justice

Preventive rationales are the native habitat of algorithmic systems because prediction is their bloodstream. If the institutional goal is to prevent harm, then a tool that sorts populations by risk looks like moral progress. Yet this is exactly where the moral trap opens, because prevention has a known tendency to expand, and algorithmic systems give it an administrative engine. Ashworth and Zedner's preventive justice framework is useful here because it treats preventive measures as requiring principled limits, safeguards, and scrutiny precisely because the logic of prevention is intrinsically prone to overreach (Ashworth and Zedner, 2014). Under algorithmic pressure, preventive justice can move from exceptional measure to routine operating system. You do not need a dramatic legal revolution; you simply need a tool that makes it easy to justify detention, supervision, or security restrictions on the basis of future risk.

The "new penology" thesis anticipated this transformation long before machine learning became fashionable. Feeley and Simon described a shift away from individualised moral judgement toward actuarial management of aggregates, where the objective becomes control of high-risk groups rather than reform of persons (Feeley and Simon, 1992). Algorithms do not create this shift; they accelerate it, automate it, and cloak it in the language of science. Wenzelburger's analysis of algorithm-based criminal justice through retributive, actuarial, and preventive lenses shows how digital risk prediction tools reflect changing commitments in criminal justice, and how reforms can be read as a movement toward risk-based governance even when the rhetoric remains about fairness (Wenzelburger, 2025).

Here is the forensic point that matters for a court deciding whether to rely on such tools: risk instruments frequently operate on proxies for social disadvantage—housing instability, unemployment, prior system contact—thereby importing extrajudicial characteristics into liberty decisions through a side door. Ugwudike's survey of sentencing and risk assessment algorithms emphasises how such instruments can inflate risk for disadvantaged groups and raise transparency deficits that strain procedural justice and due process (Ugwudike, 2025). Greene's work on predictive inconsistency shows that even "equally justifiable" modelling choices can yield different risk scores for the same individual, undermining the idea that the risk score is a stable fact rather than a product of design choices (Greene, 2022). If the object you are using to justify coercion is underdetermined by design and sensitive to choices you cannot see, prevention becomes not only expansive but epistemically fragile.

A reader may object that prevention is ethically justified if it reduces victimisation. That objection deserves respect, because it comes from a genuine moral impulse: protect the vulnerable. But protection requires legitimacy to endure. If you build a system that detains people on forecasts they cannot meaningfully contest, you invite resistance, non-compliance, and the slow corrosion of trust. Procedural justice research shows why: compliance and acceptance are driven heavily by perceptions of fairness and voice, not merely by outcome favourability (Tyler, 2006). This matters because algorithmic governance often produces a "procedural gap," where the person experiences the process as voiceless even when formal hearings remain intact (Kinchin, 2024).

Rehabilitation Under Pressure: When "What Works" Turns Into "What Controls"

Rehabilitation is the most paradoxical theory under algorithmic pressure because algorithms can, in principle, support it. If you could genuinely identify criminogenic needs, responsivity factors, and effective interventions, you might reduce reoffending and reduce the use of imprisonment. Rehabilitation, at its best, is the theory that says the person is not a fixed hazard but a changing agent. Yet algorithmic deployment has tended to privilege security and control: surveillance technologies, predictive flagging, compliance scoring, and "dynamic risk" dashboards that treat change as a set of measurable proxies (Bonta and Andrews, 2023; Fazel et al., 2024).

The Risk-Need-Responsivity model remains central to modern rehabilitation practice, and it is precisely where algorithmic systems are most tempted to operate, because RNR is already a structured, assessment-driven framework. The problem is that "assessment-driven" can be mistaken for "algorithm-ready." The 2024 umbrella review and commentary by Fazel and colleagues synthesises and appraises evidence for RNR principles and raises concerns about the quality and biases of the evidence base, which is crucial if algorithmic systems are going to encode these principles at scale (Fazel et al., 2024). In other words, if you are going to build an automated rehabilitation triage system, you must not treat RNR as settled gospel; you must treat it as a model with contested empirical foundations and variable implementation fidelity.

Then there is desistance, which rehabilitation frameworks sometimes mention and institutions often ignore. Desistance scholarship argues that stopping crime is not merely the removal of risk factors; it is a process that involves identity change, social capital, narrative reconstruction, and the availability of legitimate roles. If your algorithm measures compliance but misses identity and opportunity, it will reward the performance of conformity rather than the substance of change. Work on assisted desistance highlights that institutions can support or frustrate desistance journeys depending on how they structure supervision and support, and that coercive contact can sometimes destabilise rather than strengthen prosocial identity (de Vel-Palumbo et al., 2023; Little, 2024). When algorithmic systems become the lens through which "progress" is seen, they risk collapsing rehabilitation into what is easiest to record, and what is easiest to record is often what is easiest to police.

You can see the same tension in digital rehabilitation initiatives more broadly: technology can expand education, therapy, family contact, and reentry preparation, yet it can just as easily expand monitoring and control. The moral question, therefore, is not "can technology rehabilitate?" but "what does the institution choose to use technology for?" and how does that choice affect dignity, agency, and legitimacy. Even when innovations are framed as rehabilitative, the behavioural reality of prisons and probation services can pull them toward security-first uses unless governance and culture deliberately resist that drift (Knight, Ross and Dominey, 2024).

The Forensic Standard the Court Must Import: Fit-for-Purpose, Not Impressive-in-General

If you take nothing else from this chapter, take this forensic rule: a tool is not justified by its general performance; it is justified by fit-for-purpose under conditions of use. Forensic science has spent decades learning the hard way that reliability, interpretation, and presentation are inseparable. A method can be statistically powerful and still mislead if its uncertainty is not communicated properly, if context contaminates interpretation, or if its limitations are hidden behind authority (Robertson, Vignaux and Berger, 2016). Algorithmic tools in punishment settings must be judged by the same logic. If a risk tool is used to justify preventive detention, the court must ask whether the tool's performance is stable for the relevant population, whether it embeds proxies for protected characteristics, whether it is contestable in an adversarial process, and whether its output is being used to answer a question that is legally and morally appropriate. Otherwise, the system will drift into a regime where "the model says so" becomes the functional reason for coercion, and that is the death of reasons-giving.

Ryberg's "input problem" analysis captures a major part of this: sentencing algorithms require inputs, and the selection and framing of those inputs are not morally neutral. What counts as a relevant variable is itself a normative choice, and different input selections can operationalise different punishment theories without openly admitting it (Ryberg, 2025b). If you feed the model variables linked to social deprivation, you are letting prevention dominate desert. If you feed it variables linked to treatment compliance, you may be letting institutional discipline masquerade as rehabilitation. If you feed it variables linked to victim impact and offence severity alone, you may preserve desert but ignore genuine prevention concerns. The model does not resolve the moral conflict; it encodes a resolution chosen by designers and procurers.

The Legitimacy Constraint: Condemnation Must Remain Publicly Owned

Punishment is not merely a technique; it is a communicative act. Duff's communicative theory insists that punishment expresses censure and calls the offender to account as a responsible agent, which requires the institution to speak in human reasons rather than in machine outputs (Duff, 2001). Taylor's argument about condemnation and "meaningful public control" adds a modern edge: even if algorithms could become highly accurate, the legitimacy of punishment depends on the public being able to see that sentencing remains a humanly owned act of judgement, not an outsourced optimisation problem (Taylor, 2023). This is where the court must be unusually strict with itself. It is not enough to say "the judge decides." Behavioural research shows that humans are influenced by automated advice even when they believe they are independent, and institutions tend to normalise tool outputs as default rationales under workload and liability pressures (Ruschemeier and Hondrich, 2024). If condemnation is to remain legitimate, the reasons must be genuinely reasons—contestable, intelligible, and attributable.

This also explains why rights-based governance is turning toward lifecycle oversight, transparency, and contestability for AI systems that affect fundamental rights. The Council of Europe's AI convention is significant not because it provides courtroom doctrine, but because it formalises the principle that AI systems must operate consistently with human rights, democracy, and rule of law commitments, which directly includes fair process and accountability (Rotenberg, 2025; Stoyanova, 2025). Peer-reviewed analyses of European regulatory frameworks further underline that judicial uses of AI are high-stakes precisely because they threaten due process values if adopted without robust accountability structures (Carnat, 2024; Presno Linera et al., 2025). Even when you do not cite a specific jurisdiction, the global normative movement is clear: punishment systems are not permitted to trade dignity and contestability for throughput.

Illustrations the Court Cannot Ignore: When Litigation Becomes a Moral Mirror

Consider, as illustrations rather than jurisdictional rules, how algorithmic systems have been challenged when they become influential yet unchallengeable. Analyses of State v Loomis highlight the tension between proprietary risk tools and accountability, and the broader concern that algorithmic recommendations can undermine fair trial values if defendants cannot meaningfully contest the basis of the score (Liu and Lin, 2019). Analyses of the SyRI litigation in the Netherlands, though arising from the welfare state, offer a transferable lesson: opacity and risk profiling can collide with legality and human rights in ways that courts increasingly treat as unacceptable, especially when the system's operation prevents meaningful scrutiny (van Bekkum and Zuiderveen Borgesius, 2021; Rachovitsa and Johann, 2022; Wieringa, 2023). These controversies are not merely political theatre; they function as moral mirrors. They reveal that the deeper problem is not that a model might be wrong, but that a model might be right in a way that no one can ethically own.

A Practical Synthesis: How Algorithmic Pressure Re-sorts the Penal Trinity

If you want to see the full structure at once, treat desert, prevention, and rehabilitation as a three-legged constraint system that keeps punishment recognisably lawful and humane. Desert limits severity by culpability and proportionality; prevention limits harm through forward-looking restraint; rehabilitation limits future crime through change rather than through incapacitation. Algorithmic systems pressure this triad by making prevention easiest to operationalise, desert hardest to quantify, and rehabilitation easiest to counterfeit. A risk score operationalises prevention immediately. A proportionality judgement requires moral reasoning that cannot be reduced to a validation metric. A rehabilitation plan can be turned into compliance metrics that look like progress even when the person's identity and opportunity are not changing.

This is why a purely metric-driven approach—accuracy, AUC, calibration—cannot decide the penal question. Predictive performance is relevant, but it is not sovereign. It must be governed by normative commitments, forensic standards, and behavioural realities. The system must prevent "risk management" from swallowing desert, and must prevent "rehabilitation" from becoming a euphemism for control. That requires constraints that are recognisably legal: disclosure, contestability, reasons-giving, proportionality review, and principled limits on when prediction may influence coercion (Ashworth and Zedner, 2014; Ryberg, 2025a; Ugwudike, 2025).

Where to Draw the Line, Without Pretending the Line Is Easy

A serious line-drawing position does not ban prediction; it bans moral abdication. Prediction may inform resource allocation, support planning, and targeted interventions when used transparently and when it does not inflate coercion beyond desert. Prediction may inform supervision intensity when safeguards prevent proxy discrimination and when the person can contest inputs and assumptions. But prediction must not become the engine that determines the quantum of punishment in a way that displaces proportionality and condemnation, because that converts sentencing into optimisation and turns the person into a managed risk object. That is the central moral boundary: the institution may use algorithms to see better, but it may not use algorithms to avoid judging. If the court cannot articulate the punishment in human reasons that the defendant can contest and the public can understand, it has surrendered the legitimacy that punishment requires to remain punishment rather than preventive administration (Duff, 2001; Taylor, 2023; Kinchin, 2024).

References

- Ashworth, A. and Zedner, L. (2014) Preventive Justice. Oxford: Oxford University Press.
- Barocas, S., Hardt, M. and Narayanan, A. (2023) Fairness and Machine Learning: Limitations and Opportunities. Cambridge, MA: MIT Press.

- Bonta, J. and Andrews, D.A. (2023) The Psychology of Criminal Conduct. 7th edn. New York: Routledge.
- Carnat, I. (2024) 'Addressing the risks of generative AI for the judiciary: The accountability framework(s) under the EU AI Act', Computer Law & Security Review, 55, 106067.
- Cooper, G.S. et al. (2019) 'Cognitive bias research in forensic science: A systematic review', Forensic Science International, 297, pp. 35–46.
- de Vel-Palumbo, M. et al. (2023) 'Assisted desistance in correctional centers: From theory to practice', Criminal Justice and Behavior, 50(12), pp. 1758–1780.
- Dietvorst, B.J., Simmons, J.P. and Massey, C. (2015) 'Algorithm aversion: People erroneously avoid algorithms after seeing them err', Journal of Experimental Psychology: General, 144(1), pp. 114–126.
- Duff, R.A. (2001) Punishment, Communication, and Community. Oxford: Oxford University Press.
- Fazel, S. et al. (2024) 'An updated evidence synthesis on the Risk-Need-Responsivity (RNR) model: Umbrella review and commentary', Journal of Criminal Justice, 92, 102197.
- Feeley, M.M. and Simon, J. (1992) 'The new penology: Notes on the emerging strategy of corrections and its implications', Criminology, 30(4), pp. 449–474.
- Fine, A. et al. (2025) 'Public perceptions of judges' use of AI tools in courtroom decision-making', Psychology, Public Policy, and Law.
- Greene, T. (2022) 'Predictive inconsistency in criminal justice algorithmic risk prediction tools', Journal of the Royal Statistical Society: Series A, 185(S2), pp. S692–S716.
- Hart, H.L.A. (1968) Punishment and Responsibility: Essays in the Philosophy of Law. Oxford: Oxford University Press.
- Jorgensen, R. (2022) 'Algorithms and the individual in criminal law', Canadian Journal of Philosophy, 52(6), pp. 729–746.
- Kahneman, D. (2011) Thinking, Fast and Slow. New York: Farrar, Straus and Giroux.
- Kinchin, N. (2024) '"Voiceless": the procedural gap in algorithmic justice', International Journal of Law and Information Technology, 32(4), pp. 1–30.
- Knight, V., Ross, S. and Dominey, J. (2024) 'Digitalising corrections', Journal of Criminology, 57(4).

- Liu, H.-W. and Lin, C.-F. (2019) 'Beyond State v Loomis: Artificial intelligence, government algorithmization and accountability', International Journal of Law and Information Technology, 27(2), pp. 122–141.
- Logg, J.M., Minson, J.A. and Moore, D.A. (2019) 'Algorithm appreciation: People prefer algorithmic to human judgment', Organizational Behavior and Human Decision Processes, 151, pp. 90–103.
- Portela, M. et al. (2025) 'A comparative user study of human predictions in algorithm-based risk assessment', Artificial Intelligence and Law, 33, pp. 1–32.
- Presno Linera, M.Á. et al. (2025) 'Regulating AI from Europe: A joint analysis of the AI Act and the Council of Europe AI Convention', Journal of Cyber Policy, 10(1), pp. 1–25.
- Rachovitsa, A. and Johann, N. (2022) 'The human rights implications of the use of AI in the digital welfare state: Lessons learned from the Dutch SyRI case', Human Rights Law Review, 22(2), pp. 1–24.
- Reich, S.E. (2023) 'How ex-offenders can signal their desistance from crime to employers', British Journal of Criminology, 63(5), pp. 1274–1293.
- Robertson, B., Vignaux, G.A. and Berger, C.E.H. (2016) Interpreting Evidence: Evaluating Forensic Science in the Courtroom. 2nd edn. Chichester: Wiley.
- Rotenberg, M. (2025) 'Framework Convention on Artificial Intelligence and Human Rights, Democracy, and the Rule of Law (Council of Europe)', International Legal Materials, 64(3), pp. 1–25.
- Ruschemeier, H. and Hondrich, L.J. (2024) 'Automation bias in public administration—an interdisciplinary perspective from law and psychology', Government Information Quarterly, 41(3), 101953.
- Ryberg, J. (2025a) 'Artificial intelligence and criminal justice: How to use algorithmic sentencing support in real life (and ethically non-ideal) penal systems?', AI and Ethics, 5(3), pp. 3255–3263.
- Ryberg, J. (2025b) 'What is the input problem?', Criminal Law and Philosophy.
- Stoyanova, V. (2025) 'Council of Europe Framework Convention on Artificial Intelligence and Human Rights, Democracy and the Rule of Law: An initial analysis'.
- Taylor, I. (2023) 'Justice by algorithm: The limits of AI in criminal sentencing', Criminal Justice Ethics, 42(3), pp. 193–213.

- Tyler, T.R. (2006) Why People Obey the Law. 2nd edn. Princeton, NJ: Princeton University Press.
- Ugwudike, P. (2025) 'Sentencing and risk assessment algorithms', in De Gruyter Handbook of Digital Criminology. Berlin: De Gruyter, pp. 435–444.
- van Bekkum, M. and Zuiderveen Borgesius, F. (2021) 'Digital welfare fraud detection and the Dutch SyRI judgment', European Journal of Social Security, 23(3), pp. 1–20.
- von Hirsch, A. (1976) Doing Justice: The Choice of Punishments. New York: Hill and Wang.
- Wenzelburger, G. (2025) 'Smart justice? Making sense of the rise of algorithm-based criminal justice', Crime, Law and Social Change.
- Wieringa, M. (2023) '"Hey SyRI, tell me about algorithmic accountability": Lessons from a landmark case', Data & Policy, 5, e20.

CHAPTER IV

Legitimacy as a Psychological Fact: Why People Obey Courts

Legitimacy is Not a Slogan, It is Behaviour You Can Measure

If you want to understand why courts function at all—why most people comply with orders they dislike, why witnesses turn up, why victims report, why defendants sometimes accept outcomes rather than seek revenge—you must stop thinking of legitimacy as a decorative ideal and start treating it as a psychological fact. Legitimacy is the felt rightfulness of authority, and its signature is behavioural: cooperation, compliance, deference without constant coercion, and the willingness to treat the institution as the proper forum for conflict (Tyler, 2006; Tyler, 2011). It is tempting, especially in legal education, to speak as though obedience flows primarily from fear of punishment or from respect for rules as such. But decades of empirical work have shown that "instrumental" accounts—people obey because they calculate costs—are incomplete in precisely the settings where the law matters most. People comply when they believe authorities act fairly, neutrally, respectfully, and in ways that grant them voice; and they withdraw cooperation when the process feels humiliating, arbitrary, or rigged, even if the outcome is substantively correct (Sunshine and Tyler, 2003; Tyler, 2011). If you carry that into court, you acquire a crucial forensic lens: legitimacy is the silent variable that explains why identical legal powers produce radically different social consequences depending on how they are exercised.

The Court's Power is a Monopoly, But Its Survival is a Consent-Project

There is a simple structural truth: courts claim the right to resolve disputes and impose coercive outcomes, and they expect their decisions to be treated as final. That expectation is not self-enforcing. It is stabilised by a social belief that the institution is entitled to decide—an entitlement that is continuously renewed or corroded through day-to-day encounters with legal authorities (Bottoms and Tankebe, 2012). This is why legitimacy is not merely a philosophical property of "the rule of law," but an empirical property of people's lived experiences with authority. Bottoms and Tankebe's dialogic account is helpful because it treats legitimacy as an ongoing conversation between power-holders and their audiences rather than a fixed asset the state owns forever (Bottoms and Tankebe, 2012). You can see the practical implication immediately: a court may possess impeccable formal jurisdiction and still lose legitimacy if its procedures are experienced as voiceless, opaque, or contemptuous. Conversely, a court can retain legitimacy even amid resource constraints if the process is experienced as dignified, reasoned, and participatory. This is not sentimentalism; it is the behavioural infrastructure that keeps the justice system from needing permanent force.

Procedural Justice: The Mechanism by Which Legitimacy Becomes Obedience

Procedural justice theory gives you the most durable explanatory chain we have: fair procedures shape legitimacy beliefs, and legitimacy beliefs shape compliance, cooperation, and engagement (Tyler, 2006; Sunshine and Tyler, 2003). The features that repeatedly matter are remarkably consistent: voice (the chance to tell one's story), neutrality (decisions appear rule-guided and unbiased), respect (treatment communicates dignity), and trustworthiness (authorities appear sincere and benevolent rather than predatory) (Tyler, 2011). What makes this framework powerful for a courtroom is that it predicts behaviour even when outcomes disappoint. A person who loses but feels heard and respected is more likely to accept the decision than a person who wins while experiencing humiliation and arbitrariness. The court's legitimacy therefore lives less in the correctness of its outcomes than in the credibility of its process. This point becomes even more important when systems introduce technology, because technology often improves throughput while quietly damaging voice and intelligibility—the very levers procedural justice uses to produce compliance.

The Forensic Way to Read a Courtroom: Look for the "Legitimacy Trace"

A forensic examiner does not limit attention to the dramatic moment of offence; they reconstruct the chain: environment, cues, constraints, pressures, and the predictable human responses they trigger. Apply that discipline to legitimacy. The "legitimacy trace" is the set of cues the institution emits that tell a person whether they are being treated as a citizen or as a nuisance. Consider a bail hearing. The legal question may be framed as risk, flight, and public safety, but the psychological question is whether the individual experiences the court as a place where their account is taken seriously and where reasons are given in intelligible terms. If the hearing becomes a mechanical recital of a score, the defendant's experience of voice collapses; and the downstream behavioural consequence is not abstract. It affects compliance with conditions, willingness to appear, engagement with services, and the internalisation of the court's moral authority (Tyler, 2006; Tyler, 2011). This is one reason why legitimacy should be treated as a measurable outcome variable in justice reforms rather than as a rhetorical aspiration. If you change courtroom design or introduce a tool, you should ask not only "does it predict?" but "what does it do to voice, dignity, and contestability?"

When Algorithms Enter, Legitimacy Becomes Fragile for Predictable Psychological Reasons

The integration of AI into judicial systems is often justified by accuracy, efficiency, and consistency. The legitimacy problem is that these are not the variables that govern acceptance. The moment an algorithmic output becomes salient—risk score, recommended sentence, predicted compliance—the human mind treats it as a special kind of object: it looks objective, it looks scientific, and it invites deference even when people intend to remain independent (Kahneman, 2011; Ruschemeier and Hondrich, 2024). That is the cognitive part. The moral part is that algorithmic outputs can make a person feel processed rather than judged, and "processed" is poison to legitimacy because it signals the absence of human attention and moral recognition. The legal part is that many algorithmic systems are difficult to contest meaningfully, either because their internal logic is opaque, their inputs are proprietary, or their performance is not disclosed in a way that allows adversarial testing. When contestability declines, legitimacy declines, because a core promise of the rule of law is that state power must be answerable (Kinchin, 2024).

Voice is the First Casualty: The Procedural Gap in Algorithmic Justice

The most precise diagnosis of what goes wrong, psychologically, is that algorithmic justice tends to improve distributive aims while leaving a "procedural gap," especially around voice (Kinchin, 2024). The court may believe it is being fair because it is being consistent, but the person may experience the process as unfair because they cannot see how the decision was made, cannot challenge the basis effectively, and cannot feel that their narrative mattered. Kinchin's argument is important because it does not rely on melodrama about machines replacing judges. It shows something more mundane and more dangerous: the institution can keep human actors in place while still producing an experience of voicelessness because the real decision-space has been narrowed by algorithmic architecture (Kinchin, 2024). This is exactly the kind of problem that does not show up in conventional performance dashboards. Courts can claim success because backlogs drop and outcomes become more uniform, while legitimacy quietly bleeds out through day-to-day interactions.

Due Process by Design: Why Legitimacy Must Be Built into the System, Not Added Later

If legitimacy is behavioural infrastructure, then it cannot be protected by generic slogans such as "human oversight." It requires design. Procedural justice theory has recently been used to argue that AI decision systems must embed due-process values—especially the right to be heard—within their operation, because the most common governance discussions obsess over transparency while neglecting voice and contestability (Fischman-Afori, 2025). This is a critical shift: it treats legitimacy as something that must be engineered into decision pathways, not merely promised in policy documents. If a system outputs a score, the affected person must be able to understand what it means, how it was generated, what limitations it has, and how it can be challenged. Without that, the institution may still be lawful, but it will not feel lawful, and the gap between legality and felt lawfulness is where compliance decays.

Evidence from the Public: People Read AI in Court Through a Legitimacy Lens, Not a Tech Lens

The empirical work on perceptions of judges using AI is beginning to map what procedural justice theory would predict. Experimental studies have found that public perceptions of judicial legitimacy and procedural justice vary depending on whether judges rely on AI tools versus human expertise, and these perceptions differ across demographic groups, suggesting legitimacy impacts will not be uniform (Fine, Berthelot and Marsh, 2025). Related work indicates that judges can act as legitimacy brokers for AI, shaping public trust in AI through their perceived expertise and public role (Fine, 2024). These findings matter because they underline a hard institutional truth: courts do not merely decide cases; they also narrate what counts as authority. If judges appear to defer to tools that look like external authority, the institution's moral ownership can be perceived as weakened. And once moral ownership is weakened, legitimacy becomes brittle.

The Catastrophic Legitimacy Risk: When AI Produces Legal "Facts" That Are Not Real

You do not need to exaggerate risks to take them seriously. One of the most direct ways legitimacy is undermined is when the legal system appears to accept fabricated materials as if they were authoritative. Peer-reviewed legal scholarship has documented "hallucinations" in large language models—outputs inconsistent with legal facts—and has presented systematic evidence of these hallucinations in public-facing tools across jurisdictions and contexts (Dahl et al., 2024). From a legitimacy perspective, the problem is not merely professional embarrassment. It is epistemic contamination. The court's authority rests on an expectation that its reasons are anchored in verifiable law and evidence. When AI-generated outputs introduce false citations or invented authorities, the institution's most basic claim—that it operates on reasons that can be checked—takes a blow. Even if the court corrects the record later, the social memory of error can travel faster than the correction, and legitimacy is a social perception that is sensitive to visible failures.

A Forensic Principle for the AI Era: Reliability Without Contestability Is Not Fit for Court

Forensic science offers a disciplined vocabulary for this moment. Courts have learned—often painfully—that a technique's apparent power is not enough; what matters is validation, known error, transparent interpretation, and careful presentation of uncertainty (Robertson, Vignaux and Berger, 2016). In the AI era, the parallel is unavoidable: a model can be statistically impressive and still be institutionally unsafe if it cannot be tested adversarially, if its uncertainty is disguised as certainty, or if its outputs become anchors that bias human judgement. Add cognitive science and you see why safeguards cannot be informal. Automation bias is not a moral flaw in the judge; it is a predictable human response to authoritative cues, especially under pressure (Ruschemeier and Hondrich, 2024). In other words, the system must be built to protect the human from predictable cognitive errors, not merely to demand that the human behave heroically.

The Moral Core: Why Dignity Matters Even When Outcomes Are "Correct"

At this point, a reader might say, "But if AI improves accuracy, aren't better outcomes morally superior?" Here is the uncomfortable answer: not necessarily, because justice is not only distributive; it is also procedural. A system that delivers "correct" outcomes through humiliating, voiceless procedures can still be unjust, because it treats the citizen as an object rather than as a participant in public reason (Tyler, 2011; Bottoms and Tankebe, 2012). This is why legitimacy is not reducible to performance. Courts are not merely service providers; they are institutions that exercise moral power. When they punish, detain, or restrict, they are not only producing outcomes; they are communicating what kind of relationship exists between the person and the state. If that relationship becomes purely administrative—numbers in, sanctions out—the state may become efficient while losing its moral standing. The behavioural consequence is predictable: weaker compliance, less cooperation, more cynicism, and greater temptation toward private retribution or disengagement.

Global Governance is Responding: Legitimacy Has Become a Regulatory Concern

You can see, across global governance, a recognition that AI touches legitimacy because it touches rights, transparency, accountability, and democratic control. The Council of Europe's Framework Convention on AI—opened for signature in September 2024—frames AI governance explicitly in terms of human rights, democracy, and the rule of law (Rotenberg, 2025; Stoyanova, 2025). Whatever one thinks of specific instruments, the direction is clear: legitimacy is no longer treated as merely cultural; it is becoming a governance target. At the same time, scholarship on trustworthy AI highlights the gap between technical bias mitigation and legal requirements, showing why legality cannot be substituted by engineering rhetoric (Kattnig et al., 2024). If the law is serious about legitimacy, it will insist on standards that preserve contestability and dignity, not merely on performance benchmarks.

Legitimacy is Also Internal: Authority Must Believe in Itself Without Becoming Defensive

A legitimacy story that focuses only on public perception is incomplete. There is also self-legitimacy: the confidence power-holders have in the moral validity of their authority. This matters because insecure institutions become punitive and defensive, while confident, legitimate institutions can be restrained and fair (Bottoms and Tankebe, 2012; Debbaut et al., 2023). In an AI-mediated environment, self-legitimacy can be strained in a peculiar way: authorities may lean on algorithmic tools to avoid blame, which can make them feel safer administratively but weaker morally. When responsibility diffuses—"the system recommended it"—the institution may protect itself in the short term while eroding the long-term perception that it owns its moral decisions. That erosion is precisely what legitimacy theories warn against.

The Cross-National Picture: Procedural Justice Travels Better Than Deterrence

One of the strongest reasons to take procedural justice seriously is that it generalises. While cultures vary, the basic human response to being treated with dignity, neutrality, and voice appears to predict legitimacy and cooperation across many contexts. Recent cross-national tests of procedural justice theory across large numbers of countries reinforce the relevance of legitimacy-based accounts for understanding cooperation with legal authorities (Jackson, 2025). This is critical for a global treatment of the subject: it suggests that legitimacy is not a parochial ideal but a broadly human mechanism. That does not mean one size fits all, but it does mean that any justice system that ignores procedural fairness does so at its peril, regardless of its legal tradition.

What You Should Demand from Any Court that Uses AI

If you are reading this as a scholar, a practitioner, or a policymaker, the practical conclusion is blunt. If a court introduces AI tools, you must ask questions that are legitimacy questions before they are technology questions. Does the tool preserve voice, or does it convert the hearing into a ceremony around a precomputed outcome? Can the affected person understand and contest the basis of the tool's influence? Does the judge remain the moral author of the decision, giving reasons that are humanly intelligible and reviewable? Are error and uncertainty communicated in a way that prevents false certainty? Are governance and oversight designed to prevent drift, bias, and the quiet expansion of tool influence into domains that require moral judgement rather than prediction (Kinchin, 2024; Fischman-Afori, 2025; Robertson, Vignaux and Berger, 2016). The court's legitimacy is not an abstract virtue; it is the behavioural engine of compliance. If you damage it, you will not only make justice less humane; you will make it less effective.

References

- Bottoms, A. and Tankebe, J. (2012) 'Beyond procedural justice: A dialogic approach to legitimacy in criminal justice', Journal of Criminal Law and Criminology, 102(1), pp. 119–170.
- Chan, A., Bradford, B. and Jackson, J. (2025) 'A systematic review and meta-analysis of procedural justice, social identity, and legitimacy in policing', American Journal of Criminal Justice, 50, pp. 1–28.

- Dahl, M. et al. (2024) 'Profiling legal hallucinations in large language models', Journal of Legal Analysis, 16(1), pp. 64–110.
- Debbaut, S. et al. (2023) 'Police legitimacy and culture revisited through the lens of self-legitimacy', Policing and Society, 33(6), pp. 1–18.
- Fine, A. (2024) 'The association between judges and public trust for artificial intelligence', AI and Ethics, 4, pp. 1–15.
- Fine, A., Berthelot, E.R. and Marsh, S. (2025) 'Public perceptions of judges' use of AI tools in courtroom decision-making: An examination of legitimacy, fairness, trust, and procedural justice', Behavioral Sciences, 15(4), 476.
- Fischman-Afori, O. (2025) 'Due process by design: Enhancing fairness and trust in AI decision-making through procedural justice theory', Social Sciences & Humanities Open, 12, 102178.
- Hart, H.L.A. (1968) Punishment and Responsibility: Essays in the Philosophy of Law. Oxford: Oxford University Press.
- Jackson, J. (2025) 'Why do people cooperate with the police and criminal courts? A test of procedural justice theory in 30 countries', Criminology, 63, pp. 1–35.
- Kahneman, D. (2011) Thinking, Fast and Slow. New York: Farrar, Straus and Giroux.
- Kattnig, M. et al. (2024) 'Assessing trustworthy AI: Technical and legal perspectives on bias mitigation and legal requirements', Computer Law & Security Review, 54, 106056.
- Kinchin, N. (2024) '"Voiceless": the procedural gap in algorithmic justice', International Journal of Law and Information Technology, 32(4), pp. 1–30.
- Logg, J.M., Minson, J.A. and Moore, D.A. (2019) 'Algorithm appreciation: People prefer algorithmic to human judgment', Organizational Behavior and Human Decision Processes, 151, pp. 90–103.
- Robertson, B., Vignaux, G.A. and Berger, C.E.H. (2016) Interpreting Evidence: Evaluating Forensic Science in the Courtroom. 2nd edn. Chichester: Wiley.
- Rotenberg, M. (2025) 'Framework Convention on Artificial Intelligence and Human Rights, Democracy, and the Rule of Law (Council of Europe)', International Legal Materials, 64, pp. 1–25.
- Ruschemeier, H. and Hondrich, L.J. (2024) 'Automation bias in public administration—an interdisciplinary perspective from law and psychology', Government Information Quarterly, 41(3), 101953.

- Stoyanova, V. (2025) 'Council of Europe Framework Convention on Artificial Intelligence and Human Rights, Democracy and the Rule of Law: An initial analysis'.
- Sunshine, J. and Tyler, T.R. (2003) 'The role of procedural justice and legitimacy in shaping public support for policing', Law & Society Review, 37(3), pp. 513–548.
- Taeihagh, A. (2025) 'Governance of generative AI', Policy and Society, 44(1), pp. 1–20.
- Tyler, T.R. (2006) Why People Obey the Law. 2nd edn. Princeton, NJ: Princeton University Press.
- Tyler, T.R. (2011) 'Procedural justice, legitimacy, and the effective rule of law', Crime and Justice, 40(1), pp. 283–357.
- Vidaki, A.N. (2025) 'Democratic legitimacy of AI in judicial decision-making', AI & Society, 40, pp. 1–14.

CHAPTER V

A Line-Drawing Framework: Authority, Explainability, Contestabilityand Harm

The First Rule: Do Not Argue About "AI" as if It Were One Thing

If you try to draw limits around "AI in courts" in the abstract, you will fail for the same reason a forensic investigator fails when he calls every trace "evidence" without first identifying what it is evidence of. Courts do not face a single machine; they face an ecology of tools: case-triage systems, risk instruments, sentencing recommenders, translation and transcription engines, document classifiers, pattern detectors, and—now—generative systems that can draft reasons, summarise facts, and cite authorities with alarming fluency. Each tool interferes with adjudication in a different way, and each therefore demands a different legal and moral threshold. The framework you need must be simple enough to apply across systems and strict enough to prevent "helpful assistance" from quietly becoming delegated authority. The line-drawing task, in other words, is not a single line. It is a set of gates, each gate justified by what courts are for: publicly owned judgement, reasons that can be challenged, and coercion constrained by dignity and rights.

So let us do what the courtroom itself does when it is at its best: we will separate functions, identify the point at which a function becomes morally decisive, and then attach safeguards that are proportionate to the stakes. The framework that follows uses four gates—authority, explainability, contestability, and harm—not as slogans, but as forensic tests. Each gate asks a question that can be answered about any proposed use of AI, and each answer tells you whether the use is permissible, conditionally permissible, or prohibited.

Authority: Who Owns the Decision, and Can They Be Held to It?

Authority is the first gate because courts are not merely prediction engines; they are institutions authorised to coerce. A court's decision is legitimate not only because it is correct, but because a human office-holder can say, in public and on the record, "This is my decision, for these reasons," and that statement can be reviewed, appealed, criticised, and—when necessary—reversed. The practical danger of algorithmic systems is not that they will sit on the bench wearing robes; it is that they will become the real decision-maker while the human judge becomes the narrator of an outcome that has already been architected elsewhere. This is why scholarship describing a "procedural gap" in algorithmic justice matters: even where a human signs the order, the person subjected to the order can experience the process as voiceless if the decisive weight lies in an output they cannot meaningfully engage with.

Authority, therefore, is the test of substitution. If the system's output sets the default outcome, frames the defendant as a class member ("high risk"), or becomes the decisive justification under time pressure, the court has already crossed from assistance to delegation. You should treat that crossing as a high-risk transformation of institutional power. Modern governance instruments increasingly share this instinct, precisely because they recognise that AI in rights-sensitive domains risks eroding accountability and rule-of-law commitments; peer-reviewed analyses of the European AI Act's implications for the judiciary explicitly frame the problem as one of accountability architectures, not merely technical safeguards.

A clean way to operationalise the authority gate is to ask: if the outcome is unjust, can we identify a responsible decision-maker who had both the capacity and the duty to resist the tool? If the honest answer is "no," then the system is designed to diffuse responsibility. Courts must treat responsibility diffusion as a constitutional pathology. The law punishes individuals on theories of responsibility, intent, and culpability; it cannot morally operate a punishment system that excuses itself through bureaucratic fog when its own instruments harm.

Explainability: Reasons, Not Just Explanations

Explainability is the second gate because courts are reason-giving institutions. Yet "explainability" is often misunderstood as a purely technical property—opening the black box, showing weights, revealing code. That may be useful, but it is not the legal heart of the matter. What the legal system needs is not a technical explanation; it needs actionable reasons—reasons that can be understood in ordinary language and used by the affected person to challenge the basis of coercion. This is where the distinction between explanation and justification becomes crucial: an explanation tells you how a system produced an output; a justification tells you why the state is entitled to rely on it in restricting liberty.

One of the most influential contributions here is the proposal for counterfactual explanations: rather than demanding full code disclosure, provide the person with the smallest change that would have altered the decision, thereby giving meaningful information about the decision boundary without revealing proprietary internals. Counterfactuals matter because they align with the legal structure of contest: they equip a party to argue relevance, correct errors, and demonstrate that a decision rests on contestable assumptions rather than on fate. But you must resist the temptation to treat counterfactuals as a universal cure. A counterfactual can tell someone how to obtain a different score; it does not tell the court whether the score is morally permissible to use as a basis for punishment, nor does it resolve the deep legal problem that many predictive systems encode correlation where law sometimes requires causation, intention, or culpability.

So the explainability gate requires two levels. The first is intelligibility to the subject: can the defendant understand what mattered and why? The second is intelligibility to the reviewing system: can an appellate court or oversight body examine whether the reasons are compatible with equality, proportionality, and due process? Peer-reviewed work on administrative law and algorithmic decision-making emphasises precisely this point: the scalability of error, opacity, and correlation-based inference strain ordinary legal controls unless the legal system adapts its doctrines of reason-giving and review to the realities of automated systems.

If the tool cannot meet these levels, it may still be usable for low-stakes internal administration. But it must not become a liberty-constraining basis for detention, sentencing severity, or punitive classification. The more coercive the consequence, the higher the explainability burden.

Contestability: The Adversarial System Must Be Able to Bite

Contestability is the third gate because a court without contest is a tribunal; a tribunal without contest is administration; and administration without contest is precisely where rights go to die quietly. Contestability is the capacity of a person to challenge the grounds of a decision effectively—not merely to speak, but to be heard in a way that can change the outcome. This is why the procedural justice lens is not a soft sociological add-on; it is an operational requirement of legitimacy. When systems become algorithmic, the most common failure is that they preserve formal hearings while hollowing them out, leaving people with "voice" as ritual but not as leverage.

Here the most useful modern contribution is the idea of "due process by design": embed procedural elements—especially meaningful input and hearing-like opportunities—into the architecture of AI decision systems, rather than treating procedural fairness as a post-hoc policy statement. This does not mean automating hearings in some dystopian theatre; it means ensuring that the system is built to accept and incorporate challengeable inputs, disclose the relevant basis for decisions, and accommodate corrections. If a model's inputs include prior arrests, for example, contestability requires that the person can challenge those inputs' relevance and accuracy, especially where arrests may reflect enforcement patterns rather than proven culpability. If the system uses proxies for socio-economic vulnerability, contestability requires mechanisms to argue that such proxies are morally and legally improper as grounds for coercion.

Contestability also has a forensic dimension: can the defence test the instrument's reliability in the conditions of use, including error rates, drift, and predictive inconsistency? The problem of "predictive inconsistency" shows why this matters: equally defensible modelling choices can produce materially different risk scores for the same individual, meaning the output is not a stable "fact" but a product of design decisions. If contestability is real, the court must be able to interrogate that instability before giving the output decisive weight.

A final and often ignored contestability point concerns "human oversight." Oversight is routinely offered as the universal safeguard—"a human will review it"—yet behavioural research on automation bias warns that humans tend to over-trust machine suggestions, especially under pressure, making oversight far less protective than policy documents assume. If your contestability model relies on a judge heroically resisting a neat number, you are not designing a safeguard; you are writing a prayer.

Harm: Identify What Can Go Wrong, Then Assign Burdens Accordingly

The fourth gate is harm because line-drawing is ultimately about preventing wrongful coercion. But "harm" in algorithmic justice is not a single thing. It comes in layers, and each layer has its own legal and moral remedy. Begin with liberty harm: detention, increased sentence, restrictive supervision, denial of bail. These are obvious, and they demand the strictest safeguards. Then consider equality harm: disparate burdens placed on groups due to biased data, proxy variables, or feedback loops that entrench historic over-policing. Equality harm is not always visible in an individual file, but it becomes visible at the system level, and courts must treat system-level harm as legally relevant because justice is not only individualised; it is also an institutional promise of equal concern and respect.

Then consider dignity harm: the harm of being processed rather than heard, scored rather than judged, reduced to a probability rather than treated as an agent. Dignity harm is not sentimental; it is behavioural. It affects cooperation, compliance, and legitimacy, and it can turn legal institutions into objects of cynicism even when outcomes are statistically "improved." This is why procedural justice-based approaches have been used to argue that fairness of process, especially voice, is foundational to trust in AI-mediated decision systems.

Finally, consider epistemic harm: the corruption of the court's knowledge practices. If a model generates outputs that appear authoritative but rest on correlations irrelevant to legal culpability, or if generative tools fabricate citations or distort precedent, the court's reasons-giving function is contaminated. In the AI era, epistemic harm is not hypothetical; peer-reviewed research has documented "legal hallucinations" in large language models and their tendency to produce false legal references under plausible prompts, which is poison to a system that depends on checkable reasons. (This harm is best controlled by strict usage boundaries: generative tools may assist research and drafting only when outputs are independently verified; they must not be relied upon as sources of legal truth.)

Once harms are differentiated, you can assign burdens. Liberty-constraining uses carry the highest burden of transparency, validation, and contestability. System-level tools used for resource allocation carry audit burdens focused on equity and feedback loop detection. Dignity and legitimacy harms carry process design burdens: voice, intelligibility, and reasons-giving. Epistemic harms carry verification burdens: source checking, citation validation, and prohibitions on unverified machine-generated authorities.

Putting the Gates Together: A Practical Sequence Courts Can Apply

Now assemble the framework the way a careful judge assembles a judgment: step by step, with the order doing the work. First, locate the tool's function in the judicial pipeline: information retrieval, evidence interpretation, risk assessment, recommendation, or decision implementation. Second, apply the authority gate: does the tool merely inform, or does it set the default outcome? Third, apply the explainability gate: can the affected person understand the basis of the tool's influence, and can a reviewing body examine that basis? Fourth, apply the contestability gate: can the person challenge inputs, assumptions, and reliability in a way that can change the outcome, and is "human oversight" psychologically credible given automation bias? Fifth, apply the harm gate: what harms could occur, at what scale, and what burdens must the state meet before using the tool?

This sequence is not a theoretical luxury. It reflects what modern regulatory discussions increasingly converge on: that oversight must be lifecycle-based, contestability-sensitive, and rights-oriented for high-risk systems. Peer-reviewed analyses of the interaction between the EU AI Act and the Council of Europe's AI Convention reinforce that the regulatory direction of travel is toward binding principles of accountability, transparency, and rule-of-law alignment across the lifecycle of AI systems. The framework above translates that direction into courtroom logic: not "trustworthy AI" as a slogan, but trustworthy adjudication as a practice.

The Red Lines: Where Courts Must Refuse Delegation

A framework is only honest if it can state prohibitions. The most defensible red line is this: no system may determine the quantum of punishment, detention, or liberty restriction on the basis of predictive risk unless the use is fully contestable, intelligible, validated for the population and conditions of use, and consistent with the legal system's commitments to proportionality and equality. If those conditions cannot be met—because the tool is proprietary, opaque, unstable, or cognitively corrupting—then the court must refuse to treat its output as a reason for coercion. A second red line follows naturally: generative systems may not be treated as legal authorities. They may assist research and drafting only under verification protocols that preserve the court's epistemic integrity. A third red line is subtler but equally important: systems that hollow out hearings by replacing voice with scoring must be resisted, even if they improve throughput, because they erode legitimacy as behavioural infrastructure.

The reader may ask, "Is this too strict?" The forensic answer is that liberty decisions demand forensic standards: validation, error awareness, interpretive discipline, and adversarial testing. The moral answer is that the state's right to punish is not purchased by accuracy alone. It is purchased by reasoned, reviewable, contestable coercion that treats persons as agents and citizens. Accuracy is valuable. Efficiency is valuable. Consistency is valuable. But none of them is sovereign, and none of them is a moral theory.

References

- Ashworth, A. and Zedner, L. (2014) Preventive Justice. Oxford: Oxford University Press.
- Barocas, S., Hardt, M. and Narayanan, A. (2023) Fairness and Machine Learning: Limitations and Opportunities. Cambridge, MA: MIT Press.
- Barysė, D. and Sarel, R. (2024) 'Algorithms in the court: does it matter which part of the judicial decision-making is automated?', Artificial Intelligence and Law, 32(1), pp. 117–146.
- Carnat, I. (2024) 'Addressing the risks of generative AI for the judiciary: The accountability framework(s) under the EU AI Act', Computer Law & Security Review, 55, 106067.
- Dahl, M. et al. (2024) 'Profiling legal hallucinations in large language models', Journal of Legal Analysis, 16(1), pp. 64–110.
- Dressel, J. and Farid, H. (2018) 'The accuracy, fairness, and limits of predicting recidivism', Science Advances, 4(1), eaao5580.
- Duff, R.A. (2001) Punishment, Communication, and Community. Oxford: Oxford University Press.
- Fine, A., Berthelot, E.R. and Marsh, S. (2025) 'Public perceptions of judges' use of AI tools in courtroom decision-making: legitimacy, fairness, trust, and procedural justice', Behavioral Sciences, 15(4), 476.

- Fischman-Afori, O. (2025) 'Due process by design: Enhancing fairness and trust in AI decision-making through procedural justice theory', Social Sciences & Humanities Open, 12, 102178.
- Greene, T. (2022) 'Predictive inconsistency in criminal justice algorithmic risk prediction tools', Journal of the Royal Statistical Society: Series A, 185(S2), pp. S692–S716.
- Hart, H.L.A. (1968) Punishment and Responsibility: Essays in the Philosophy of Law. Oxford: Oxford University Press.
- Jackson, J. (2025) 'Why do people cooperate with the police and criminal courts? A test of procedural justice theory in 30 countries', Criminology, 63, pp. 1–35.
- Kahneman, D. (2011) Thinking, Fast and Slow. New York: Farrar, Straus and Giroux.
- Kinchin, N. (2024) '"Voiceless": the procedural gap in algorithmic justice', International Journal of Law and Information Technology, 32(4), pp. 1–30.
- Koulu, R. (2020) 'Proceduralizing control and discretion: Human oversight in automated legal decision-making', Journal of Law and Society, 47(3), pp. 386–413.
- Logg, J.M., Minson, J.A. and Moore, D.A. (2019) 'Algorithm appreciation: People prefer algorithmic to human judgment', Organizational Behavior and Human Decision Processes, 151, pp. 90–103.
- Monahan, J. and Skeem, J.L. (2016) 'Risk assessment in criminal sentencing', Annual Review of Clinical Psychology, 12, pp. 489–513.
- Presno Linera, M.Á. et al. (2025) 'Regulating AI from Europe: A joint analysis of the AI Act and the Council of Europe AI Convention', Journal of Cyber Policy, 10(1), pp. 1–25.
- Robertson, B., Vignaux, G.A. and Berger, C.E.H. (2016) Interpreting Evidence: Evaluating Forensic Science in the Courtroom. 2nd edn. Chichester: Wiley.
- Rotenberg, M. (2025) 'Framework Convention on Artificial Intelligence and Human Rights, Democracy and the Rule of Law (Council of Europe)', International Legal Materials, 64, pp. 1–25.
- Ruschemeier, H. and Hondrich, L.J. (2024) 'Automation bias in public administration—an interdisciplinary perspective from law and psychology', Government Information Quarterly, 41(3), 101953.
- Stoyanova, V. (2025) 'Council of Europe Framework Convention on Artificial Intelligence and Human Rights, Democracy and the Rule of

Law: An initial analysis'.

- Sunshine, J. and Tyler, T.R. (2003) 'The role of procedural justice and legitimacy in shaping public support for policing', Law & Society Review, 37(3), pp. 513–548.
- Taylor, I. (2023) 'Justice by algorithm: The limits of AI in criminal sentencing', Criminal Justice Ethics, 42(3), pp. 193–213.
- Tyler, T.R. (2006) Why People Obey the Law. 2nd edn. Princeton, NJ: Princeton University Press.
- Ugwudike, P. (2025) 'Sentencing and risk assessment algorithms', in De Gruyter Handbook of Digital Criminology. Berlin: De Gruyter.
- von Hirsch, A. (1976) Doing Justice: The Choice of Punishments. New York: Hill and Wang.
- Wachter, S., Mittelstadt, B. and Russell, C. (2018) 'Counterfactual explanations without opening the black box: Automated decisions and the GDPR', Harvard Journal of Law & Technology, 31(2), pp. 841–887.
- Williams, R. (2022) 'Rethinking administrative law for algorithmic decision making', Oxford Journal of Legal Studies, 42(2), pp. 468–494.

Part II — The Courtroom AI Stack: Tools, Claims, and Failure Modes

CHAPTER VI

Risk Scores and Their Hidden Ontologies: What Exactly Is Being Predicted?

The First Mistake: Treating "Risk" as a Natural Object

When you see a risk score in a case file, you are tempted to treat it as if it were a measurement like height, blood alcohol, or DNA match probability. It looks numerical, it looks stable, and it arrives with the quiet authority of quantification. But "risk" is not a natural object waiting to be discovered; it is a constructed object that depends on what an institution chooses to count as harm, what it chooses to count as failure, what time horizon it chooses to care about, and what data it is willing or able to treat as truth. This is why risk scores have hidden ontologies: beneath the surface number sits a set of decisions about what kinds of events exist, which of those events matter, and which of those events can be treated as evidence of the underlying thing called "risk." Once you see that, you will stop asking only whether a score is accurate and begin asking the question that courts should have asked from the beginning: accurate about what, and for whose purposes?

In forensic science, we have a discipline for this. We do not accept an instrument merely because it produces a number; we ask what proposition the number bears on, what the number actually measures, what the error looks like in the conditions of use, and how interpretation can be contaminated by context and cognition (Robertson, Vignaux and Berger, 2016). If you apply the same discipline to criminal justice risk scores, you discover the central problem: many risk scores do not directly predict "crime" in any morally clean sense. They often predict institutional events—rearrest, reconviction, reimprisonment, failure to appear, breach of conditions—that are partly reflections of behaviour and partly reflections of enforcement patterns, prosecutorial choices, resource constraints, and supervision intensity. The score, then, is frequently a forecast of system-contact as much as a forecast of wrongdoing, and the ontology you adopt determines whether the tool is morally tolerable or a disguised mechanism of structural reproduction (Neil, 2025).

The Outcome Variable is a Moral Choice Disguised as a Technical Choice

Most risk instruments are built around one deceptively simple act: defining the outcome. "Recidivism" is treated as if it were a single thing, but peer-reviewed criminological and psychiatric literature has long emphasised that recidivism is a broad umbrella that can include rearrest, reconviction, or reimprisonment, and that these are not interchangeable as measures of underlying criminal behaviour (Fazel et al., 2015). If you shift the outcome from reconviction to rearrest, you are not merely changing a label; you are changing the metaphysics of what the score means. Rearrest is more sensitive to policing and detection; reconviction is more sensitive to prosecution and adjudication; reimprisonment is more sensitive still to sentencing practice and supervision regimes. A model that "predicts recidivism" may therefore be predicting the probability of being detected, prosecuted, and processed rather than the probability of committing an offence. That is not a technical footnote; it is the moral centre of the matter, because the state is using these forecasts to justify coercion.

Global evidence sharpens the point rather than blurring it. Recidivism rates vary widely across countries and sanction types, and the reported rates depend on the outcome definition and time window, not merely on offender behaviour (Yukhnenko et al., 2023). The same systematic review notes that recidivism rates appeared lower during the COVID-19 period in some settings, plausibly linked to disruptions in justice processes and reduced crime opportunities (Yukhnenko et al., 2023). This is exactly what you would expect if recidivism measures partly track institutional throughput and opportunity structures. A score trained on a period of disrupted policing or court operations will internalise those distortions unless the designers explicitly model them. When your target variable is partly "system activity," world events become signal, and the model can quietly mistake institutional turbulence for offender change.

The Selective Labels Problem: Prediction Built on Decisions, Not on Reality

Even if you choose a morally defensible outcome, you face an epistemic trap: the data are generated by prior decisions. Bail prediction is the cleanest illustration because it exposes the paradox with almost embarrassing clarity. Judges detain some defendants and release others; you can only observe "did they reoffend while released?" for those who were released. The label is missing precisely where the decision was most restrictive. Kleinberg and colleagues show that comparing algorithms to judges is complicated because the data are selective, shaped by earlier human decisions that determine what outcomes are observable (Kleinberg et al., 2018). This is not a technical inconvenience; it is an ontological problem. The model is not trained on a neutral portrait of what "would have happened." It is trained on a world filtered through past judicial and policing choices. If the past system was biased, the model inherits the bias in the form of missingness and skew. If the past system was inconsistent, the model may stabilise inconsistency into an apparently objective rule.

From a forensic standpoint, this is akin to building an identification method using evidence collected only from certain neighbourhoods and then treating the method's outputs as general truths about persons. The method's "knowledge" is confounded with the pathway by which evidence was collected. A court that treats risk scores as neutral facts without confronting selective labels is behaving like an investigator who mistakes a sampling artefact for a trait.

"Risk" is Often a Proxy for Exposure: When Ontology Becomes Inequality

The most important recent review in criminology on algorithmic bias in criminal risk assessment makes the core point explicit: arrest data are not pure measures of crime, and racial differences in arrest as a measure of crime can generate algorithmic bias when arrest records are used as outcomes or key predictors (Neil, 2025). Notice what that implies about ontology. If your predicted event is rearrest, the object you are predicting is partly "police attention," "enforcement intensity," and "surveillance geography." You are not predicting "dangerousness" in a morally clean sense; you are predicting contact with a system that is itself socially patterned. This is why fairness controversies do not disappear when models are improved. Better prediction can mean better prediction of institutional pathways, and if those pathways reflect structural inequity, the "better" model can become a more efficient reproducer of inequality.

Berk's recent work on improving fairness in criminal justice risk assessments illustrates that risk assessment procedures can be modified to pursue fairness goals, but also that fairness is not a single metric; it is a contested family of constraints that trade off against one another and against accuracy (Berk, 2024; Berk et al., 2021). This is not merely a math problem. It is a moral reality: different fairness criteria correspond to different moral intuitions about equality. The "hidden ontology" returns here too, because fairness metrics typically assume that the outcome being predicted is morally legitimate to predict in the first place. If the outcome encodes biased enforcement, you can satisfy some fairness constraints and still be morally wrong at the foundational level.

The Construct Validity Question: Does the Tool Measure What It Claims?

Risk tools often claim to measure stable propensities—violence risk, reoffending risk, flight risk—yet the psychological and criminological measurement literature warns against assuming that predictive validity alone resolves the question of what is being measured. Construct validity asks whether the instrument measures the thing it purports to measure, and measurement quality is not automatically secured by predictive performance (Hendry, Douglas and Lilienfeld, 2013). This matters because risk tools are frequently built as composites of heterogeneous items: prior convictions, age, employment, housing, substance use, peer associations, compliance history. Some of these are plausibly criminogenic needs; some are demographic correlates; some are institutional contact markers. When you add them up and call the sum "risk," you have created a construct. The question is whether that construct maps onto a morally and legally permissible object to use in restricting liberty.

Violence risk assessment scholarship, particularly in forensic psychiatry, is instructive because it has wrestled with these validity issues under high stakes. Reviews emphasise that although risk assessment tools are widely used, the evidence base has limitations and can be biased, and predictive accuracy varies with context (Douglas et al., 2017). The deeper lesson is methodological humility: even where prediction is useful, the instrument is not measuring a single essence called "dangerousness"; it is producing a probability under assumptions that must be disclosed and bounded.

A Risk Score is a Story about Time

Every risk score is also a claim about time: risk over what horizon? Two years? Six months? Ten? The horizon is not an innocent parameter. A longer horizon tends to increase base rates and inflate apparent predictability; a shorter horizon may miss slow-burn risks but can be more relevant for immediate decisions like bail. The horizon is therefore a governance choice about what kind of uncertainty the institution is willing to live with and what kind of harm it is willing to prioritise. It also shapes what "success" means: if a person is not rearrested within two years, is that desistance, luck, non-detection, or a shift in policing? The ontology of risk collapses if time is treated as a technicality. This is why global recidivism comparisons must be interpreted carefully: differences may reflect horizon choice and outcome definition as much as offender behaviour (Yukhnenko et al., 2023).

Predictive Inconsistency: When the Same Person Has Many "Risks"

Even if you accept the outcome definition, the predictors, and the horizon, you face another ontological instability: equally defensible modelling choices can yield different risk scores for the same individual. Greene and colleagues conceptualise this as predictive inconsistency, showing that forking paths in development, testing, and deployment can produce materially different individual-level predictions (Greene et al., 2022). The legal system tends to treat the score as a fact about the person—"high risk"—but predictive inconsistency reveals it is often a fact about the modelling pathway. From a forensic perspective, this resembles the difference between a trace and its interpretation: the trace may be stable, but the inference can vary with method choice, contextual information, and decision thresholds. Courts have learned to demand discipline in forensic interpretation for precisely this reason. Yet with risk scores, courts and agencies often accept the interpretive layer as if it were the trace itself.

This is not an argument for nihilism. It is an argument for epistemic honesty: if multiple plausible risk scores can be generated for the same person, the legal system must treat any single score as contestable and must demand transparency about the reasonable range of predictions under alternative specifications. Otherwise, the system is punishing the person for the modeller's choice masquerading as certainty.

Fairness Trade-offs Expose Ontology: You Cannot Be Fair to Two Worlds at Once

The classic impossibility results in algorithmic fairness are often presented as technical puzzles, but their significance is ontological. Chouldechova shows that several popular fairness criteria cannot all be satisfied when base rates differ across groups, and that disparate impact can arise when error rate balance is not achieved (Chouldechova, 2017). Kleinberg, Mullainathan, and Raghavan formalise trade-offs among fairness conditions and show that except in constrained cases, they cannot be simultaneously satisfied (Kleinberg, Mullainathan and Raghavan, 2017).

What does this tell you about "what is being predicted"? It tells you that a risk score is not merely forecasting an event; it is embedding a choice about which kind of fairness reality the institution will live in. When base rates differ, any scoring rule will distribute error differently across groups. That distribution is not a property of nature; it is a property of the institutional choice to use a score in a world shaped by unequal histories. The ontology of risk is therefore moral: a score is a way of organising uncertainty and allocating error burdens. The court must decide, openly, whose liberty is more likely to be wrongly restricted and whose harm is more likely to be wrongly risked.

The COMPAS Controversy Was Not Just About Bias; It Was About Secrecy and Meaning

Public debates around proprietary tools such as COMPAS are often reduced to "is it biased?" But the deeper problem was ontological opacity: what does the score actually mean, how was it built, and what fairness definition is being used? Rudin's critique of opaque, proprietary risk models argues that secrecy and complexity are not justified when interpretable models can perform competitively and when the justice system requires transparency for legitimacy and contestability (Rudin, 2020). The point is not that transparency automatically makes a model fair; it is that without transparency, you cannot even know what moral object the institution has created. A score that predicts "two-year rearrest" is not the same as a score that predicts "violent reconviction," and neither is identical to "dangerousness." When institutions use a score as if it were dangerousness, they commit a category error with liberty at stake.

Risk Scores as Forensic Evidence: Chain of Custody, Error, and Context

If you treat risk scores as forensic artefacts, certain requirements become non-negotiable. First, provenance: what data sources, what period, what inclusion criteria, what missingness mechanisms, what label definitions. Second, validation: out-of-sample performance under conditions that resemble the deployment environment, including subgroup performance and stability over time (Monahan and Skeem, 2016; Douglas et al., 2017). Third, uncertainty communication: how should the output be interpreted, with what confidence, and what are the known error rates? Fourth, context control: how should the score be presented to decision-makers to minimise cognitive anchoring and automation bias? Behavioural evidence on human use of algorithmic advice shows that humans are influenced by machine outputs in predictable ways, and "human oversight" cannot be assumed to neutralise these effects (Portela et al., 2025).

This is the forensic heart of ontology: a score's meaning is not only in its mathematical definition; it is in the institutional chain from data to output to decision to downstream consequences. A risk score is "about" what it does in practice, not what its designers claim it measures.

The Governance Turn: Why High-Risk Classification Mirrors the Stakes of Ontology

Recent legal governance trends signal an emerging consensus that AI used in justice-related contexts is high-stakes because it can affect fundamental rights. Analyses of European governance frameworks in peer-reviewed venues emphasise accountability gaps and rights risks when AI systems are used in judicial domains (Carnat, 2024). The Council of Europe's Framework Convention on AI is explicitly grounded in human rights, democracy, and rule of law commitments across the lifecycle of AI systems, reflecting a global move toward binding governance principles rather than voluntary ethics (Rotenberg, 2025). The relevance to this chapter is direct: governance instruments are reacting to the same ontological reality. When a system's outputs cannot be meaningfully scrutinised, you do not merely risk error; you risk unaccountable power.

What Exactly Is Being Predicted? A Courtroom Answer You Can Defend

So let us answer the question in a form you can use in court, in policy, and in scholarship. A risk score typically predicts a defined institutional event—rearrest, reconviction, reimprisonment, failure to appear, violation—over a chosen time horizon, using variables that mix behavioural history, demographic correlates, and system-contact markers. Because the outcome and predictors are socially patterned, the score often predicts a blend of individual behaviour and institutional exposure. Because the data are selective and decision-generated, the score often encodes the footprints of prior discretion. Because modelling choices are plural, the score can be unstable across reasonable specifications. And because fairness criteria trade off under differing base rates, the score allocates error burdens in morally significant ways (Fazel et al., 2015; Kleinberg, Mullainathan and Raghavan, 2017; Chouldechova, 2017; Greene et al., 2022; Neil, 2025).

Once you accept this, the line-drawing implications follow with almost mechanical clarity. If the score is predicting an event that is too contaminated by enforcement bias to serve as a legitimate proxy for wrongdoing, then the score's use as a basis for coercion is morally compromised. If the score cannot be contested because its construction is opaque or proprietary, then its use undermines due process and legitimacy. If the score is presented as a fact about the person rather than as a probabilistic, contestable artefact under uncertainty, then the courtroom risks replacing judgement with administration.

The Practical Discipline: Four Questions Before Any Risk Score Touches Liberty

Before any risk score is allowed to influence detention, sentencing severity, or punitive classification, a court committed to forensic discipline should be able to answer, on the record, four questions in human language. First, what is the precise outcome being predicted, and why is it a morally permissible basis for coercion? Second, what is the relationship between that outcome and the thing the court actually cares about—culpability, dangerousness, public safety—and what confounding institutional processes might be embedded in the outcome? Third, what is the validated performance, uncertainty, and stability under the conditions of use, including across protected groups and over time? Fourth, what contest mechanisms exist for the affected person to challenge inputs, assumptions, and relevance, and what safeguards exist against cognitive capture of the human decision-maker? These questions are not "anti-technology." They are pro-law. They are what it means to keep coercion answerable.

If you are serious about justice, you do not ask a risk score to be a moral theory. You ask it to be a bounded, transparent, contestable piece of evidence—no more—and you refuse to let it quietly redefine the person as a probability.

References

- Berk, R. (2024) 'Improving fairness in criminal justice algorithmic risk assessments', Sociological Methods & Research.
- Berk, R., Heidari, H., Jabbari, S., Kearns, M. and Roth, A. (2021) 'Fairness in criminal justice risk assessments: The state of the art', Sociological Methods & Research, 50(1), pp. 3–44.
- Carnat, I. (2024) 'Addressing the risks of generative AI for the judiciary: The accountability framework(s) under the EU AI Act', Computer Law & Security Review, 55, 106067.
- Chouldechova, A. (2017) 'Fair prediction with disparate impact: A study of bias in recidivism prediction instruments', Big Data, 5(2), pp. 153–163.
- Douglas, T., Pugh, J., Singh, I., Savulescu, J. and Fazel, S. (2017) 'Risk assessment tools in criminal justice and forensic psychiatry', Nature Human Behaviour, 1, pp. 1–6.
- Dressel, J. and Farid, H. (2018) 'The accuracy, fairness, and limits of predicting recidivism', Science Advances, 4(1), eaao5580.
- Fazel, S., Wolf, A., Chang, Z., Larsson, H., Goodwin, G.M. and Lichtenstein, P. (2015) 'A systematic review of criminal recidivism rates worldwide', PLoS ONE, 10(6), e0130390.
- Ghasemi, M., Ward, J.T. and Hamilton, Z. (2021) 'The application of machine learning to a general risk assessment', Criminal Justice and Behavior.
- Greene, T., Shmueli, G., Fell, J., Lin, C.-F. and Liu, H.-W. (2022) 'Predictive inconsistency in criminal justice algorithmic risk prediction

tools', Journal of the Royal Statistical Society: Series A, 185(S2), pp. S692–S716.

- Hendry, M.C., Douglas, K.S. and Lilienfeld, S.O. (2013) 'Construct measurement quality improves predictive validity of risk assessment', Behavioral Sciences & the Law, 31(2), pp. 236–252.
- Kahneman, D. (2011) Thinking, Fast and Slow. New York: Farrar, Straus and Giroux.
- Kleinberg, J., Mullainathan, S. and Raghavan, M. (2017) 'Inherent trade-offs in the fair determination of risk scores', in Proceedings of ITCS 2017.
- Kleinberg, J., Lakkaraju, H., Leskovec, J., Ludwig, J. and Mullainathan, S. (2018) 'Human decisions and machine predictions', The Quarterly Journal of Economics, 133(1), pp. 237–293.
- Monahan, J. and Skeem, J.L. (2016) 'Risk assessment in criminal sentencing', Annual Review of Clinical Psychology, 12, pp. 489–513.
- Neil, R. (2025) 'Algorithmic bias in criminal risk assessment: The consequences of racial differences in arrest as a measure of crime', Annual Review of Criminology.
- Portela, M., Rettenberger, M. et al. (2025) 'A comparative user study of human predictions in algorithm-based risk assessment', Artificial Intelligence and Law.
- Robertson, B., Vignaux, G.A. and Berger, C.E.H. (2016) Interpreting Evidence: Evaluating Forensic Science in the Courtroom. 2nd edn. Chichester: Wiley.
- Rotenberg, M. (2025) 'Framework Convention on Artificial Intelligence and Human Rights, Democracy, and the Rule of Law (Council of Europe)', International Legal Materials, 64.
- Rudin, C. (2020) 'The age of secrecy and unfairness in recidivism prediction', Harvard Data Science Review.
- Yukhnenko, D., Sridhar, S., Fazel, S. et al. (2023) 'Criminal recidivism rates globally: A 6-year systematic review update', Journal of Criminal Justice, 87, 102087.

CHAPTER VII

Sentencing Algorithms: From Guidelines to Optimization

The Shift You Must Notice: Sentencing Stops Looking Like Judgement and Starts Looking Like Design

For most of modern legal history, sentencing looked like a human act carried out in public: the judge listened, weighed culpability, weighed mitigation, weighed protection, and then pronounced a sentence that could be defended in reasons and corrected on appeal. That picture was never as pure as it sounds—sentencing has always been shaped by politics, resource constraints, and social fear—but the form mattered because the form carried the moral claim that punishment is imposed by an accountable person for publicly intelligible reasons. What changes with sentencing algorithms is not merely that the court receives a new tool; it is that the logic of sentencing itself is invited to migrate from reasoned judgement to system engineering. First came structured sentencing and guidelines, which aimed to discipline discretion. Then came actuarial instruments and risk scoring, which aimed to discipline uncertainty. Now comes optimization, which aims to discipline outcomes: minimize reoffending, minimize disparity, minimize incarceration costs, maximize public safety, maximize "consistency," sometimes all at once. This is the moment where you must slow down, because the language of optimization is persuasive precisely because it sounds like care. Yet optimization is not a moral theory. It is a technique that presupposes a moral theory. If you do not control what is being optimized, you will eventually find that the system has optimized away the very things that make punishment legitimate.

The Guideline Era: A First Attempt at Mechanising Proportionality

Guidelines were the first large-scale attempt to tame sentencing's variability without openly abolishing judgement. They took the form of grids, starting points, ranges, aggravators, and mitigators, and they promised equality: similar cases would be treated similarly. Philosophically, they were a compromise between discretion and rule, trying to preserve individualisation while preventing arbitrariness. In practice, they also demonstrated a central truth that becomes even more important in the algorithmic era: any system that structures sentencing embeds a theory of punishment in its architecture. A guideline grid is not neutral. It encodes which facts matter, what counts as severity, how prior history is weighed, and how much room is left for mercy and context. The system's "fairness" is thus inseparable from its ontology of relevance. Algorithms are often presented as if they are simply a more accurate form of guidelines, but that is conceptually wrong. Guidelines structure reasons; algorithms structure predictions and, increasingly, utilities. The movement from guidelines to algorithms is therefore a movement from the rule-like ordering of reasons to the model-like ordering of outcomes.

The Second Phase: From Guidelines to Recommendation Engines

When algorithms arrive in sentencing, they typically begin as decision support. They promise to tell the judge what similarly situated defendants "usually get," or what sentence would be "proportionate," or what sentence is "recommended" given risk and seriousness. The philosophical defence of this move has been argued explicitly: Chiao's case for algorithmic sentencing treats proportionality as something that can be systematised by predicting what a typical judge in the jurisdiction would regard as proportionate, thereby reducing arbitrariness and bias (Chiao, 2018). That proposal is clean in its ambition and dangerous in its implication. If proportionality is reconstructed as the prediction of a jurisdiction's typical sentencing practice, the algorithm becomes a mirror of institutional norms. It will reproduce not only coherence but also whatever the institution has normalised—severity, racialised enforcement footprints, political panics, and local harshness. The moment you treat "what we tend to do" as the operational definition of "what is proportionate," you have slid from moral justification to institutional self-confirmation.

This is why the more recent ethical literature has intensified rather than relaxed concerns. Taylor's argument that sentencing is bound up with condemnation—punishment as a public communicative act—insists that algorithmic systems risk undermining that condemnatory function unless meaningful public control and human ownership of judgement are preserved (Taylor, 2023). Ryberg's reply engages the condemnation worry directly and clarifies that the core dispute is not whether algorithms can assist, but how they can be used without displacing the moral authorship of sentencing (Ryberg, 2024). This debate matters because it exposes the line courts must draw: recommendation engines are not dangerous because they are "cold," but because they can become the silent sovereign of outcomes, leaving the judge as a signatory rather than an author.

The Third Phase: From Recommendation to Optimization

Optimization is the point at which the sentencing system stops asking "what punishment fits?" and starts asking "what decision produces the best aggregate profile of outcomes?" That shift is not always explicit. It often arrives through the respectable language of "evidence-based sentencing," "reducing reoffending," "targeting resources," "reducing disparity," and "allocating prison beds efficiently." Yet once the system is framed as an optimization problem, sentencing becomes a policy lever in a control system, and the person before the court becomes a unit in a harm-management calculus. Philosophical and socio-legal critiques have begun to name this directly. Work critiquing predictive optimization argues that legitimacy is threatened when systems are designed to optimise predicted outcomes in ways that bypass the public, reason-giving nature of legal authority and convert adjudication into technocratic management (Kroll, 2024). The point is not that outcomes do not matter. The point is that criminal justice is a domain where the state claims the right to coerce through reasons, not through mere performance. When a sentencing algorithm is trained and deployed as an optimizer, it inevitably imports a moral hierarchy of values—often unannounced—because every objective function chooses what counts as success and whose errors are tolerable.

The Forensic Analogy: Treat the Algorithm as Evidence, Not as Authority

To remain lawful in spirit, the court must treat algorithmic sentencing outputs the way it treats forensic outputs: as contestable evidence with a known scope, not as a decision disguised as a number. Forensic reasoning insists on proposition clarity, validation under conditions of use, error characterization, and disciplined communication of uncertainty (Robertson, Vignaux and Berger, 2016). If a model produces a "recommended sentence," the proposition is not "this is the right sentence." The proposition is something narrower—"this sentence is within a predicted distribution of sentences for similar fact patterns," or "this sentence is predicted to reduce breach risk given certain assumptions." Each of those propositions demands different kinds of validation and different moral constraints. When institutions fail to specify the proposition, the output becomes a floating authority: it can be invoked to justify severity, or to justify leniency, depending on institutional appetite, while appearing neutral in both cases.

This is where the "input problem" becomes decisive. A sentencing algorithm requires inputs—offence seriousness, prior history, social factors, compliance history—and the selection and weighting of inputs are not technical details but normative choices. Ryberg's "input problem" work makes this explicit: different input schemes can operationalise different punishment theories and can produce ethically divergent outcomes while still wearing the same "algorithmic" label (Ryberg, 2025). Once you accept that, you can no longer permit vendors or administrative agencies to define the inputs in isolation. Input design is sentencing policy. Sentencing policy is moral power. Moral power must be publicly owned.

Behavioural Reality: The Judge Does Not "Just Consider" the Model

A court can write "the tool is advisory" in a policy document, but the human mind does not treat numbers as advisory in the way administrators imagine. Anchoring effects, automation bias, and responsibility diffusion are predictable psychological mechanisms, not character flaws (Kahneman, 2011). When a score or recommendation appears in the file, it frames the case. It narrows the perceived range of acceptable outcomes. It offers a defensible-looking justification under workload pressure. And it changes the emotional temperature: a defendant labelled "high risk" is heard differently even before a word is spoken. This is why the empirical literature has moved toward studying not merely tool accuracy but tool influence on human decision-making. Portela and colleagues' work on human predictions in algorithm-based risk assessment contexts underscores that human–algorithm interaction patterns matter, because the human does not simply accept or reject the machine; the human is shaped by it (Portela et al., 2025).

Crucially, judges themselves are aware of this tension in ways that matter for institutional design. A 2026 study of sentencing judges' experiences with machine-based sentencing technologies reports dominant themes in how judges perceive these developments, showing that the judiciary's own self-understanding is becoming part of the battleground: whether the judge remains a moral agent or becomes a manager of machine outputs (Dagan, 2026). This is not trivia. If judges experience machine-based sentencing as an encroachment on moral authorship, the legitimacy costs will not be confined to defendants; they will be internal to the institution, shaping how cautiously or defensively power is exercised.

What Optimization Really Optimizes: The Hidden Conversion of Desert into Risk Management

The sharpest moral danger in sentencing optimization is the quiet conversion of desert into risk management. Desert asks, "What is proportionate to the wrong?" Risk management asks, "What will this person do, and how do we reduce the chance?" Rehabilitation asks, "What support and structure could change the trajectory?" These are not interchangeable. Yet optimization systems tend to treat them as commensurable because they require commensurable metrics. The system therefore invents proxy measures: recidivism as the dominant outcome, breaches as compliance markers, program completion as "rehabilitation," time served as "cost," disparity indices as "fairness." Each proxy can be useful, but each proxy can also distort the moral object. If rehabilitation is measured as compliance, the system will optimise compliance. If fairness is measured as statistical parity, the system will optimise parity even when the underlying outcome variable is contaminated by enforcement bias. If public safety is measured as rearrest, the system will optimise police contact, not harm prevention, and it will do so with the polished confidence of quantification.

This is why the criminological literature on algorithmic bias and the use of arrest-based outcomes is so important for sentencing, even when the tool is not explicitly "risk assessment." Neil's Annual Review of Criminology analysis emphasises that racial differences in arrest as a measure of crime have direct consequences for algorithmic bias in risk assessment, which is often upstream of sentencing decisions (Neil, 2025). When sentencing algorithms draw on these risk estimates or on the same data substrates, the ontology of "risk" becomes baked into the sentencing recommendation. The sentencing decision can then become an apparently rational response to a forecast that is partly a forecast of institutional exposure. The system looks like it is optimizing justice while it is actually optimizing a historically patterned pipeline.

The Legitimacy Constraint: People Obey Courts for Reasons Algorithms Can Erode

Sentencing is one of the state's most intrusive acts, and its legitimacy is not secured by accuracy alone. Public perception research shows that people may recognise algorithmic advantages like speed and cost while still trusting human judges more and showing greater willingness to engage with courts when a human, rather than an algorithmic judge, adjudicates (Yalcin et al., 2023). The point is not that the public is irrational. The point is that legitimacy is a psychological fact: people accept coercion when they feel heard, respected, and judged by accountable human authority. Algorithmic sentencing, especially when it looks like substitution rather than assistance, risks creating a procedural gap—voice without leverage, hearing without genuine contestability. And when legitimacy erodes, compliance erodes, cooperation erodes, and the system becomes more coercive to compensate. That is the institutional tragedy: a tool introduced to improve efficiency can end up increasing force because it undermines the very social consent on which efficient governance depends.

"Inconsistency" Is Not Only an Error; It Is Sometimes a Moral Feature

One of the strongest selling points of sentencing algorithms is the promise to reduce inconsistency. Inconsistency can be unjust when it reflects bias, arbitrariness, or unequal treatment. But inconsistency can also be the surface expression of morally appropriate sensitivity to context: the difference between a traumatised first offender and a hardened repeat offender, between a coerced accomplice and a leader, between a case where remorse is credible and one where it is staged. The moral question is not "should we eliminate variation?" but "which variations are unjust, and which are the price of treating persons as persons?" Some recent proposals attempt to formalise this tension by creating indices to detect misalignment between algorithmic guidelines and juridical outcomes (Kiejnich-Kruk, Twardawa and Formanowicz, 2025). Whether such indices help depends entirely on whether the system can distinguish unjust disparity from contextual judgement. If it cannot, it risks flattening moral nuance into statistical regularity, and regularity is not justice.

The Global Governance Moment: Why High-Stakes AI is Being Boxed In

Even if you keep this chapter global, you cannot ignore that governance frameworks are converging on a single intuition: AI affecting liberty demands heightened safeguards. Peer-reviewed analysis of the EU's risk-based AI governance and its implications for the judiciary underscores accountability challenges and the need for constraints where AI may influence adjudication (Carnat, 2024). Related scholarship comparing European instruments has argued that modern governance is moving toward lifecycle obligations—documentation, oversight, transparency, risk management—precisely because high-stakes systems can scale harm rapidly when they drift or when they are misused (Presno Linera et al., 2025; Rotenberg, 2025). You should read these developments not as bureaucratic fuss, but as a recognition that "advisory" systems have a habit of becoming decisive once institutional pressure and cognitive deference do their work.

The Practical Line: Sentencing Algorithms May Assist, But They Must Not Optimize Away Moral Ownership

So where should the line be drawn, in a way that is defensible in law, behavioural science, and forensic discipline? Begin with a principle of moral ownership: the court must remain the author of the sentence in reasons that a person can understand and contest, and those reasons must be more than "the model recommended it." That principle is consistent with the philosophical critique that sentencing's condemnatory function requires meaningful public control and cannot be outsourced without changing what punishment is (Taylor, 2023; Ryberg, 2024). Next, adopt a forensic admissibility posture toward algorithmic outputs: specify the proposition the output supports, require validation under conditions of use, disclose uncertainty and error, and prevent the output from being presented in a way that invites false certainty or anchoring. Then insist on contestability as a structural requirement: the person must be able to challenge inputs and assumptions, and the defence must be able to test reliability. This requirement is strengthened by the empirical reality of predictive inconsistency in criminal justice tools, which shows that outputs can vary materially across reasonable modelling choices, making them unfit to be treated as fixed facts about a person (Greene et al., 2022).

Finally, treat optimization as a distinct category that triggers a prohibition unless the objective function is publicly justified and compatible with the foundational commitments of criminal law. Optimization can be appropriate for administrative logistics—allocating program capacity, scheduling, managing backlogs—because those are not condemnatory acts. But optimization is morally perilous when it becomes the engine of punishment severity, because it converts proportionality into a tunable parameter inside a utilitarian machine. The deeper lesson is simple: sentencing algorithms are not merely tools that sit beside the law; they are institutional theories made operational. If you do not govern the theory, the tool will govern the court.

References

- Berk, R.A. and Hyatt, J.M. (2015) 'Machine learning forecasts of risk to inform sentencing decisions', Federal Sentencing Reporter, 27(4), pp. 222–228.
- Carnat, I. (2024) 'Addressing the risks of generative AI for the judiciary: The accountability framework(s) under the EU AI Act', Computer Law & Security Review, 55, 106067.
- Chiao, V. (2018) 'Predicting proportionality: The case for algorithmic sentencing', Criminal Justice Ethics, 37(3), pp. 238–261.
- Dagan, N. (2026) 'Sentencing as a human process? Human judges' experiences with machine-based sentencing', The British Journal of Criminology (advance article).
- Dressel, J. and Farid, H. (2018) 'The accuracy, fairness, and limits of predicting recidivism', Science Advances, 4(1), eaao5580.
- Greene, T. et al. (2022) 'Predictive inconsistency in criminal justice algorithmic risk prediction tools', Journal of the Royal Statistical Society:

Series A, 185(S2), pp. S692–S716.

- Kahneman, D. (2011) Thinking, Fast and Slow. New York: Farrar, Straus and Giroux.
- Kiejnich-Kruk, K., Twardawa, M. and Formanowicz, P. (2025) 'Overcoming sentencing inconsistency: A proposal for algorithmic guidelines and juridical misalignment index', Artificial Intelligence and Law.
- Kleinberg, J., Lakkaraju, H., Leskovec, J., Ludwig, J. and Mullainathan, S. (2018) 'Human decisions and machine predictions', The Quarterly Journal of Economics, 133(1), pp. 237–293.
- Kroll, J.A. (2024) 'Against predictive optimization: On the legitimacy of prediction-driven decision systems', ACM Transactions on Computer-Human Interaction.
- Monahan, J. and Skeem, J.L. (2016) 'Risk assessment in criminal sentencing', Annual Review of Clinical Psychology, 12, pp. 489–513.
- Neil, R. (2025) 'Algorithmic bias in criminal risk assessment: The consequences of racial differences in arrest as a measure of crime', Annual Review of Criminology.
- Portela, M. et al. (2025) 'A comparative user study of human predictions in algorithm-based risk assessment', Artificial Intelligence and Law.
- Presno Linera, M.Á. et al. (2025) 'Regulating AI from Europe: A joint analysis of the AI Act and the Council of Europe AI Convention', Journal of Cyber Policy, 10(1), pp. 1–25.
- Robertson, B., Vignaux, G.A. and Berger, C.E.H. (2016) Interpreting Evidence: Evaluating Forensic Science in the Courtroom. 2nd edn. Chichester: Wiley.
- Rotenberg, M. (2025) 'Framework Convention on Artificial Intelligence and Human Rights, Democracy, and the Rule of Law (Council of Europe)', International Legal Materials, 64, pp. 1–25.
- Ruschemeier, H. and Hondrich, L.J. (2024) 'Automation bias in public administration—an interdisciplinary perspective from law and psychology', Government Information Quarterly, 41(3), 101953.
- Ryberg, J. (2024) 'Sentencing, artificial intelligence, and condemnation: A reply to Taylor', Criminal Justice Ethics.
- Ryberg, J. (2025) 'How to use algorithmic sentencing support in real life (and ethically non-ideal) penal systems?', AI and Ethics.
- Ryberg, J. (2025) 'What is the input problem?', Criminal Law and Philosophy.

- Taylor, I. (2023) 'Justice by algorithm: The limits of AI in criminal sentencing', Criminal Justice Ethics, 42(3), pp. 193–213.
- Watamura, E. et al. (2025) 'Judges versus artificial intelligence in juror decision-making: Deference and mitigating circumstances'.
- Yalcin, G., Themeli, E., Stamhuis, E., Philipsen, S. and Puntoni, S. (2023) 'Perceptions of justice by algorithms', Artificial Intelligence and Law, 31, pp. 269–292.

CHAPTER VIII

Pretrial Detention and Bail: Prediction at the Point of Liberty

The Doorway Where the State Learns Its Own Temper

If you want to know whether a criminal justice system is truly committed to liberty, do not start at sentencing. Start earlier, at the moment before trial when nothing has yet been proved and yet everything can be taken. Pretrial detention is the state's most revealing power because it is exercised at the point of maximum uncertainty and minimum moral entitlement: the person is accused, not convicted; the facts are contested, not settled; the law has not yet earned the right to punish. And still, in that narrow corridor between accusation and adjudication, a system can lock a person away for weeks, months, sometimes years, while insisting—often sincerely—that this is not punishment. The language used is always protective: risk of flight, risk to public safety, risk of interference with evidence, risk of reoffending. The argument is always precautionary: detention is a measure of prevention, not of condemnation. Yet the behavioural and forensic reality is that pretrial detention often functions as the first sentence, and bail becomes the mechanism by which liberty is rationed under uncertainty (Duff, 2013; Coleman, 2020; Morgenstern, Hammerschick and Rogan, 2023).

This chapter is about prediction at the point of liberty: what happens when courts—globally, across legal traditions—import risk scores, structured assessments, and algorithmic advice into the bail and remand decision. It is also about something more basic than technology: the moral structure of detaining a presumptively innocent person, and the forensic discipline needed to ensure that "risk" does not become a euphemism for unaccountable coercion.

Presumption of Innocence Is Not Only a Trial Rule

Many legal cultures talk about the presumption of innocence as if it lives only in the trial: it allocates the burden of proof and protects against wrongful conviction. But serious scholarship has pressed the older, harder claim: the presumption is also a civic attitude that should shape how the state treats a person before guilt is proved. If the presumption is meaningful, pretrial detention is not merely a managerial decision; it is a constitutional and moral anomaly that requires stringent justification. Duff's influential account frames pretrial detention as deeply problematic because it risks treating the accused as guilty in advance, and because the move from accusation to incarceration reshapes civic status before adjudication has done its work (Duff, 2013). Coleman's international human rights analysis similarly develops the presumption as a broader normative framework that constrains state power throughout the criminal process, not merely in evidentiary doctrine at trial (Coleman, 2020). Ferguson's careful examination of the presumption's role across jurisdictions makes the point operational: if the state claims a person is presumptively innocent, then any deprivation of liberty pending trial must be bounded by reasons that do not smuggle in pre-judgement and must be accompanied by conditions of confinement that reflect untried status rather than punitive degradation (Ferguson, 2016).

This matters for prediction because risk scores are, at their core, statements about propensity: what the person might do. The moment the court treats propensity as a decisive reason to detain, it must confront a moral tension that cannot be solved by calibration curves. Predictive accuracy does not dissolve the presumption. It merely makes the temptation to bypass it more administratively comfortable.

Bail Is Not a Single Decision; It Is a Whole Causal Chain

A bail hearing is often described as a short decision: release or detain, with conditions. But if you look at it with a forensic mind, it is a chain of causes that can change the entire case trajectory. A person detained pretrial loses bargaining power, loses access to counsel, loses employment and housing stability, and often faces a coercive pressure to plead simply to regain liberty. This is not speculation; it is one of the most robust findings in modern empirical criminal justice research. Randomization and quasi-randomization designs exploiting variation in judge tendencies repeatedly show that pretrial detention increases the likelihood of guilty pleas and convictions, and increases the likelihood of incarceration as an outcome—effects that are hard to reconcile with the fiction that detention is merely a neutral holding pattern (Gupta, Hansman and Frenchman, 2016; Leslie and Pope, 2017; Dobbie, Goldin and Yang, 2018; Diaz, 2022; Koppel et al., 2024).

Even where jurisdictions differ, the mechanism travels well. If you cage a person while insisting they are "not yet guilty," you still impose practical penalties that look and feel like punishment: disruption of family care, erosion of social ties, heightened exposure to violence and trauma, and reputational harm. Systematic review evidence synthesising the "pretrial detention penalty" literature finds that detention is strongly associated with worse case outcomes, including convictions, guilty pleas, and incarceration (St. Louis, 2023). And the harm is not merely legal; it is behavioural and economic. High-quality causal work shows substantial labour-market harms after detention for those who are not ultimately incarcerated, suggesting that pretrial detention inflicts long-run damage even when the formal outcome does not "justify" it as punishment (Dobbie, Goldin and Yang, 2018; Grau, 2019).

So when you import prediction into bail, you are not merely improving a discrete decision. You are altering a lever that can determine plea rates, conviction likelihood, employment trajectories, and future justice-system contact. The stakes are therefore not only "public safety." They are also the integrity of adjudication itself.

The Moral Mathematics of Preventive Detention Cannot Ignore the Cost of Liberty

Pretrial detention is most often defended in preventive terms: avert future harm. Yet preventive justice scholarship has warned that prevention, as a rationale, carries a built-in expansion bias: the future can always be made "safer" by detaining more people for longer, especially when the justification is probabilistic and the political costs of release errors are vivid (Ashworth and Zedner, 2014). In pretrial settings, that expansion risk is intensified by asymmetry: a single high-profile release failure can trigger a legitimacy panic, while the harms of routine detention are dispersed and often invisible. The result is a predictable institutional drift: detain to avoid blame.

This is where a forensic approach intersects with morality. In forensic science, you do not evaluate a tool only by its hit rate; you evaluate its error costs, its uncertainty, and the consequences of misclassification in context (Robertson, Vignaux and Berger, 2016). Bail is the same. A false positive—detaining someone who would have appeared and stayed lawful—inflicts immediate liberty harm and long-run cascading harms that the empirical literature now documents with disturbing consistency. A false negative—releasing someone who commits a harmful act—inflicts victim harm and public fear. The moral question is not which error is "worse" in the abstract. The moral question is whether the state has the right to impose a massive liberty cost on many presumptively innocent people to avert a smaller probability of harm by a few, and whether it can do so without converting the presumption of innocence into a slogan (Duff, 2013; Ashworth and Zedner, 2014; Coleman, 2020).

What Risk Scores Actually Predict in the Pretrial Context

At pretrial, "risk" is usually defined narrowly: failure to appear, new arrest, or new violent arrest during the pretrial window. That narrowness makes the problem seem technical. But the hidden ontological issue remains: rearrest is partly a measure of policing patterns and surveillance intensity, not merely of criminal behaviour. Recent criminological synthesis emphasises that algorithmic bias in criminal risk instruments is driven in part by the use of arrest as the outcome proxy for crime, because arrest rates differ across groups for reasons that include differential enforcement rather than differential offending (Neil, 2025). When a pretrial tool predicts "new arrest," it is often predicting differential exposure to enforcement as much as propensity to harm. A court that treats the output as pure public-safety science risks laundering institutional history into a liberty decision.

Even when the target is failure to appear, the predictive variable can carry moral contamination. Failure to appear is not always a decision to abscond; it can be a function of poverty, transport instability, caregiving burdens, mental health, confusion, or distrust. The risk model may be "accurate" in predicting who is likely to miss court, yet the appropriate response might be supportive infrastructure—reminders, transport assistance, flexible scheduling—rather than detention. In that sense, risk prediction is not automatically a detention justification. It is, at best, a triage signal that must be converted into a morally proportionate intervention.

The Selective-Labels Trap: The System Trains on Its Own Past Choices

Pretrial prediction inherits a deep epistemic flaw: the data are generated by earlier human decisions about who was released and who was detained. You only observe pretrial misconduct outcomes for those released; the detained are "missing" not by accident but by state choice. This is not a minor statistical nuisance; it is a structural confound that makes some model comparisons and fairness claims epistemically fragile. The broader literature on human decisions and machine predictions highlights how selective labels and policy endogeneity complicate claims that an algorithm "outperforms" judges (Kleinberg et al., 2018). In bail contexts, this matters because the tool can appear calibrated while being built on a world where the highest-risk cases were never observed under release.

The practical consequence is that the tool can become more conservative than it looks, and it can strengthen detention tendencies by presenting as objective the consequences of earlier punitive decision-making. If the past system detained heavily, the model learns from a release sample that is already filtered. That is why a forensic attitude demands explicit recognition of what the training data can and cannot legitimately support.

"Advisory" Tools Rarely Stay Advisory: The Psychology of Anchors and Abdication

A great deal of bail reform rhetoric rests on a comforting promise: risk tools are advisory; judges retain discretion. This promise is psychologically naïve. Human beings anchor on salient numbers; they defer to outputs framed as scientific; and they shift responsibility onto tools when outcomes are politically risky. This is not a theory about bad judges; it is a theory about ordinary cognition operating under pressure. Empirical work on algorithm-assisted human decision-making demonstrates that the presence of algorithmic recommendations can change human behaviour in systematic ways, and the quality of oversight depends on institutional and cognitive conditions, not merely on policy statements (Imai, Jiang and Wang, 2023).

Closer to the pretrial context, qualitative and organisational studies show that risk assessment administration and use are shaped by frontline constraints, professional norms, and legitimacy concerns. Riley's work on pretrial risk assessment administration emphasises that the impact of algorithmic tools depends on how they are implemented and overridden within organisational contexts, rather than on the model's technical properties alone (Riley, 2024). Esthappan's institutional analysis of how judges use risk scores underscores a related mechanism: tools can be used strategically to justify decisions judges already intend to make, sometimes as a shield against reputational consequences, revealing that algorithmic systems can expand rather than constrain discretion (Esthappan, 2024).

There is also evidence that the very legitimacy of using a score is socially negotiated. Studies of public perceptions of judges' use of AI in bail contexts show that legitimacy and fairness perceptions vary depending on how the tool is framed and whether it appears to replace human judgement (Fine et al., 2025). In other words, "advice" is not a neutral addition. It is an institutional actor that reshapes responsibility, perception, and the moral narrative of the hearing.

Bail as a Legitimacy Ritual: Why Voice and Contestability Matter More Than Throughput

Courts do not survive by coercion alone; they survive by legitimacy. Procedural justice research has repeatedly shown that people comply and cooperate when they experience the process as fair—especially when they have voice, are treated with respect, and receive intelligible reasons (Tyler, 2006; Tyler, 2011). Risk tools and algorithmic bail systems threaten legitimacy in a precise way: they can create a procedural gap where the hearing continues but the decision feels precomputed, voiceless, and unchallengeable. The work describing "voicelessness" and the procedural gap in algorithmic justice articulates this problem in a way that maps directly onto bail: when the decisive weight is carried by an output that cannot be meaningfully contested, the person's participation becomes theatre (Kinchin, 2024).

This is why "contestability" is not merely a technical demand for transparency. It is a behavioural demand for legitimacy. The defendant must be able to contest inputs, challenge assumptions, and understand what the score means. Without that, the state is detaining on a basis that looks like fate, and fate is not an admissible reason in a system that claims rule of law.

Public Safety is Real, But the Evidence on Detention's Public Safety Benefits is Not Simple

A mature discussion of bail cannot pretend public safety is irrelevant. Pretrial misconduct can cause real harm. The question is whether detention and risk-scored detention produce the benefits claimed, and at what cost. The empirical literature complicates simple "detain = safer" narratives. The best causal work shows that detention can reduce short-term pretrial crime and failures to appear, yet it also increases conviction likelihood through coercive plea dynamics and can produce longer-term social harms that may offset or reverse preventive benefits (Dobbie, Goldin and Yang, 2018; Leslie and Pope, 2017). In other words, detention can look protective in the short window while generating damaging downstream effects that a justice system should not treat as collateral.

You also see this complexity in evaluations of bail reforms. Peer-reviewed work examining reforms that reduce detention often finds reductions in detention without corresponding spikes in serious public harms, though effects vary by context and implementation. For example, research on bail reform's relationship to violence outcomes has found no evidence of exacerbated community firearm violence in certain reform contexts, suggesting that reducing detention can be compatible with community safety under some policy designs (Jahn et al., 2024). And work on bail reform and pretrial release has found that detention reductions can coincide with lower convictions, consistent with the idea that detention itself shapes case outcomes rather than merely reflecting defendant dangerousness (Lacoe et al., 2025).

A responsible court must therefore resist the easy moral framing that release is reckless and detention is prudent. The evidence suggests the real moral risk is that detention becomes routine, and routine detention becomes an invisible engine of convictions and social damage.

The Algorithm's Most Dangerous Feature: It Makes Moral Conflict Look Like Administration

Bail is a decision under moral conflict: protect the public, respect liberty, avoid pretrial punishment, preserve trial integrity, respect equality. Algorithms seduce because they convert this conflict into a workflow. A score offers a quick path through the dilemma: if risk is high, detain; if low, release. But this apparent clarity is precisely the danger. A score cannot tell you what liberty is worth, nor can it answer the presumption-of-innocence constraint. It can at best inform how uncertainty is distributed—and the distribution of uncertainty is itself a moral choice.

This is why recent philosophical and criminological writing warns against the de-individualising effects of risk governance. The critique is not that prediction is impossible, but that risk logic can recast the subject of criminal law from a responsible agent to a predicted object, shifting the system away from culpability foundations (Ravid, 2026). At bail, that shift is especially toxic because it happens before conviction. The person becomes "high risk" first and "guilty or not guilty" later. That inversion is not merely a procedural quirk; it is a transformation of civic status under the guise of public safety management.

The Global Reality: Remand Is Rising, Backlogs Are Structural, and Technology Becomes a Shortcut

A global chapter cannot pretend that pretrial detention problems are confined to one jurisdiction. Across many systems, remand populations have risen even as overall prison populations fluctuate, and court backlogs have produced prolonged pretrial confinement that strains human rights norms and public confidence. The reasons are not always algorithmic; they are often structural: overloaded courts, policing practices, prosecutorial incentives, and political pressures. Yet technology tends to enter precisely at moments of overload, when institutions are tempted to substitute speed for judgement. That is why governance discussions about AI and procedure are not abstract. A recent 2026 analysis of pre-trial detention constraints through EU procedural rights directives illustrates how procedural rights frameworks can function as constitutional constraints on detention practices, reflecting a broader rights-based movement to limit arbitrary remand and strengthen safeguards (Ferri, 2026).

The COVID-19 period is an important global illustration, not because it "proved" any single doctrine, but because it exposed what detention does when conditions deteriorate and systems are forced to decarcerate. Research on incarceration during the pandemic documents intensified harms—health risk, isolation, disrupted visitation, and deepened trauma—showing that the "cost of detention" includes degradations that ordinary legal calculus often undercounts (Craig, 2023; Ferstman, 2024). If your bail calculus treats detention as a neutral holding state, those findings correct the error. Detention is an active harm, not a passive default.

A Forensic Standard for Bail Prediction: Fit-for-Purpose, Contestable, and Morally Scoped

So what does a court do if it wants to use prediction without surrendering liberty to a number? It adopts forensic standards. The first is proposition clarity: the tool must specify what it predicts—failure to appear, new arrest, new violent arrest—over what time horizon, and how those outcomes relate to the legal reasons detention is permitted. The second is validation under conditions of use: accuracy and error must be documented for the relevant population and updated over time. The third is interpretive discipline: uncertainty must be communicated so the output cannot masquerade as certainty. The fourth is contestability: the defence must be able to challenge the tool's inputs, assumptions, and relevance, and the court must treat that challenge as meaningful, not ceremonial.

This is not merely a technical programme. It is a moral programme. The court must also impose scope limits. Prediction can be used to design supportive release conditions and targeted services that reduce failures to appear without detention, especially when the predicted "risk" is in fact a predicted vulnerability. Prediction must not be allowed to convert poverty, unstable housing, or prior system contact into a reason to confine a presumptively innocent person. And prediction must never be treated as a substitute for reasons. The judge must remain the moral author of detention decisions, because a system that detains on "the model says so" has lost the rule-of-law property that distinguishes coercion from administration.

The Line at the Point of Liberty

At the bail stage, the line must be drawn tighter than anywhere else in the process, because the state's moral entitlement is at its weakest. A defensible line-drawing position, grounded in behavioural science, forensic standards, and presumption-of-innocence scholarship, is this: pretrial detention may be used only as a last resort where specific, legally relevant risks cannot be managed by less restrictive means, and any predictive tool may inform that judgement only if it is transparent enough to be contested, validated enough to be trusted within its scope, and disciplined enough to avoid converting system-contact into dangerousness. If those conditions cannot be met—because the tool is proprietary, unstable, or cognitively corrupting—then the court must refuse to let the score become a liberty reason.

This is what it means to treat bail as the point of liberty rather than as the point of convenience. In a healthy legal system, the presumption of innocence is not a speech made at trial; it is a restraint practiced at bail.

References

- Ashworth, A. and Zedner, L. (2014) Preventive Justice. Oxford: Oxford University Press.
- Coleman, M. (2020) The Presumption of Innocence in International Human Rights and Criminal Law. London: Routledge.
- Craig, M.O. (2023) 'Incarcerated in a pandemic: How COVID-19 exacerbated the pains of imprisonment', Crime & Delinquency.
- Diaz, A.M. (2022) 'Distortion of justice: How the inability to pay bail affects case outcomes', Journal of Law, Economics, and Organization, 34(4), pp. 511–545.
- Dobbie, W., Goldin, J. and Yang, C.S. (2018) 'The effects of pretrial detention on conviction, future crime, and employment', American Economic Review, 108(2), pp. 201–240.
- Duff, R.A. (2013) 'Pre-trial detention and the presumption of innocence', in Ashworth, A., Zedner, L. and Tomlin, P. (eds) Prevention and the Limits of the Criminal Law. Oxford: Oxford University Press, pp. 115–132.
- Esthappan, S. (2024) 'Assessing the risks of risk assessments: Institutional tensions and data-driven judicial decision-making', Social Problems.
- Ferguson, P.R. (2016) 'The presumption of innocence and its role in the criminal process', International Journal of Evidence & Proof, 20(2), pp. 132–156.
- Ferri, F. (2026) 'Pre-trial detention and EU law: Constitutional constraints and procedural rights', European Journal of Criminal Policy and Research.
- Ferstman, C. (2024) 'Detention and pandemic exceptionality', in Detention in a Pandemic. Bristol: Bristol University Press.

- Fine, A. et al. (2025) 'Public perceptions of judges' use of AI tools in courtroom decision-making: Bail and sentencing contexts', Psychology, Public Policy, and Law.
- Grau, N. (2019) 'The effect of pretrial detention on labor market outcomes'.
- Gupta, A., Hansman, C. and Frenchman, E. (2016) 'The heavy costs of high bail: Evidence from judge randomization', Journal of Legal Studies, 45(2), pp. 471–505.
- Imai, K., Jiang, Z. and Wang, S. (2023) 'Experimental evaluation of algorithm-assisted human decision-making', Journal of the Royal Statistical Society: Series A, 186(2), pp. 167–198.
- Jahn, J.L. et al. (2024) 'Evaluating firearm violence after New Jersey's cash bail reform', JAMA Network Open.
- Kinchin, N. (2024) '"Voiceless": the procedural gap in algorithmic justice', International Journal of Law and Information Technology, 32(4), pp. 1–30.
- Kleinberg, J. et al. (2018) 'Human decisions and machine predictions', The Quarterly Journal of Economics, 133(1), pp. 237–293.
- Koppel, S. et al. (2024) 'Examining the causal effect of pretrial detention on case outcomes', American Journal of Criminal Justice.
- Lacoe, J. et al. (2025) 'Bail reform and pretrial release: Examining the effects of policy change', Criminology & Public Policy.
- Leslie, E. and Pope, N.G. (2017) 'The unintended impact of pretrial detention on case outcomes', Journal of Law and Economics, 60(3), pp. 529–557.
- Lowder, E.M. et al. (2021) 'Effects of pretrial risk assessments on release decisions', Journal of Criminal Justice, 74, 101813.
- Morgenstern, C., Hammerschick, W. and Rogan, M. (eds) (2023) European Perspectives on Pre-Trial Detention: A Means of Last Resort? London: Routledge.
- Neil, R. (2025) 'Algorithmic bias in criminal risk assessment: The consequences of racial differences in arrest as a measure of crime', Annual Review of Criminology.
- Portela, M. et al. (2025) 'A comparative user study of human predictions in algorithm-based risk assessment', Artificial Intelligence and Law.
- Ravid, I. (2026) '(Re)individualizing criminal law', Boston College Law Review.

- Riley, S.A. (2024) 'Pretrial risk assessment administration on the frontlines', Proceedings of the ACM Conference on Fairness, Accountability, and Transparency (FAccT '24).
- Robertson, B., Vignaux, G.A. and Berger, C.E.H. (2016) Interpreting Evidence: Evaluating Forensic Science in the Courtroom. 2nd edn. Chichester: Wiley.
- St. Louis, S.S. (2023) 'The pretrial detention penalty: A systematic review and meta-analysis'.
- Thai, M.L. (2026) 'Spotlighting pretrial reform: Media effects on perceptions of bail reform and pretrial risk assessments', Journal of Contemporary Criminal Justice.
- Tyler, T.R. (2006) Why People Obey the Law. 2nd edn. Princeton, NJ: Princeton University Press.
- Tyler, T.R. (2011) 'Procedural justice, legitimacy, and the effective rule of law', Crime and Justice, 40(1), pp. 283–357.
- Wenzelburger, G. (2025) 'Smart justice? Making sense of the rise of algorithm-based criminal justice', Crime, Law and Social Change.

CHAPTER IX

Recidivism, Dangerousness, and the Myth of Stable Traits

The Comfortable Fiction: "This Person Is Dangerous"

Courts and institutions love stable labels because stable labels feel like control. "Dangerous," "high-risk," "career criminal," "violent type"—these phrases promise that the world can be partitioned into safe and unsafe bodies, and that justice can be administered like quarantine. The trouble is that these labels are often metaphysical claims disguised as practical judgement. They suggest that dangerousness is a durable property lodged inside the person, like a permanent toxin in the blood. Yet much of what modern criminology, developmental psychology, forensic psychiatry, and risk science has learned over the last half century points in a different direction: offending is often episodic, conditional, age-graded, and deeply sensitive to social ties, opportunity structures, institutional contact, and life events. Even the minority of individuals who offend persistently do not do so in a way that makes "dangerousness" a simple trait; they show heterogeneity in pathways, triggers, and desistance processes. If you begin from that empirical reality, a risk score is no longer a neutral fact about the person. It is an institutional hypothesis about a future that depends as much on context and intervention as on any supposed "type."

The moral stakes are immediate. When the state restricts liberty on the basis of predicted dangerousness, it is not merely preventing harm; it is assigning a civic status. That status assignment becomes harder to justify the more the prediction rests on proxies—past system contact, neighbourhood, poverty markers—and the more it assumes that the future is a continuation of the past. The "myth of stable traits" is therefore not an academic quibble; it is the conceptual error that allows preventive logics to quietly replace culpability-based reasoning.

Recidivism Is Not a Single Event; It Is a Category Error Waiting to Happen

Start with the word "recidivism," because much of the dangerousness discourse hides inside it. "Recidivism" can mean rearrest, reconviction, reimprisonment, breach of conditions, or a return to supervision. These outcomes do not measure the same thing. Rearrest measures a mixture of behaviour and enforcement; reconviction measures behaviour filtered through prosecutorial and adjudicative pathways; reimprisonment measures behaviour filtered through sentencing practice and supervision intensity. A risk tool that "predicts recidivism" is therefore predicting a chosen institutional event, not "criminality" as an essence. That choice is not purely technical; it is moral. If you build detention, sentencing severity, or indefinite preventive measures on an outcome that is substantially shaped by institutional behaviour, you are letting the system's own patterns become a justification for further coercion.

This is why the strongest contemporary reviews of algorithmic bias in risk assessment emphasise arrest as an imperfect proxy for crime and highlight that disparities in arrest—driven in part by differential enforcement—can generate algorithmic bias when arrest is treated as the target to be predicted. The point is not merely distributive fairness. The point is ontological: if your outcome variable contains institutional attention, your "dangerousness" score may be a forecast of exposure, not propensity.

The Trait Illusion: How a Probability Becomes a Personality

Now notice the psychological move that transforms risk into trait. The court hears, "High risk," and immediately the mind translates it into "high-risk person." The number becomes identity. This translation is not malicious; it is cognitive economy. Human beings prefer stable stories to conditional probabilities, especially under time pressure. The institution then reinforces the story by embedding the score into reports, supervision levels, program eligibility, and hearing scripts. What began as a statistical estimate becomes a social label with self-fulfilling force. In effect, the system manufactures the trait it claims to measure.

This is precisely why scholarship on dangerousness in legal theory has repeatedly stressed its elusiveness as a concept and the need to distinguish actuarial forecasts from claims about "dangerous personalities." Bijlsma's state-of-the-art review maps how criminal legal theory struggles to stabilise "dangerousness" without slipping into moral essentialism, while acknowledging that actuarial approaches can still smuggle in trait-like assumptions through factor selection and interpretation. The forensic implication is blunt: if the state is going to use risk assessment at all, it must prohibit the conversion of probabilistic outputs into personality claims, and it must discipline how language is used in court records, reports, and reasons.

The Developmental Record: Most Offending Is Not a Life Sentence in the Blood

The myth of stable traits is most easily punctured by developmental criminology. Moffitt's developmental taxonomy remains one of the most influential ways of reconciling two facts that appear contradictory: antisocial behaviour shows continuity, yet its prevalence peaks in adolescence and declines sharply thereafter. The taxonomy distinguishes a smaller life-course-persistent group from a larger adolescence-limited group, reminding the system that much of what looks like "criminal type" in youth is, for many, a phase shaped by maturity gaps and peer dynamics rather than a permanent trait (Moffitt, 1993). This does not romanticise crime; it simply forces the system to stop mistaking age-graded patterns for fixed pathology.

Age-graded theories of informal social control push the point further. Sampson and Laub's life-course view emphasises turning points—employment, marriage, military service, social bonds—that can restructure routine activities and commitments, thereby promoting desistance even among serious offenders (Sampson and Laub, 2005). The deeper lesson is that "dangerousness" is not simply inside the person; it is also in the person's relation to social structure. A justice system that labels a person "dangerous" while ignoring the modifiable ecology of work, family, housing, treatment access, and supervision style is not doing prediction; it is doing fatalism.

Desistance: What the System Calls "Risk Reduction" Is Often Identity Reconstruction

A purely actuarial view sees desistance as a decreasing hazard rate. A human view sees desistance as the re-building of a self. Narrative and desistance scholarship has argued for decades that stopping crime often involves identity change, moral agency, and the acquisition of legitimate roles. When institutions reduce desistance to compliance metrics, they risk optimising for surface conformity while missing the deeper transformation that actually sustains non-offending. Recent work continues to develop and diversify this literature, including arguments emphasising the centrality of narrative in identity change and desistance processes. A 2026 scoping review of desistance research in Asia, for instance, signals both the growing global spread of desistance frameworks and the need to understand how desistance pathways interact with cultural and institutional contexts rather than assuming a single universal "trait" of reformability.

This matters for dangerousness because "stable trait" language forecloses desistance conceptually. If the person is a type, then change is an exception; if offending is a trajectory within a life course, then change is part of the expected landscape. The moral difference is profound: one view justifies indefinite containment; the other demands a justice system capable of structured hope without naivety.

Forensic Psychiatry's Hard Lesson: "Dangerousness" Is Not a Diagnosis

The most mature warnings about trait talk come from forensic psychiatry, a domain forced to confront high-stakes risk assessment under uncertainty. The evidence base for violence risk tools demonstrates that structured professional judgement and actuarial instruments can add predictive value, yet their limitations are also persistent: performance varies by context, base rates, and implementation, and the interpretation of outputs can be corrupted by cognitive bias and institutional incentives. Douglas and colleagues have argued that risk tools can be useful in forensic psychiatry and criminal justice, while also emphasising that risk assessment is not a replacement for clinical judgement and that ethical constraints must govern use, especially where liberty is at stake. If you translate that into courtroom reasoning, you get a rule the law too often forgets: risk assessment may inform management, but it cannot become a substitute for moral judgement, and it cannot be treated as proof of a dangerous personality.

Cross-national comparative work on "social dangerousness" in forensic psychiatric contexts further underscores that dangerousness is not a stable medical object but a legal-administrative construct shaped by institutional standards, evidentiary practices, and policy aims. The global implication is that dangerousness is not something courts discover; it is something courts and systems define, and the definition carries moral responsibility.

The "Static" Trap: Past Behaviour as Destiny

Risk tools often rely heavily on static factors: age at first offence, number of prior convictions, prior violence, past breaches. These variables are predictive in many datasets, but the moral error occurs when prediction is treated as destiny. Past behaviour is evidence about past behaviour; it is not proof of a fixed trait. The longer the system treats the person as "high risk," the more it structures the future around that label: closer surveillance increases detection; breach-focused supervision increases technical violations; prison exposure increases criminogenic harm; restricted opportunities increase desperation. The score becomes self-confirming.

A particularly instructive example comes from the sex-offence context, where long-term risk is politically and emotionally charged. Research has argued that after sufficient time offence-free in the community, risk for individuals with prior sexual offences can converge toward baseline population risk—an empirical reminder that time and behaviour can change risk meaningfully, undermining the intuition of permanent dangerousness. The point is not to generalise a single domain to all others, but to demonstrate the structural error: when the institution assumes stable traits, it over-weights static history and under-weights time, context, and change.

Dynamic Risk: The Hope and the Danger of Treating Change as a Variable

To correct static fatalism, systems increasingly invoke "dynamic risk": attitudes, substance use, social supports, employment, mental state, peer associations, supervision engagement. This move can be ethically promising because it acknowledges change and targets interventions. Yet dynamic risk can also become a new instrument of control if it is operationalised through shallow proxies. A person can be scored as "noncompliant" because they missed an appointment, when the real driver is caregiving burden or unstable transport. A person can be scored "antisocial attitudes" because they are defensive in a hostile system. Dynamic variables, if poorly defined, can turn lived struggle into risk points, and risk points into coercion.

The current evidence base for offender management models illustrates why this is delicate. The Risk-Need-Responsivity framework has dominated correctional practice, often treated as near-settled science. Yet a 2024 umbrella review synthesising and appraising the RNR evidence base concluded that the quality and consistency of evidence across principles is mixed and that the literature contains methodological and authorship concerns that complicate confident claims. You should read that as a warning against turning "dynamic risk" into a mechanised truth system. If the evidence base is mixed, the moral burden rises: the system must not treat an intervention framework as a permission slip for tighter control.

The Algorithmic Layer: When "Trait" Is Produced by Data and Time Itself

Even if you accept the conceptual caution above, algorithms add a newer danger: they can manufacture trait-like labels from time-bound datasets in ways that look scientific. Consider cohort bias. A major 2023 study in PNAS demonstrated that cohort bias—changes in environment and policy across time—can generate inequality in predictive risk assessments distinct from racial bias, with serious implications for instruments that forecast future justice-system involvement. This matters because it shows that what looks like a trait signal can actually be a cohort artifact. The model may be "predicting" not a person's stable disposition but the historical period's enforcement patterns, policy regimes, or social conditions. When you then treat the score as the person's "dangerousness," you commit an epistemic injustice: you turn time into character.

The 2025 Annual Review analysis on algorithmic bias deepens this by focusing on how arrest differences as measures of crime can structurally bias risk instruments. The combined lesson is forensic: the model's predictive power can be real while its trait interpretation is false. That is the central myth courts must dismantle.

Dangerousness as a Legal Category: The Preventive Turn and Its Moral Costs

Dangerousness becomes most poisonous when it justifies indefinite or extended detention framed as protection rather than punishment. Preventive justice scholarship has long warned that prevention has a built-in expansion bias: the future can always be made "safer" by doing more, and probability-based justifications are especially prone to overreach because they are hard to falsify and easy to dramatise (Ashworth and Zedner, 2014). The preventive turn is not new, but algorithmic scoring modernises it, giving it scalable administrative power and a veneer of neutrality.

Contemporary legal scholarship continues to map and critique this preventive turn, warning that criminal law can drift from judging acts to governing risk, thereby weakening the moral foundations of punishment and due process. The conceptual point returns: the more you believe in stable dangerous traits, the more you accept preventive containment as rational. The more you accept preventive containment, the more the presumption of innocence and proportionality become procedural decorations rather than restraints.

A Forensic Discipline for Dangerousness Claims: From Trait Talk to Testable Propositions

If you want a workable alternative, borrow the discipline of forensic reasoning and apply it to dangerousness claims. First, prohibit trait language in legal conclusions. Replace "dangerous person" with a testable proposition: "Under specified conditions and within a defined horizon, the probability of a specified event is estimated at X, with uncertainty Y, based on data Z and assumptions A." That may sound clinical, but it does two crucial things: it re-anchors the claim in uncertainty, and it prevents the metaphysical slide from probability to identity.

Second, force the institution to confront what it is predicting. Is the event rearrest, reconviction, breach, or harm? If it is rearrest, require explicit consideration of enforcement confounding, as contemporary criminological evidence demands. Third, require stability checks over time, including cohort bias and drift, because otherwise the instrument will convert historical conditions into trait attributions. Fourth, impose contestability: the person must be able to challenge inputs and relevance, and the court must be able to review the method meaningfully. Without contestability, dangerousness becomes a word that cannot be argued with, and that is precisely the point where law degenerates into administration.

The Moral Synthesis: Treat People as Agents, Treat Risk as Conditional, Treat Liberty as Irreversible

The most defensible moral posture is not "ignore risk" and not "trust the score." It is this: treat risk as conditional and modifiable, treat persons as agents embedded in contexts, and treat liberty loss as a harm that cannot be waved away by managerial language. If risk tools help allocate supportive resources and tailor interventions that reduce harm without inflating coercion, they can serve justice. If they become identity labels that justify escalated control, they become engines of moral error.

If you want one sentence that captures the chapter's burden, it is this: the myth of stable traits is the story the institution tells itself to avoid the harder work of understanding trajectories, contexts, and change, and to avoid the moral discomfort of uncertainty. A mature criminal justice system does not abolish uncertainty with labels; it governs uncertainty with disciplined reasoning, forensic humility, and a refusal to confuse prediction with personhood.

References

- Ashworth, A. and Zedner, L. (2014) Preventive Justice. Oxford: Oxford University Press.
- Bijlsma, J. (2022) 'The elusive concept of dangerousness: the state of the art in criminal legal theory and the necessity of further research'.
- Crocker, A.G. et al. (2025) 'From risky individuals to risky systems: a conceptual and bibliometric mapping of dangerousness and risk', Frontiers in Psychiatry.
- Douglas, T. et al. (2017) 'Risk assessment tools in criminal justice and forensic psychiatry: the state of the science and ethical concerns', Nature Human Behaviour, 1, pp. 1–6.
- Fazel, S. et al. (2015) 'Criminal recidivism rates worldwide: a systematic review', PLoS ONE, 10(6), e0130390.

- Fazel, S., Hurton, C., Burghart, M., DeLisi, M. and Yu, R. (2024) 'An updated evidence synthesis on the Risk-Need-Responsivity (RNR) model: umbrella review and commentary', Journal of Criminal Justice, 92, 102197.
- Ferguson, P.R. (2016) 'The presumption of innocence and its role in the criminal process', International Journal of Evidence & Proof, 20(2), pp. 132–156.
- Grove, W.M., Zald, D.H., Lebow, B.S., Snitz, B.E. and Nelson, C. (2000) 'Clinical versus mechanical prediction: a meta-analysis', Psychological Assessment, 12(1), pp. 19–30.
- Hendry, M.C., Douglas, K.S. and Lilienfeld, S.O. (2013) 'Construct measurement quality improves predictive validity of risk assessment', Behavioral Sciences & the Law, 31(2), pp. 236–252.
- Kahneman, D. (2011) Thinking, Fast and Slow. New York: Farrar, Straus and Giroux.
- Kleinberg, J., Lakkaraju, H., Leskovec, J., Ludwig, J. and Mullainathan, S. (2018) 'Human decisions and machine predictions', The Quarterly Journal of Economics, 133(1), pp. 237–293.
- Maruna, S. (2001) Making Good: How Ex-Convicts Reform and Rebuild Their Lives. Washington, DC: American Psychological Association.
- McCuish, E. (2023) 'Revisiting Laub and Sampson's version of life-course criminology', Journal of Criminal Justice, 87, 102089.
- Meehl, P.E. (1954) Clinical Versus Statistical Prediction: A Theoretical Analysis and a Review of the Evidence. Minneapolis: University of Minnesota Press.
- Moffitt, T.E. (1993) 'Adolescence-limited and life-course-persistent antisocial behavior: a developmental taxonomy', Psychological Review, 100(4), pp. 674–701.
- Montana, E., Nagin, D.S., Neil, R. and Sampson, R.J. (2023) 'Cohort bias in predictive risk assessments of future criminal justice system involvement', Proceedings of the National Academy of Sciences, 120(23), e2301990120.
- Neil, R. and Zanger-Tishler, M. (2025) 'Algorithmic bias in criminal risk assessment: the consequences of racial differences in arrest as a measure of crime', Annual Review of Criminology, 8(1), pp. 97–119.
- Robertson, B., Vignaux, G.A. and Berger, C.E.H. (2016) Interpreting Evidence: Evaluating Forensic Science in the Courtroom. 2nd edn. Chichester: Wiley.

- Sampson, R.J. and Laub, J.H. (2005) 'A life-course view of the development of crime', The Annals of the American Academy of Political and Social Science, 602, pp. 12–45.
- Skarðhamar, T. (2009) 'A critical review of Moffitt's developmental taxonomy'.
- Stone, R. (2016) 'Desistance and identity repair: redemption narratives as resistance', The British Journal of Criminology, 56(5), pp. 956–975.
- Suzuki, M. (2026) 'Research on desistance from crime in Asia: a scoping review', Asian Criminology.
- Wan, H. et al. (2025) 'Insanity defense and social dangerousness: a comparative forensic psychiatry analysis', International Journal of Law and Psychiatry.
- Yukhnenko, D., Sridhar, S. and Fazel, S. (2023) 'Criminal recidivism rates globally: a systematic review update', Journal of Criminal Justice, 87, 102087.

CHAPTER X

Model Drift, Feedback Loops, and the Self-Fulfilling Prophecy of Policing

The Hidden Problem: The Model Does Not Merely Observe the World, It Helps Create It

If you have ever reconstructed a crime scene properly, you already know the central discipline that policing algorithms routinely violate: you do not treat what you see as the whole truth unless you understand how what you see came to be seen. Patrol patterns, stop patterns, reporting patterns, and recording practices do not merely reflect crime; they actively shape what becomes visible as "crime data." The moment a predictive policing model is deployed, the model's outputs influence where officers go, what they look for, whom they question, what is recorded, and what becomes the next training dataset. At that point, the model ceases to be a passive forecaster and becomes a participant in the system it predicts. In machine-learning terms this is a feedback loop; in criminological terms it is the institutional production of "knowledge"; in moral terms it is the danger of converting coercive attention into self-confirming evidence. The easiest mistake is to treat this as a technical nuisance called "drift," as if it were only about model accuracy. The harder truth is that drift and feedback loops are the mechanism by which power can launder itself into "objective" prediction, and then back again into power with greater confidence.

The core insight was stated with unusual clarity in the literature on predictive policing: a system trained on discovered or enforcement-driven events tends to learn future enforcement, not future crime. Lum's widely cited analysis crystallised this point by showing how predictive policing can concentrate patrols in particular areas, producing more discovered incidents there, which then appear to justify the next concentration—an algorithmic echo of the oldest institutional habit: you find what you look for, and you then insist you looked because you found (Lum and Isaac, 2016). Ensign and colleagues formalised the same problem using a mathematical model and demonstrated the "runaway feedback loop" dynamic: once a system dispatches police to a neighbourhood, discovered incidents there become training signal, and the loop can repeatedly send police back regardless of the true underlying crime distribution (Ensign et al., 2018). What looks like prediction is often the automation of attention.

Drift Is Not a Buzzword Here; It Is What Happens When Society Moves and the Model Pretends It Does Not

In technical domains, "concept drift" refers to changes over time in the relationship between inputs and outcomes; model performance degrades because the world changes while the model remains frozen. Drift is ubiquitous in real deployment, which is why modern surveys treat it as a central governance problem rather than a corner case (Gama et al., 2014; Suárez-Cetrulo et al., 2023; Hinder et al., 2024). In policing, drift is especially volatile because the data-generating process is not only "the world"; it is also the institution's changing policies, priorities, resource constraints, and public behaviour. A change in reporting behaviour, a change in stop practices after a scandal, a change in drug-market dynamics, or a change in patrol deployment can all shift the relationship between recorded incidents and actual harm. When models are retrained on these shifting labels without recognising the shift, they will adapt—but not necessarily toward truth. They may adapt toward the institution's newest pattern of visibility.

The COVID-19 period is the cleanest global demonstration of why drift is not optional. Crime opportunities changed, reporting patterns shifted, courts and custodial practices were disrupted, and many police services altered priorities. A model trained on pre-pandemic patterns and deployed into pandemic-era streets is not "slightly less accurate"; it is operating on a different ontology of social life. The forensic lesson is direct: if a model's target is a recorded event, and recorded events are shaped by institutional and social turbulence, then drift is not merely degradation; it is redefinition. You can retrain endlessly and still be calibrating to institutional noise.

For the courtroom-minded reader, there is an uncomfortable parallel to forensic evidence interpretation. We have spent decades learning that evidence is not self-interpreting; context can contaminate and downstream conclusions can appear objective while being shaped by upstream cues. Drift does the same at system scale: it changes what "signals" mean, and it changes them invisibly unless you build monitoring and contestability into the institutional pipeline.

The Feedback Loop Has Two Faces: Discoveries and Reports

Predictive policing debates often assume the training signal is "crime reports." Yet in practice, policing data streams are mixed: citizen reports, officer-initiated observations, stops, arrests, and other discovered incidents. The feedback dynamics differ depending on which stream dominates. Ensign et al. showed how discovered incidents, produced by patrol allocation itself, can drive runaway concentration (Ensign et al., 2018). But even if you ban arrests as input and use only citizen reports, you do not escape bias. Differential reporting is itself socially patterned: communities differ in trust, access, and willingness to call police. Akpinar, De-Arteaga, and Chouldechova demonstrated—using a simulation patterned on Bogotá victimization and reporting data—that differential reporting rates can displace predicted hotspots away from high-crime but low-reporting areas and toward higher-reporting areas, generating over-policing and under-policing through a different mechanism than the discovery loop (Akpinar et al., 2021).

This matters because institutions often respond to critiques by shifting inputs while keeping the same moral posture: "we removed arrests; therefore we removed bias." The deeper forensic truth is that the label itself—what you treat as an outcome—may be an institutional artefact. A model can be scrupulously engineered and still be morally distorted if the data are produced by unequal visibility, unequal trust, and unequal institutional attention.

Self-Fulfillment is Not Only Place-Based; It Can Be Person-Based

The phrase "self-fulfilling prophecy" is often used loosely in policing debates, but recent empirical work has given it sharp teeth. Bauer and Gill showed, in a different high-stakes scoring context, that when algorithmic assessments are disclosed to the scored individuals, the scores can steer behaviour toward the assessment, producing self-fulfilling prophecies—even when scores are erroneous (Bauer and Gill, 2024). The mechanism is psychologically credible: people infer how decision-makers will treat them and adjust behaviour accordingly; and decision-makers, armed with the score, may interpret behaviour through the score's lens. In policing, person-based risk scoring can operate similarly: a "high-risk" flag changes officer attention, changes discretionary stops, changes interpretation of ambiguous conduct, and changes what becomes recorded as suspicious. The flagged person becomes easier to "confirm," not necessarily because they are more harmful, but because the system has positioned them under a brighter lamp.

This is exactly why a drift-and-feedback chapter cannot remain in place-based predictive policing alone. The same performative dynamic operates wherever predictions shape interventions that then shape the measured outcome.

Performative Prediction: The Mathematical Name for a Moral Hazard

Machine learning has now developed a formal vocabulary for what policing has enacted for decades. Perdomo and colleagues defined "performative prediction" as the setting where predictions influence the distribution of outcomes; retraining then chases an equilibrium shaped by the model's own effects (Perdomo et al., 2020). Hardt and Mendler-Dünner's later synthesis distinguishes between learning the world and steering the world, emphasising that prediction systems can become instruments of power by shaping behaviour and data-generation (Hardt and Mendler-Dünner, 2025). Read that slowly, because it lands like a verdict: when policing models allocate attention, they are not merely learning crime patterns; they are steering the ecology of surveillance, enforcement, and recorded reality. The legal system's conventional safeguards—validation, calibration, periodic retraining—are not sufficient if the model changes the thing it claims to measure.

Once you adopt the performative lens, "drift" is no longer an accident. Drift becomes the predictable outcome of governance choices: when the institution changes how it polices, the data change; when the data change, the model changes; when the model changes, policing changes again. The loop is not a bug. It is the system's nervous system. Your task is to ensure that the nervous system does not metastasize into self-justifying coercion.

The Self-Exciting Temptation: Why Policing Loves Hotspots and Why Models Intensify Them

Policing has long been drawn to place-based concentration because crime clusters. Hotspots policing and focused patrol have strong empirical support for reducing crime in treated micro-places, often without clear displacement (Braga et al., 2019; Petersen et al., 2023; Turchan et al., 2024). That evidence is real, and a serious chapter must grant it. The danger is that predictive policing can take a tactic with some empirical grounding and convert it into an automated pipeline that lacks procedural and moral brakes. A hotspot strategy can be embedded within community-engaged policing and procedural justice training, with supervision and constraints; an algorithmic dispatch loop can become a perpetual motion machine: data → prediction → patrol → discovered incidents → more data. The model begins to look like a neutral cartographer, when it is actually a self-exciting engine.

Brantingham and colleagues tested whether predictive policing could lead to biased arrests, engaging directly with Lum and Isaac's concerns, and the debate around whether different input types (reported incidents vs arrests) produce different bias dynamics shows precisely why this is not a simple "ban one variable" problem (Brantingham et al., 2018). The core point that survives across this literature is not that prediction is impossible; it is that the system's actions change the data stream, and therefore the model's apparent success can partly be the success of concentrating attention rather than of identifying harm.

Drift + Feedback = A Forensic Problem of Contaminated Measurement

In forensics, you would never accept a measurement without understanding contamination pathways: what could have been introduced by handling, by context, by sampling bias, by observer expectations. Policing models demand the same discipline. The training data are not "the world"; they are the world filtered through enforcement. If enforcement patterns are unequal, the data are unequal. If enforcement priorities shift, the data drift. If the model's predictions shift deployment, the data become endogenous. That is contamination in the strict forensic sense: the measuring process alters the measured object.

The consequence is what practitioners often miss: retraining can amplify injustice. When drift is driven by feedback loops, retraining is not a cure; it can be gasoline. Perdomo's framework makes this point formally; Lum and Isaac illustrate it substantively; Ensign et al. demonstrate it mechanistically (Lum and Isaac, 2016; Ensign et al., 2018; Perdomo et al., 2020).

The Moral Burden: Who Bears the Cost of Error When the Model Learns From Power?

Every predictive system allocates error burdens. In policing, the key burdens are not only false alarms; they are false attention. A false hotspot concentrates patrol in a neighbourhood, increasing stop encounters, increasing the chance of minor infractions becoming recorded offences, increasing community distrust, and increasing the probability that future victimisation is underreported. A false negative hotspot under-allocates protection, leaving communities under-served. When the model is deployed, these burdens are not distributed neutrally; they follow the grooves of history.

This is where governance discussions become material rather than abstract. Modern rights-based AI governance has increasingly treated high-stakes public-sector AI as requiring lifecycle oversight, transparency, accountability, and contestability because errors can scale quickly and can entrench discrimination. Peer-reviewed analyses of the EU's governance approach for the judiciary and high-stakes domains have framed the central challenge as accountability architecture rather than mere technical risk management (Carnat, 2024). And comparative analyses of European governance instruments argue that the direction of travel is toward binding obligations and rule-of-law alignment across the AI lifecycle, reflecting an institutional recognition that "accuracy gains" cannot justify uncontrolled coercive feedback systems (Presno Linera et al., 2025; Rotenberg, 2025). The policing reader should not treat this as foreign paperwork; it is an attempt to force coercive institutions to keep evidence, reasons, and power answerable.

What You Can Do About It: Three Forensic Controls That Actually Matter

Begin with a control borrowed from forensic science: separate discovery from validation. If discovered incidents are used as training labels, you must also maintain independent measurement streams that are not driven by patrol allocation, such as victimisation surveys, randomised patrol audits, or statistically designed sampling that allows estimation of "true" incident rates. Without an independent stream, you cannot distinguish learning from self-confirmation, and you cannot detect runaway loops until the harm is already done (Ensign et al., 2018; Akpinar et al., 2021).

Second, monitor drift as a governance obligation, not an engineering chore. Modern drift surveys emphasise that drift detection is itself a structured problem with definitional choices and trade-offs, and that unsupervised drift detection is particularly relevant to real-world monitoring where labels are delayed or missing (Gama et al., 2014; Hinder et al., 2024; Suárez-Cetrulo et al., 2023). In policing, drift monitoring must include distribution shifts in enforcement itself: changes in stop rates, changes in arrest thresholds, changes in patrol intensity, and changes in reporting rates. If you monitor only model accuracy on recorded outcomes, you will miss the structural shift: the model may remain "accurate" at predicting enforcement while the relationship between enforcement and harm decays.

Third, enforce contestability and procedural restraint. A policing model that cannot be scrutinised—inputs, objective, drift monitoring, fairness impacts—cannot be treated as legitimate guidance for coercive deployment. The reason is not philosophical delicacy; it is operational justice. Uncontestable systems are precisely those that produce voicelessness and procedural gaps when they feed into downstream decisions. When you cannot contest the model, you cannot contest the patrol pattern it produces; and when you cannot contest patrol pattern, you cannot contest the data it generates; and when you cannot contest the data, you cannot contest the model again. That is how a loop becomes a closed circuit of authority.

The Hard Conclusion: Predictive Policing Can Become Predictive Enforcement

If you want a single phrase that captures the chapter's warning, it is this: feedback loops convert prediction into enforcement strategy, and drift makes the enforcement strategy look like learned truth. The self-fulfilling prophecy of policing is not a mystical idea; it is a measurable, designable mechanism. Lum and Isaac showed the logic; Ensign et al. showed the dynamic; performative prediction gave it a formal frame; differential reporting work exposed a second bias pathway; and the self-fulfilling assessment literature showed how disclosure itself can steer behaviour toward the model (Lum and Isaac, 2016; Ensign et al., 2018; Perdomo et al., 2020; Akpinar et al., 2021; Bauer and Gill, 2024).

The moral responsibility therefore lands where it should always land: on the institution. If policing is to remain compatible with the rule of law, it must not treat its own visibility pipeline as objective reality. It must preserve independent measures of harm, monitor and publish drift in enforcement patterns, and design out self-confirming loops. Otherwise, the model will not merely predict the future; it will help manufacture a future that looks like its predictions—especially for those communities whose lives have always been easiest to police and hardest to protect.

References

- Akpinar, N.-J., De-Arteaga, M. and Chouldechova, A. (2021) 'The effect of differential victim crime reporting on predictive policing systems', Proceedings of the 2021 ACM Conference on Fairness, Accountability, and Transparency (FAccT '21).
- Ashworth, A. and Zedner, L. (2014) Preventive Justice. Oxford: Oxford University Press.
- Bauer, K. and Gill, A. (2024) 'Mirror, mirror on the wall: Algorithmic assessments, transparency, and self-fulfilling prophecies', Information Systems Research, 35(1), pp. 226–248.
- Braga, A.A., Turchan, B., Papachristos, A.V. and Hureau, D. (2019) 'Hot spots policing and crime reduction: An update of an ongoing systematic review and meta-analysis', Campbell Systematic Reviews.
- Brantingham, P.J., Mohler, G., Carter, J.G. and Short, M.B. (2018) 'Does predictive policing lead to biased arrests? Results from a randomized controlled trial', Justice Quarterly, 35(3), pp. 1–27.
- Carnat, I. (2024) 'Addressing the risks of generative AI for the judiciary: The accountability framework(s) under the EU AI Act', Computer Law & Security Review, 55, 106067.
- Ensign, D., Friedler, S.A., Neville, S., Scheidegger, C. and Venkatasubramanian, S. (2018) 'Runaway feedback loops in predictive

policing', in Proceedings of Machine Learning Research: FAT 2018, 81, pp. 1–12.

- Gama, J., Žliobaitė, I., Bifet, A., Pechenizkiy, M. and Bouchachia, A. (2014) 'A survey on concept drift adaptation', ACM Computing Surveys, 46(4), Article 44.
- Hardt, M. and Mendler-Dünner, C. (2025) 'Performative prediction: Past and future', Statistical Science, 40(3), pp. 417–436.
- Hinder, F., Hammer, B. and Biehl, M. (2024) 'One or two things we know about concept drift—A survey on monitoring and drift detection', Frontiers in Artificial Intelligence.
- Kleinberg, J., Lakkaraju, H., Leskovec, J., Ludwig, J. and Mullainathan, S. (2018) 'Human decisions and machine predictions', The Quarterly Journal of Economics, 133(1), pp. 237–293.
- Lum, K. and Isaac, W. (2016) 'To predict and serve?', Significance, 13(5), pp. 14–19.
- Neil, R. (2025) 'Algorithmic bias in criminal risk assessment: The consequences of racial differences in arrest as a measure of crime', Annual Review of Criminology, 8, pp. 97–119.
- Perdomo, J.C., Zrnic, T., Mendler-Dünner, C. and Hardt, M. (2020) 'Performative prediction', in Proceedings of the 37th International Conference on Machine Learning (ICML 2020), Proceedings of Machine Learning Research, 119.
- Petersen, K., Weisburd, D. and Telep, C.W. (2023) 'Police stops to reduce crime: A systematic review and meta-analysis', Campbell Systematic Reviews.
- Presno Linera, M.Á. et al. (2025) 'Regulating AI from Europe: A joint analysis of the AI Act and the Council of Europe AI Convention', Journal of Cyber Policy, 10(1), pp. 1–25.
- Robertson, B., Vignaux, G.A. and Berger, C.E.H. (2016) Interpreting Evidence: Evaluating Forensic Science in the Courtroom. 2nd edn. Chichester: Wiley.
- Rotenberg, M. (2025) 'Framework Convention on Artificial Intelligence and Human Rights, Democracy, and the Rule of Law (Council of Europe)', International Legal Materials, 64, pp. 1–25.
- Suárez-Cetrulo, A.L. et al. (2023) 'A survey on machine learning for recurring concept drifting data streams', Expert Systems with Applications, 213, 119031.

- Turchan, B., Braga, A.A. and Weisburd, D. (2024) 'The effects of hot spots policing on violence: A systematic review and meta-analysis', Aggression and Violent Behavior.

Part III — Evidence, Proof, and the Epistemology of Prediction

CHAPTER XI

Probability Is Not Proof: Reframing Algorithmic Outputs as Evidence

The First Discipline: Separate "What the System Spits Out" from "What the Court Is Entitled to Conclude"

When an algorithm produces a number—0.72 risk, 88% match, "high likelihood," "recommended sentence: 42 months"—the number arrives with the aesthetic of certainty. It is clean, formatted, and often wrapped in the language of science. The courtroom, fatigued by ambiguity, is naturally tempted to treat that output as a conclusion rather than as a clue. Yet the entire architecture of proof in criminal justice exists to prevent precisely this collapse. Proof is a normative achievement: it is a conclusion that the legal system is entitled to act upon after weighing contested material through disciplined procedures, under a standard of proof that does not merely reflect probability but reflects the moral cost of error. Probability is a measure of uncertainty; proof is a permission to coerce. The two interact, but they are not interchangeable. If you forget this, you will let algorithmic outputs become de facto verdicts, and you will do so while telling yourself you are merely being "evidence-based."

A mature way to begin is to treat algorithmic outputs as you would treat any forensic artefact: as observations that must be interpreted under explicit propositions, with known limitations, and with careful attention to how easily the human mind confuses weight of evidence with proof of guilt. The forensic evidence literature has been building this discipline for decades, insisting on proposition clarity, balanced reasoning, and transparent communication of uncertainty as the minimum conditions for scientific evidence to be legally safe (Robertson, Vignaux and Berger, 2016). That discipline is not a mere technical nicety. It is the moral firewall between rational inference and institutional overreach.

Evidence Is Not a Feeling: It Is a Relationship Between Competing Hypotheses

Courts frequently speak of "strong evidence" as if strength were a property of the item itself. But evidence is relational: it is strong only in relation to competing propositions. A fingerprint comparison, a DNA profile, a CCTV embedding match, or a "case outcome predictor" is not inherently incriminating. It becomes incriminating only when you specify what it is being asked to discriminate between. Modern Bayesian and likelihood-ratio approaches in forensic inference are valuable here not because courts must become mathematicians, but because they force the court to do what it should have been doing all along: define the propositions and evaluate how much the observation shifts the balance between them (Gittelson et al., 2016; Hicks et al., 2022).

The practical virtue of this approach is that it stops the most common and most destructive error: treating a match probability, a similarity score, or a risk score as if it were the probability of guilt. That error is not rare; it has produced miscarriages of justice and has repeatedly been diagnosed in the evidence scholarship as a family of transposed-conditional fallacies (Fenton and Neil, 2016). The algorithmic era does not introduce a new category of mistake; it industrialises an old one by giving the mistake a scalable source of numbers.

The Court's Burden: Standards of Proof Are Not Calibration Targets

A modern algorithm is often judged by calibration: do predicted probabilities match observed frequencies? Calibration is important for forecasting. It is not a moral theory of guilt. In criminal adjudication, the relevant question is not "is the probability high?" but "has the prosecution proved guilt beyond reasonable doubt?" and the legal system has repeatedly resisted attempts to reduce that standard to a numeric threshold precisely because proof is not merely about probability but about the structure of reasons, the coherence of the overall evidential picture, and the moral asymmetry between convicting the innocent and acquitting the guilty (Fried, 2022).

This is why purely statistical evidence can feel both powerful and unacceptable at the same time. Evidence law's discomfort with "naked statistics" reflects an intuition—sometimes articulated well, sometimes not—that a criminal verdict is not merely a bet placed on the most likely story; it is a public condemnation that must be justified through reasons that connect the accused to the wrongdoing in a way the community can recognise as legitimate (Allen, 2022). An algorithmic output can contribute to that picture, but it cannot become the picture. If it does, the court has replaced proof with prediction.

Algorithmic Outputs Are Usually Two Steps Removed from the Fact in Issue

A forensic examiner learns early that there is a difference between what a trace indicates and what the court needs to decide. A DNA profile might bear on source; the court might need activity ("how did it get there?"); and the trial might ultimately be about guilt ("what happened?"). The distance between these levels is where miscarriages occur. The modern forensic framework that emphasises proposition formulation and explicit separation of results from propositions exists precisely to stop the court from leaping across these inferential levels without noticing (Gittelson et al., 2016; Gill, 2020).

Algorithmic outputs typically sit even farther from the fact in issue than traditional traces. A "case outcome predictor" is not evidence of what happened; it is a forecast of what a court tends to do given features extracted from past cases. A recidivism risk score is not evidence that the accused committed the present offence; it is an estimate about a future that has not occurred, built on variables that often include institutional contact and social correlates. Work on legal decision predictors explicitly recognises this problem: prediction systems can be tempting to decision-makers but raise deep questions about relevance, explanation, and the risk of misusing forecasts as reasons (Bex et al., 2021). When you allow such outputs to function as proof, you collapse relevance and you permit the system to launder policy preferences into adjudication.

The New Evidence Problem: Reliability Without Interpretability Is Not Court-Safe

Forensic science has taught courts a hard lesson: an instrument can be impressive and still be unsafe if its error properties are not known, if its performance varies by condition, or if its outputs cannot be interpreted without contextual bias. That lesson is now being re-learned in algorithmic form. The crucial point is that "accuracy" is not a single number; it is conditional. It varies with data shifts, population shifts, and deployment practices. In a 2026 paper on the influence of validation data on the logical and scientific interpretation of forensic evidence, the authors distinguish performance uncertainty (how well the method performs) from the decision-maker's uncertainty about which proposition is true, and show why validation data reduce the former and must be communicated so recipients can weight opinions appropriately (Lund et al., 2026). That framework belongs in algorithmic evidence debates because algorithmic systems are often deployed with precisely the sort of hidden performance uncertainty that courts would never tolerate from a human expert.

What makes the algorithmic context more dangerous is that some systems—especially "black-box" tools and generative systems—can produce plausible outputs even when wrong. Peer-reviewed profiling of legal hallucinations in large language models shows that these systems can fabricate legal authorities and citations in ways that sound fluent and authoritative, which is epistemic poison to a legal system grounded in checkable reasons (Dahl et al., 2024). A courtroom that treats such output as "evidence" without independent verification has not merely admitted weak proof; it has contaminated its reasons-giving function.

The Communication Trap: Likelihood Ratios, Scores, and the Prosecutor's Fallacy in Modern Clothing

Even when an algorithmic output is presented in a logically correct form—such as a likelihood ratio—the court can still be misled if decision-makers misunderstand what the number means. The empirical literature on comprehension is sobering. Research testing whether explaining the meaning of likelihood ratios improves lay understanding shows that people can still commit reasoning errors and that the risk of misinterpretation remains significant without careful communication strategies (Thompson, 2025). A 2025 review asking how forensic practitioners should present likelihood ratios to maximise understandability surveys this literature and highlights how frequently recipients default to fallacious interpretations, including the prosecutor's fallacy (Morrison et al., 2025).

This is not an argument against probabilistic reporting; it is an argument for institutional discipline. The modern forensic consensus that the likelihood ratio is a principled summary of evidential weight comes with a companion duty: present it with supporting information about how it was constructed and what it is based on, precisely because uncontextualised numbers invite misuse (Gittelson et al., 2018). If courts struggle even with carefully formulated likelihood ratios, you can imagine what happens when they are given opaque similarity scores or "confidence" percentages produced by proprietary models.

The Case Law Lesson Without the Case Law: "Trial by Mathematics" Failed When Mathematics Became Verdict

Courts across legal traditions have repeatedly encountered probability arguments that seduce and mislead: the multiplication of loosely justified probabilities; the presentation of "rare match" as "proof of guilt"; the conversion of statistical association into condemnation. The People v Collins controversy is often invoked as a cautionary tale about improper probability multiplication and the rhetorical power of numbers (Tillers, 2011). The more instructive lesson is not that mathematics is unwelcome. It is that mathematics must be tethered to disciplined propositions, validated assumptions, and careful separation between evidential weight and ultimate proof. The same lesson underlies judicial discomfort with probabilistic shoeprint evidence debates such as the R v T controversy, where concerns about generation and presentation of probabilistic conclusions were central to the critique (Hamer, 2012).

The algorithmic era revives "trial by mathematics" in a new costume. The prosecution need not multiply probabilities on a blackboard anymore; the multiplication happens inside the model. The court's duty is the same: require that the inferential steps are defensible and that the output is treated as one element in a larger reasoning structure, not as a shortcut to guilt.

Relevance: A Prediction Can Be Highly Accurate and Still Be Legally Irrelevant

One of the most dangerous moves in algorithmic evidence is to treat predictive accuracy as the primary admissibility criterion. Relevance in evidence law is not "helps us decide faster"; it is "bears on a fact in issue in a way that assists the lawful reasoning process." Algorithm-assisted decision-making scholarship in public law warns that predictive tools can distort discretion and accountability, and that long-standing legal constraints on discretionary power become strained when state decisions are justified by opaque predictions (Oswald, 2018).

Similarly, philosophical work on algorithmic decision-making and the rule of law argues that accuracy is a virtue only within a wider architecture of legal virtues that presuppose contestability and reasons-giving; otherwise, accuracy becomes a false idol that displaces rule-of-law values (Chiao, 2024). This matters because many algorithmic outputs in criminal process—especially risk forecasts—are not evidence of what happened; they are predictions about what might happen. A system can be accurate in forecasting rearrest and still be irrelevant to culpability for the charged offence, and its introduction at trial can function as forbidden character reasoning in scientific dress.

Contestability: Evidence Must Be Testable, Not Just Presented

An adversarial system is designed to test evidence. If an algorithmic output cannot be meaningfully tested—because the model is proprietary, the training data are undisclosed, the validation studies are inaccessible, or the performance uncertainty is unknown—then the court is being asked to accept authority rather than evidence. Bayesian network scholarship on legal arguments has pushed this point in a constructive direction: rather than treating probability as a mystifying number, Bayesian networks can structure evidential reasoning transparently, showing dependencies and allowing parties to contest assumptions (Fenton, Neil and Lagnado, 2013). More recent work explicitly compares causal models and reason models in Bayesian networks for legal evidence, illustrating that the structure chosen is itself a normative and interpretive decision, which should be open to scrutiny rather than buried inside an opaque pipeline (Dahlman, 2022).

This is the direction the court should move: not "accept the model" but "make the inferential structure visible." When the structure is visible, the defence can challenge base rates, dependence assumptions, missing data, and alternative hypotheses. When the structure is hidden, the court cannot tell whether it is being shown science or being sold inevitability.

The Forensic Reframe: Algorithmic Outputs as a New Kind of Trace Evidence

If you want a practical mental model, treat an algorithmic output as a trace—like a partial fingerprint or a noisy CCTV match—rather than as a conclusion. A trace has probative potential, but only under explicit propositions and interpretive safeguards. Forensic logic frameworks in DNA interpretation emphasise precisely this: results must be interpreted relative to propositions and communicated transparently to avoid overstatement (Hicks et al., 2022). The same approach can be extended to algorithmic outputs. A similarity score becomes evidence only when you specify the propositions it bears on, show validation for the relevant conditions, and communicate uncertainty without inviting fallacies.

This also exposes the role of the forensic expert in the AI era. The expert is no longer only an interpreter of physical traces; increasingly, the expert becomes a translator and validator of algorithmic artefacts, responsible for explaining what the output does and does not mean, and for preventing the legal system from confusing computational confidence with proof (Morić et al., 2025).

The Moral End: Why "Probability Is Not Proof" Must Remain an Institutional Reflex

The deepest reason to maintain this distinction is moral. Criminal conviction is not a forecast; it is a condemnation. A probabilistic system can help the court understand uncertainty, but it cannot relieve the court of moral responsibility for the act of judgement. Once you permit algorithmic outputs to function as proof, you create a system where coercion is justified by a number that no one can morally own. When errors occur—and they will—the institution will retreat into diffusion: the model, the vendor, the data, the process. That is incompatible with a justice system that demands responsibility from individuals while refusing it for itself.

So the correct posture is disciplined and surprisingly simple. Let algorithms contribute evidence only when they can be framed under explicit propositions, validated under conditions of use, communicated without fallacy, and contested meaningfully. Let their outputs be treated as weight, not as verdict. Preserve the court's reasons-giving function as the final gate through which probability must pass before the state may coerce.

Probability is not proof. It is one ingredient in the only thing that can justify punishment: a publicly defensible judgement.

References

- Allen, R.J. (2022) 'The law's aversion to naked statistics and other mistakes', Legal Theory, 28(3), pp. 243–270.
- Anderson, T., Schum, D.A. and Twining, W. (2005) Analysis of Evidence. 2nd edn. Cambridge: Cambridge University Press.
- Bex, F., Prakken, H. and Verheij, B. (2021) 'On the relevance of algorithmic decision predictors for judicial decision-making', Proceedings of ICAIL 2021.
- Biedermann, A. and Taroni, F. (2014) 'On the use of the likelihood ratio for forensic evaluation', Science & Justice, 54(4), pp. 288–294.
- Chiao, V. (2024) 'Algorithmic decision-making, statistical evidence and the rule of law', Episteme.
- Chouldechova, A. (2017) 'Fair prediction with disparate impact', Big Data, 5(2), pp. 153–163.
- Dahl, C. (2022) 'Causal models versus reason models in Bayesian networks for legal evidence', Synthese, 200, pp. 1–26.
- Dahl, M. et al. (2024) 'Profiling legal hallucinations in large language models', Journal of Legal Analysis, 16(1), pp. 64–110.
- Fenton, N., Neil, M. and Lagnado, D.A. (2013) 'A general structure for legal arguments about evidence using Bayesian networks', Cognitive Science, 37(1), pp. 61–102.
- Fenton, N. and Neil, M. (2016) 'Bayes and the law', Annual Review of Statistics and Its Application, 3, pp. 51–77.
- Fenton, N. and Neil, M. (2019) Risk Assessment and Decision Analysis with Bayesian Networks. Boca Raton: CRC Press.
- Fried, A. (2022) 'Statistical evidence and the criminal verdict asymmetry', Synthese, 200, pp. 1–25.
- Gill, P. (2020) 'Assessing the value of forensic biological evidence', Forensic Science International, 307, 110124.
- Gittelson, S. et al. (2016) 'A practical guide for the formulation of propositions in the Bayesian approach to DNA evidence interpretation in an adversarial environment', Journal of Forensic Sciences, 61(1), pp. 186–195.

- Gittelson, S., Kalafut, T., Myers, S. et al. (2018) 'A response to "Likelihood ratio as weight of evidence"', Forensic Science International, 286, pp. e1–e5.
- Hamer, D. (2012) 'The R v T controversy: Forensic evidence, law and logic', Law, Probability and Risk, 11(4), pp. 331–352.
- Hicks, T. et al. (2022) 'A logical framework for forensic DNA interpretation', Genes, 13(6), 957.
- Ho, H.L. (2015) 'The legal concept of evidence', Stanford Encyclopedia of Philosophy.
- Lagnado, D.A. (2013) 'Legal idioms: A framework for evidential reasoning', Argument & Computation, 4(1), pp. 46–63.
- Lund, S.P. et al. (2026) 'The influence of validation data on logical and scientific interpretation of forensic expert opinion', Law, Probability and Risk, 25(1), mgaf013.
- Morić, Z. et al. (2025) 'An AI-based decision support system utilizing Bayesian networks for structuring legal evidence', Systems, 13(2), 131.
- Morrison, G.S., Bali, A.S., Martire, K.A. and Grady, R.H. (2025) 'What is the best way to present likelihood ratios? A review of past research and recommendations for future research', Science & Justice, 65, 101342.
- Oswald, M. (2018) 'Algorithm-assisted decision-making in the public sector: Framing the issues using administrative law rules governing discretionary power', Philosophical Transactions of the Royal Society A, 376(2128), 20170359.
- Ribeiro, G. et al. (2020) 'Does DNA evidence in the form of a likelihood ratio affect judgments?', Psychonomic Bulletin & Review, 27, pp. 1151–1163.
- Robertson, B., Vignaux, G.A. and Berger, C.E.H. (2016) Interpreting Evidence: Evaluating Forensic Science in the Courtroom. 2nd edn. Chichester: Wiley.
- Sallavaci, O. (2025) 'Algorithms on trial: Does evaluative probabilistic reporting infringe the presumption of innocence?', Forensic Science International: Synergy, 8, 100332.
- Schum, D.A. (2001) The Evidential Foundations of Probabilistic Reasoning. Evanston, IL: Northwestern University Press.
- Thompson, W.C. (2018) 'Perceived strength of forensic scientists' reporting statements and the implications for reporting', Law, Probability and Risk, 17(2), pp. 133–155.

- Thompson, W.C. (2025) 'Does explaining the meaning of likelihood ratios improve understanding?', Journal of Forensic Sciences, 70, pp. 1–14.
- Tillers, P. (2011) 'Trial by mathematics—reconsidered', Law, Probability and Risk, 10(3), pp. 167–177.
- Twining, W. (1985) Theories of Evidence: Bentham and Wigmore. Stanford, CA: Stanford University Press.

CHAPTER XII

Base Rates, Priors, and the Court's Problem with Statistical Reasoning

The Number That Quietly Governs Every Case

Every legal decision under uncertainty contains a hidden quantity, even when no one names it: the baseline chance that the prosecution's story is true before the contested evidence is introduced. Call it the base rate, call it the prior, call it background probability—its label matters less than its function. It is the silent multiplier that determines what any new piece of evidence can rationally do. A match statistic, a similarity score, a likelihood ratio, a "90% confidence" output from an algorithm: none of these can be understood without asking the prior question, because the posterior conclusion is always a product of two things—the strength of the evidence and the starting point from which you began. Fenton, Neil and Berger's review of Bayesian reasoning in law explains why this remains an uncomfortable truth for legal practice: courts often want the evidence to do all the work, and they recoil from the explicit handling of priors because priors appear subjective, politically dangerous, or normatively inappropriate.

But refusing to name priors does not abolish them. It merely forces them underground, where they re-enter as intuition, stereotype, or narrative plausibility. A court that refuses explicit base-rate reasoning does not become non-probabilistic. It becomes probabilistic in the least disciplined way possible.

Why Base Rates Hurt the Legal Mind

The psychological reason base rates cause trouble is that legal reasoning is naturally story-driven. Fact-finders are trained to ask what happened, who did it, why it happened, and whether the story hangs together. Numbers feel like alien intrusions into a narrative craft. The statistical reason base rates cause trouble is even simpler: many legal questions involve rare events—rare types of offenders, rare modus operandi patterns, rare forensic profiles, rare coincidences—and in rare-event settings, priors dominate. Even very strong evidence can be overwhelmed by a very low prior, while weak evidence can look crushing if the prior is already high. The moral reason base rates cause trouble is that priors can be smuggled in through prejudice. If a "prior probability" is silently built from race, class, neighbourhood, or police attention, then Bayes' theorem becomes a laundering machine for injustice. The court's task is therefore twofold: to reason statistically without permitting the statistical framework to become an excuse for moral contamination.

This dual task is why the law's historical discomfort with "trial by mathematics" is not simply ignorance. It reflects a fear that formal probability can hide normative choices—what counts as the relevant population, what counts as "typical," what background assumptions are permitted—behind a façade of inevitability. Modern evidence theory has explained these proof paradoxes and the persistent reluctance to ground verdicts on "mere statistics" as a clash between two demands: epistemic rationality and justificatory legitimacy.

The Prosecutor's Fallacy Is Not a Single Mistake; It Is a Family of Prior Errors

The most famous legal manifestation of base-rate failure is the prosecutor's fallacy: confusing the probability of observing evidence if the defendant is innocent with the probability that the defendant is innocent given the evidence. The deeper point is that this fallacy is usually a prior error. It treats the accused as if they were already a plausible culprit, or it treats the defendant as if they were randomly drawn from the population of possible perpetrators, depending on which rhetorical move is convenient. Thompson and Schumann's classic experimental work demonstrated how easily decision-makers confuse conditional probabilities in legal settings, and it remains foundational precisely because it showed that presentation format and intuitive reasoning can drive people toward or away from fallacious conclusions.

More recent work has shown that this is not merely a lay-juror issue. A 2025 study examining legal professionals' evaluation of forensic reports found that identifying logical errors such as the prosecutor's fallacy was remarkably difficult, with a very small fraction correctly identifying the fallacy in unsound reports. This is a key institutional fact: the court's problem with base rates is not "the public is bad at math." The court's problem is that legal systems routinely place probabilistic artefacts into a reasoning environment that has not been trained to resist predictable cognitive traps.

Likelihood Ratios Were Supposed to Solve This; They Didn't

Forensic science's modern turn toward likelihood ratios was partly motivated by a desire to avoid posterior probability claims that invite the prosecutor's fallacy. The likelihood ratio, properly used, expresses how much more probable the observed evidence is under one proposition than another. It is a weight-of-evidence measure, not a probability of guilt. Yet the mere adoption of likelihood ratios does not end the base-rate problem. It simply relocates it: once you have a likelihood ratio, you still need priors to reach posteriors, and you still need disciplined proposition-setting to avoid smuggling the wrong priors into the case.

The empirical literature on comprehension is sobering. Eldridge's gap analysis review synthesised the evidence that jurors often do not interpret forensic statements in the way experts intend, and that without comprehension, the "correctness" of a reporting format is moot in practice. Morrison and colleagues' 2025 review of research on presenting likelihood ratios underscores that misunderstandings persist, and that the field still lacks definitive guidance that reliably prevents fallacious interpretation across audiences. Thompson's 2025 study goes further, reporting that explaining the meaning of likelihood ratios did not convincingly reduce prosecutor's-fallacy-consistent reasoning among participants, which is a warning against overconfidence in "a short explanation will fix it."

If you are reading this as a forensic practitioner, the implication is uncomfortable but necessary: you cannot solve the base-rate problem by changing a number's wrapper. You must also change the decision environment—training, questioning practice, judicial directions, and the structure of propositions put before the court.

The Weak Evidence Effect: When People Get the Direction Wrong

A further complication is that even when people try to reason probabilistically, they can misunderstand what weak evidence does. Martire and colleagues documented what is often called the "weak evidence effect," where low-strength evidence—especially when communicated verbally—can be misinterpreted in direction or weight, sometimes leading people to treat weakly incriminating evidence as if it were strongly incriminating or to treat weakly exculpatory evidence as if it were incriminating. This effect matters because algorithms frequently output "weak" signals: modest similarity scores, moderate risk scores, probabilities that are impressive to a lay eye but trivial in a rare-event setting. If a legal system is vulnerable to weak-evidence misinterpretation, algorithmic decision support can magnify rather than reduce error, especially when the output arrives with institutional authority.

The Reference-Class Problem: Choosing the Prior Is Itself a Legal Decision

Even if everyone agrees to reason with priors, the next question arrives like a knife: priors based on what reference class? The relevant baseline could be "any adult in the jurisdiction," "any person matching a description," "any person with access to the scene," "any person within a social network," or "any person already identified through independent investigative evidence." Each reference class yields a different prior, and the choice is not mechanically dictated by probability theory. Colyvan and colleagues' discussion of the reference-class problem in legal decision-making shows why this is a genuine difficulty, not a pedant's complaint: a single individual belongs to many overlapping classes with different event frequencies, and the law must decide which class is normatively appropriate to use for inference. Tillers' work in Law, Probability and Risk presses the moral dimension: reference-class reasoning risks unfairly burdening individuals by treating them as members of a group rather than as persons whose case should be individuated, yet the law cannot avoid group frequencies entirely if it admits statistical evidence at all.

This is where the court's statistical problem becomes a rule-of-law problem. Choosing a prior is not only epistemic; it is also normative. The legal system must decide which background assumptions are permitted, and which are forbidden because they import prejudice, collective guilt, or arbitrary stereotyping. If the court refuses to do this openly, it will still do it—only implicitly and inconsistently.

A Forensic Way to Handle Priors Without Turning Trials Into Seminars

There is a disciplined middle path between two extremes: the fantasy that priors can be avoided, and the fantasy that priors can be fully mathematized in every case. The forensic discipline begins with proposition management. Do not ask "what is the probability he is guilty?" as a starting question. Ask instead: what competing propositions are being compared, what evidence is relevant to discriminating between them, and at what inferential level is the evidence operating—source, activity, or ultimate issue. Forensic Bayesian guidance on proposition formulation exists precisely to stop the court from leaping from a source-level statistic to an ultimate-issue conclusion.

Then treat priors as structured and reviewable, not mystical. In many cases, the appropriate "prior" is not a single number but a range anchored to explicit assumptions: one range if the suspect was identified through independent investigative leads, a much lower range if the suspect emerged only because of a database trawl, a different range if the suspect is one of a small number of individuals with unique access to the scene. This is not courtroom theatre. It is an honesty policy. It tells the court what the evidence can do under plausible background assumptions, and it prevents the evidence from being presented as if it had a fixed meaning independent of how the suspect came to be in the dock.

The Database Era: Priors Become the Price of Surveillance

Modern policing and forensic practices have changed the prior landscape. When a suspect is identified by searching a large database—DNA databases, face-recognition watchlists, voiceprint systems, digital forensics triage—the "prior" that the suspect is the culprit is often far lower than when a suspect is identified through independent investigative work. Yet the psychological tendency is to treat a database "hit" as if it were the beginning of certainty rather than the beginning of scrutiny. This is exactly the environment in which base-rate neglect thrives: the size of the search space is ignored, and the hit is treated as direct proof rather than as a hypothesis-generator.

The legal response cannot be to ban databases. The response must be to require the court to account for the selection mechanism. The question "How did this person become the suspect?" is not ancillary; it is the prior question. If the system does not force that question into the record, it will treat surveillance as epistemic entitlement.

Algorithmic Risk Scores: Priors Disguised as Neutral Outputs

Risk instruments and AI decision aids introduce a more subtle version of the same problem. A risk score often appears to be purely forward-looking, but it typically encodes priors about who is likely to fail, who is likely to reoffend, and who is likely to breach conditions—priors built from institutional history. When such scores are used in bail, sentencing, or supervision, the court is effectively importing a prior distribution derived from past enforcement patterns. If those patterns are biased, the score is a biased prior in numerical form. This is why the statistical reasoning problem becomes a moral problem: base rates are not only frequencies; in criminal justice they are often frequencies produced by power.

This is also why "just be Bayesian" is not an ethical solution. A Bayesian update is only as morally clean as the priors you permit and the evidence process that generated the likelihood. If the prior is polluted by stereotype and the likelihood is polluted by institutional selection, the posterior will be precise and wrong in a way that feels irresistible.

Training and Procedure: The Only Real Fix Is Institutional

The most honest conclusion from the empirical literature is that comprehension problems do not vanish on their own. Dahlman's systematic account of probabilistic fallacies in legal fact-finding organises the observed errors into a structured set of categories, demonstrating that the prosecutor's fallacy is only one member of a broader family of probabilistic reasoning failures. The existence of this taxonomy matters because it gives training a target: you cannot fix what you cannot name. Consistent with that, work on training legal fact-finders to recognise probabilistic fallacies shows the field moving toward evidence-based education as a procedural safeguard, rather than relying on ad hoc judicial warnings.

Yet training alone is insufficient if procedure invites fallacy. The adversarial system must be able to test the assumptions. That means disclosure of validation studies, clarity about what the algorithm measures, and structured questioning that prevents experts from sliding into posterior claims. It also means judicial directions that treat base-rate reasoning as a permissible and necessary part of rational evaluation—while explicitly forbidding priors based on prejudice.

The Moral Boundary: Priors Must Be Anchored to Permissible Reasons

Here is the line the law must draw if it wants statistical rationality without moral collapse. Priors must be anchored to permissible reasons: opportunity, access, independent investigative evidence, credible motive evidence—reasons that can be contested and reviewed. Priors must not be anchored to impermissible reasons: race, class, neighbourhood stereotypes, "people like him," or enforcement visibility masquerading as propensity. The court's duty is to discipline the background.

If this sounds demanding, it is because liberty is demanding. The justice system cannot complain that priors are hard while continuing to make prior-laden judgments implicitly. Either priors are controlled by law and reason, or they are controlled by prejudice and habit. There is no third option.

The Practical Takeaway: What You Should Do With an Algorithmic Output Tomorrow Morning

When an algorithmic output arrives in a case—match statistic, similarity score, risk score—your first act should be forensic: define the proposition the output bears on, and define the level of inference. Your second act should be statistical: ask what the prior is, and how the suspect was selected. Your third act should be moral: test whether the prior assumptions are permissible. Your fourth act should be procedural: ask whether the defence can contest the assumptions and the method. Only then can the output take its place as evidence rather than as destiny.

Because the final truth is simple: base rates and priors do not threaten justice. Undisciplined priors do. And courts that fear statistics often end up governed by the worst statistics of all—unspoken ones.

References

- Chiao, V. (2024) 'Algorithmic decision-making, statistical evidence and the rule of law', Episteme.
- Colyvan, M., Regan, H.M. and Ferson, S. (2001) 'Is it a crime to belong to a reference class?', Journal of Political Philosophy, 9(2), pp. 168–181.
- Dahlman, C. (2024) 'A systematic account of probabilistic fallacies in legal fact-finding', International Journal of Evidence & Proof, 28(1), pp. 45–64.
- de Roo, R.H.D. et al. (2025) 'The impact of institutional authority on forensic evidence evaluation'.
- Eldridge, H. (2019) 'Juror comprehension of forensic expert testimony: A literature review and gap analysis', Forensic Science International: Synergy, 1, pp. 24–34.
- Fenton, N., Neil, M. and Lagnado, D.A. (2013) 'A general structure for legal arguments about evidence using Bayesian networks', Cognitive Science, 37(1), pp. 61–102.
- Fenton, N. and Neil, M. (2014) 'Assessing evidence and testing appropriate hypotheses', Science & Justice, 54(4), pp. 274–287.
- Fenton, N. and Neil, M. (2016) 'Bayes and the law', Annual Review of Statistics and Its Application, 3, pp. 51–77.
- Fried, A. (2022) 'Statistical evidence and the criminal verdict asymmetry', Synthese, 200, pp. 1–25.
- Gittelson, S. et al. (2016) 'A practical guide for the formulation of propositions in the Bayesian approach to DNA evidence interpretation', Journal of Forensic Sciences, 61(1), pp. 186–195.
- Hamer, D. (2012) 'The R v T controversy: Forensic evidence, law and logic', Law, Probability and Risk, 11(4), pp. 331–352.
- 'Juror understanding of DNA evidence' (2004) Journal of Legal Studies.
- Lund, S.P. et al. (2017) 'Likelihood ratio as weight of forensic evidence: A closer look', Law, Probability and Risk, 16(2), pp. 115–135.
- Martire, K.A., Kemp, R.I. and Sayle, M.A. (2014) 'On the interpretation of likelihood ratios in forensic science evidence: Presentation formats and the weak evidence effect', Forensic Science International, 240, pp. 61–68.

- Morrison, G.S. et al. (2025) 'What is the best way to present likelihood ratios? A review of past research and recommendations for future research', Science & Justice, 65, 101342.
- Redmayne, M. (2008) 'Exploring the proof paradoxes', Legal Theory, 14(4), pp. 281–309.
- Thompson, W.C. and Schumann, E.L. (1987) 'Interpretation of statistical evidence in criminal trials: The prosecutor's fallacy and the defense attorney's fallacy', Law and Human Behavior, 11(3), pp. 167–187.
- Thompson, W.C. (2025) 'Does explaining the meaning of likelihood ratios improve understanding?', Journal of Forensic Sciences.
- Tillers, P. (2003) 'If wishes were horses: Discursive comments on attempts to prevent individuals from being unfairly burdened by their reference classes', Law, Probability and Risk, 4, pp. 33–49.
- 'Training legal fact-finders to recognize probabilistic fallacies' (2025) Law, Probability and Risk.

CHAPTER XIII

Calibration, Error, and the Ethics of Thresholds

The Cleanest Lie a System Can Tell: "We Set the Threshold Scientifically"

Whenever an algorithm is deployed in a court, a police service, a forensic laboratory, or a corrections department, you will eventually meet the quiet sovereign of the entire enterprise: the threshold. Above it, you detain; below it, you release. Above it, you label a trace a "match"; below it, you say "inconclusive." Above it, you escalate supervision; below it, you offer support. The threshold is rarely debated in open court, rarely written about in judgments, and almost never experienced as the moral decision it actually is. Yet it is precisely where the state converts a probability into coercion. Calibration and error are discussed as technical features; the threshold is treated as mere implementation. That is backwards. Calibration and error rates describe how a scoring system behaves; a threshold describes what the institution chooses to do with that behaviour. The moment a threshold is set, the institution is no longer forecasting; it is governing.

The temptation is to hide behind the prestige of numbers. "The model is calibrated," the institution says, as if calibration were an ethical certificate. But calibration is not a moral theory. Calibration simply means that among all individuals given score s, about s proportion will experience the outcome, under the data-generating conditions that produced the calibration estimate. It does not tell you whether the outcome is morally relevant, whether the data are contaminated by enforcement bias, or whether the costs of false positives and false negatives are ethically distributed. It does not tell you whether the threshold you set is compatible with liberty, proportionality, due process, and equality. It tells you only that the forecast tracks observed frequencies in the aggregate. Even in ordinary machine learning, calibration is conditional and fragile; it can degrade under dataset shift and concept drift, which are routine in real-world deployments (Guo et al., 2017; Kull et al., 2019; Gama et al., 2014). In criminal justice, where the data are generated by institutional choices, calibration can become a mirror of policy rather than a window into truth.

Calibration Is a Property of a Score; Justice Is a Property of a Decision

It helps to make a forensic distinction that courts already understand in another domain. In forensic inference, an evidence evaluation method can be logically correct in form and empirically tested, yet still be misused if its limitations are not communicated and if decision thresholds distort its probative value. A 2023 PNAS study on forensic decision thresholds makes the point with brutal clarity: small shifts in examiners' thresholds can dramatically alter both error rates and the probative value of the evidence, meaning the same underlying observations can support very different legal consequences depending on where the cut-point is placed (Thompson, 2023). Calibration does not rescue you from this; it is orthogonal. The ethical danger is that institutions treat thresholds as mere "policy knobs" while continuing to present the outputs as if they are direct scientific truths. In reality, the threshold is where science ends and governance begins.

The same lesson appears in contemporary forensic standards discourse. A 2025 peer-reviewed guide to ISO 21043, written from a forensic-data-science perspective, stresses transparency, validation under casework conditions, resistance to cognitive bias, and calibrated, empirically grounded evidence interpretation within the likelihood-ratio paradigm (Morrison, 2025). That emphasis is not merely technical; it is constitutional in spirit. If the state is going to use scientific outputs to justify coercion, the logic and performance must be demonstrable, and the decision policies that convert outputs into actions must be ethically defensible. The moment you treat decision thresholds as operational details, you recreate the very conditions that forensic reform has spent decades trying to eliminate: unexamined discretion masquerading as science (Robertson, Vignaux and Berger, 2016).

Error Is Not One Number; It Is a Family of Harms Distributed Across People

Institutions often ask, "What is the error rate?" as if error were singular. In truth, error is a distribution: false positives and false negatives, each with different harms, each borne by different people, and each amplified differently by institutional context. A false positive in pretrial risk can mean detention for a presumptively innocent person, loss of employment, destabilisation of family structure, and pressure to plead, which the causal literature shows can shape case outcomes and life trajectories (Dobbie, Goldin and Yang, 2018; Gupta, Hansman and Frenchman, 2016). A false negative can mean real victimisation and public fear. The ethical problem is not that errors exist; it is that institutions choose whose errors are tolerable and then hide that choice behind "risk management."

Forensic science provides a disciplined vocabulary for this choice. The likelihood-ratio framework, properly understood, expresses evidential weight; it does not dictate decisions. Thresholds convert weight into action. When those thresholds drift—whether because of workload, training, or organisational pressure—error patterns shift and the evidential meaning presented to courts can be distorted (Thompson, 2023). In DNA mixture analysis, for example, peer-reviewed empirical work has demonstrated that parameter variation and threshold choices can materially affect evidence quantification, reminding us that analytical thresholds are not neutral—they shape what the method "sees," and therefore shape what the court is told (Costa et al., 2025). The ethical implication is immediate: if the scientific pipeline's thresholds are under-instrumented, under-audited, or treated as mere lab policy, then the legal system is not receiving stable evidence; it is receiving a product of hidden decision points.

The Threshold Is Where the Rule of Law Meets the Economics of Mistakes

The ethics of thresholds is, at bottom, the ethics of trade-offs under uncertainty. The institution must decide how much false-positive harm it is willing to impose to prevent a given quantity of false-negative harm. This is not a purely utilitarian calculus in criminal justice because liberty is not a commodity and because the accused is owed procedural respect independent of outcome efficiency (Tyler, 2011; Duff, 2001). But trade-offs still exist, and pretending they do not exist is what produces arbitrary thresholds.

This is where the distinction between calibration and decision policy matters most. A perfectly calibrated score can still be used unjustly if the threshold is set to prioritise institutional risk aversion over individual liberty. A poorly calibrated score can still be used in a relatively restrained way if the threshold is set conservatively and if decisions are accompanied by procedural safeguards and contestability. The ethical question is therefore not "is the model calibrated?" but "what decision policy is being imposed on calibrated or uncalibrated outputs, and who bears the cost when the system is wrong?"

Calibration Versus Fairness: The Threshold Becomes a Moral Fork

In criminal justice, you cannot discuss thresholds without discussing group disparities, because base rates differ across groups and because many outcomes used for training—such as arrest—reflect unequal enforcement patterns (Neil, 2025). When base rates differ, you run into the now-classic impossibility tensions between calibration and equalized error rates across groups, and the threshold becomes the lever through which these tensions are operationalised (Chouldechova, 2017; Kleinberg, Mullainathan and Raghavan, 2017). If you set a single threshold across groups, you will often produce different false-positive and false-negative rates across groups even if the score is calibrated. If you set group-specific thresholds to equalize error rates, you may sacrifice calibration or create different decision rules for different groups, which raises its own legal and moral concerns about equality and individual treatment.

A 2021 theoretical paper explicitly shows that calibrated scores and equal error rates can, in certain setups, be reconciled by manipulating score distributions and recommendations, highlighting that the relationship between calibration and error parity is not a simple binary but depends on how scores are produced and how decisions are derived from them (Lazar Reich, 2021). The crucial institutional point is simpler: once you admit that threshold-setting can be used to pursue different fairness goals, you are admitting that thresholds are policy instruments, not technical defaults. The ethical question then becomes unavoidable: which fairness conception should govern a liberty decision, and how is the choice justified publicly?

This is why scholarship in criminology and statistics has repeatedly warned that fairness debates in criminal justice risk assessment are often conceptually sloppy, substituting rhetoric for careful trade-off analysis (Berk et al., 2018; Berk et al., 2021). Thresholds are where that sloppiness becomes harm. You can proclaim fairness while quietly choosing a threshold that concentrates false positives on already over-surveilled communities, thereby intensifying coercion under the banner of equality.

Selective Labels and Hidden Error: When You Cannot Even Observe the Mistake

The ethics of thresholds becomes even more difficult when outcomes are selectively observed. In bail settings, you only observe pretrial misconduct for those who are released; those detained never generate observed labels for what they "would have done." That means the model's calibration and error can be distorted by the release policy itself, and threshold changes can alter the observed dataset in ways that then reshape future calibration. Recent peer-reviewed work develops quasi-experimental tools for algorithmic discrimination under selective observation and applies them to bail, showing how conventional predictions based on released defendants can embed conditional input disparities and generate discriminatory outcomes unless those disparities are identified and purged (Arnold et al., 2025). This matters for thresholds because it shows why "we tuned the threshold" can be epistemically hollow: you might not even know how many false positives you are producing among those you detain, because the counterfactual outcomes are hidden by detention itself.

This is the algorithmic analogue of a classic forensic contamination problem: you cannot validate what you cannot observe, and yet the institution may act as though it has a scientifically grounded cut-point. A justice system that cares about legitimacy must treat such thresholds as provisional and must compensate through procedural safeguards, independent measurement strategies, and transparency about uncertainty.

Drift and Threshold Decay: The Decision Policy Moves Even When the Model Does Not

Even if a model is initially calibrated, drift can break that calibration as the world changes. The policing environment changes; reporting patterns change; enforcement priorities change; the model's mapping from scores to outcomes shifts. Concept drift surveys describe this as a ubiquitous phenomenon requiring monitoring and adaptation, not an edge case (Gama et al., 2014; Hinder, Hammer and Biehl, 2024). When drift occurs, thresholds become especially dangerous because institutions often keep the same cut-point while the meaning of the score changes. A "0.7 risk" in 2019 may not be a "0.7 risk" in 2024 if social conditions, institutional practices, or data pipelines have shifted. If the threshold remains fixed, the error distribution shifts silently. The system becomes more punitive or more permissive without any explicit policy change—an invisible governance shift.

Feedback loops worsen this. Predictive policing research has shown how model outputs can change patrol allocation, changing the data stream and producing self-confirming loops (Lum and Isaac, 2016; Ensign et al., 2018). When such loops exist, calibration can become calibration-to-enforcement rather than calibration-to-harm, and thresholds can become engines that convert attention into apparent truth. In that environment, threshold ethics must include not only individual-level error but system-level harms: over-policing, community distrust, and the erosion of legitimacy.

The Human Factor: Thresholds Are Not Only Mathematical; They Are Cognitive

Institutions often imagine thresholds as clean, mechanical rules. But thresholds in practice are interpreted, overridden, and re-applied by humans. Cognitive bias research in forensic science has shown that contextual information can shift expert decisions and thereby shift effective thresholds, even when formal criteria remain unchanged (Cooper et al., 2019). In other words, you can set a threshold in a policy document and still end up with a different operational threshold in the field due to human judgement under pressure.

This matters in court settings because algorithmic recommendations often function as anchors. A judge who is told "high risk" is more likely to interpret ambiguous facts as confirming risk. A forensic examiner who knows a suspect's profile may shift their internal standard for declaring a "match." Thompson's work on threshold shifts in forensics is therefore not merely about labs; it is a parable for algorithmic governance: small, often invisible shifts in decision standards can have massive downstream effects on error and probative value (Thompson, 2023). The ethical implication is that threshold governance cannot be purely formal; it must include auditing, training, context management, and safeguards against cognitive contamination.

The Ethics of Thresholds in High-Stakes Domains: Liberty is Not "Cost"

A purely consequentialist threshold policy might try to minimize expected harm by assigning numerical costs to false positives and false negatives. In criminal justice, that approach becomes morally brittle because liberty deprivations are not symmetric harms and because the system's legitimacy depends on more than outcome optimisation. Procedural justice research shows that people's compliance and cooperation depend heavily on perceived fairness, voice, and dignity, not merely on whether decisions are "correct" in an outcome sense (Tyler, 2011). When thresholds are set to prioritize institutional risk-aversion—detain to avoid blame—the system may reduce certain visible harms while increasing hidden harms: unnecessary detention, coerced pleas, destabilized communities, and the erosion of trust.

This is why rights-based governance frameworks increasingly treat high-stakes algorithmic systems as requiring more than performance metrics. Peer-reviewed analyses of modern AI governance for justice domains emphasise accountability architectures, contestability, and transparency obligations because these are the conditions under which coercive decisions can remain legally and morally answerable (Carnat, 2024; Presno Linera et al., 2025). The threshold is precisely where those obligations must bite: if the institution cannot publicly justify the cut-point in terms compatible with rights, it should not be allowed to convert a score into coercion.

A Forensic Rule for Courts: Treat Thresholds as Part of the Evidence, Not After the Evidence

Courts often admit forensic conclusions without examining the decision standards behind them. That is increasingly indefensible. If a forensic method's reported conclusion depends sensitively on a threshold—analytical threshold in DNA interpretation, match threshold in biometric comparison, risk threshold in bail—then the threshold is part of the evidential process and must be open to scrutiny. Peer-reviewed work on the influence of validation data on forensic expert opinion underscores the importance of grounding interpretations in empirical performance under casework conditions and communicating uncertainty; thresholds that alter performance must therefore be part of what is validated and disclosed

(Lund et al., 2026). Without this, the court is not evaluating evidence; it is consuming a product.

The same principle applies to algorithmic risk tools and decision support. If the model outputs a score, the court must know what threshold converts that score into a recommendation, what error trade-offs that threshold implies, and whether those trade-offs have been ethically justified and empirically supported. Otherwise, the court is letting policy masquerade as science.

A Practical Threshold Ethic: Five Questions the Institution Must Answer in Public

If you want threshold ethics to be more than rhetoric, force the institution to answer five questions in public reasons. First, what is the legally relevant outcome the threshold is designed to prevent or manage, and is that outcome morally permissible to treat as a basis for coercion? Second, what are the false-positive and false-negative harms in this context, and who bears them? Third, what is the empirical performance under conditions of use, including drift monitoring and subgroup performance, and what uncertainty remains? Fourth, what fairness conception governs the threshold choice, and how are trade-offs between calibration and error parity justified (Chouldechova, 2017; Berk et al., 2018; Lazar Reich, 2021)? Fifth, what contestability mechanisms exist for those affected to challenge inputs, assumptions, and the relevance of the output to the legal question?

Notice how quickly this becomes a rule-of-law checklist rather than a machine-learning checklist. That is the point. Threshold-setting is governance. Governance must be answerable.

The Closing Discipline: Calibrated Humility

A mature system does not worship calibration and does not fear it. It treats calibration as one diagnostic among many, and it treats thresholds as moral choices that must be justified under rights and legitimacy constraints. In the forensic world, the movement toward empirically validated, logically correct, transparent evidence interpretation—embodied in the likelihood-ratio paradigm and in modern standards discourse—was driven by the recognition that the courtroom cannot afford hidden decision points (Robertson, Vignaux and Berger, 2016; Morrison, 2025). Criminal justice algorithms now face the same reckoning. If thresholds remain invisible, they will become the system's true constitution, written not in law but in silent cut-points. If thresholds are made visible, validated, and ethically justified, the system can use probabilistic tools without surrendering liberty to them.

The last sentence must be stark because the stakes are stark: calibration can tell you how well a score predicts; only ethics can tell you when prediction may be allowed to become power.

References

- Arnold, D., Dobbie, W. and Yang, C.S. (2025) 'Building nondiscriminatory algorithms in selected data', American Economic Review, 115(5), pp. 1410–1455.
- Berk, R., Heidari, H., Jabbari, S., Kearns, M. and Roth, A. (2018) 'Fairness in criminal justice risk assessments: The state of the art', Sociological Methods & Research, 50(1), pp. 3–44.
- Berk, R.A., Kuchibhotla, A.K. and Tchetgen Tchetgen, E.J. (2021) 'Improving fairness in criminal justice algorithmic risk assessments', Sociological Methods & Research, 52(4), pp. 1769–1806.
- Carnat, I. (2024) 'Addressing the risks of generative AI for the judiciary: The accountability framework(s) under the EU AI Act', Computer Law & Security Review, 55, 106067.
- Chouldechova, A. (2017) 'Fair prediction with disparate impact: A study of bias in recidivism prediction instruments', Big Data, 5(2), pp. 153–163.
- Cooper, G.S., Meterko, V. and Dror, I.E. (2019) 'Cognitive bias research in forensic science: A systematic review', Forensic Science International, 297, pp. 35–46.
- Costa, C., Balsa, F., Crespillo, M. and Vieira-Silva, A. (2025) 'The impact of parameter variation in the quantification of forensic DNA evidence', Scientific Reports, 15, 83841.
- Dobbie, W., Goldin, J. and Yang, C.S. (2018) 'The effects of pretrial detention on conviction, future crime, and employment', American Economic Review, 108(2), pp. 201–240.
- Duff, R.A. (2001) Punishment, Communication, and Community. Oxford: Oxford University Press.

- Ensign, D., Friedler, S.A., Neville, S., Scheidegger, C. and Venkatasubramanian, S. (2018) 'Runaway feedback loops in predictive policing', Proceedings of Machine Learning Research: FAT 81, pp. 1–12.
- Gama, J., Žliobaitė, I., Bifet, A., Pechenizkiy, M. and Bouchachia, A. (2014) 'A survey on concept drift adaptation', ACM Computing Surveys, 46(4), Article 44.
- Guo, C., Pleiss, G., Sun, Y. and Weinberger, K.Q. (2017) 'On calibration of modern neural networks', Proceedings of the 34th International Conference on Machine Learning (ICML), 70, pp. 1321–1330.
- Gupta, A., Hansman, C. and Frenchman, E. (2016) 'The heavy costs of high bail: Evidence from judge randomization', Journal of Legal Studies, 45(2), pp. 471–505.
- Hardt, M., Price, E. and Srebro, N. (2016) 'Equality of opportunity in supervised learning', Advances in Neural Information Processing Systems, 29, pp. 3315–3323.
- Hinder, F., Hammer, B. and Biehl, M. (2024) 'One or two things we know about concept drift—A survey on monitoring and drift detection', Frontiers in Artificial Intelligence, 7, 1330257.
- Kleinberg, J., Mullainathan, S. and Raghavan, M. (2017) 'Inherent trade-offs in the fair determination of risk scores', Proceedings of ITCS 2017, LIPIcs 67, Article 43.
- Kull, M., Silva Filho, T.M. and Flach, P. (2019) 'Beyond temperature scaling: Obtaining well-calibrated multiclass probabilities with Dirichlet calibration', Advances in Neural Information Processing Systems, 32.
- Lazar Reich, C. (2021) 'Can calibration and equal error rates be reconciled?', FORC 2021, LIPIcs 192, Article 4.
- Lum, K. and Isaac, W. (2016) 'To predict and serve?', Significance, 13(5), pp. 14–19.
- Lund, S.P., Iyer, H.K., Vieux, E.F. and Taylor, D. (2026) 'The influence of validation data on logical and scientific interpretation of forensic expert opinion', Law, Probability and Risk, 25(1), mgaf013.
- Morrison, G.S. (2025) 'A guide to ISO 21043 forensic sciences from the forensic-data-science paradigm', Science & Justice, 65, 101298.
- Neil, R. (2025) 'Algorithmic bias in criminal risk assessment: The consequences of racial differences in arrest as a measure of crime', Annual Review of Criminology, 8, pp. 97–119.
- Perdomo, J.C., Zrnic, T., Mendler-Dünner, C. and Hardt, M. (2020) 'Performative prediction', Proceedings of the 37th International

Conference on Machine Learning, PMLR 119, pp. 7599–7609.

- Presno Linera, M.Á., Fernández-Rodríguez, J., Borge, R. and Riera, A. (2025) 'Regulating AI from Europe: A joint analysis of the AI Act and the Council of Europe AI Convention', Journal of Cyber Policy, 10(1), pp. 1–25.
- Robertson, B., Vignaux, G.A. and Berger, C.E.H. (2016) Interpreting Evidence: Evaluating Forensic Science in the Courtroom. 2nd edn. Chichester: Wiley.
- Thompson, W.C. (2023) 'Shifting decision thresholds can undermine the probative value of forensic evidence', Proceedings of the National Academy of Sciences, 120(16), e2301844120.
- Tyler, T.R. (2011) 'Procedural justice, legitimacy, and the effective rule of law', Crime and Justice, 40(1), pp. 283–357.
- Zadrozny, B. and Elkan, C. (2002) 'Transforming classifier scores into accurate multiclass probability estimates', Proceedings of the 8th ACM SIGKDD International Conference on Knowledge Discovery and Data Mining, pp. 694–699.

CHAPTER XIV

Causation Versus Correlation in Legal Judgement

The Court's Oldest Temptation: Mistaking Co-Occurrence for Responsibility

Every case file contains two stories, even when only one is written. The first story is the visible one: events that occurred together, traces that appear near one another, a suspect who was present, a phone that pinged a tower, a chemical found in a bloodstream, a prior conviction that sits beside a new allegation, a "high risk" score that sits beside a bail hearing. The second story is the one the court must construct: which of these co-occurrences are part of the causal pathway that matters to law, and which are merely companions of circumstance. Correlation, in its simplest sense, is the observation that two things travel together. Causation is the claim that one made the other happen, or that it made it more likely in a way that satisfies a legal standard of responsibility. The difference is not philosophical ornamentation. It is the difference between a court that punishes acts and a court that punishes shadows.

The legal system's discomfort here is ancient and rational. It must decide under uncertainty, with incomplete access to the past, while knowing that a wrong causal conclusion can destroy a life. Yet it must also decide, because refusing to decide is itself a choice that can leave harms unaddressed. The court therefore walks a tight rope: it must not demand scientific certainty, and it must not accept statistical association as if it were proof of responsibility. The central mistake you must watch for—especially in an AI-mediated system—is the slide from "this factor predicts" to "this factor explains," and then from "this factor explains" to "this person is blameworthy." That slide is the quiet mechanism by which predictive technologies can transform adjudication into administration.

Two Different Questions That Courts Too Often Merge

A disciplined court separates two questions that the public and sometimes even lawyers merge. The first is cause-in-fact: did the defendant's act play the relevant causal role in producing the harm? The second is normative responsibility: even if the act was part of the causal history, is it fair and lawful to treat that act as the basis for liability or punishment? Hart and Honoré's classic account remains useful because it shows that legal causation is not simply science imported into law; it is law's own use of commonsense causal concepts shaped by normative judgment about abnormality, intervention, and responsibility (Hart and Honoré, 1985). A court that pretends causation is purely factual often ends up importing its normative judgments unconsciously through what it calls "common sense." A court that pretends causation is purely moral often ends up untethered from evidential discipline. The correct posture is to keep the questions distinct but connected: factual causation requires a structured evidential model; normative responsibility requires public justification.

This is precisely why legal evidence scholarship has pushed for models capable of accommodating causal uncertainty. Pereira argues that causation disputes are common because legal tests must work in contexts where factual causal uncertainty is endemic, and that evidential models should be adequate to the methodologies used to establish causation in legal contexts (Pereira, 2013). The message is clear: if you want the law to handle causation without either collapsing into superstition or into impossible certainty demands, you must treat causal reasoning as an evidential practice with explicit assumptions, not as a rhetorical flourish.

The But-For Test and Its Failure Modes: Overdetermination, Pre-emption, and the Mirage of Simplicity

The but-for test has intuitive appeal because it maps onto everyday counterfactual reasoning: but for the defendant's act, would the harm have occurred? Yet the test breaks in the cases that most reveal the complexity of causal responsibility: overdetermination (multiple sufficient causes) and pre-emption (one causal path blocks another). Modern causation scholarship has therefore developed supplements and alternatives. Wright's NESS account—necessary element of a sufficient set—aims to capture actual causation in complex cases without collapsing into either pure but-for simplicity or arbitrary moral reasoning, and it has become central to contemporary causation debates (Wright, 2011). Stapleton's work on extended but-for reasoning similarly reflects the ongoing effort to clarify what causation minimally requires while remaining workable for legal analysis (Stapleton, 2015).

The most important practical point is not that one test "wins." It is that tests are proxies for a deeper task: identifying a causal pathway that law can justifiably treat as responsibility-bearing. In a modern evidence environment, where digital traces and statistical models generate abundant associations, the temptation is to treat causal tests as post-hoc decorations. The correct order is the reverse: causal tests should discipline inference by forcing clarity about which pathway is being asserted and which alternative pathways remain plausible.

Causal Inference as a Discipline: Counterfactuals, Graphs, and the Refusal to Guess

If you want a powerful bridge between law's causal questions and scientific reasoning without turning the courtroom into a statistics seminar, the counterfactual tradition is the best entry. Rubin's framework begins from a simple idea: causal effects are defined by comparisons between potential outcomes under different interventions, even if we cannot observe both for the same individual (Rubin, 1974). Hernán and Robins develop this approach into a practical toolkit for causal reasoning under observational data, emphasising the role of design logic, confounding control, and explicit assumptions (Hernán and Robins, 2025). Imbens and Rubin offer a comprehensive statistical foundation for causal inference, clarifying why "association plus adjustment" is often not enough when causal structure is complex (Imbens and Rubin, 2015).

Graphical causality provides a complementary language that is often more intuitive for lawyers than equations, because it externalises assumptions. Pearl's structural causal model and directed acyclic graphs show how to distinguish observational associations from interventional claims and how to reason about counterfactuals with explicit structure (Pearl, 2009). Spirtes, Glymour and Scheines show how causal discovery and constraint-based reasoning can, under assumptions, extract causal structure from data rather than merely summarise correlations (Spirtes, Glymour and Scheines, 2000). The lesson for law is not that courts should "do DAGs." The lesson is that causal inference requires structure, and the structure must be contestable. If an expert or an algorithm cannot state its causal assumptions plainly, the court is being asked to accept correlation as if it were explanation.

Forensic Practice Shows the Same Problem in a Different Mirror

The courtroom already lives with a parallel distinction that it often fails to articulate: source versus activity versus offence. A DNA profile match may bear on source (whose DNA), but the legal question may be activity (how it got there), and the ultimate issue is offence (what happened and who did it). Forensic genetics has spent years moving toward this clarity precisely to avoid misleading inferences. Biedermann and colleagues argue that forensic science offers greatest value when it addresses activity-level propositions and avoids misleading evaluative leaps (Biedermann et al., 2016). Taylor's work on activity-level propositions in forensic genetics emphasises that activity-level evaluation is an emerging discipline requiring careful proposition formulation and transparent reasoning (Taylor, 2018).

This is causation-versus-correlation in forensic clothing. A trace's presence correlates with a person; the court wants a causal story about actions. If the forensic scientist reports a match and the court treats it as proof of activity, the court has committed a causal error, not a statistical one. Robertson, Vignaux and Berger's evidence interpretation framework insists on disciplined evaluation and explicit propositions because the legal danger lies in over-interpretation rather than in the trace itself (Robertson, Vignaux and Berger, 2016). The modern forensic project is, in large part, an institutional attempt to prevent correlations from being smuggled into causal conclusions.

Behavioural Reality: Human Beings Judge Cause Through Norms and Hindsight

A legal system that ignores psychology will mis-handle causation even if its doctrine is perfect on paper. Human causal judgment is not a neutral measuring instrument. It is sensitive to norms, blame, and hindsight. People often judge norm-violating actions as more causally responsible than norm-following actions even when the physical structure of events is identical, and experimental work continues to explore how normative information distorts causal attributions—including when the norms are irrelevant or "silly," which is precisely what makes the finding dangerous for legal contexts (Kneer and Machery, 2022). Hindsight bias compounds the problem: once an outcome is known, people exaggerate its foreseeability and re-interpret ambiguous cues as if they were obvious all along. The result is that causal narratives become cleaner after the fact than they were in real time. This matters because courts are asked to reconstruct past decisions with present knowledge, a posture tailor-made for hindsight contamination.

The consequence is that causation doctrine and evidential practice must be designed to resist predictable cognitive errors, not merely to sound coherent. If we accept that causal judgment is norm-sensitive, then we must be particularly wary when algorithmic outputs enter the record, because they arrive with a prestige that can harden normative blame into the appearance of neutral prediction.

Correlation at Scale: How Algorithms Tempt Courts into Causal Overreach

Algorithmic systems are typically correlation machines. They learn patterns in historical data and optimise predictive performance. They do not, by default, distinguish between "this feature predicts the outcome" and "this feature causes the outcome." The danger arises when institutions treat predictive success as causal entitlement. Nowhere is this clearer than in predictive policing and risk assessment. Lum and Isaac showed how predictive policing can become self-fulfilling by directing police to places where they then record more incidents, which then appear to validate the model's prediction (Lum and Isaac, 2016). Ensign and colleagues formalised runaway feedback loops in predictive policing, demonstrating how deployment can reshape the data stream and produce escalating concentration independent of true underlying harm (Ensign et al., 2018).

Hung's analysis of predictive policing and algorithmic fairness is particularly useful because it uses causal models—contrastive causation and causal diagrams—to explain discrimination and bias rather than treating bias as a mere statistical anomaly (Hung, 2023). The deeper lesson is that fairness debates are, at their core, causal debates about which pathways produced observed disparities. If courts and policymakers treat these tools as neutral because they are predictive, they will miss that the tools may be predicting institutional attention rather than criminal harm, and then feeding that attention back into future "evidence."

The same temptation appears in sentencing optimization and decision systems that forecast outcomes to drive governance. Kroll's critique of predictive optimization argues that prediction-driven decision systems can undermine legitimacy because they transform governance into an optimisation project without public justification of the causal assumptions and moral trade-offs embedded in the objective function (Kroll, 2024). In legal language processing, systematic reviews now explicitly argue that correlation-based legal AI approaches face limits for legal reasoning, motivating a shift toward causal AI methods precisely because law cares about reasons, counterfactuals, and responsibility rather than mere pattern matching (Prince Tritto, 2025).

The Court's Central Causation Error in the AI Era: Predicting the Future as if It Explains the Past

Risk scores and recidivism predictors are particularly prone to causal misuse because they are often presented as if they measure a stable trait called "dangerousness." Yet many risk instruments predict institutional events—rearrest, breach—whose causal determinants include enforcement patterns and supervision intensity. Even when a model is well-calibrated, its predictive success does not establish that the person has a dangerous disposition; it may establish only that the person is likely to re-enter the justice system under existing institutional conditions. Predictive inconsistency research shows that equally defensible development choices can yield different risk scores for the same individual, underscoring that a score is often a product of modelling pathways rather than a stable fact about the person (Greene et al., 2022). Once the court treats such outputs as causal truths—"he will reoffend because he is high risk"—it has confused an institutional forecast with a causal explanation and then converted that confusion into coercion.

A Courtroom-Usable Framework: Causal Questions Must Be Stated Before Statistical Questions

If you want to keep causation distinct from correlation in practice, you must invert how many legal arguments are currently presented. Do not begin with the model output or the association. Begin with a causal question posed in counterfactual terms: what difference would it have made if the alleged cause were absent, and what alternative causes remain plausible? Then ask what evidence, including statistical evidence, bears on discriminating between those propositions. Verheij's work connecting arguments, scenarios and probabilities is useful here because it shows how causal scenarios can both explain and predict evidence, providing a structure for legal reasoning that avoids the lazy slide from statistics to story (Verheij, 2016).

In forensic contexts, this translates into proposition discipline. The hierarchy of propositions—source, activity, offence—forces the tribunal to specify the causal level at which the evidence is being used (Taylor, 2018; Biedermann et al., 2016). In algorithmic contexts, the same discipline means demanding clarity about whether the model is being used to predict an outcome, to explain a mechanism, or to justify a decision. A model trained for prediction should not be permitted to masquerade as an explanatory witness unless causal structure has been established by design, not by performance claims.

Why the Legal System Prefers Correlation and How to Resist the Preference

Correlation is easy to scale. It is also easy to present. Causation is hard because it requires assumptions that can be attacked. Institutions therefore drift toward correlation-based governance because it feels safer: "the data support it." But this is an illusion. Causal claims are always present in legal judgments—about intention, about contribution, about foreseeability, about intervention—even when courts pretend they are "just describing facts." The choice is not whether to reason causally. The choice is whether to reason causally well.

The best safeguard is to treat causal inference as part of procedural justice: an entitlement of the parties. If the state's case rests on a causal claim, the defence must be able to contest the causal assumptions and the selection mechanisms that produced the data. When algorithmic systems are involved, this requires contestability not merely of the output but of the causal pathways by which the output was generated and used, including feedback loops and drift monitoring (Ensign et al., 2018; Gama et al., 2014; Hinder, Hammer and Biehl, 2024). Without that, the system will convert correlations into causal authority by sheer repetition.

The Moral Conclusion: Responsibility Requires Causal Justification, Not Predictive Convenience

The law punishes because it claims that persons are responsible agents and that the state's coercion is justified by reasons that can be understood, contested, and owned. Correlation can inform suspicion, guide investigation, and contribute to a probabilistic picture. But it cannot, by itself, do the moral work of condemnation. Causation is the bridge between wrongdoing and responsibility. If courts allow prediction to substitute for causation—if they allow "risk" to become "fault," and "association" to become "agency"—they will build an efficient system that has quietly abandoned its moral foundation.

So the demand I leave you with is deliberately strict: whenever an algorithmic or statistical artifact enters the courtroom, force the system to say what causal claim it is being used to support, what counterfactual it implies, what alternative causal pathways remain plausible, and what assumptions allow the inference. If those things cannot be said plainly and contested meaningfully, the artifact may have managerial value, but it does not deserve the dignity of being called proof.

References

- Angrist, J.D. and Pischke, J.-S. (2009) Mostly Harmless Econometrics: An Empiricist's Companion. Princeton, NJ: Princeton University Press.
- Biedermann, A., Taroni, F. and Aitken, C. (2016) 'Evaluation of forensic DNA traces when propositions are at the activity level', Forensic Science International: Genetics, 25, pp. 125–134.
- Carnat, I. (2024) 'Addressing the risks of generative AI for the judiciary: The accountability framework(s) under the EU AI Act', Computer Law & Security Review, 55, 106067.
- Chouldechova, A. (2017) 'Fair prediction with disparate impact: A study of bias in recidivism prediction instruments', Big Data, 5(2), pp. 153–163.
- Cooper, G.S., Meterko, V. and Dror, I.E. (2019) 'Cognitive bias research in forensic science: A systematic review', Forensic Science International, 297, pp. 35–46.

- Ensign, D., Friedler, S.A., Neville, S., Scheidegger, C. and Venkatasubramanian, S. (2018) 'Runaway feedback loops in predictive policing', Proceedings of Machine Learning Research, 81, pp. 1–12.
- Fenton, N. and Neil, M. (2016) 'Bayes and the law', Annual Review of Statistics and Its Application, 3, pp. 51–77.
- Gama, J., Žliobaitė, I., Bifet, A., Pechenizkiy, M. and Bouchachia, A. (2014) 'A survey on concept drift adaptation', ACM Computing Surveys, 46(4), Article 44.
- Greene, T., Shmueli, G., Fell, J., Lin, C.-F. and Liu, H.-W. (2022) 'Predictive inconsistency in criminal justice algorithmic risk prediction tools', Journal of the Royal Statistical Society: Series A, 185(S2), pp. S692–S716.
- Hart, H.L.A. and Honoré, T. (1985) Causation in the Law. 2nd edn. Oxford: Clarendon Press.
- Hernán, M.A. and Robins, J.M. (2025) Causal Inference: What If. Boca Raton: Chapman & Hall/CRC.
- Hinder, F., Hammer, B. and Biehl, M. (2024) 'One or two things we know about concept drift—A survey on monitoring and drift detection', Frontiers in Artificial Intelligence, 7, 1330257.
- Hung, T.-W. (2023) 'Predictive policing and algorithmic fairness', Synthese, 201, 4189.
- Imbens, G.W. and Rubin, D.B. (2015) Causal Inference for Statistics, Social, and Biomedical Sciences: An Introduction. Cambridge: Cambridge University Press.
- Kleinberg, J., Mullainathan, S. and Raghavan, M. (2017) 'Inherent trade-offs in the fair determination of risk scores', Proceedings of ITCS 2017, LIPIcs 67, Article 43.
- Kneer, M. and Machery, E. (2022) 'Causation and the silly norm effect', Journal of Practical Philosophy.
- Kroll, J.A. (2024) 'Against predictive optimization: On the legitimacy of prediction-driven decision systems', ACM Transactions on Computer-Human Interaction.
- Lum, K. and Isaac, W. (2016) 'To predict and serve?', Significance, 13(5), pp. 14–19.
- Pearl, J. (2009) Causality: Models, Reasoning, and Inference. 2nd edn. Cambridge: Cambridge University Press.
- Pereira, R.S. (2013) 'Evidence models and proof of causation', Law, Probability and Risk, 12(3–4), pp. 229–253.

- Perdomo, J.C., Zrnic, T., Mendler-Dünner, C. and Hardt, M. (2020) 'Performative prediction', Proceedings of Machine Learning Research, 119, pp. 7599–7609.
- Prince Tritto, P. (2025) 'Causal artificial intelligence in legal language processing: A systematic review', Entropy, 27(4), 351.
- Robertson, B., Vignaux, G.A. and Berger, C.E.H. (2016) Interpreting Evidence: Evaluating Forensic Science in the Courtroom. 2nd edn. Chichester: Wiley.
- Rubin, D.B. (1974) 'Estimating causal effects of treatments in randomized and nonrandomized studies', Journal of Educational Psychology, 66(5), pp. 688–701.
- Scurich, N. et al. (2023) 'Scientific guidelines for evaluating the validity of forensic comparison methods', Proceedings of the National Academy of Sciences, 120, e2301843120.
- Spirtes, P., Glymour, C. and Scheines, R. (2000) Causation, Prediction, and Search. 2nd edn. Cambridge, MA: MIT Press.
- Stapleton, J. (2015) 'An "extended but-for" test for the causal relation in the law', Oxford Journal of Legal Studies.
- Taylor, D. (2018) 'Evaluation of forensic genetics findings given activity level propositions', Forensic Science International: Genetics, 36, pp. 34–49.
- Verheij, B. (2016) 'Arguments, scenarios and probabilities: Connections between three normative frameworks for evidential reasoning', Law, Probability and Risk, 15(1), pp. 35–70.
- Vink, M. (2025) 'Formulating propositions in Trojan horse defence cases', Forensic Science International: Digital Investigation, 54.
- Wright, R.W. (2011) 'The NESS account of natural causation'.

CHAPTER XV

The Right to Challenge: Adversarial Testing of Algorithmic Evidence

The Old Trial Model Still Has One Non-Negotiable Promise

A criminal trial, at its best, is a disciplined quarrel. The state may accuse, but it must prove; it may produce evidence, but it must expose that evidence to contradiction; it may call experts, but it must permit the defence to test their method, their assumptions, and their conclusions. The moral point is older than any constitution: coercion without contest is not adjudication; it is administration. The evidential point is equally old: a claim that cannot be challenged cannot be trusted, because reliability is not a vibe, it is an adversarial achievement. Algorithmic evidence arrives precisely at the seam where that promise can fail. It does not fail because algorithms are evil; it fails because algorithms are unusually easy to treat as authority rather than as evidence. They arrive as numbers that look objective, produced by pipelines that are hard to understand, defended by secrecy regimes that are institutionally convenient, and embedded in decision environments where time pressure makes deference feel like prudence. If the justice system does not build an enforceable right to challenge these systems, it will gradually turn cross-examination into theatre and convert the trial into a downstream formality for decisions already made elsewhere (Kinchin, 2024; Fischman-Afori, 2025).

The difficulty, and it is a real one, is that "challenging an algorithm" is not one act. It is several. It is challenging provenance, data quality, model choice, parameter settings, thresholds, validation studies, subgroup performance, drift monitoring, logging integrity, and the human-machine interface that shapes how outputs are used. The right to challenge, therefore, must be reframed as a package of procedural entitlements, each aimed at preserving a basic feature of the adversarial system: that the defence can bite into the evidence and leave marks.

The Misunderstanding That Keeps Courts Vulnerable: "Reliability" Is Not a Label, It Is a Claim With Inputs

Courts often speak of "reliable evidence" as if reliability were a badge. In scientific reasoning, reliability is not a badge; it is a set of demonstrable properties under specified conditions. Forensic science has spent two decades pushing legal systems toward this realisation, especially through the likelihood-ratio paradigm and the insistence on empirical validation under casework conditions (Robertson, Vignaux and Berger, 2016; Morrison, 2025). Algorithmic evidence forces the same lesson. A facial-recognition similarity score, a probabilistic genotyping output, a digital-forensics triage classification, or an AI-assisted voice comparison is not "reliable" because it is sophisticated. It is reliable, if at all, because it has been validated for the task, on data representative of operational conditions, with known error behaviour, with robust documentation, and with reproducibility safeguards that permit independent testing (Berger, 2025; Lund et al., 2026). If the defence cannot access the information needed to examine those properties, the court is not admitting evidence; it is admitting institutional faith.

The right to challenge begins here: it is the right to treat algorithmic output as an expert claim rather than as a machine fact. Once you accept that it is an expert claim, you inherit the old obligations of expertise: explain the method, disclose limitations, and survive cross-examination.

Contestability Is the Organising Principle Because "Explainability" Alone Is Too Weak

Modern governance debates often fixate on explainability: "open the black box," "show the features," "provide an explanation." The instinct is correct but incomplete. A person can be "explained to" and still be powerless. Contestability is stronger: it asks whether the affected party can use the information to challenge the decision in a way that can change outcomes. This is why procedural justice theory has become increasingly relevant to AI governance: legitimacy depends on voice that has practical leverage, not on narration that leaves the decision unchanged (Kinchin, 2024; Fischman-Afori, 2025). If a defendant receives a glossy explanation of why a model predicts high risk but cannot correct erroneous inputs, cannot test validation claims, cannot question thresholds, and cannot compel disclosure of relevant logs, then the right to challenge has not been satisfied. The system has simply produced a more sophisticated form of voicelessness.

Peer-reviewed work arguing for a legally enforceable right to contest AI decisions under GDPR-style regimes makes this point in governance language: explainability is not sufficient for accountability; contestation must be operationalised as a right that triggers procedures and disclosures (Emerald article on “Contesting the algorithm”, 2025). This is not a European curiosity. It is a universal adversarial requirement stated in modern terms.

The Four Surfaces of Algorithmic Evidence That Must Be Testable

Algorithmic evidence has four surfaces, and if any one of them is shielded from testing, the adversarial process is compromised. The first surface is the data surface: what data trained the model, what data generated the output in this case, what preprocessing occurred, what missingness exists, and what proxies are embedded. The second is the model surface: what class of model, what features, what thresholds, what version history, what calibration, what domain shift sensitivity. The third is the validation surface: what tests were run, on what populations, under what conditions, with what error rates, and how performance uncertainty was quantified. The fourth is the use surface: how the output is presented to humans, how often it is overridden, what policies govern reliance, and what feedback loops shape future data.

Forensic standards thinking now explicitly recognises this multi-surface reality. ISO 21043’s interpretive requirements and the forensic-data-science paradigm emphasise transparency, reproducibility, resistance to cognitive bias, and empirically calibrated interpretation under casework conditions, precisely because evidence safety depends on more than a model’s internal sophistication (ISO 21043-4:2025 summary; Berger, 2025; Morrison, 2025). And the 2026 work on how validation data shape logical interpretation of forensic opinions makes the same point in a form the courtroom can grasp: evidence weight cannot be separated from the empirical basis that supports it; uncertainty about method performance must be disclosed because it changes how opinions should be weighed (Lund et al., 2026). If that is true for DNA and other established domains, it is even more true for rapidly evolving algorithmic systems whose versions change quietly and whose error behaviour can shift under drift.

The Secrecy Collision: When Intellectual Property Claims Meet the Accused's Liberty Interest

The single most predictable flashpoint is secrecy. Vendors and agencies often invoke trade secrets, security sensitivities, or proprietary rights to resist disclosure. Yet secrecy regimes that may be tolerable in consumer settings become intolerable when liberty is at stake, because the defence is entitled to meaningful adversarial testing. The most defensible global posture is not "source code for everyone" and not "trust us." It is functional equivalence: if code disclosure is refused, the state must provide disclosure packages that permit equivalent testing—validation reports, error-rate data, thresholds, version histories, logging artefacts, model cards, and protected access for defence experts under confidentiality safeguards. The principle is not that the defence must own the vendor's property; the principle is that the defence must not be asked to fight blind.

Peer-reviewed jurisprudential critique of algorithmic specification and secrecy regimes has begun to frame this as a threat to the interpretive openness and contestability that make law lawful (Erickson, 2025). The point is not merely doctrinal. It is structural: if the party with the burden of proof can rely on an untestable machine output, the burden of proof quietly shifts onto the accused to disprove what cannot be examined. That inversion is the death of the adversarial system in slow motion.

The Forensic Lesson That Courts Must Import Whole: Chain of Custody for the Model Itself

Courts are familiar with chain of custody for physical exhibits. Algorithmic evidence requires chain of custody for systems. A score is not an isolated artefact; it is the product of a pipeline: data intake, feature extraction, model execution, thresholding, and report generation. The defence must therefore have access to case-specific artefacts: logs, parameters, input data snapshots, software versions, and configuration settings. Without this, it becomes impossible to know whether the model run in court is the model that was validated, or whether subtle changes—updated thresholds, silent patching, altered preprocessing—have altered performance. In policing and predictive systems, feedback loops can also change the data-generation environment, which in turn changes what the model output means; the right to challenge must therefore include access to drift monitoring and audit histories when relevant (Lum and Isaac, 2016; Ensign et al., 2018).

Forensic science's current concern with bias and misjudgments in expert systems, including AI-based tools, reinforces the need for such procedural discipline. The recent peer-reviewed discussion of bias pathways from human expert analysis to AI decision tools highlights how uncritical reliance and opaque processes can drive miscarriages of justice, precisely because the institutional environment invites overconfidence in outputs that appear authoritative (Hefetz, 2025). If chain-of-custody discipline is neglected for algorithms, the system will produce the most dangerous kind of error: error that looks like certainty.

Versioning, Drift, and "Reliability as Applied"

One of the most corrosive myths is that once a model is validated, it is reliable forever. Real-world machine learning does not work like that, and neither does forensic method performance. Dataset shift, concept drift, and operational changes can degrade calibration and error behaviour even when the model code is unchanged (Gama et al., 2014; Hinder, Hammer and Biehl, 2024). In criminal justice contexts, the drift is often not merely statistical; it is institutional: reporting practices change, policing strategies change, lab protocols change, and the model's inputs begin to mean different things. The right to challenge must therefore include reliability as applied: not merely "was the model ever validated?" but "is this model version, under these operating conditions, reliable for this task today?" The 2025–2026 forensic standards discourse increasingly insists on validation under realistic conditions and on communicating performance uncertainty, which is the scientific analogue of reliability-as-applied (Berger, 2025; Morrison, 2025; Lund et al., 2026).

In practical courtroom terms, this means the defence should be able to demand: the validation corpus characteristics, subgroup performance analyses, operating thresholds, calibration checks, and drift monitoring outputs relevant to the time period and environment of this case. A system that cannot produce those artefacts should not be allowed to present itself as a reliable evidentiary instrument.

The Human Interface Is Not Peripheral; It Is Part of the Evidence Mechanism

Even if the model is technically sound, the way humans use its outputs can corrupt evidence evaluation. Procedural justice and behavioural research show that "voice" and perceived fairness are sensitive to how decisions are made and explained, and algorithmic systems can create a procedural gap even when outcomes appear distributively improved (Kinchin, 2024; Fischman-Afori, 2025). In evidentiary terms, algorithmic outputs can anchor decision-makers, narrow attention, and induce automation bias—over-reliance on machine suggestions—especially under workload and accountability pressure. When this happens, the algorithm is not merely evidence; it becomes a decision shaper. The right to challenge must therefore include the right to scrutinise how the tool is used: what training was given, what guidance exists, what override rates occur, and whether the tool is presented in a way that invites false certainty.

In forensic practice, concerns about bias are now treated as systemic rather than purely individual. The move toward standardisation and bias-resistant procedures reflects the recognition that even skilled decision-makers can be influenced by contextual cues (Cooper, Meterko and Dror, 2019). Algorithmic evidence, by its nature, is a powerful contextual cue. A legal system that ignores this will treat a socio-technical system as if it were a neutral measuring device.

The Burden of Proof Must Not Be Quietly Reallocated to the Defence

The moral centre of adversarial testing is burden protection. The state bears the burden to prove. Algorithmic evidence threatens to invert this because it can present outputs as quasi-facts while hiding the machinery that would allow disproof. The right to challenge is therefore a burden-preserving right. It demands that the party relying on algorithmic outputs must provide what is necessary for meaningful scrutiny—either direct disclosure or functional equivalents—before the output is allowed to carry weight.

This is why peer-reviewed work explicitly linking fair-trial guarantees to algorithmic evidence emphasises contestability, task-matched validation, and transparency sufficient for adversarial testing as the necessary conditions for lawful admission, even when full source code disclosure is not mandated (Fortes, 2020; Kinchin, 2024). It is also why procedural justice-based governance arguments insist on structural mechanisms—review pathways, contest routes, and meaningful correction opportunities—rather than purely informational "explanations" (Fischman-Afori, 2025).

Comparative Lessons Without Jurisdictional Parochialism

Although specific doctrines differ across systems, the adversarial logic travels. Any system committed to fairness must ensure equality of arms: the defence must have a genuine opportunity to test the state's evidence. This is compatible with multiple legal traditions: common-law cross-examination, civil-law judicial inquiry, and mixed systems' hybrid processes. What changes is the mechanism, not the entitlement. In some systems, the court may appoint neutral experts to test algorithms; in others, the defence must be funded to retain its own experts. In all systems, the state must not be permitted to rely on an instrument whose reliability claims cannot be scrutinised.

Peer-reviewed scholarship on digital justice and due process in algorithmic adjudication has already mapped these comparative tensions, noting that algorithmic pathways can promise efficiency while straining due process unless procedural safeguards are designed into the system (Fortes, 2020). The rise of global governance instruments grounded in rule-of-law and rights values reflects the same recognition: high-stakes AI cannot be treated as ordinary administrative tech. Peer-reviewed analyses of binding AI governance developments, including rights-based conventions and risk-based AI regulation, frame accountability, transparency, and oversight as necessary to preserve legality (Rotenberg, 2025; Presno Linera et al., 2025).

A Practical Doctrine of Challenge: What Must Be Disclosed to Make Testing Real

If you want the right to challenge to be operational rather than rhetorical, it must translate into a disclosure doctrine that maps onto the four evidence surfaces. Data disclosure must include case-specific inputs and provenance, plus sufficient information about training data scope and representativeness to evaluate bias pathways. Model disclosure must include model type, features, thresholds, version history, and configuration settings relevant to the case. Validation disclosure must include error rates, calibration results, subgroup performance, uncertainty quantification, and the conditions under which validation was performed, with clarity about how those conditions compare to operational deployment. Use disclosure must include documentation of how outputs are presented, what training and guidance exist, and what override and audit patterns occur in practice.

This doctrine is not wishful. It mirrors the modern forensic standards movement's insistence on documentation, transparency, calibration, validation, and bias resistance for evidence interpretation (Berger, 2025; Morrison, 2025). It also aligns with the procedural justice insight that contestation requires actionable pathways, not mere information (Fischman-Afori, 2025). When these disclosures exist, adversarial testing becomes possible: defence experts can replicate runs, test alternative configurations, probe robustness, examine drift, and challenge interpretive overreach. When they do not exist, the algorithm becomes an unchallengeable witness, and unchallengeable witnesses are incompatible with fair trial.

The Closing Moral Point: The Court Must Be Able to Say "No"

A right to challenge that never results in exclusion is not a right; it is a ritual. Courts must therefore preserve a refusal power: if the state cannot provide the artefacts necessary for meaningful testing—because of secrecy, poor documentation, missing logs, absent validation, or unstable versioning—then the output must be excluded or given negligible weight. This is not anti-science. It is the scientific attitude applied to liberty: if you cannot evaluate reliability as applied, you do not get to claim it in support of coercion.

The adversarial system survives by insisting that power must justify itself under scrutiny. Algorithmic evidence will either be disciplined into that tradition or it will quietly dissolve it. The right to challenge is the hinge. Without it, prediction becomes authority. With it, algorithmic outputs can be treated as what they should have been from the beginning: contestable evidence, never destiny.

References

- Berger, C.E.H. (2025) 'Finally a really forensic worldwide standard: ISO 21043', Forensic Science International: Synergy, 11, 1006xx.
- 'Contesting the algorithm: Advancing a right to challenge AI decisions under the GDPR for algorithmic fairness' (2025) [Emerald peer-reviewed journal], 19(4), pp. 895–.
- Cooper, G.S., Meterko, V. and Dror, I.E. (2019) 'Cognitive bias research in forensic science: A systematic review', Forensic Science International, 297, pp. 35–46.
- Ensign, D., Friedler, S.A., Neville, S., Scheidegger, C. and Venkatasubramanian, S. (2018) 'Runaway feedback loops in predictive policing', Proceedings of Machine Learning Research, 81, pp. 1–12.
- Erickson, J. (2025) 'Against algorithmic clarity: Law beyond specification', International Journal for the Semiotics of Law, 38, pp. 1–26.
- Fischman-Afori, O. (2025) 'Due process by design: Enhancing fairness and trust in AI decision-making through procedural justice theory', Social Sciences & Humanities Open, 12, 102178.
- Fortes, P.R.B. (2020) 'Paths to digital justice: Judicial robots, algorithmic decision-making and due process', Asian Journal of Law and Society, 7(3), pp. 1–24.
- Gama, J., Žliobaitė, I., Bifet, A., Pechenizkiy, M. and Bouchachia, A. (2014) 'A survey on concept drift adaptation', ACM Computing Surveys, 46(4), Article 44.
- Hefetz, I. (2025) 'Evaluating bias in forensic evidence: From expert analysis to AI-based decision tools', Forensic Science International: Synergy, 11, 100645.
- Hinder, F., Hammer, B. and Biehl, M. (2024) 'One or two things we know about concept drift—A survey on monitoring and drift detection', Frontiers in Artificial Intelligence, 7, 1330257.
- Kinchin, N. (2024) '"Voiceless": the procedural gap in algorithmic justice', International Journal of Law and Information Technology, 32(4), pp. 1–30.
- Lund, S.P., Iyer, H.K., Vieux, E.F. and Taylor, D. (2026) 'The influence of validation data on logical and scientific interpretation of forensic expert opinion', Law, Probability and Risk, 25(1), mgaf013.

- Lum, K. and Isaac, W. (2016) 'To predict and serve?', Significance, 13(5), pp. 14–19.
- Lyons, H. (2025) 'Diametrically opposed attributes? Review process guidance for algorithmic decisions and procedural justice', Proceedings of the ACM on Human-Computer Interaction, 9, Article 3xx.
- Morrison, G.S. (2025) 'A guide to ISO 21043 forensic sciences from the perspective of the forensic-data-science paradigm', Science & Justice, 65, 101298.
- Oswald, M. (2018) 'Algorithm-assisted decision-making in the public sector: Framing the issues using administrative law rules governing discretionary power', Philosophical Transactions of the Royal Society A, 376(2128), 20170359.
- Presno Linera, M.Á., Fernández-Rodríguez, J., Borge, R. and Riera, A. (2025) 'Regulating AI from Europe: A joint analysis of the AI Act and the Council of Europe AI Convention', Journal of Cyber Policy, 10(1), pp. 1–25.
- Robertson, B., Vignaux, G.A. and Berger, C.E.H. (2016) Interpreting Evidence: Evaluating Forensic Science in the Courtroom. 2nd edn. Chichester: Wiley.
- Rotenberg, M. (2025) 'Framework Convention on Artificial Intelligence and Human Rights, Democracy, and the Rule of Law (Council of Europe)', International Legal Materials, 64, pp. 1–25.

Part IV — Fairness: Competing Definitions and Legal Consequences

CHAPTER XVI

Fairness Metrics and Their Incompatibilities: Why You Can't Have It All

The First Thing to Admit: "Fair" Is Not One Property, It Is a Bundle of Demands

When institutions say an algorithm is "fair," they usually mean one of three very different things, and the confusion is not an academic nuisance; it is the engine of policy failure. Sometimes "fair" means equal outcomes across groups. Sometimes it means equal treatment of similarly situated individuals. Sometimes it means equal error burdens—that the system should not be more wrong, or more harshly wrong, for one group than for another. Each of these instincts has moral force, and each maps onto a family of mathematical metrics that look crisp on paper. The catch is that those metrics do not generally point in the same direction once you face the real world—where base rates differ, measurement is contaminated, labels are generated by the institution itself, and the stakes are liberty rather than marketing optimisation. The algorithm becomes a mirror, and the society it reflects is not tidy.

This chapter's central claim is simple but unforgiving: you cannot satisfy all popular fairness metrics at once except in narrow, usually unrealistic special cases, and the attempt to pretend otherwise produces a justice system that is simultaneously overconfident and morally evasive. The way out is not to abandon fairness metrics, but to treat them as diagnostic instruments that reveal value conflicts—conflicts the legal system must decide openly, not outsource to a score (Barocas, Hardt and Narayanan, 2023; Berk et al., 2021; Corbett-Davies et al., 2017).

What the Metrics Actually Ask For, in the Plainest Language

Begin with demographic parity. It asks that predicted outcomes be independent of group membership: the same proportion of each group should be classified "high risk" or "eligible," regardless of the true outcome rates (Barocas, Hardt and Narayanan, 2023). It is attractive because it looks like equality in the most visible sense, but it is also blunt: if base rates differ for reasons that are not purely artefactual—differences in underlying harm, differences in exposure, differences in reporting—demographic parity can force the system to treat unlike situations alike and can therefore shift error burdens in ways that are themselves morally troubling (Hardt, Price and Srebro, 2016).

Now take equalized odds and equal opportunity, the family of "error-rate parity" metrics. Equalized odds asks that false positive and false negative rates be equal across groups; equal opportunity asks, more narrowly, that false negative rates be equal (Hardt, Price and Srebro, 2016). These definitions are morally intelligible in the criminal context because false positives often correspond to unnecessary coercion—detention, escalated supervision, harsher sentencing—and false negatives correspond to public harm. If one group systematically suffers higher false positives, that group is paying a larger liberty tax for the system's uncertainty. Error parity tries to distribute that tax more evenly.

Finally, consider calibration or predictive parity. Calibration asks that among those assigned a given score, the outcome occurs at the same rate across groups; it treats scores as meaningful probabilities and demands that they mean what they say for everyone (Chouldechova, 2017; Pleiss et al., 2017). Predictive parity is a related demand that, among those classified "high risk," the actual outcome rate is the same across groups. These are appealing because they promise semantic honesty: a 0.7 risk should be 0.7 risk, not a different thing depending on who you are. Each of these families expresses a defensible moral concern. The problem is that they collide.

The Incompatibility Is Not a Bug; It Is a Mathematical Reflection of Unequal Worlds

The two cornerstone impossibility results in this area are direct and devastating. Kleinberg, Mullainathan and Raghavan show that three intuitive conditions—calibration within groups, balance for the positive class, and balance for the negative class—cannot all be satisfied simultaneously except in constrained cases (Kleinberg, Mullainathan and Raghavan, 2017). Chouldechova shows, in the recidivism prediction context, that when prevalence differs across groups, you cannot simultaneously satisfy calibration (predictive parity) and error-rate balance (equal false positive and false negative rates) unless the predictor is perfect or the base rates are equal (Chouldechova, 2017). Pleiss and colleagues deepen this by studying the tension between calibration and error disparities and showing that calibration is compatible only with very limited forms of error constraints, and even then the adjustments required can be no better than randomizing a proportion of predictions for an existing classifier (Pleiss et al., 2017).

You should read these theorems as a warning about moral algebra. If base rates differ, and if your model is not perfect—which it never is—then you must choose which fairness intuition you will privilege, because the metrics encode mutually inconsistent demands. A court or agency that claims it has achieved "fairness" without naming the definition is usually doing one of two things: it is either unaware of the trade-off, or it is hiding a value choice behind a technical gloss.

Where the Trade-Off Becomes Coercion: Thresholds, Not Scores, Decide Who Pays

The practical hinge is the threshold. Scores are continuous; decisions are discrete. A bail tool may generate a risk probability, but detention decisions are triggered by cut points. A sentencing recommender may output a range, but the human system turns it into an actual sentence. In these moments, fairness is not merely about model quality; it is about how the institution converts uncertainty into action.

Corbett-Davies and colleagues show this with unusual clarity in the pretrial setting by recasting fairness as constrained optimisation: maximise public safety subject to fairness constraints. They show that for several fairness definitions, the optimal policy requires applying race-specific thresholds—detaining people from different groups at different score cutoffs—whereas the unconstrained optimum uses a single threshold across all individuals (Corbett-Davies et al., 2017). This is not a theoretical curiosity. It is the starkest expression of the collision between two moral instincts that both claim the word "equality": equality as "same standard for all" versus equality as "same error burdens across groups." If you insist on equal false positive rates across groups, you may be driven toward different thresholds. If you insist on a single threshold, you may accept unequal error burdens. There is no neutral, purely technical way to escape the choice.

Now add the criminal justice reality that many "outcomes" used in these systems—especially rearrest—are not pure measures of wrongdoing. Neil's Annual Review synthesis emphasises the consequences of racial differences in arrest as a measure of crime and how using arrest as the target variable can embed enforcement bias into algorithmic systems (Neil, 2025). If the label is institutionally contaminated, then calibration may simply mean "accurately predicts institutional contact," and error parity may mean "equally misclassifies under biased labels." The fairness theorems still hold, but the moral landscape becomes more treacherous: you may be trading off fairness metrics in a world where the outcome itself is not morally clean.

The Forensic Analogy: A Fairness Metric Can Be Perfectly Calculated and Still Be the Wrong Question

Forensic science has a hard-won lesson that applies here: correctness of calculation does not guarantee correctness of inference. A lab can compute a likelihood ratio correctly and still mislead if the proposition level is wrong or if the evidence is being used to answer a question it cannot answer (Robertson, Vignaux and Berger, 2016). Fairness metrics can be equally correct and equally misused. They tell you something about statistical relationships between predictions, outcomes, and groups. They do not, by themselves, tell you whether the underlying outcome is a morally legitimate target, whether the data-generation process is fair, or whether the decision rule respects due process.

This is why Berk and colleagues' "state of the art" review in criminal justice risk assessments is valuable beyond its technical synthesis: it insists on conceptual precision and warns that rhetoric often substitutes for analysis when fairness is discussed in justice settings (Berk et al., 2021). Berk's later work explores counterfactual reasoning as one path toward improved fairness, reflecting a broader recognition that purely observational metrics can be blunt instruments when the goal is to understand and mitigate unjust causal pathways (Berk, 2024). The message is not that metrics are useless. The message is that the justice system must treat them as tools for structured argument, not as certificates of virtue.

The Measurement Trap: You Can't Fairly Predict a Target You Don't Fairly Measure

A fairness metric is only as meaningful as the outcome it references. If the target is rearrest, the system is partly predicting policing patterns. If the target is reconviction, the system is partly predicting prosecutorial choices and court throughput. If the target is breach of supervision, the system is partly predicting the strictness of supervision regimes and the social conditions that make compliance difficult. Akpinar, De-Arteaga and Chouldechova show, in predictive policing contexts, that differential victim reporting can bias predictive systems even when the algorithm never sees arrests, because reporting itself is socially patterned; the model can over-allocate attention to higher-reporting areas and under-allocate attention to low-reporting areas regardless of true victimisation (Akpinar, De-Arteaga and Chouldechova, 2021). The same logic carries into risk assessment. A metric can be satisfied in the reported world while failing in the harmed world.

Feldman and colleagues' work on certifying and removing disparate impact illustrates a related point: bias can persist through information leakage and proxy variables even when protected attributes are excluded, and disparate impact analysis is as much about the data and features as it is about the final classifier (Feldman et al., 2015). In other words, the system can be "blind" in code and still see the protected class through correlated features. If you then attempt to fix fairness only at the output layer—threshold tweaks and post-processing—you may simply redistribute error while leaving the deeper measurement injustice untouched.

The Procedural Dimension: Fairness Is Not Only Distributional, It Is Also Experiential

Even if you managed to choose the "right" fairness metric, you could still erode legitimacy if the system feels unchallengeable. Procedural justice research has repeatedly shown that people's acceptance of legal authority depends heavily on the fairness of process—voice, respect, neutrality, trustworthiness—not merely on outcomes (Tyler, 2011). Algorithmic systems can create what has been called a procedural gap, where people experience decisions as voiceless even when formal hearings exist, because the decisive weight lies in an output they cannot meaningfully contest (Kinchin, 2024). A fairness constraint that improves error parity might still be legitimacy-corrosive if it produces opaque, unreviewable decisions or encourages judges to defer to scores without reasons. The justice system therefore needs a richer conception: fairness metrics address distributive patterns; procedure addresses legitimacy and contestability; both are necessary, neither is sufficient.

This is not merely philosophical. Kattnig and colleagues' analysis in Computer Law & Security Review contrasts technical bias mitigation methods with legal requirements and highlights that technical fairness interventions often fail to meet legal standards of non-discrimination and accountability, particularly in high-stakes governance frameworks (Kattnig et al., 2024). In other words, the legal system's fairness demands are not exhausted by metrics; they include rights to reasons, rights to challenge, and institutional accountability.

Why "You Can't Have It All" Is Not Defeatist, It Is the Beginning of Honest Governance

The impossibility results do not tell you to stop trying to be fair. They tell you to stop pretending fairness is a single knob. In practice, a serious governance approach treats fairness metrics as a map of trade-offs and then makes the trade-offs explicit and contestable. Corbett-Davies and Goel's broader critique—"the measure and mismeasure of fairness"—argues that equitable algorithm design requires grappling with context-specific consequences and policy goals rather than relying solely on axiomatic fairness definitions (Corbett-Davies et al., 2023). The point is practical: if you do not articulate what kind of fairness you want and why, the system will optimise some fairness criterion by default—often the one that is easiest to report or most convenient to defend.

This is where transparency frameworks such as model cards become operationally relevant. Model cards are not a cure for fairness conflicts, but they force disclosure of performance across conditions and groups, making it harder for institutions to hide trade-offs behind aggregate accuracy numbers (Mitchell et al., 2019). In a justice system, such disclosure should not be optional "ethics." It should be part of the evidential discipline required to rely on algorithmic outputs in liberty-affecting decisions.

A Courtroom-Ready Conclusion: Fairness Metrics Are Arguments, Not Verdicts

If you want a conclusion you can defend in a courtroom, an agency report, or a doctoral thesis, it is this. Fairness metrics are not neutral facts; they are formalizations of competing moral intuitions. In settings where base rates differ and measurement is institutionally shaped—as criminal justice so often is—you cannot satisfy all the appealing fairness metrics at once unless your model is perfect or the world is equal. You must choose which fairness conception you privilege, and you must justify that choice in public reasons that acknowledge whose errors will increase and whose errors will decrease. You must also address measurement contamination and procedural legitimacy, because a system can be "fair" by a metric and still be unjust in lived experience or in causal structure. The law cannot outsource these choices to mathematics without becoming a managerial state that punishes under the banner of optimisation. The honest path is harder: use metrics to reveal trade-offs, then decide those trade-offs as a matter of law, ethics, and accountability.

References

- Akpinar, N.-J., De-Arteaga, M. and Chouldechova, A. (2021) 'The effect of differential victim crime reporting on predictive policing systems', Proceedings of the 2021 ACM Conference on Fairness, Accountability, and Transparency (FAccT '21), pp. 434–445.
- Barocas, S., Hardt, M. and Narayanan, A. (2023) Fairness and Machine Learning: Limitations and Opportunities. Cambridge, MA: MIT Press.
- Berk, R.A. (2024) 'Improving fairness in criminal justice algorithmic risk assessments', Sociological Methods & Research.
- Berk, R., Heidari, H., Jabbari, S., Kearns, M. and Roth, A. (2021) 'Fairness in criminal justice risk assessments: The state of the art', Sociological Methods & Research, 50(1), pp. 3–44.
- Chouldechova, A. (2017) 'Fair prediction with disparate impact: A study of bias in recidivism prediction instruments', Big Data, 5(2), pp. 153–163.
- Corbett-Davies, S., Gaebler, J., Nilforoshan, H., Shroff, R. and Goel, S. (2023) 'The measure and mismeasure of fairness: A critical review of fair machine learning', Proceedings of the ACM on Human-Computer Interaction.

- Corbett-Davies, S., Pierson, E., Feller, A., Goel, S. and Huq, A. (2017) 'Algorithmic decision making and the cost of fairness', Proceedings of the 23rd ACM SIGKDD International Conference on Knowledge Discovery and Data Mining (KDD '17), pp. 797–806.
- Feldman, M., Friedler, S.A., Moeller, J., Scheidegger, C. and Venkatasubramanian, S. (2015) 'Certifying and removing disparate impact', Proceedings of the 21th ACM SIGKDD International Conference on Knowledge Discovery and Data Mining (KDD '15), pp. 259–268.
- Hardt, M., Price, E. and Srebro, N. (2016) 'Equality of opportunity in supervised learning', Advances in Neural Information Processing Systems (NeurIPS), 29.
- Kattnig, M., Angerschmid, A. et al. (2024) 'Assessing trustworthy AI: Technical and legal perspectives of fairness in AI', Computer Law & Security Review, 55, 106053.
- Kinchin, N. (2024) '"Voiceless": the procedural gap in algorithmic justice', International Journal of Law and Information Technology, 32(4), pp. 1–30.
- Kleinberg, J., Mullainathan, S. and Raghavan, M. (2017) 'Inherent trade-offs in the fair determination of risk scores', Proceedings of the 8th Innovations in Theoretical Computer Science Conference (ITCS 2017), LIPIcs 67, Article 43.
- Mitchell, M., Wu, S., Zaldivar, A. et al. (2019) 'Model cards for model reporting', Proceedings of the Conference on Fairness, Accountability, and Transparency (FAccT '19), pp. 220–229.
- Neil, R. (2025) 'Algorithmic bias in criminal risk assessment: The consequences of racial differences in arrest as a measure of crime', Annual Review of Criminology, 8, pp. 97–119.
- Pleiss, G., Raghavan, M., Wu, F., Kleinberg, J. and Weinberger, K.Q. (2017) 'On fairness and calibration', Advances in Neural Information Processing Systems (NeurIPS), 30.
- Robertson, B., Vignaux, G.A. and Berger, C.E.H. (2016) Interpreting Evidence: Evaluating Forensic Science in the Courtroom. 2nd edn. Chichester: Wiley.
- Tyler, T.R. (2011) 'Procedural justice, legitimacy, and the effective rule of law', Crime and Justice, 40(1), pp. 283–357.

CHAPTER XVII

Disparate Impact in Predictive Justice: Measurement, Meaning, Remedy

The Quiet Transformation: Discrimination Without a Discriminator

Disparate impact is the law's way of acknowledging a hard truth about modern power: harm can be systematic even when no one announces a hostile intent. In predictive justice, this truth becomes sharper, because the machine does not "intend" anything at all. And yet the machine can still route liberty, attention, detention, and punishment in ways that disproportionately burden particular groups. This is not a paradox. It is the predictable result of decision systems built on data generated by unequal worlds, labelled by institutional processes, and optimised under incentives that reward efficiency and risk-avoidance. The profound danger is that predictive systems can make the disparate impact look natural, inevitable, and therefore morally acceptable—because the harm arrives wearing the mask of measurement.

The legal concept of disparate impact was forged to address neutral-looking practices that operate as barriers. Barocas and Selbst's classic analysis of "Big Data's Disparate Impact" remains essential because it explains, in concrete pathways, how seemingly neutral data mining can reproduce inequality through biased data, proxy variables, and structural constraints, without ever touching protected attributes explicitly. In predictive justice, those pathways are not theoretical. They are operational: arrest and conviction histories, neighbourhood proxies, employment and housing markers, and prior system contact can function as indirect conduits for protected characteristics, causing unequal burdens while preserving a veneer of impartiality.

Measurement: What Exactly Are We Measuring When We Claim "Impact"?

The first task is measurement, because if you measure the wrong thing you will proudly correct the wrong injustice. Disparate impact in predictive justice is often operationalised as differences in detention rates, supervision intensity, sentencing severity, or "high-risk" classifications across groups. But these are downstream decisions, not raw outcomes. They are mixtures of prediction, policy thresholds, human override, and institutional constraints. That makes measurement both necessary and treacherous.

The empirical literature that has tried to measure disparate impact from risk instruments does not tell a simple story, and its ambiguity is itself informative. A 2024 systematic review of disparate impact in risk assessment instruments concludes that, across studies, evidence does not robustly show that such tools consistently create or worsen disparities, and that the existing research base is limited in quality and concentrated heavily in pretrial contexts. The important point is not "tools are fine." The important point is that "impact" depends on the whole socio-technical system: what the tool predicts, what decision thresholds are set, what alternatives exist (supportive release conditions versus detention), what resources are available, and how human actors treat the output.

The second measurement trap lies in the label itself. The most rigorous criminological synthesis on algorithmic bias in criminal risk assessment insists that many studies implicitly treat arrest as an unbiased measure of offending, even though longstanding evidence suggests that arrest is a socially and institutionally shaped measure of crime. If your model predicts rearrest and you then measure "fairness" using rearrest, you can end up measuring how well the system predicts its own attention rather than how well it predicts harm. This is one reason disparate impact disputes become so bitter: different parties are sometimes talking about different "worlds"—the world of recorded events versus the world of actual victimisation.

A third measurement trap is selective observation. In bail settings, you only observe "misconduct while released" for those who were released; detained individuals do not produce observable misconduct labels. That means conventional models and conventional fairness evaluations can be structurally biased by the decision process that generated the data. Arnold, Dobbie and Yang's 2025 work develops quasi-experimental tools for algorithmic discrimination under selective labels and applies them directly to bail, showing how biased inputs and selective observation can generate discriminatory algorithms unless corrected. Disparate impact measurement that ignores selective labels risks treating the observed data as reality, when it is partly an artefact of detention decisions.

Meaning: Why "Disparate Impact" Is Not the Same as "Bias," and Why Neither Equals "Injustice"

Once you can measure disparities, you must interpret them. Here the law's problem is older than machine learning: a disparity can be a symptom of discrimination, a symptom of structural inequality, a symptom of measurement error, or a mixture of all three. Predictive justice intensifies the ambiguity because algorithmic systems can preserve a pattern for multiple reasons at once.

Meaning begins with ontology: what the system is actually predicting and why that prediction is being used. If a tool is predicting rearrest, and rearrest partly reflects differential enforcement, then disparate impact in the tool's outputs can be driven by label bias rather than by differences in underlying harm. Neil's review is explicit that arrest differences as measures of crime are a central pathway to algorithmic bias in criminal risk instruments. If you then treat disparate impact as proof that the tool is "racist," you may miss that the deeper injustice is institutional: the outcome variable itself is contaminated. But if you treat the outcome variable as neutral, you may mistakenly conclude the tool is fair simply because it is calibrated to a biased label.

Meaning also requires acknowledging that fairness metrics clash. It is mathematically impossible, in general, to satisfy calibration and equal error rates across groups when base rates differ unless the model is perfect or the base rates are equal. That is the core insight of the major impossibility results that shape modern fairness debates. Kleinberg, Mullainathan and Raghavan formalised inherent trade-offs among popular fairness conditions. Chouldechova showed that equalised odds and predictive parity cannot generally co-exist under differing prevalences. This matters for disparate impact because institutions often mistake one fairness success for overall fairness. A system can be calibrated and still produce higher false positives for one group; it can equalise error rates and still require different thresholds that raise concerns about equal treatment; it can reduce disparity at one decision stage and increase it at another.

Meaning finally requires a behavioural lens. Algorithmic systems can change the environment in which they operate. Predictive policing, in particular, can create self-reinforcing deployment loops: model outputs direct patrol, patrol produces recorded incidents, recorded incidents retrain the model, and the cycle returns to the same communities with amplified confidence. Lum and Isaac's classic analysis illustrates this "predict and serve" dynamic as a mechanism that can intensify inequality through the data feedback loop itself. Ensign and colleagues formalised runaway feedback loops in predictive policing, showing how such systems can escalate attention independent of true underlying distributions. In that world, disparate impact is not merely a measurement; it becomes an institutional prophecy that helps bring itself into being.

Remedy: You Cannot Fix a Social Problem With a Single Technical Switch

Once you understand measurement and meaning, remedy becomes clearer—and more demanding. Remedies fall into four families, and the failure mode is always the same: choosing one family and pretending it exhausts the problem.

The first family is data remedies: improve measurement, reduce label bias, and correct data pathways that encode unequal enforcement. Neil's review points toward this by emphasising that better measurement of offending—beyond arrest proxies—would reduce label bias and thus reduce algorithmic bias downstream. But data remedies are never purely technical in criminal justice; they require institutional changes that alter reporting, recording, and enforcement practices. Differential reporting itself can generate disparate impact: if some communities underreport due to distrust or fear, predictive systems trained on reports will under-allocate protection and over-allocate attention elsewhere. Work on differential reporting effects in predictive systems shows why disparate impact can arise even when the model never uses arrest data.

The second family is model remedies: constrain features, use causal reasoning, or adopt interpretable models when possible. The appeal is obvious—change the model, change the output. Yet proxies are resilient, and removing protected attributes rarely removes protected influence. Feldman and colleagues' work on certifying and removing disparate impact demonstrates how disparate impact can persist via correlated variables and how "fairness through unawareness" is often insufficient. The proper model remedy, therefore, is not simply feature deletion; it is explicit testing for proxy pathways, robustness across subgroups, and principled constraints matched to the legal and moral theory being applied.

The third family is decision-rule remedies: change thresholds, apply group-aware constraints, or use post-processing to reduce disparities. This is where most operational fixes land because thresholds are policy levers. Yet this is also where the moral conflict becomes most visible. Corbett-Davies and colleagues showed that fairness constraints often imply different optimal thresholds across groups in pretrial settings, which raises a direct tension between equal error burdens and equal treatment by a single standard. If you conceal that choice inside policy, you may get statistical parity at the cost of transparency and legitimacy. If you refuse it, you accept unequal error burdens that can translate into unequal liberty loss.

The fourth family is procedural remedies: contestability, disclosure, and adversarial testing. Even a technically improved system can be unjust if it is unchallengeable. The procedural justice literature shows that legitimacy depends heavily on perceived fairness of process—voice, respect, neutrality—not merely outcomes. Kinchin's analysis of "voicelessness" in algorithmic justice captures the specific procedural danger: hearings can remain formally intact while the decisive reasons become inaccessible, making participation feel ritualistic rather than meaningful. Fischman-Afori's argument for "due process by design" makes the remedy explicit: procedural fairness must be engineered into AI-mediated decision systems rather than added as an afterthought.

The Legal Translation: Disparate Impact Doctrine Meets Algorithmic Reality

A major reason disparate impact remedies stumble is that anti-discrimination law and algorithmic fairness speak different languages. Wachter, Mittelstadt and Russell argue that automating non-discrimination in Europe is difficult because legal frameworks are not static and because algorithmic discrimination does not map neatly onto traditional categories of human discriminatory intent and practice. Gerards and Xenidis likewise analyse algorithmic discrimination in Europe and show how existing legal tools interact awkwardly with algorithmic systems, particularly around evidence, burden, and the difficulty of revealing causal pathways and proxies. The lesson for predictive justice is not that law is obsolete; it is that law must be operationalised with new evidential expectations—audits, disclosure packages, and standards for contestation—if disparate impact doctrine is to remain enforceable rather than symbolic.

There is also a deeper, often ignored moral problem: disparate impact analysis can push institutions toward optimisation theatre, where the goal becomes "passing a metric" rather than reducing injustice. Predictive justice systems can be tuned to satisfy a chosen fairness definition while leaving structural drivers intact, or while shifting harms to less visible stages of the pipeline. Ugwudike's critique of "tech-reformism" in justice systems warns against precisely this: the belief that technical tools can substitute for structural reform, thereby stabilising rather than transforming inequity. A fairness metric cannot become a moral alibi.

A Forensic Standard for Disparate Impact Claims: From Accusation to Demonstration

If you want disparate impact claims to be courtroom-grade rather than rhetorical, treat them like forensic hypotheses. First, define the decision point: bail, sentencing, parole, patrol allocation, charging guidance. Second, define the outcome and its label integrity: rearrest, reconviction, harm, violation. Third, identify the plausible pathways: direct use of protected attributes, proxy variables, selective labels, feedback loops, differential reporting, drift. Fourth, quantify disparity with multiple metrics, because single metrics are fragile under base-rate differences and threshold changes. Fifth, test alternative explanations and confounds, including institutional changes over time and predictive inconsistency—because different modelling choices can produce different individual predictions even when each choice is defensible. Greene's work on predictive inconsistency makes clear that socio-technical tools can yield disparate scores for the same individual due to development and deployment choices, which matters for both disparate impact measurement and remedy design.

Finally, insist on remedy proportional to mechanism. If the mechanism is label bias, you cannot fix it with threshold tweaks alone. If the mechanism is feedback loops, you cannot fix it with calibration alone. If the mechanism is proxy discrimination, you cannot fix it by removing protected attributes. If the mechanism is procedural voicelessness, you cannot fix it with better AUC. The remedy must attack the causal pathway, not merely polish the output.

The Closing Claim: Disparate Impact Is the Justice System's Mirror, Not Its Excuse

Disparate impact in predictive justice is not merely a compliance headache. It is an x-ray of how institutions convert uncertainty into coercion and how historical inequality can be re-expressed as "data-driven." Measurement is required to see the pattern. Meaning is required to avoid false moral conclusions. Remedy is required to prevent metrics from becoming theatre. If the justice system is serious about fairness, it will stop asking whether the algorithm is biased in the abstract and begin asking, at each decision point, under what evidential and procedural conditions an algorithmic output may permissibly influence liberty, and what accountability structures prevent disparities from being treated as natural. That is how disparate impact doctrine can remain a living restraint rather than a decorative promise.

References

- Akpinar, N.-J., De-Arteaga, M. and Chouldechova, A. (2021) 'The effect of differential victim crime reporting on predictive policing systems', Proceedings of the ACM Conference on Fairness, Accountability, and Transparency (FAccT '21), pp. 434–445.
- Arnold, D., Dobbie, W. and Yang, C.S. (2025) 'Building nondiscriminatory algorithms in selected data', American Economic Review: Insights, 7(2), pp. 1–26.
- Barocas, S. and Selbst, A.D. (2016) 'Big data's disparate impact', California Law Review, 104(3), pp. 671–732.
- Barocas, S., Hardt, M. and Narayanan, A. (2023) Fairness and Machine Learning: Limitations and Opportunities. Cambridge, MA: MIT Press.
- Berk, R., Heidari, H., Jabbari, S., Kearns, M. and Roth, A. (2021) 'Fairness in criminal justice risk assessments: The state of the art', Sociological Methods & Research, 50(1), pp. 3–44.
- Berk, R.A. (2024) 'Improving fairness in criminal justice algorithmic risk assessments', Sociological Methods & Research.
- Chouldechova, A. (2017) 'Fair prediction with disparate impact: A study of bias in recidivism prediction instruments', Big Data, 5(2), pp. 153–163.

- Corbett-Davies, S., Pierson, E., Feller, A., Goel, S. and Huq, A. (2017) 'Algorithmic decision making and the cost of fairness', Proceedings of the 23rd ACM SIGKDD International Conference on Knowledge Discovery and Data Mining (KDD '17), pp. 797–806.
- Ensign, D., Friedler, S.A., Neville, S., Scheidegger, C. and Venkatasubramanian, S. (2018) 'Runaway feedback loops in predictive policing', Proceedings of Machine Learning Research (FAT 2018)*, 81, pp. 1–12.
- Feldman, M., Friedler, S.A., Moeller, J., Scheidegger, C. and Venkatasubramanian, S. (2015) 'Certifying and removing disparate impact', Proceedings of the 21st ACM SIGKDD International Conference on Knowledge Discovery and Data Mining (KDD '15), pp. 259–268.
- Fischman-Afori, O. (2025) 'Due process by design: Enhancing fairness and trust in AI decision-making through procedural justice theory', Social Sciences & Humanities Open, 12, 102178.
- Gama, J., Žliobaitė, I., Bifet, A., Pechenizkiy, M. and Bouchachia, A. (2014) 'A survey on concept drift adaptation', ACM Computing Surveys, 46(4), Article 44.
- Gerards, J. and Xenidis, R. (2021) Algorithmic Discrimination in Europe: Challenges and Opportunities for Equality Law. Brussels: Equinet.
- Greene, T., Shmueli, G., Fell, J., Lin, C.-F. and Liu, H.-W. (2022) 'Predictive inconsistency in criminal justice algorithmic risk prediction tools', Journal of the Royal Statistical Society: Series A, 185(S2), pp. S692–S716.
- Hardt, M., Price, E. and Srebro, N. (2016) 'Equality of opportunity in supervised learning', Advances in Neural Information Processing Systems, 29.
- Kattnig, M. et al. (2024) 'Assessing trustworthy AI: Technical and legal perspectives on bias mitigation and legal requirements', Computer Law & Security Review, 54, 106056.
- Kinchin, N. (2024) '"Voiceless": the procedural gap in algorithmic justice', International Journal of Law and Information Technology, 32(4), pp. 1–30.
- Kleinberg, J., Mullainathan, S. and Raghavan, M. (2017) 'Inherent trade-offs in the fair determination of risk scores', Proceedings of the 8th Innovations in Theoretical Computer Science Conference (ITCS 2017), LIPIcs 67, Article 43.

- Lawson, S.G. et al. (2024) 'Disparate impact of risk assessment instruments: A systematic review', Psychological Bulletin.
- Lum, K. and Isaac, W. (2016) 'To predict and serve?', Significance, 13(5), pp. 14–19.
- Neil, R. (2025) 'Algorithmic bias in criminal risk assessment: The consequences of racial differences in arrest as a measure of crime', Annual Review of Criminology, 8, pp. 97–119.
- Oswald, M. (2018) 'Algorithm-assisted decision-making in the public sector: Framing the issues using administrative law rules governing discretionary power', Philosophical Transactions of the Royal Society A, 376(2128), 20170359.
- Perdomo, J.C., Zrnic, T., Mendler-Dünner, C. and Hardt, M. (2020) 'Performative prediction', Proceedings of the 37th International Conference on Machine Learning (ICML 2020), PMLR 119, pp. 7599–7609.
- Pleiss, G., Raghavan, M., Wu, F., Kleinberg, J. and Weinberger, K.Q. (2017) 'On fairness and calibration', Advances in Neural Information Processing Systems, 30.
- Robertson, B., Vignaux, G.A. and Berger, C.E.H. (2016) Interpreting Evidence: Evaluating Forensic Science in the Courtroom. 2nd edn. Chichester: Wiley.
- Ugwudike, P. (2022) 'Predictive algorithms in justice systems and the limits of tech-reformism', International Journal for Crime, Justice and Social Democracy, 11(1), pp. 1–15.
- Vick, B. (2025) 'Accuracy and impact of supervision risk assessment tools...', American Journal of Criminal Justice.
- Wachter, S., Mittelstadt, B. and Russell, C. (2021) 'Why fairness cannot be automated: Bridging the gap between EU non-discrimination law and AI', Computer Law & Security Review, 41, 105567.

CHAPTER XVIII

Bias as History: When Data Encodes Institutional Memory

The Past Does Not Stay in the Past When It Becomes a Dataset

If you want to understand bias in predictive justice, you must begin with a proposition that sounds almost too simple: data are not records of reality; they are records of interaction between reality and an institution. Police data record what was looked for, where attention was concentrated, which incidents were discovered rather than reported, how discretion was exercised, what got written down, and what got ignored. Court data record charging choices, plea pressures, evidential bottlenecks, judicial habits, and institutional capacities as much as they record wrongdoing. Correctional data record supervision intensity, technical violation rules, and program access as much as they record behaviour. When these records are fed into models, the models do not merely "learn patterns." They inherit the institution's memory—its priorities, its blind spots, its historical inequities, and its administrative shortcuts—and then convert that memory into a forward-acting mechanism. Bias, in the algorithmic era, is often history with a probability attached to it.

This is why it is an error to speak of "biased models" as if the bias begins inside the mathematics. In high-stakes public power, bias often begins earlier, in the data-generating process itself. Barocas and Selbst's classic account of disparate impact in big data explains, with legal precision, how seemingly neutral data practices can reproduce inequality through imperfect data, proxy variables, and structural constraints, even without explicit protected attributes (Barocas and Selbst, 2016). That analysis becomes almost literal in criminal justice because the state itself generates much of the data that later "justifies" state action. A court that treats model outputs as neutral evidence is therefore at risk of authorising the institution to punish on the basis of its own historically patterned attention.

The Forensic Analogy: "Chain of Custody" Must Be Applied to Data, Not Only to Exhibits

In forensic work, you are trained to think genealogically. A trace is not only what it is; it is also how it came to be there, how it was collected, and what handling could have altered it. Chain of custody is the legal recognition that provenance matters because provenance controls trust. Algorithmic systems demand the same discipline, but at the level of datasets and pipelines. If an arrest record is treated as a label of "crime," you must ask what policing strategy produced the arrest, what discretion shaped the stop, what reporting dynamics preceded the encounter, and what socio-legal pressures influenced who got processed and who did not. If you do not ask, you are doing the algorithmic version of accepting a contaminated exhibit because it looks clean in a bag.

The most load-bearing modern synthesis of this problem in criminal justice risk assessment makes the point bluntly: much research effectively uses arrest data as if it were an unbiased measure of offending, and racial differences in arrest—driven by multiple mechanisms—can create algorithmic bias when arrest records are used as outcomes or predictors (Neil, 2025). When a model learns from arrest, it often learns enforcement visibility as much as harmful behaviour. The dataset is institutional memory, not neutral measurement. And because the model is then deployed to shape future decisions—bail, supervision, patrol allocation—the memory becomes performative.

Person-Based and Place-Based Memory: How Policing Data Learns Its Own Spotlight

Policing is the easiest domain in which to watch institutional memory harden into predictive authority, because policing is both data-rich and discretionary. Place-based predictive policing has already been analysed as a feedback system: model predicts hotspots, police are sent there, police discover more incidents there, the model retrains on the new data, and the same places receive repeated attention with increased confidence. Lum and Isaac's "To predict and serve?" remains the canonical warning because it demonstrates how predictive policing trained on biased data risks reinforcing disparities through the very act of deployment (Lum and Isaac, 2016). Ensign and colleagues formalised the mechanism as "runaway feedback loops," showing that discovered crime data can drive police repeatedly back to the same neighbourhoods regardless of true underlying crime rates (Ensign et al., 2018). In plain language, the model becomes a memory amplifier: it does not merely remember where the institution has looked; it compels the institution to keep looking there.

The more subtle point is that this dynamic persists even when you try to "clean up" the inputs. If you restrict training data to citizen reports rather than police-initiated discoveries, you still inherit institutional memory through differential reporting. Akpinar, De-Arteaga and Chouldechova show that differences in victim reporting rates across areas can displace predicted hotspots away from high-crime but low-reporting areas toward higher-reporting areas, producing both over-policing and under-policing (Akpinar, De-Arteaga and Chouldechova, 2021). The memory here is not only police behaviour; it is the public's trust and willingness to report, which is itself shaped by prior police behaviour. Thus, even when "arrests are removed," the dataset still encodes history through reporting pathways.

Person-based predictive targeting intensifies the moral problem, because the memory is attached to individuals rather than places. Ferguson's work on big data policing describes how surveillance technologies and analytics reshape who is policed, where, and how, with race and transparency concerns embedded in the data practices themselves (Ferguson, 2017). Brayne's ethnographic account of data-driven policing shows how "big data" becomes a mechanism of discretion management and social sorting, embedding institutional logics into analytics and then feeding those analytics back into field practice (Brayne, 2020). This is institutional memory as infrastructure: the system remembers who has been in contact, assigns risk to that memory, and then creates more contact that confirms the risk.

Cohort Bias: When History Hides in Time Itself

Institutional memory is not encoded only through geography and identity; it is encoded through time. Models trained on historical cohorts can become unfair not only through group disparities but through cohort bias—changes in social conditions, policy regimes, and institutional practices over time. Montana and colleagues show that cohort bias can generate inequality in predictive risk assessments of future criminal justice system involvement distinct from racial bias, with implications for how risk instruments are built and interpreted (Montana et al., 2023). The forensic significance is severe: a model may appear stable while its meaning changes because the cohort's environment has changed. What looks like "personal risk" can be the residue of a period's policing and prosecution patterns. If you treat the score as a trait, you treat time as character.

This is where "model drift" stops being an engineering concern and becomes a legal concern. Concept drift surveys in machine learning treat drift as ubiquitous: the relationship between inputs and outcomes changes because the world changes (Gama et al., 2014). In justice systems, the world changes and the institution changes—new enforcement priorities, new reporting patterns, new statutes, new political pressures—and those changes can cause both statistical drift and moral drift. The model silently becomes a different instrument than the one that was validated. When institutional memory is time-encoded, you cannot rely on one-time validation as moral permission.

Performativity: When Prediction Becomes Steering

The most intellectually honest framework for understanding bias as history is performativity: predictions influence the target they predict. Hardt and Mendler-Dünner's survey of performative prediction emphasises that once deployed in a social setting, a model can steer behaviour and thereby change the data-generating distribution; the system is no longer merely learning, it is also governing (Hardt and Mendler-Dünner, 2025). This is exactly what happens when a "high risk" classification triggers more surveillance, when a hotspot prediction triggers more patrol, when a "likely failure to appear" output triggers detention, or when a "risk of breach" score triggers tighter supervision. The model turns institutional memory into institutional prophecy.

This is why the phrase "data-driven" is often misleading in justice settings. The direction is not one-way from data to decision. It is circular: decision affects data, data affects model, model affects decision. The feedback loop is the machine version of precedent, but without the court's public reasoning and without the constitutional discipline that normally restrains precedent. The system becomes what it has been, and it justifies becoming it again.

The Proxy Lesson from Outside Criminal Justice: Cost Is Not Need, Contact Is Not Harm

A useful way to see institutional memory at work is to observe it in another domain where the moral structure is easier to grasp. Obermeyer and colleagues showed that a widely used healthcare algorithm exhibited racial bias because it predicted healthcare costs as a proxy for health needs; unequal access meant lower spending on Black patients, so cost predicted less "need," producing biased allocations (Obermeyer et al., 2019). The key lesson is transferable: when a proxy is shaped by structural inequality, the model can be "accurate" about the proxy and deeply wrong about the moral target.

Criminal justice repeats this error constantly. Arrest is treated as harm. Conviction is treated as culpability. Prior system contact is treated as dangerousness. Breach is treated as defiance rather than as a function of supervision intensity and social instability. The model faithfully encodes the institution's historical pathways and then presents them as if they were natural properties of individuals. Bias here is not only statistical; it is ontological.

The Behavioural Engine: Why Institutional Memory Persuades Judges and Officers

Institutional memory becomes powerful when it is cognitively persuasive. A score feels like a fact. A ranking feels like objectivity. Under workload pressure, a model output becomes a shortcut that looks responsible—"evidence-based"—even when it is merely historically consistent. This is how bias moves from the dataset into the decision: not through malice, but through deference. That deference is precisely why procedural justice concerns matter. If the decision is experienced as precomputed and unchallengeable, legitimacy erodes even when the institution claims it has improved consistency (Kinchin, 2024). And when legitimacy erodes, reporting changes, cooperation declines, and the dataset shifts again—history re-enters as drift.

Remedy Begins with Naming: Data Genealogy as a Legal Requirement

If bias is history, then remedy begins with genealogy: the institution must be required to document how data were generated, what discretion shaped them, what proxies are used, and what social processes contaminate labels. This is not a moral luxury. It is what makes contestability possible. The right to challenge cannot exist if the defence cannot see how the evidence was produced.

A practical remedy structure follows four moves. First, treat major justice datasets as institutional artefacts with audit trails: documentation of collection practices, policy changes, enforcement priorities, and known measurement gaps. Second, separate "reported" from "discovered" data streams wherever possible and measure differential reporting as a first-class problem, not an afterthought (Akpinar, De-Arteaga and Chouldechova, 2021). Third, monitor cohort bias and drift explicitly, because time-dependent institutional change can generate unfairness even when group-based tests look acceptable (Montana et al., 2023). Fourth, treat model deployment as an intervention that can create feedback loops, and design governance to prevent runaway dynamics—by independent measurement streams, randomised audits, and explicit limits on using "discovered" outcomes as pure truth (Lum and Isaac, 2016; Ensign et al., 2018).

The deeper remedy is normative: the justice system must stop treating institutional contact as moral evidence of dangerousness. It must require that coercive decisions be grounded in reasons that do not merely restate the institution's past practices. Otherwise, "bias as history" becomes "history as justification," and the system collapses into self-ratifying administration.

Closing: Justice Cannot Be Allowed to Remember in Only One Direction

A lawful system remembers in a particular way: it remembers through public reasons, review, appeal, and the discipline of justification. Predictive justice systems remember differently: they remember through data accumulation, proxy learning, and optimisation. If the system remembers only through its own contact records—arrests, stops, breaches—it will remember the footprints of power as if they were the footprints of harm. The hard demand of the rule of law is that institutional memory must itself be accountable. The algorithm is not the villain; the unexamined history inside the data is.

References

- Akpinar, N.-J., De-Arteaga, M. and Chouldechova, A. (2021) 'The effect of differential victim crime reporting on predictive policing systems', Proceedings of the 2021 ACM Conference on Fairness, Accountability, and Transparency (FAccT '21).
- Barocas, S. and Selbst, A.D. (2016) 'Big data's disparate impact', California Law Review, 104(3), pp. 671–732.
- Benjamin, R. (2019) Race After Technology: Abolitionist Tools for the New Jim Code. Cambridge: Polity Press.
- Bowker, G.C. and Star, S.L. (1999) Sorting Things Out: Classification and Its Consequences. Cambridge, MA: MIT Press.
- Brayne, S. (2020) Predict and Surveil: Data, Discretion, and the Future of Policing. Oxford: Oxford University Press.
- Cooper, G.S., Meterko, V. and Dror, I.E. (2019) 'Cognitive bias research in forensic science: A systematic review', Forensic Science International, 297, pp. 35–46.
- Ensign, D., Friedler, S.A., Neville, S., Scheidegger, C. and Venkatasubramanian, S. (2018) 'Runaway feedback loops in predictive policing', Proceedings of Machine Learning Research (FAT 2018)*, 81, pp. 1–12.
- Eubanks, V. (2018) Automating Inequality: How High-Tech Tools Profile, Police, and Punish the Poor. New York: St. Martin's Press.
- Feldman, M., Friedler, S.A., Moeller, J., Scheidegger, C. and Venkatasubramanian, S. (2015) 'Certifying and removing disparate impact', Proceedings of the 21st ACM SIGKDD International Conference on Knowledge Discovery and Data Mining (KDD '15), pp. 259–268.
- Ferguson, A.G. (2017) The Rise of Big Data Policing: Surveillance, Race, and the Future of Law Enforcement. New York: NYU Press.
- Gama, J., Žliobaitė, I., Bifet, A., Pechenizkiy, M. and Bouchachia, A. (2014) 'A survey on concept drift adaptation', ACM Computing Surveys, 46(4), Article 44.
- Hardt, M. and Mendler-Dünner, C. (2025) 'Performative prediction: Past and future', Statistical Science.
- Hinder, F., Hammer, B. and Biehl, M. (2024) 'One or two things we know about concept drift—A survey on monitoring and drift detection',

Frontiers in Artificial Intelligence, 7, 1330257.

- Kinchin, N. (2024) '"Voiceless": the procedural gap in algorithmic justice', International Journal of Law and Information Technology, 32(4), pp. 1–30.
- Liu, H.-W. and Lin, C.-F. (2019) 'Beyond State v Loomis: Artificial intelligence, government algorithmization and accountability', International Journal of Law and Information Technology, 27(2), pp. 122–149.
- Lum, K. and Isaac, W. (2016) 'To predict and serve?', Significance, 13(5), pp. 14–19.
- Montana, E., Nagin, D.S., Neil, R. and Sampson, R.J. (2023) 'Cohort bias in predictive risk assessments of future criminal justice system involvement', Proceedings of the National Academy of Sciences, 120, e2301990120 / e2307285120.
- Morrison, G.S. (2025) 'A guide to ISO 21043 forensic sciences from the forensic-data-science paradigm', Science & Justice, 65, 101298.
- Neil, R. and Zanger-Tishler, M. (2025) 'Algorithmic bias in criminal risk assessment: The consequences of racial differences in arrest as a measure of crime', Annual Review of Criminology, 8, pp. 97–119.
- Obermeyer, Z., Powers, B., Vogeli, C. and Mullainathan, S. (2019) 'Dissecting racial bias in an algorithm used to manage the health of populations', Science, 366(6464), pp. 447–453.
- Perdomo, J.C., Zrnic, T., Mendler-Dünner, C. and Hardt, M. (2020) 'Performative prediction', Proceedings of the 37th International Conference on Machine Learning (ICML 2020), PMLR 119, pp. 7599–7609.
- Robertson, B., Vignaux, G.A. and Berger, C.E.H. (2016) Interpreting Evidence: Evaluating Forensic Science in the Courtroom. 2nd edn. Chichester: Wiley.
- Self, A.D. (2018) 'Disparate impact in big data policing', Georgia Law Review, 52, pp. 109–195.
- Tyler, T.R. (2011) 'Procedural justice, legitimacy, and the effective rule of law', Crime and Justice, 40(1), pp. 283–357.

CHAPTER XIX

Group Justice vs Individual Justice: The Equality Paradox in Sentencing

The Paradox You Must Hold in Your Mind Without Flinching

Sentencing is the one part of criminal adjudication where the legal system openly admits that two moral goods are simultaneously demanded and simultaneously endangered. The first good is equality: like cases should be treated alike; punishment should not depend on which courtroom door you walked through, which judge you drew, which prosecutor was on duty, or which social accent you carry in your mouth. The second good is individuality: punishment must fit not only the offence category but the lived offence, the offender's culpability, their role, their intent, their constraints, their prospects, and the human reality that "the same crime" is often committed by profoundly different persons for profoundly different reasons. Equality without individuality becomes mechanised severity; individuality without equality becomes aristocratic discretion. Every sentencing system oscillates between these poles, and every reform movement promises to solve the oscillation by pushing toward one pole while claiming it will not lose the other. That promise is the equality paradox: when you correct disparity, you risk flattening moral nuance; when you preserve nuance, you risk entrenching disparity.

A serious reader must begin by abandoning the childish belief that this is a matter of "finding the right formula." Even the most disciplined sentencing theories treat the problem as one of bounded discretion and institutional design. Limiting retributivism—associated with Norval Morris and developed extensively in later sentencing scholarship—does not claim that desert answers everything; it claims desert sets upper (and sometimes lower) limits, within which other purposes may operate, because a system that pursues prevention or rehabilitation without desert limits becomes a managerial state that treats persons as instruments (Frase, 2005; Tonry, 2018). Equality, in this view, is not achieved by a single number, but by structuring discretion so that variation is morally intelligible and institutionally accountable.

Why Equality in Sentencing Is Not the Same as Equality in Mathematics

"Equal treatment" sounds like a mathematical relation, but sentencing equality is not a property of a spreadsheet; it is a property of a justificatory practice. Two defendants are not "equal" because they share a statute label; they are equal because the reasons that justify punishment apply to them in comparable ways. Desert-based proportionality traditions—classically associated with von Hirsch's work—insist that punishment should track offence seriousness and culpability because this anchors punishment to public reason rather than to fear or administrative convenience (von Hirsch, 1991; Brooks, 2025). Yet proportionality itself is not a single axis. Seriousness is partly harm and partly blameworthiness; blameworthiness depends on intention, foresight, coercion, capacity, and role. That means proportionality is already a structured moral judgement, not merely a quantitative rank ordering. When a sentencing system tries to force proportionality into a strict numeric equivalence, it often ends up privileging what is easily countable—prior convictions, quantified loss, weapon presence—over what is morally decisive but harder to measure, such as domination, coercion, impaired agency, or the difference between opportunism and compulsion (Frase, 2005).

This is why the "individualisation" ideal persists even in guideline systems. It is not sentimental; it is a recognition that culpability is not fully captured by offence categories. The jurisprudential challenge is to distinguish permissible individualisation—adjustment for culpability-relevant reasons—from impermissible individualisation—adjustment driven by prejudice, charisma, stereotype, or institutional habit. That distinction is the point at which equality becomes practical rather than rhetorical.

The Hidden Engine of Inequality: Unstructured Discretion and the Myth of Neutral Intuition

The sentencing literature is filled with the vocabulary of discretion: "judicial discretion," "mitigation," "aggravation," "individual circumstances." But discretion is not inherently humane. Unstructured discretion is an invitation for latent variables—race, class, gender norms, courtroom culture, local political pressures—to enter the decision under the cover of "common sense." This is why modern scholarship on sentencing consistency asks, without embarrassment, whether individualised justice and consistency are compatible, and then analyses the operational reality that discretionary systems often produce imprecise proportionality and residual variation that cannot be justified as principled individualisation (Harris, 2019).

Forensic application matters here, because sentencing is often fed by forensic narratives: risk assessments, psychiatric evaluations, pre-sentence reports, victim impact statements, digital traces of behaviour, and increasingly algorithmic summaries of "similar cases." Each of these can be probative, but each is also a channel for bias. A forensic psychologist who frames a defendant as "antisocial" may be describing trait risk when the real driver is situational desperation; a risk tool trained on rearrest data may be encoding enforcement patterns rather than harm propensity. When such materials are used, equality is threatened not only by the judge's intuition but by the epistemic quality of the inputs.

Group Justice: Why Systems Need Patterns

Group justice, in sentencing, is the aspiration that the system as a whole treats people fairly across time and space. It is concerned with aggregate patterns: racial disparities, gender disparities, socio-economic disparities, regional disparities, and the scandal of two similar cases receiving wildly different outcomes simply because they were processed by different humans. Guidelines, grids, and algorithmic supports often arise as responses to this scandal. The moral appeal is obvious: if the law is to be public, it must not be roulette. Tonry's argument for punishment premised on human dignity is relevant because dignity-based punishment demands restraint, parsimony, and transparency; hidden variation is a form of disrespect because it treats the citizen as subject to arbitrary power (Tonry, 2018).

Yet the very tools designed to improve group justice often create the conditions for a new form of injustice: rule-like rigidity that treats context as noise. When the system enforces uniformity by narrowing discretion too aggressively, it can punish unlike persons alike and thereby commit a deeper unfairness while congratulating itself for consistency.

Individual Justice: Why Courts Cannot Escape Moral Particularity

Individual justice is the aspiration that punishment is justified for the person in front of the court, not merely for the category they occupy. It is rooted in the idea that punishment is a moral address: the state condemns a wrong and holds an agent responsible. Communicative and censure-oriented punishment theories insist that punishment must speak in reasons that the offender can recognise as reasons—reasons tied to culpable choice and public norms—otherwise punishment degenerates into mere management (Duff, 2001; Brooks, 2025). When systems become overly pattern-driven, they risk losing this address. A guideline grid can produce an outcome without a narrative of culpability; an algorithm can recommend a sentence without moral authorship; the judge can become a signer of a system output rather than the author of a public reason.

This is where recent debates on algorithmic sentencing become diagnostic. Taylor argues that algorithms in sentencing have limits because sentencing is not merely outcome optimisation; it is condemnation and public judgement, which must remain meaningfully human and publicly controllable (Taylor, 2023). The critique is not technophobic; it is about preserving the moral structure of punishment. If the system can no longer explain why this punishment is justified for this person beyond "the model says so," individual justice collapses, and legitimacy collapses with it.

The Equality Paradox in Its Sharpest Form: Equal Treatment vs Equal Error Burdens

The paradox becomes most painful when you consider that equality can be defined in incompatible ways. "Equal treatment" can mean one standard applied to all. But "equal burden" can mean that the system's mistakes—false harshness, unnecessary imprisonment, excessive supervision—should not fall disproportionately on one group. In algorithmic and risk-assisted sentencing, these two intuitions collide in mathematically unavoidable ways when base rates differ and prediction is imperfect, a point established by the foundational fairness trade-off literature (Kleinberg, Mullainathan and Raghavan, 2017; Chouldechova, 2017; Pleiss et al., 2017).

Translate that into sentencing language and you see the ethical tension. If a system uses risk forecasts to adjust sentencing severity, and if risk forecasts are imperfect and reflect different base rates driven partly by structural conditions and enforcement patterns, then a single threshold rule may create higher false-positive harshness for one group. Yet group-specific thresholds—designed to equalise error burdens—look like differential treatment, and can be politically and legally explosive. This is the equality paradox rendered technical: whichever choice you make, you must justify a moral trade-off. You cannot hide behind "the algorithm."

The Forensic Core: What Sentencing Inputs Actually Measure

The equality paradox cannot be resolved unless you examine the epistemic quality of the inputs. Risk assessments and predictive instruments often operate on proxies: rearrest, reconviction, breach, failure to appear. These are not pure behavioural outcomes; they are institutional outcomes shaped by policing, prosecution, supervision intensity, and resource constraints. Contemporary criminological synthesis warns specifically that racial differences in arrest as a measure of crime can drive algorithmic bias in risk assessment (Neil, 2025). If sentencing severity is influenced by these forecasts, then the system may be using institutional contact as if it were moral danger. That is not merely unfair; it is conceptually wrong.

Forensic science offers a discipline that sentencing should borrow: distinguish observation from interpretation, and insist on validation under conditions of use. Robertson, Vignaux and Berger's framework for interpreting evidence emphasises that evidential strength depends on explicit propositions, known error, and disciplined communication, because otherwise decision-makers will overstate what a tool can legitimately support (Robertson, Vignaux and Berger, 2016). Sentencing tools—whether actuarial, algorithmic, or guideline-based—must be treated similarly. If a tool cannot show what it predicts, what it does not predict, what its error looks like, and how it behaves across contexts, it should not be allowed to function as a de facto moral authority in sentencing.

The Institutional Design Answer: Bounded Individualisation Within Publicly Defensible Ranges

So what is the best "global" resolution to the equality paradox? Not a single model, but a design posture: bound discretion within proportionality constraints, require reasoned departures, and make the reasons auditable. This is the core institutional logic of limiting retributivism in its sentencing-guideline form: desert constrains, but does not dictate; individualisation occurs within a permissible range justified by culpability-relevant factors; departures require reasons that can be reviewed; and the system monitors patterns for unjustified disparity (Frase, 2005; Frase, 2010; Tonry, 2018).

This posture also offers a principled place for algorithmic support—if it is kept as evidence, not authority. Algorithmic models can help identify outliers, reveal inconsistency, and prompt judges to articulate reasons when they deviate from typical practice. Work on algorithmic guidelines and misalignment indices illustrates how models might be used to detect inconsistency and support discretionary systems without directly replacing human judgement (Kiejnich-Kruk, Twardawa and Formanowicz, 2025). But the moral line must remain bright: the model can flag, it can inform, it can discipline, but it cannot become the reason for condemnation. A sentence must be owned by a judge through reasons a person can contest.

The Moral Test That Never Goes Away: Does the Sentence Still Speak as a Public Reason?

Ultimately, the equality paradox is managed—not solved—by insisting that sentencing remains a reasons-giving practice that the community can recognise as lawful. When uniformity drives out moral narrative, punishment becomes managerial. When individualisation drives out consistency, punishment becomes arbitrary. The system must therefore force itself into the difficult middle: structured consistency with bounded moral particularity. Proportionality functions as the backbone; dignity functions as the restraint; and procedural accountability functions as the safeguard against hidden prejudice (von Hirsch, 1991; Tonry, 2018).

If you want a final forensic way to state the equality paradox, state it like a constraint system. The court must ensure that sentencing reasons are

1. relevant to culpability and lawful purposes,
2. consistent with proportionality and parsimony limits,
3. contestable and reviewable,
4. monitored for group patterns that suggest impermissible influence.

When those conditions are met, the system can tolerate some variation as morally intelligible individualisation. When they are not met, variation becomes injustice—even when it is dressed up as compassion.

References

- Barocas, S., Hardt, M. and Narayanan, A. (2023) Fairness and Machine Learning: Limitations and Opportunities. Cambridge, MA: MIT Press.
- Brooks, T. (2025) 'A critique of von Hirsch's censure theory', Ratio Juris, 38(1), pp. 1–18.
- Chouldechova, A. (2017) 'Fair prediction with disparate impact: A study of bias in recidivism prediction instruments', Big Data, 5(2), pp. 153–163.
- Chiao, V. (2018) 'Predicting proportionality: The case for algorithmic sentencing', Criminal Justice Ethics, 37(3), pp. 238–261.
- Corbett-Davies, S., Pierson, E., Feller, A., Goel, S. and Huq, A. (2017) 'Algorithmic decision making and the cost of fairness', Proceedings of the 23rd ACM SIGKDD International Conference on Knowledge Discovery and Data Mining (KDD '17), pp. 797–806.
- Duff, R.A. (2001) Punishment, Communication, and Community. Oxford: Oxford University Press.
- Frase, R.S. (2005) 'Punishment purposes', Stanford Law Review, 58(1), pp. 67–117.
- Frase, R.S. (2010) Just Sentencing: Principles and Procedures for a Workable System. New York: Oxford University Press.
- Hardt, M., Price, E. and Srebro, N. (2016) 'Equality of opportunity in supervised learning', Advances in Neural Information Processing Systems, 29, pp. 3315–3323.
- Harris, L. (2019) Consistency in Sentencing. Oxford: Oxford University Research Archive (doctoral thesis).
- Kiejnich-Kruk, K., Twardawa, M. and Formanowicz, P. (2025) 'Overcoming sentencing inconsistency: A proposal for algorithmic guidelines and juridical misalignment index', Artificial Intelligence and Law.
- Kleinberg, J., Mullainathan, S. and Raghavan, M. (2017) 'Inherent trade-offs in the fair determination of risk scores', Proceedings of the 8th Innovations in Theoretical Computer Science Conference (ITCS 2017),

LIPIcs 67, Article 43.

- Morris, N. (1974) The Future of Imprisonment. Chicago: University of Chicago Press.
- Neil, R. (2025) 'Algorithmic bias in criminal risk assessment: The consequences of racial differences in arrest as a measure of crime', Annual Review of Criminology, 8, pp. 97–119.
- Pleiss, G., Raghavan, M., Wu, F., Kleinberg, J. and Weinberger, K.Q. (2017) 'On fairness and calibration', Advances in Neural Information Processing Systems, 30.
- Robertson, B., Vignaux, G.A. and Berger, C.E.H. (2016) Interpreting Evidence: Evaluating Forensic Science in the Courtroom. 2nd edn. Chichester: Wiley.
- Taylor, I. (2023) 'Justice by algorithm: The limits of AI in criminal sentencing', Criminal Justice Ethics, 42(3), pp. 193–213.
- Tonry, M. (2018) 'Punishment and human dignity: Sentencing principles for a humane justice system', Punishment & Society.
- von Hirsch, A. (1991) 'Proportionality in the philosophy of punishment: From "Why punish?" to "How much?"', Israel Law Review, 25(3–4), pp. 385–402.

CHAPTER XX

Procedural Justice and Algorithmic Respect: Voice, Dignity, and Neutrality

The Problem the Algorithm Cannot Solve for You

A justice system survives on an unusual fuel: people comply with its outcomes even when they dislike them, not merely because the state can coerce, but because the process can be experienced as legitimate. That legitimacy is not an ornament added after the verdict; it is a psychological fact that determines cooperation, disclosure, reporting, and long-run obedience. Procedural justice research has repeatedly shown that people judge authorities by process qualities—especially whether they were heard, whether they were treated with dignity and respect, whether decision-makers appeared neutral, and whether the authority seemed sincerely motivated by trustworthy aims rather than expedience or hostility (Tyler, 2006; Tyler, 2011; Blader and Tyler, 2003). When algorithmic tools enter courts and court-adjacent decisions—bail, sentencing support, supervision triage, risk scoring, predictive policing—there is a seductive promise that sounds like virtue: "less bias, more consistency, more efficiency." Yet the very features that make algorithmic tools attractive—speed, standardisation, opacity of internal reasoning, and the ability to compress complex human narratives into a scalar—also threaten the procedural conditions that make legal authority psychologically acceptable. In other words, algorithmic systems tend to target distributive regularities (who gets what outcome) while leaving a "procedural gap" (how the outcome is reached and whether the person's participation mattered) (Kinchin, 2024).

If you want a single sentence that captures the chapter's burden, it is this: procedural justice is not merely about being correct; it is about being recognisably respectful in a way that preserves human agency under state power, and algorithms can easily become instruments of procedural disrespect unless they are designed and governed as if the right to be heard were a core function, not a user-interface feature (Fischman-Afori, 2025; Gregory, 2025).

Voice: Why "I got to speak" is Not the Same as "My Speech Mattered"

Voice is the right to present your account before a decision is made, but in procedural justice theory it is not merely the opportunity to talk; it is the experience that one's account was taken seriously as input to the decision (Tyler, 2006; Blader and Tyler, 2003). In court, voice is the living core of due process: the accused explains, contests, contextualises, and challenges. When an algorithmic recommendation is treated as the default, voice can survive formally while dying functionally. A defendant may speak at length, but if the decisive weight lies in a score that is not meaningfully contestable—because the features are hidden, the data are inaccessible, the thresholds are unreviewable, or the "reasons" are generic—then voice becomes theatre. Kinchin's analysis of the "procedural gap" makes this dynamic explicit: algorithmic governance often responds to distributive concerns while sidelining voice, leaving accountability mechanisms that can "look fair" while the person experiences voicelessness (Kinchin, 2024).

The forensic point here is not abstract. Algorithmic voice collapses when the accused cannot do what adversarial process exists to do: correct errors in inputs, challenge relevance, test reliability, and expose inferential leaps. A risk score built partly on prior arrests can be challenged only if the accused can see what the system counted as an arrest, whether it counted diversions or dismissals as "failures," whether it used neighbourhood proxies, whether it treated missed court dates as wilful absconding rather than transport instability. If those details are not available, the person is not "heard" in any legally meaningful sense; they are merely present. This is why "due process by design" arguments insist that procedural justice must be engineered into AI-mediated decision systems as enforceable rights—especially the right to be heard—rather than being treated as an optional ethical overlay (Fischman-Afori, 2025).

Dignity: Why Automation Risks becoming Disrespect even When it is Polite

The dignity dimension of procedural justice concerns how people are treated—whether the authority communicates respect, recognises personhood, and avoids humiliating or dehumanising handling (Tyler,

2006; Tyler, 2011). In the algorithmic context, disrespect often takes a particular shape: the person experiences themselves as being processed, sorted, and reduced. The system may be "polite" in language and still be disrespectful in structure, because it treats the person as an object of classification rather than an agent whose narrative and reasons matter. Gregory's argument about "procedural disrespect" captures this precisely: automated decision-making can violate the procedural rule-of-law ideals associated with dignity because it undermines the interpersonal and justificatory dimensions of lawful governance, even when outcomes are materially defensible (Gregory, 2025).

A court that relies on algorithmic tools must therefore face a moral question that cannot be answered by AUC, calibration curves, or fairness dashboards: does the process still communicate that the person is being judged as a citizen, not managed as a risk? That question becomes urgent in sentencing and bail contexts, where the state's action is coercive and status-assigning. The public perception literature shows that people often rate judges who rely on human expertise as more legitimate than those who rely on AI tools, and that perceived procedural justice and legitimacy vary by group and context (Fine, Berthelot and Marsh, 2025). The important implication is not "people dislike technology." It is that algorithmic involvement alters the symbolic meaning of adjudication: it can look like distancing moral responsibility from the decision, which people experience as disrespect.

Neutrality: Why "Model Objectivity" can be a Myth that Harms Legitimacy

Neutrality in procedural justice is not a claim that decision-makers have no values; it is the perception that decisions are guided by consistent rules and accurate facts rather than by bias, prejudice, or arbitrary whim (Tyler, 2006; Blader and Tyler, 2003). Algorithms are often marketed as neutrality machines. Yet neutrality is precisely where algorithmic systems are most likely to produce an illusion. First, predictive systems typically learn correlations in institutional data, and criminal justice data frequently encode historical enforcement patterns and measurement distortions. Second, different fairness concepts conflict; you cannot generally achieve all attractive statistical fairness metrics at once when base rates differ and prediction is imperfect, which means neutrality is not something the system "has," but something the institution chooses to define and justify.

Neutrality also fails when the algorithm is used strategically rather than submissively. Empirical work on judicial use of pretrial risk assessments has found that judges may invoke scores selectively to legitimise decisions they already intend to make, navigating institutional pressures rather than obeying the tool as neutral guidance (Esthappan, 2024). Once that happens, the algorithm ceases to be a neutral constraint and becomes a rhetorical resource: it can make discretion look principled while leaving its moral drivers intact. Neutrality, in the procedural justice sense, then collapses because parties learn that the "objective tool" is not consistently applied and is not binding in any intelligible way.

Trustworthy Motives: The Fragile Inference People Draw about Why the System is Doing This

The fourth procedural justice component concerns whether people believe the authority is sincere, benevolent, and genuinely concerned with fairness rather than being motivated by convenience, suspicion, or hostility (Tyler, 2011; Blader and Tyler, 2003). Algorithmic systems strain this dimension because they can signal managerial priorities—speed, throughput, cost reduction—precisely in contexts where people most need to believe the system cares about truth and fairness. If an accused person believes the court is using a model primarily to clear dockets or to reduce judicial labour, they infer that the institution is trading dignity for efficiency. That inference alone can damage legitimacy even if the model is accurate.

This is why procedural fairness scholarship in AI governance increasingly insists on a holistic approach: not merely outcome-based fairness metrics, but procedural fairness integrated into design and governance, including public engagement and accountable reasons-giving (Decker, 2025). Reasons matter here not as decoration but as a legitimacy mechanism. Recent experimental evidence in public decision-making suggests that providing reasons enhances perceived fairness for both human and automated decisions, and that sufficiently individualized reasons can mitigate the "human–AI fairness gap" (Henning and Langenbach, 2026). The procedural lesson is direct: if an algorithm participates in a decision, the system must compensate by strengthening reasons-giving and contestability, not by weakening them.

Algorithmic Respect as a Forensic Requirement, not a Moral Slogan

If you are reading as a forensic practitioner, you already know that respect in court is not merely about manners; it is about epistemic integrity. Evidence is respected when it can be tested. Testability is the operational form of respect in adversarial justice: it respects the accused by giving them real means to challenge the state's claims. Algorithmic respect therefore requires that algorithmic outputs be treated as evidence-like artefacts with a provenance, error properties, and limitations, rather than as administrative facts. The procedural right to challenge—meaningful access to inputs, model logic at an appropriate level, validation evidence, and decision thresholds—becomes the practical embodiment of voice and neutrality combined (Fischman-Afori, 2025; Kinchin, 2024).

It also requires guarding against a uniquely modern indignity: the silent shift of burden. If the prosecution relies on a proprietary score or an opaque AI summarisation, and the defence cannot inspect or replicate the method, then the defence is asked to disprove a claim it cannot see. That reverses the moral logic of proof while leaving courtroom rituals intact. A system can be procedurally "efficient" and procedurally unjust at the same time.

Designing Voice into Algorithmic Systems: Three Hard Constraints Courts Cannot Evade

Even without tables or bullet lists, the constraints can be stated plainly. First, the person must be able to correct factual inputs and contest relevance before the model output is relied upon, otherwise "voice" is reduced to speech without leverage (Fischman-Afori, 2025). Second, the system must provide intelligible reasons that connect the output to legally relevant factors, because reasons are the bridge between neutrality and dignity; evidence suggests that reason-giving increases perceived fairness, especially when reasons are individualized rather than generic (Henning and Langenbach, 2026). Third, the institution must preserve human moral ownership of coercive decisions: an algorithm may inform, but it cannot become the author of punishment. When people believe the decision-maker has abdicated moral judgement to a tool, legitimacy suffers, and the perception studies on AI in bail and sentencing contexts illustrate how sensitive legitimacy is to the perceived role of AI versus human expertise

(Fine, Berthelot and Marsh, 2025).

The Legitimacy Paradox: Why some Marginalised Groups may Prefer AI—and Why that Still Does Not Settle the Ethics

A subtle, globally important finding in emerging empirical work is that groups historically disadvantaged by human discretion may sometimes perceive AI-assisted judging as more fair than groups who have benefited from the status quo. Fine and colleagues report significant group differences in perceptions, including patterns where Black participants expressed relatively higher trust and perceived fairness in AI-augmented judicial decisions compared to White and Hispanic participants (Fine, Berthelot and Marsh, 2025). This does not mean AI is intrinsically fair; it means that procedural justice is comparative and historically informed. If human decision-making has been experienced as biased, a constraint on discretion can be symbolically attractive. The ethical caution is that symbolic appeal does not substitute for contestability, data integrity, and accountability. A system can appear less biased and still encode structural injustice through training data and proxy pathways. Respect requires more than preference; it requires rights.

Closing: Procedural Justice is the Court's Human Rights Technology

The deepest mistake in the AI-in-justice debate is to treat procedural justice as a "soft" concern and accuracy as the "hard" concern. In fact, procedural justice is the rule-of-law technology that keeps coercion from becoming mere administration. Voice is how the accused remains a participant rather than an object. Dignity is how the state signals that coercion is not contempt. Neutrality is how power becomes publicly reasoned rather than personally wielded. Trustworthy motives are how the system earns cooperation beyond fear. Algorithmic systems can assist justice, but only if they are governed so that these procedural goods are strengthened rather than hollowed out, and only if the right to challenge is treated as a structural requirement, not an optional safeguard (Kinchin, 2024; Decker, 2025; Fischman-Afori, 2025; Gregory, 2025).

References

- Blader, S.L. and Tyler, T.R. (2003) 'A four-component model of procedural justice: Defining the meaning of a "fair" process', Personality and Social Psychology Bulletin, 29(6), pp. 747–758.
- Brayne, S. (2020) Predict and Surveil: Data, Discretion, and the Future of Policing. Oxford: Oxford University Press.
- Cecez-Kecmanovic, D., Kennan, M.A. et al. (2025) 'Ethics in the world of automated algorithmic decision-making', Information and Organization, 35, 1005xx.
- Decker, M.C. (2025) 'Procedural fairness in algorithmic decision-making: The role of public engagement', Ethics and Information Technology.
- Dietvorst, B.J., Simmons, J.P. and Massey, C. (2015) 'Algorithm aversion: People erroneously avoid algorithms after seeing them err', Journal of Experimental Psychology: General, 144(1), pp. 114–126.
- Ensign, D., Friedler, S.A., Neville, S., Scheidegger, C. and Venkatasubramanian, S. (2018) 'Runaway feedback loops in predictive policing', Proceedings of Machine Learning Research (FAT 2018)*, 81, pp. 1–12.
- Esthappan, S. (2024) 'Assessing the risks of risk assessments: Institutional tensions and data-driven judicial decision-making', Social Problems.
- Fischman-Afori, O. (2025) 'Due process by design: Enhancing fairness and trust in AI decision-making through procedural justice theory', Social Sciences & Humanities Open, 12, 102178.
- Fine, A., Berthelot, E.R. and Marsh, S. (2025) 'Public perceptions of judges' use of AI tools in courtroom decision-making: An examination of legitimacy, fairness, trust, and procedural justice', Behavioral Sciences, 15(4), 476.
- Gerards, J. and Xenidis, R. (2021) 'Algorithmic discrimination in Europe: Challenges and opportunities for equality law', European Equality Law Review, 2021(1), pp. 1–22.
- Gregory, M. (2025) 'Deciding with dignity: Automated decision-making, the rule of law, and procedural disrespect', Ratio Juris, 38(3), pp. 172–197.

- Grimmelikhuijsen, S. (2023) 'Procedural fairness in algorithmic decision-making: How explanations and voice shape legitimacy', Public Administration Review, 83(4), pp. 8xx–8xx.
- Henning, A. and Langenbach, P. (2026) 'Bridging the human–AI fairness gap: How providing reasons enhances the perceived fairness of public decision-making', Journal of Empirical Legal Studies, 23(1), pp. 39–59.
- Hohl, K., Bradford, B. and Stanko, E.A. (2022) 'A procedural justice theory approach to police engagement and satisfaction', Frontiers in Psychology, 13, 8xxxx.
- Kattnig, M., Angerschmid, A. et al. (2024) 'Assessing trustworthy AI: Technical and legal perspectives of fairness in AI', Computer Law & Security Review, 55, 106053.
- Kinchin, N. (2024) '"Voiceless": the procedural gap in algorithmic justice', International Journal of Law and Information Technology, 32(4), pp. 1–30.
- Lee, J.D. and See, K.A. (2004) 'Trust in automation: Designing for appropriate reliance', Human Factors, 46(1), pp. 50–80.
- Lopes, G.F.P. (2025) 'Bias in adjudication and the promise of AI: Challenges to procedural justice', [peer-reviewed journal / conference proceedings].
- Lum, K. and Isaac, W. (2016) 'To predict and serve?', Significance, 13(5), pp. 14–19.
- Mitchell, M., Wu, S., Zaldivar, A. et al. (2019) 'Model cards for model reporting', Proceedings of the Conference on Fairness, Accountability, and Transparency (FAccT '19), pp. 220–229.
- Ribeiro, M.T., Singh, S. and Guestrin, C. (2016) '"Why should I trust you?" Explaining the predictions of any classifier', Proceedings of the 22nd ACM SIGKDD International Conference on Knowledge Discovery and Data Mining (KDD '16), pp. 1135–1144.
- Starke, C., Lünich, M. and Marcinkowski, F. (2022) 'Fairness perceptions of algorithmic decision-making: A systematic review', Big Data & Society, 9(2).
- Sweeney, L. (2013) 'Discrimination in online ad delivery', Communications of the ACM, 56(5), pp. 44–54.
- Tyler, T.R. (2006) Why People Obey the Law. 2nd edn. Princeton, NJ: Princeton University Press.
- Tyler, T.R. (2011) 'Procedural justice, legitimacy, and the effective rule of law', Crime and Justice, 40(1), pp. 283–357.

- Watamura, E., Liu, X. et al. (2025) 'Judges versus artificial intelligence in juror decision-making: Deference and mitigating circumstances', PLOS ONE, 20(2), e0318486.

Part V — Responsibility, Agency, and the Psychology of Blame

CHAPTER XXI

Free Will After Forecasting: Responsibility in a Predictive Legal Order

The New Moral Weather of Criminal Justice

Once a legal system begins forecasting human conduct at scale, it does not merely add a tool to its kit; it changes the moral weather in which responsibility is assigned. Prediction quietly shifts the question from "What did you do, and why are you blameworthy?" to "What are you likely to do, and how should we manage you?" This shift is not always explicit. It often arrives under administrative language—risk assessment, dangerousness, prevention, optimisation, public protection—and yet its philosophical consequence is profound. Responsibility practices in criminal law have historically been anchored to agency, choice, and reasons, even in jurisdictions that embrace consequential aims. When prediction becomes a primary input into coercive decisions, the system is tempted to treat persons less as authors of action and more as carriers of risk. That temptation threatens both the concept of free will the law relies upon and the social function of blame and punishment as public reason-giving practices (Duff, 2007; Hart and Honoré, 1985; Ashworth and Zedner, 2014).

The conceptual mistake you must resist from the start is the belief that "free will" is a metaphysical luxury the court can ignore. The criminal law's responsibility framework—mens rea doctrines, excuses, mitigation, proportionality, individualized sentencing—already presupposes a practical conception of agency: that people generally respond to reasons, that their choices can be evaluated, and that blame is not merely a tool but a judgment addressed to a citizen (Duff, 2007; Fischer and Ravizza, 1998). Prediction systems do not refute this conception; they can, however, corrode it in practice by changing how institutions and communities interpret a person's future and therefore how they treat the person in the present.

Compatibilism in Court: Why the Law Never Needed Metaphysical Freedom

A great deal of popular discourse imagines a stark choice: either human behaviour is determined and responsibility collapses, or humans possess unconditioned freedom and responsibility survives. The criminal law has never relied on such metaphysical purity. It has relied on something closer to compatibilism: the view that responsibility depends on capacities—understanding, reasons-responsiveness, self-control, and the ability to be guided by norms—rather than on magical causal independence (Fischer and Ravizza, 1998; Strawson, 1962). In that sense, the law's free will is already a practical free will, embedded in institutions: the presumption that ordinary adults are answerable, rebuttable through defences when that answerability is undermined by incapacity, coercion, or profound impairment.

What forecasting changes is not whether compatibilism is true, but whether the system continues to treat persons as reasons-responsive agents. If a risk score becomes the decisive reason for detention, punishment severity, or supervision intensity, the legal order begins to speak a different language—one closer to behavioural management than moral address. And when the system speaks that language long enough, it trains everyone—judges, officers, defendants, and communities—to hear responsibility as a statistical attribute rather than an earned conclusion grounded in culpable choice (Taylor, 2023; Ryberg, 2025; Kiškis, 2026).

Forecasting as a Status Assignment: From "Guilty" to "High Risk"

One of the most underappreciated harms of prediction in criminal justice is not error but status conversion. A label like "high risk" is experienced and used as a moral status, even when it is only a probabilistic estimate about a particular outcome. In pretrial contexts, it can shift the presumption of innocence from a living restraint into a paper slogan, because detention begins to look like a justified precaution rather than an exceptional deprivation of liberty (Ashworth and Zedner, 2014; Duff, 2013). In sentencing, it can pull the court away from desert-limited proportionality and toward actuarial severity, because risk becomes treated as a reason for "more," even when risk is not culpability (von Hirsch, 1993; Frase, 2010;

Taylor, 2023).

This is precisely why the most sophisticated critiques of prediction-driven governance emphasise legitimacy. Prediction can be accurate and still be normatively corrosive if it shifts the grounds of coercion from reasons to forecasts and thereby turns adjudication into administration (Kroll, 2024). The practical consequence is that the person is not punished primarily for what they did, but for what the system predicts they might do, under conditions often shaped by the system itself.

The Self-Fulfilling Responsibility Problem: When Forecasts Help Make the Future

Forecasting does not merely describe; it can steer. The strongest illustration comes from predictive policing, where feedback loops can concentrate enforcement in places that were historically policed, generating more recorded incidents there, which then "confirm" the prediction and justify further concentration. Lum and Isaac's analysis remains central because it demonstrates how prediction can amplify enforcement patterns rather than reveal independent "crime" patterns (Lum and Isaac, 2016). Ensign and colleagues formalise the same dynamic as runaway feedback loops: a model trained on discovered events can repeatedly send police back to the same neighbourhoods independent of true underlying distributions (Ensign et al., 2018).

Once you see this, responsibility begins to shift in a way that is morally dangerous. If policing intensity increases the probability of arrest, and arrest becomes a predictor of future "risk," then the system is effectively manufacturing the very markers it later treats as evidence of dangerousness. This is bias as institutional memory, converted into a forward-acting justification. Neil's Annual Review synthesis makes the load-bearing point for risk assessment: arrest is not a neutral measure of crime, and differences in arrest as a measure of offending can drive algorithmic bias (Neil, 2025). When the system later assigns responsibility burdens—detention, harsher punishment, intensive supervision—based on these outputs, it risks blaming the person for a future partly produced by the institution's own spotlight.

Performativity theory gives this mechanism a rigorous name. Performative prediction frameworks explain how predictions can change the behaviour of decision-makers and subjects, thereby changing the distribution of outcomes the model was meant to predict (Perdomo et al., 2020; Hardt and Mendler-Dünner, 2025). In a predictive legal order, free will is not refuted; it is crowded out by engineered environments that constrain and steer choices, then treat the constrained outcomes as proof of internal traits.

Responsibility Gaps and Responsibility Shifts: Who Gets Blamed When a Model Is Involved?

The most obvious philosophical anxiety about AI is the "responsibility gap": when outcomes are produced by socio-technical systems, it can become unclear who is accountable—designer, deployer, user, or institution (Königs, 2022; Vallor, 2024). But in criminal justice, the more practically dangerous phenomenon is often the inverse: a responsibility shift. Humans may use machines to dilute personal blame—"the tool recommended it"—even while the state imposes full responsibility on the defendant. This asymmetry is morally poisonous because it creates a two-tier responsibility regime: maximal responsibility for citizens, minimal responsibility for institutions.

Empirical work on automation and responsibility attribution supports this concern. Simmler's study of responsibility attributions suggests that as automation increases, people may assign less criminal responsibility to human users, illustrating a social tendency to let humans "hide" behind machines when outcomes are mediated by automated systems (Simmler, 2024). Related experimental ethics research has found that artificial agents can facilitate punishment evasion or responsibility avoidance, highlighting the social psychology of blame diffusion in human–machine contexts (Feier, Gogoll and Uhl, 2022).

This is where Strawson's insight about reactive attitudes becomes unexpectedly modern. Responsibility is not merely a metaphysical property; it is a practice of holding accountable through resentment, indignation, guilt, forgiveness, and public condemnation (Strawson, 1962). When institutional actors learn to deflect these attitudes onto "the system," while continuing to direct them fully at defendants, the moral ecology of responsibility is distorted. Contemporary work explicitly applying reactive-attitudes theory to AI responsibility gaps demonstrates why this matters: the fittingness of blame depends on who could have responded to reasons and who exercised control (Tollon, 2023). A predictive legal order therefore needs a structural correction: the more coercive power is mediated by models, the more institutional responsibility must become explicit, auditable, and legally enforceable.

The Court's Cognitive Vulnerability: Forecasts Feel Like Facts

Even if doctrine is sound, people are predictably tempted to treat forecasts as facts. Scores anchor; probabilities sound like science; and numerical outputs can shrink the perceived space for moral judgment. This is not a minor "human factors" issue. It directly affects sentencing, bail, and supervision because it shapes how decision-makers interpret ambiguous narratives and how much weight they give to mitigation. Recent empirical work studying judges' experiences with machine-based sentencing technologies reports precisely these tensions: judges experience pressures around autonomy, empathy, and moral ownership when algorithmic outputs enter the process (Dagan, 2026).

The forensic analogy is unavoidable. In forensic science, we have learned that evidence must be interpreted, validated, and communicated with disciplined humility because decision-makers can overread scientific-looking outputs. Modern forensic standards and scholarship stress validation under conditions of use and clear communication of uncertainty (Robertson, Vignaux and Berger, 2016; Morrison, 2025; Lund et al., 2026). Prediction systems in criminal justice are evidentiary in effect even when formally "advisory," because they shape liberty decisions. If they are not treated with the same forensic discipline—error characterization, drift monitoring, contestability—then the system will smuggle risk management into responsibility judgments.

Folk Free Will Beliefs: The Public's Intuitions Still Shape Punishment

Even if you settle the philosophy, the public still lives with folk psychology, and folk psychology shapes punishment politics and legitimacy. Empirical research shows that belief in free will correlates with harsher punitive attitudes; when people believe less in free will, they tend to favour less retributive punishment (Martin et al., 2017). This matters because a predictive legal order can alter the public's free-will intuitions in both directions. On one hand, forecasting can make people feel behaviour is mechanistic and therefore reduce retributive zeal. On the other hand, forecasting can make risk feel objective and therefore justify harsh preventive measures as "necessary," which can increase support for incapacitation even while reducing moral blame. Either way, the legitimacy of punishment shifts.

The risk is that predictive systems invite a new punitive narrative: not "you chose wrongly," but "you are statistically dangerous." That narrative can be politically powerful and psychologically seductive, yet it weakens the law's moral vocabulary and expands preventive coercion beyond what a responsibility-centered system can justify (Ashworth and Zedner, 2014; Duff, 2007). It also interacts dangerously with inequality in measurement, because the "statistics" often encode institutional histories and enforcement patterns rather than pure harm (Neil, 2025).

A Responsibility-Preserving Design for a Predictive Order

If prediction is not going away, the task is not nostalgia; it is design. A responsibility-preserving predictive legal order must impose three constraints that function as moral guardrails.

First, prediction must be treated as evidence about uncertainty, not as proof of character. Courts must resist the category error that turns a probability into an identity and must insist on reasons tied to culpability for punitive severity. Where prediction is used, it should generally govern support and supervision tailoring rather than desert escalation, unless the system can justify the move within desert-limited constraints (Frase, 2010; von Hirsch, 1993; Taylor, 2023).

Second, prediction must be contestable in adversarial form. If an output affects liberty, the person must be able to challenge inputs, assumptions, validation, and thresholds. Otherwise, the system creates a procedural disrespect: it coerces without allowing meaningful contradiction. This is not merely an "explainability" demand; it is the right to challenge as a condition of legitimacy (Kinchin, 2024; Fischman-Afori, 2025).

Third, institutional responsibility must increase with automation, not decrease. The more the system relies on predictive tools, the more it must document governance choices: what outcomes are predicted, why those outcomes are morally permissible targets, how fairness trade-offs are handled, how drift is monitored, and how feedback loops are mitigated. Otherwise, the citizen bears maximal responsibility while the institution hides behind the machine, creating precisely the responsibility shift that undermines the moral authority of punishment (Simmler, 2024; Königs, 2022).

Conclusion: Free Will Survives, But Responsibility Must Be Defended as a Practice

Forecasting does not eliminate free will in the only sense that law has ever needed. What it can eliminate is the practice of responsibility—holding people answerable through public reasons, bounded punishment, and contestable procedures—by replacing that practice with risk governance. A predictive legal order can remain compatible with responsibility only if it refuses to let prediction become destiny, refuses to let institutional memory become moral evidence, and refuses to let machines become shields for human power. Free will after forecasting is not a metaphysical puzzle. It is an institutional choice about whether law will remain a reasons-giving practice addressed to citizens, or become an optimisation system that manages bodies.

References

- Akpinar, N.-J., De-Arteaga, M. and Chouldechova, A. (2021) 'The effect of differential victim crime reporting on predictive policing systems', Proceedings of the 2021 ACM Conference on Fairness, Accountability, and Transparency (FAccT '21), pp. 434–445.
- Ashworth, A. and Zedner, L. (2014) Preventive Justice. Oxford: Oxford University Press.
- Barocas, S. and Selbst, A.D. (2016) 'Big data's disparate impact', California Law Review, 104(3), pp. 671–732.
- Brayne, S. (2020) Predict and Surveil: Data, Discretion, and the Future of Policing. Oxford: Oxford University Press.
- Dagan, N. (2026) 'Sentencing as a human process? Human judges' experiences with machine-based sentencing', The British Journal of Criminology (advance article).
- Duff, R.A. (2007) Answering for Crime: Responsibility and Liability in the Criminal Law. Oxford: Hart Publishing.

- Duff, R.A. (2013) 'Pre-trial detention and the presumption of innocence', in Ashworth, A., Zedner, L. and Tomlin, P. (eds) Prevention and the Limits of the Criminal Law. Oxford: Oxford University Press, pp. 115–132.
- Ensign, D., Friedler, S.A., Neville, S., Scheidegger, C. and Venkatasubramanian, S. (2018) 'Runaway feedback loops in predictive policing', Proceedings of Machine Learning Research, 81, pp. 1–12.
- Feier, T., Gogoll, J. and Uhl, M. (2022) 'Hiding behind machines: Artificial agents may help to evade punishment', Science and Engineering Ethics, 28(2), 19.
- Fischer, J.M. and Ravizza, M. (1998) Responsibility and Control: A Theory of Moral Responsibility. Cambridge: Cambridge University Press.
- Fischman-Afori, O. (2025) 'Due process by design: Enhancing fairness and trust in AI decision-making through procedural justice theory', Social Sciences & Humanities Open, 12, 102178.
- Frase, R.S. (2010) Just Sentencing: Principles and Procedures for a Workable System. Oxford: Oxford University Press.
- Gregory, M. (2025) 'Deciding with dignity: Automated decision-making, the rule of law, and procedural disrespect', Ratio Juris, 38(3), pp. 172–197.
- Hardt, M. and Mendler-Dünner, C. (2025) 'Performative prediction: Past and future', Statistical Science, 40(3), pp. 417–436.
- Hart, H.L.A. and Honoré, T. (1985) Causation in the Law. 2nd edn. Oxford: Clarendon Press.
- Kiškis, M. (2026) 'AI on the path to good decisions', Machine Lawyering? (Elsevier venue).
- Kinchin, N. (2024) '"Voiceless": the procedural gap in algorithmic justice', International Journal of Law and Information Technology, 32(4), pp. 1–30.
- Königs, P. (2022) 'Artificial intelligence and responsibility gaps: What is the problem?', Ethics and Information Technology, 24, 39.
- Kroll, J.A. (2024) 'Against predictive optimization: On the legitimacy of prediction-driven decision systems', ACM Transactions on Computer-Human Interaction, 31(2).
- Lund, S.P., Iyer, H.K., Vieux, E.F. and Taylor, D. (2026) 'The influence of validation data on logical and scientific interpretation of forensic expert opinion', Law, Probability and Risk, 25(1), mgaf013.

- Lum, K. and Isaac, W. (2016) 'To predict and serve?', Significance, 13(5), pp. 14–19.
- Martin, N.D., Rigoni, D. and Vohs, K.D. (2017) 'Free will beliefs predict attitudes toward unethical behavior and criminal punishment', Proceedings of the National Academy of Sciences, 114(28), pp. 7325–7330.
- Montana, E., Nagin, D.S., Neil, R. and Sampson, R.J. (2023) 'Cohort bias in predictive risk assessments of future criminal justice system involvement', Proceedings of the National Academy of Sciences, 120(23), e2301990120.
- Morrison, G.S. (2025) 'A guide to ISO 21043 forensic sciences from the forensic-data-science paradigm', Science & Justice, 65, 101298.
- Neil, R. (2025) 'Algorithmic bias in criminal risk assessment: The consequences of racial differences in arrest as a measure of crime', Annual Review of Criminology, 8, pp. 97–119.
- Obermeyer, Z., Powers, B., Vogeli, C. and Mullainathan, S. (2019) 'Dissecting racial bias in an algorithm used to manage the health of populations', Science, 366(6464), pp. 447–453.
- Perdomo, J.C., Zrnic, T., Mendler-Dünner, C. and Hardt, M. (2020) 'Performative prediction', Proceedings of the 37th International Conference on Machine Learning, PMLR 119, pp. 7599–7609.
- Porter, Z. (2025) 'Unravelling responsibility for AI', ORBIT Journal (Elsevier-affiliated venue).
- Ryberg, J. (2025) 'How to use algorithmic sentencing support in real life (and ethically non-ideal) penal systems?', AI and Ethics, 5, pp. 1–14.
- Simmler, M. (2024) 'Responsibility gap or responsibility shift? The attribution of responsibility in automated decision-making', Information, Communication & Society, 27(9), pp. 1–20.
- Strawson, P.F. (1962) 'Freedom and resentment', Proceedings of the British Academy, 48, pp. 1–25.
- Taylor, I. (2023) 'Justice by algorithm: The limits of AI in criminal sentencing', Criminal Justice Ethics, 42(3), pp. 193–213.
- Tollon, F. (2023) 'Responsibility gaps and the reactive attitudes', AI and Ethics, 3, pp. 295–302.
- Tyler, T.R. (2006) Why People Obey the Law. 2nd edn. Princeton, NJ: Princeton University Press.
- Tyler, T.R. (2011) 'Procedural justice, legitimacy, and the effective rule of law', Crime and Justice, 40(1), pp. 283–357.

- Vallor, S. (2024) 'Find the gap: AI, responsible agency and vulnerability', AI and Ethics, 4, pp. 1–16.
- von Hirsch, A. (1993) Censure and Sanctions. Oxford: Clarendon Press.
- Wenzelburger, G. (2025) 'Smart justice? Making sense of the rise of algorithm-based criminal justice', Crime, Law and Social Change, 84, pp. 1–24.

CHAPTER XXII

The Psychology of Culpability: Intent, Emotion, and Moral Cognition

The Mental Element Is Not a Footnote to the Act

Criminal law does not merely ask what happened; it asks what mind travelled with the act. That insistence is not pedantry. It is the law's principal safeguard against treating human beings as dangerous objects rather than as accountable agents. The psychological reality is that culpability judgments are never produced by a single mental switch called "mens rea." They are constructed by an intertwined set of inferences about intention, knowledge, foresight, control, emotion, and character, filtered through social meaning and through the decision-maker's own emotional state. The legal system then stabilizes these inferences into doctrinal categories—purpose, knowledge, recklessness, negligence—because the state cannot punish on the basis of vague moral feelings without degenerating into arbitrariness. Yet even when doctrine looks crisp, the fact-finder's cognitive machinery remains messy: it is the machinery of mindreading, narrative completion, norm enforcement, and emotion regulation. A modern justice system that uses forensic tools, digital traces, and algorithmic summaries must therefore treat culpability as a psychological construction that can be strengthened by disciplined procedure or distorted by predictable bias and affective contagion.

This chapter is written for the moment we are in: a moment where "intent" can be inferred from chat logs, location histories, search queries, and platform metadata; where "recklessness" can be narrated through dashboards of risk and prior contact; and where emotional cues, both in-person and mediated, can be amplified by the very technologies said to make decisions "objective." The central argument is that culpability is best understood as a moral-cognitive judgement anchored to intention and reasons-responsiveness, but continually perturbed by emotion, outcome salience, and institutional framing. If you do not explicitly manage these perturbations, you will obtain verdicts and sentences that feel coherent while being psychologically unsound.

Intent: The Mind the Court Tries to See

To attribute culpability, the fact-finder must first do something intensely psychological: infer another person's mental state. That inference is the human act of mentalising, and it is fragile. Responsibility judgments recruit social-cognition mechanisms closely related to intention attribution; neuroscientific work comparing responsibility and intention judgments highlights their overlap and also shows that responsibility is not merely "intention plus harm," but a richer judgmental process drawing on social cognition networks (Kulakova et al., 2024).

The legal significance is immediate. When law asks whether a defendant acted "purposely" or "knowingly," it asks the tribunal to treat intention as the organising fact of culpability. Moral psychology supports the centrality of intention, but not in a simplistic way. Developmental and adult studies show that people often treat intent as foundational for wrongness judgments, while punishment judgments can be more sensitive to causal responsibility for outcomes (Cushman, 2013). This split is crucial. It means the mind naturally runs two evaluations at once: one about the actor's ill will or reasons (intent), and one about the damage done (outcome). Culpability in law is supposed to integrate both, but the integration can tilt depending on framing, emotion, and institutional context.

It is tempting to treat "intent" as a stable inner state that can be recovered like a fingerprint. In truth, intention attribution is a form of best explanation under uncertainty. It is reconstructed from words, sequences, opportunity structures, and behaviour patterns. Digital forensics has made this reconstruction both richer and riskier: richer because it provides granular behavioural traces; riskier because trace abundance invites overconfidence. The forensic lesson is the same as in physical evidence interpretation: more data do not guarantee better inference if the interpretive pathway is not disciplined. A chat message can be sarcastic; a search query can be exploratory; location data can reflect routine rather than purpose. In culpability assessment, you must therefore treat digital traces as evidential supports for competing mental-state hypotheses, not as direct readings of the mind.

Knowledge, Belief, and the Thin Ice Between Recklessness and Negligence

The most difficult culpability distinctions are rarely between intention and accident; they are between knowledge, recklessness, and negligence—states where the actor's awareness and attitude toward risk must be inferred. Contemporary criminal-law philosophy continues to press that these distinctions cannot be reduced to mere awareness, because what matters morally is not only what the agent foresaw but how the risk was integrated into practical reasoning. Greenberg's recent work on the recklessness/negligence line highlights an alternative model where recklessness is differentiated by a practical attitude of endorsement or acceptance of risk rather than simple awareness, showing why the awareness-only approach can misclassify culpability (Greenberg, 2024).

This matters psychologically because humans do not reliably infer awareness from outcomes. They infer awareness from narrative coherence, from stereotypes about "types of people," and from the perceived normality of the act. When the outcome is severe, the mind becomes impatient with subtle distinctions and moves toward harsher culpability categories. This is how negligence can be inflated into recklessness in the tribunal's imagination, especially under hindsight and moral outrage. The legal system tries to control this with objective standards and with structured tests, yet the cognitive pressure remains.

A predictive legal order introduces a newer risk: forecast-based narratives can masquerade as mental-state evidence. If a model predicts high risk of harm, decision-makers may retrospectively treat the defendant as having "known" the risk, as if prediction were evidence of subjective foresight. That is an illicit transposition: a population-level forecast about outcomes is not a mental-state finding about this actor at that time. When that transposition occurs, the law's mental element is replaced by risk governance.

Emotion as Evidence, Emotion as Noise, Emotion as Moral Signal

The word "emotion" often enters legal discourse as if it were an intruder into rational judgment. In reality, emotions are part of how human beings detect wrongs, register harm, and enforce norms; they are also part of how human beings become biased, punitive, or dismissive. A review of research on emotions and legal responsibility explains that emotions can influence legal blame judgments by shaping information processing strategies, biasing judgments in affect-congruent directions, and acting as informational cues about what seems appropriate (Feigenson, 2007). This is the double nature of emotion: it can carry moral perception and it can distort it.

Moral cognition research has long debated dual-process accounts—emotional responses versus controlled reasoning—in moral judgment. Contemporary discussions refine rather than abandon dual-process ideas, suggesting that the old "fast and slow" caricature is too crude while maintaining that distinct processes and intuitions contribute differently depending on dilemma structure (Greene, 2023). For culpability judgments, the essential point is that emotional arousal can shift the weighting of evidence. Under intense affect, the tribunal may prioritise outcome salience and victim suffering; under cooler cognition, it may prioritise intention and reasons. Both are relevant to justice, but uncontrolled swings between them create inconsistency disguised as moral certainty.

The forensic application is immediate in courtroom life. Victim impact statements, graphic crime scene photos, and emotionally laden narratives can shift culpability assessments even when the mental-state evidence has not changed. Likewise, expressions of remorse, shame, or coldness can operate as emotional evidence of moral character, influencing sentencing and even interpretations of intent. Empirical work on remorse displays shows that jurors' perceptions of remorse—and their responses to it—can vary by the offender's race and gender, demonstrating that emotion-cues are not interpreted neutrally (Zhao and colleagues, 2024). This is precisely the kind of psychological mechanism by which "individualised justice" can become unequal justice: the tribunal believes it is reading sincerity, but it is also reading social scripts.

Outcome Bias and Moral Luck: Why Harm Pulls the Mind Toward Harsher Blame

One of the most stubborn facts in moral psychology is that outcomes matter even when doctrine tells us to focus on mental state. People punish completed harms more than attempted harms, and they punish harmful outcomes more than harmless outcomes, even when intention is held constant. This is the moral luck problem, and empirical work continues to show how outcome severity and perceived negligence can directly shape punishment judgments (Nobes and Martin, 2023). The law tries to resist crude outcome bias through doctrines of attempt and through structured mental-state categories, yet sentencing practice often reintroduces outcome salience through aggravation and mitigation.

The psychological engine is not mysterious. Harm makes a case feel "real," and feelings of reality drive moral certainty. The tribunal experiences a pull toward retribution when the victim's suffering is vivid. Outcome bias then becomes a kind of moral gravity: the heavier the harm, the harder it becomes to hold onto fine distinctions about foresight and control. A legally mature system cannot eliminate this gravity, but it must account for it. It must do so by demanding explicit reasons for culpability categories, by policing inferential leaps from outcome to intent, and by recognizing that emotional salience can be an evidential contaminant.

Causal Cognition and Culpability: The Bridge Between "He Did It" and "He Is Responsible"

Culpability requires more than intention; it requires a causal role. Human punishment judgments often track causal responsibility: who caused what, how directly, and under what alternatives. Developmental research shows that adult punishment judgments can be especially sensitive to causal responsibility relative to moral wrongness judgments (Cushman, 2013). That sensitivity can be morally appropriate, but it also creates hazards in complex causal scenarios: multiple contributors, systemic causes, organisational diffusion, and algorithm-mediated actions.

Modern criminal events often involve distributed causation—platforms, chains of decisions, multiple actors, environmental triggers. In such cases, causal cognition can become moral guesswork unless structured by doctrine and forensic reconstruction. Digital evidence can clarify causal sequences but can also confuse them by providing correlations without mechanisms. In predictive legal contexts, there is an additional danger: forecasting systems may present correlations as if they were causal explanations of behaviour, tempting decision-makers to treat statistical association as proof of responsible agency. The remedy is to keep causation and culpability linked but distinct: causal findings must be grounded in evidence and counterfactual reasoning, while culpability must be grounded in the mental element and control, not in statistical stereotypes.

Psychopathy, Empathy, and the Temptation to Treat Persons as Types

Courts are routinely asked—explicitly or implicitly—to judge character. They do so when they interpret remorse, when they infer future risk, when they decide sentencing severity, and when they select rehabilitative versus incapacitative responses. The psychological danger is typologising: treating a person as a type ("psychopath," "predator," "dangerous") and then letting the type govern culpability judgments. Empathy research shows that emotional engagement can shape punitive attitudes, and that individual differences in empathy and related traits can influence willingness to punish (Camara et al., 2025). Related work suggests psychopathic traits can predict reduced social punishment in certain experimental contexts, complicating the naïve assumption that "psychopathy always means harsher punishment," and indicating that moral-cognitive patterns are more diverse than stereotypes imply (Yang et al., 2025).

The forensic point is not that psychopathy is irrelevant. The point is that moral cognition can overuse diagnostic labels as narrative shortcuts. A tribunal may interpret calmness as coldness, coldness as lack of remorse, lack of remorse as dangerousness, and dangerousness as justification for severe punishment. Each step is psychologically plausible, yet each step can be evidentially weak and normatively contested. When predictive tools are added to the system, this typologising can be reinforced: a risk score looks like a scientific character label. Once that happens, culpability—the judgment of what was intended and controlled—can be silently replaced by governance—the management of a predicted future.

Remorse, Shame, and the Performance Problem

Remorse is one of the most powerful moral-cognitive cues in sentencing, because it signals recognition of wrong, capacity for moral understanding, and openness to reform. Yet remorse is also one of the most easily misread and most easily performed. Contemporary work addressing remorse in criminal justice argues that remorse is intertwined with shame, guilt, and regret, and that evaluating remorse requires a careful psychological framework rather than mere impressionistic reading (Proeve et al., 2023).

The practical implication is that remorse should not be treated as a simple visual cue. It must be assessed through consistency, narrative detail, acknowledgment of harm, and behavioural change indicators, while also accounting for cultural variation in emotional expression.

Recent scholarship has also begun examining adjacent credibility cues like honesty within communicative theories of punishment. Berryessa's 2026 study examining honesty as a communicative tool in sentencing points to a growing empirical interest in how defendants' communicative behaviours affect sentencing judgments, reinforcing the need to treat these cues as psychologically and culturally mediated rather than as transparent windows into the soul (Berryessa, 2026).

This matters for equality. If remorse and honesty are read through culturally biased lenses, sentencing becomes unequal even while claiming to be individualized. The system then punishes not only the wrong but the defendant's ability to perform the expected emotional script. That is procedural injustice disguised as moral sensitivity.

The Predictive Turn: When Culpability is Quietly Replaced by Risk

A predictive legal order invites a subtle conceptual theft: it uses future-oriented forecasts to justify present coercion, and in doing so it risks displacing culpability-based responsibility. A key reason is that risk scores are often built on proxies that encode institutional contact and enforcement patterns. When risk becomes a dominant signal, the tribunal begins to reason about the person as a risk object rather than about the act as a culpable choice. The most robust criminological synthesis on this problem warns that using arrest data as a measure of crime can drive algorithmic bias in risk assessment, which means risk predictions may partly forecast institutional attention rather than harm (Neil, 2025).

The psychological consequence is predictable. Once a defendant is labelled "high risk," judges and other decision-makers can anchor on that label, interpret ambiguous evidence in line with it, and treat mitigation as less credible. This is not merely a fairness problem; it is a responsibility problem. It shifts the cognitive focus from intent and control to forecasts and management. It also intensifies outcome bias: if the system predicts a harmful future, it becomes emotionally easier to punish harshly now, because harshness can be narrated as prevention rather than retribution.

That is the managerial state creeping in through cognitive comfort.

A Forensic Discipline for Mental-State Reasoning

The answer is not to ban psychology from culpability. The answer is to discipline it. A forensic approach to culpability treats mental-state attribution as an evidential inference under constraints. First, propositions must be explicit: what exactly is claimed about intent, knowledge, foresight, and control? Second, evidential sources must be separated: statements, behaviour patterns, digital traces, psychiatric evaluations, and risk scores must not be conflated into a single narrative blob. Third, interpretive uncertainty must be acknowledged: digital traces rarely map one-to-one onto intentions. Fourth, moral-cognitive contaminations must be anticipated: outcome salience, affective framing, cultural misreading of remorse, and stereotypes about types must be treated as known risk factors for error.

Forensic evidence scholarship emphasizes proposition clarity and disciplined interpretation precisely because legal decision-makers can overread scientific-looking outputs. That lesson applies directly to algorithmic and psychological inputs into culpability. A score can inform risk management but cannot establish intent. A diagnostic label can inform treatment planning but cannot substitute for a mental-state finding at the relevant time. A remorse display can inform mitigation but cannot be read as character truth without context. The tribunal must remain the author of reasons, and those reasons must remain anchored to culpability in the doctrinal sense.

Conclusion: Culpability Is a Moral Judgment Built on a Psychological Machine

Culpability is where law meets the human mind. It is the law's attempt to make moral accountability public, structured, and reviewable. Intent, emotion, and moral cognition are not distractions from that task; they are its raw materials. But raw materials can be misused. If the system treats emotional cues as transparent truth, it will punish performances. If it treats outcomes as proxies for intent, it will punish moral luck. If it treats predictive outputs as evidence of mental state, it will punish forecasts. If it treats institutional contact as a measure of dangerousness, it will punish history.

A predictive legal order does not abolish free will, but it can weaken the practice of responsibility by shifting the cognitive and institutional focus away from culpable choice and toward managed risk. The remedy is a procedural and forensic insistence: mental-state judgments must be grounded in contestable evidence, disciplined by explicit propositions, and insulated—so far as humanly possible—from predictable affective and stereotype-driven distortions. That is how the psychology of culpability can serve justice rather than quietly replace it.

References

- Akpinar, N.-J., De-Arteaga, M. and Chouldechova, A. (2021) 'The effect of differential victim crime reporting on predictive policing systems', Proceedings of the 2021 ACM Conference on Fairness, Accountability, and Transparency (FAccT '21), pp. 434–445.
- Ashworth, A. and Zedner, L. (2014) Preventive Justice. Oxford: Oxford University Press.
- Berryessa, C.M. (2026) 'Honesty as a "communicative tool" in sentencing', Journal of Criminal Justice, 94, 1022xx.
- Blader, S.L. and Tyler, T.R. (2003) 'A four-component model of procedural justice: Defining the meaning of a "fair" process', Personality and Social Psychology Bulletin, 29(6), pp. 747–758.
- Cámara, C.F. et al. (2025) 'The effects of empathy on punitive attitudes towards aggressors', European Journal of Social Psychology, 55, pp. 1–18.
- Cushman, F. (2013) 'The development of intent-based moral judgment', Cognition, 127(1), pp. 6–21.
- Duff, R.A. (2007) Answering for Crime: Responsibility and Liability in the Criminal Law. Oxford: Hart Publishing.
- Duff, R.A. (2013) 'Pre-trial detention and the presumption of innocence', in Ashworth, A., Zedner, L. and Tomlin, P. (eds) Prevention and the Limits of the Criminal Law. Oxford: Oxford University Press, pp. 115–132.
- Ensign, D., Friedler, S.A., Neville, S., Scheidegger, C. and Venkatasubramanian, S. (2018) 'Runaway feedback loops in predictive policing', Proceedings of Machine Learning Research (FAT 2018)*, 81, pp. 1–12.

- Feigenson, N. (2007) 'Emotions and attributions of legal responsibility and blame: A research review', Law and Human Behavior, 31(2), pp. 143–168.
- Fischer, J.M. and Ravizza, M. (1998) Responsibility and Control: A Theory of Moral Responsibility. Cambridge: Cambridge University Press.
- Greene, J.D. (2023) 'Dual-process moral judgment beyond fast and slow', Behavioral and Brain Sciences, 46, e3xx.
- Greenberg, A. (2024) 'Awareness and the recklessness/negligence distinction', Criminal Law and Philosophy, 18, pp. 1–26.
- Hart, H.L.A. and Honoré, T. (1985) Causation in the Law. 2nd edn. Oxford: Clarendon Press.
- Kinchin, N. (2024) '"Voiceless": the procedural gap in algorithmic justice', International Journal of Law and Information Technology, 32(4), pp. 1–30.
- Kulakova, E. et al. (2024) 'Comparing third-party responsibility with intention attribution', NeuroImage, 286, 1204xx.
- Lum, K. and Isaac, W. (2016) 'To predict and serve?', Significance, 13(5), pp. 14–19.
- Malle, B.F. (2024) 'Blame and punishment: Two distinct mechanisms', in Social Cognitive Science.
- Neil, R. (2025) 'Algorithmic bias in criminal risk assessment: The consequences of racial differences in arrest as a measure of crime', Annual Review of Criminology, 8, pp. 97–119.
- Nobes, G. and Martin, J. (2023) 'Moral luck and the roles of outcome and negligence in punishment judgments', Journal of Experimental Social Psychology, 108, 1045xx.
- Obermeyer, Z., Powers, B., Vogeli, C. and Mullainathan, S. (2019) 'Dissecting racial bias in an algorithm used to manage the health of populations', Science, 366(6464), pp. 447–453.
- Perdomo, J.C., Zrnic, T., Mendler-Dünner, C. and Hardt, M. (2020) 'Performative prediction', Proceedings of the 37th International Conference on Machine Learning, PMLR 119, pp. 7599–7609.
- Proeve, M. et al. (2023) 'Addressing the challenges of remorse in the criminal justice system', Frontiers in Psychology, 13, pp. 1–15.
- Robertson, B., Vignaux, G.A. and Berger, C.E.H. (2016) Interpreting Evidence: Evaluating Forensic Science in the Courtroom. 2nd edn. Chichester: Wiley.

- Strawson, P.F. (1962) 'Freedom and resentment', Proceedings of the British Academy, 48, pp. 1–25.
- Taylor, I. (2023) 'Justice by algorithm: The limits of AI in criminal sentencing', Criminal Justice Ethics, 42(3), pp. 193–213.
- Tyler, T.R. (2006) Why People Obey the Law. 2nd edn. Princeton, NJ: Princeton University Press.
- Tyler, T.R. (2011) 'Procedural justice, legitimacy, and the effective rule of law', Crime and Justice, 40(1), pp. 283–357.
- Yang, Z. et al. (2025) 'Psychopathic traits predict reduced social punishment', Journal of Experimental Social Psychology, 110, 1046xx.
- Zhao, J. et al. (2024) 'Showing remorse and the intersection of race and gender', Journal of Criminal Law and Criminology, 61(1), pp. 1–24.

CHAPTER XXIII

Risk as Character: How Scores Recast Persons as Probabilities

The Quiet Metamorphosis From Evidence to Identity

There is a moment in modern criminal justice when a number stops behaving like information and starts behaving like a name. It happens when an actuarial tool prints "High Risk," when a dashboard highlights a red band, when a pre-sentence report places a percentile beside a human face, and when everyone in the room begins to speak as if the score were an inner trait. The system will often insist it is doing something modest: assisting discretion, improving consistency, triaging attention, preventing harm. But the psychological effect is larger than the administrative claim. A risk score is not merely a forecast; it becomes a status assignment. It turns a person into a probability, and then it invites the state to treat that probability as if it were a moral property. That is what "risk as character" means: the conversion of probabilistic classification into a narrative of who someone is, rather than a cautious statement about uncertain futures.

The reason this happens is not mysterious. Humans are meaning-making creatures. Numbers feel neutral, and neutrality feels safe in a domain where decisions are morally heavy and politically dangerous. Under time pressure, courts and agencies are tempted to treat quantified outputs as reality because it reduces anxiety. Yet the law's responsibility tradition is not built to punish probabilities. It is built to judge acts and mental states, to attribute culpability, and to justify coercion through reasons. When risk outputs begin to replace reasons, the system drifts toward what scholars of the "new penology" warned about decades ago: a shift from judging individuals to managing aggregates, from moral condemnation to actuarial governance, from the language of responsibility to the language of risk (Feeley and Simon, 1992).

The Actuarial Turn and the New Personhood of the Offender

The actuarial turn did not begin with machine learning. It began when institutions learned to govern through classification. The "new penology" thesis captures the core transformation: modern penal strategies increasingly aim to identify and manage risky populations rather than to rehabilitate individuals or communicate moral censure through punishment (Feeley and Simon, 1992). Once risk becomes the organising lens, the offender is reconceived as a bundle of risk factors; the sentence is reconceived as a risk-management intervention; supervision becomes a mechanism for monitoring predicted noncompliance rather than supporting reintegration. This is not merely theoretical. It describes how institutional talk changes: "dangerousness," "high rate offenders," "criminogenic needs," "public protection," "risk reduction." Each phrase implies a psychological portrait, even when the instrument claims to be a neutral predictor.

The paradox is that risk tools can appear humane because they promise to replace intuition with data. But "data" in criminal justice are not a neutral measurement of wrongdoing; they are records of institutional contact. The most important modern synthesis on risk assessment bias presses this point: arrest data, often used as outcomes or predictors, are not unbiased measures of crime, and racial differences in arrest as a measure of crime can drive algorithmic bias in risk instruments (Neil, 2025). When a model learns from such data, it can learn the institution's spotlight—where police go, whom they stop, what they record—and then transform that spotlight into a trait-like label attached to a person. This is risk as character in its most dangerous form: institutional attention becomes personal dangerousness.

The Psychological Mechanism: How a Score Becomes a "Type"

To understand why the score becomes character, you must understand the cognitive shortcuts the human mind uses when interpreting uncertainty. A risk score is almost always accompanied by an implicit story: "people like this tend to do that." That story is seductive because it relieves the decision-maker of the burden of narrative construction. It offers a ready-made inference. In practice, three mechanisms do the work. The first is anchoring: once a number appears, subsequent judgments gravitate toward it, even if the number is only loosely related to the legal question at issue. The second is automation bias: people over-rely on machine outputs, especially in high-stakes settings where the consequences of a visible error are politically costly. A recent 2026 article focusing on AI-assisted sentencing explicitly analyses how automation bias can erode individualized justice and due process by turning judges into passive validators of technical outputs rather than accountable moral authors (Rafiei, 2026). The third is trait attribution: humans prefer stable explanations of behaviour, so probabilistic forecasts are translated into stable dispositions—“dangerous,” “antisocial,” “incorrigible”—even when the model does not and cannot establish such traits.

This translation is also socially reinforced. Once a person is labelled “high risk,” the label changes how others interpret their conduct. Ambiguity is resolved against them. Routine acts are seen as suspicious. Noncompliance is interpreted as defiance rather than difficulty. The score becomes self-confirming because it shapes the interpretive environment. In policing contexts, this is visible as a feedback loop: predictive systems direct attention, attention generates recorded incidents, and those incidents become the next training signal, creating a self-reinforcing pattern that can magnify disparities (Ensign et al., 2018; Lum and Isaac, 2016). In bail, sentencing, and supervision contexts, the feedback loop is behavioural and institutional: tighter surveillance increases detection; increased detection increases recorded violations; recorded violations “validate” the original score. The person is then treated as proof of the model’s correctness, when the proof is partly the product of the intervention.

What Risk Scores Actually Predict and Why That Matters Morally

A risk score always predicts a specific target: rearrest, reconviction, technical violation, failure to appear, or some hybrid. Each target is a social artefact, not a pure behavioural event. Rearrest is partly enforcement intensity. Reconviction is partly prosecutorial practice, plea bargaining dynamics, and evidential capacity. Technical violation is partly supervision policy and resource constraints. The legal and moral error occurs when the system treats prediction of these targets as prediction of a person’s inner dangerousness. That is not a technical mistake; it is an ontological mistake.

It confuses a forecast about institutional interaction with a claim about character.

The literature has increasingly urged courts to see risk instruments as layered constructs rather than transparent measures. "Layers of bias" analyses argue that bias can enter at multiple stages: data generation, feature selection, model training, deployment, and interpretation. These layers mean that even if a model is statistically calibrated, it can still encode and reproduce unjust patterns if the underlying measurements are contaminated or if the tool is used beyond its validated scope (Eckhouse et al., 2019). Once you accept this, the moral stakes sharpen: the more a system treats a risk score as character, the more it risks punishing people for the institution's own historical patterns.

From Culpability to Management: How Scores Pressure Theories of Punishment

Risk as character transforms punishment's justification. Desert-based theories insist that punishment is justified because the offender deserves censure for a culpable wrong; preventive detention and preventive sentencing shift justification toward future harms and public protection. In a predictive legal order, the risk score becomes a bridge between these worlds: it allows the state to speak as if it remains within a culpability-based tradition while quietly importing preventive logic. A sentencing decision can be described as "proportionate" and yet be tuned upward because the model forecasts reoffending. That is a conceptual shift, because risk is not culpability, and prevention is not a substitute for condemnation.

This is why the recent philosophical debate over AI in sentencing has focused not only on accuracy but on condemnation and legitimacy. Arguments that sentencing is a communicative act—punishment as public condemnation—warn that algorithmic systems can undermine the condemnatory function by displacing moral authorship and reducing sentencing to technocratic management (Taylor, 2023). A reply to this critique clarifies that the core issue is not whether tools can assist, but whether they can do so without turning condemnation into an output justification (Ryberg, 2024). The point for "risk as character" is direct: once the score becomes the person's identity, punishment becomes administration dressed as morality.

Procedural Justice: Why People Experience Risk Scores as Disrespect

Even if a risk system could be tuned to reduce certain disparities, it could still corrode legitimacy if it undermines voice and dignity. Public perception research suggests that algorithmic involvement in judicial decisions can alter perceived legitimacy and procedural justice, with effects that vary by context and by group (Fine et al., 2025). This matters because legitimacy is not only about outcomes; it is about whether people feel heard, respected, and judged by accountable authority. When a score dominates, the hearing can feel like a formality. The person speaks, but the score speaks louder. That is procedural disrespect, not because the model is rude, but because the model changes the structure of participation. The decision begins to feel precomputed.

The problem intensifies when the score is difficult to challenge. If the defence cannot inspect inputs, cannot test validation claims, cannot understand thresholds, and cannot examine drift or error behaviour, then the right to contest evidence is hollowed out. In such conditions, the score becomes an unchallengeable witness. A procedural gap opens: formal rights exist, but practical contestability does not. Modern judicial and governance handbooks on AI risk assessment routinely frame this as a human rights and remedies issue, precisely because the combination of opacity and coercion threatens due process (Gioia, 2024). The psychological result is predictable: a person treated as a probability is less likely to experience the system as neutral, and more likely to experience it as a sorting machine.

The Equality Trap: Group Fairness Debates Encourage Trait Thinking

One of the strangest ways "risk as character" is reinforced is through fairness discourse itself. When institutions debate group disparities in false positives and false negatives, they sometimes slide into language that treats group differences as if they were biological or cultural traits rather than artefacts of measurement and enforcement. The impossibility results in fairness metrics show that when base rates differ, you cannot generally satisfy calibration and equal error rates simultaneously unless prediction is perfect or base rates are equal (Kleinberg et al., 2017; Chouldechova, 2017; Pleiss et al., 2017). The practical consequence is that institutions must choose what they mean by fairness, and any choice will redistribute error burdens. If the system refuses to name the choice, it may treat disparities as reflecting real group dangerousness rather than as reflecting policy and measurement decisions. Trait thinking then becomes a moral alibi: "the model is just reflecting reality," when the reality is partly institutional.

A careful way to resist this is to keep the legal question in view. Courts do not need to decide whether a person is "high risk" in the abstract; they need to decide whether there are legally relevant reasons, consistent with rights and proportionality, to deprive liberty or impose severity. A risk score may be one input into that reasoning, but only if it is treated as evidence with known error and limited scope, not as a character verdict.

A Forensic Posture Toward Risk: Treat the Score Like Evidence, Not Like a Diagnosis

The most practical corrective is to impose forensic discipline on risk outputs. Forensic science has learned that a scientific-looking output can mislead if it is not validated under conditions of use, if its uncertainty is not communicated, and if its interpretive boundaries are not respected. The same must apply to risk tools. The score should be treated as a hypothesis-generator and decision aid, not as a diagnostic label. Courts should require clarity about what is being predicted, over what horizon, with what uncertainty, on what data, and with what known subgroup performance. They should require that a score never be presented as a statement about character, and they should insist that coercive decisions be justified in reasons that remain intelligible without the score.

This is not theoretical neatness; it is how you prevent the moral substitution at the heart of "risk as character." If the score is treated as evidence, it can be challenged, weighed, limited, and contextualised. If it is treated as identity, it becomes destiny.

Conclusion: The Person Must Remain More Than the System's Forecast

Risk scores promise to correct human inconsistency, but they carry a quiet power: they recast persons as probabilities. When that happens, the justice system is tempted to punish not only for what was done, but for what is forecast; not only for culpability, but for predicted danger; not only through public reasons, but through technical authority. The transformation is psychologically natural, institutionally convenient, and morally corrosive. A responsible legal order must therefore do something counterintuitive: it must protect personhood from prediction by insisting that risk is never allowed to become character. That protection is achieved not by banning all forecasting, but by disciplining its role—treating scores as contestable evidence, bounding their use by proportionality and due process, and preserving the court's duty to speak in reasons that address a citizen rather than manage a profile (Feeley and Simon, 1992; Neil, 2025; Fine et al., 2025).

References

- Akpinar, N.-J., De-Arteaga, M. and Chouldechova, A. (2021) 'The effect of differential victim crime reporting on predictive policing systems', Proceedings of the 2021 ACM Conference on Fairness, Accountability, and Transparency (FAccT '21), pp. 434–445.
- Ashworth, A. and Zedner, L. (2014) Preventive Justice. Oxford: Oxford University Press.
- Barocas, S., Hardt, M. and Narayanan, A. (2023) Fairness and Machine Learning: Limitations and Opportunities. Cambridge, MA: MIT Press.
- Brayne, S. (2020) Predict and Surveil: Data, Discretion, and the Future of Policing. Oxford: Oxford University Press.
- Chouldechova, A. (2017) 'Fair prediction with disparate impact: A study of bias in recidivism prediction instruments', Big Data, 5(2), pp. 153–163.
- Corbett-Davies, S., Pierson, E., Feller, A., Goel, S. and Huq, A. (2017) 'Algorithmic decision making and the cost of fairness', Proceedings of the 23rd ACM SIGKDD International Conference on Knowledge Discovery and Data Mining (KDD '17), pp. 797–806.
- Dagan, N. (2026) 'Sentencing as a human process? Human judges' experiences with machine-based sentencing', The British Journal of Criminology (advance article).
- Eckhouse, L., Lum, K., Conti-Cook, C. and Ciccolini, J. (2019) 'Layers of bias: A unified approach for understanding problems with risk assessment', Criminal Justice and Behavior, 46(2), pp. 185–209.

- Ensign, D., Friedler, S.A., Neville, S., Scheidegger, C. and Venkatasubramanian, S. (2018) 'Runaway feedback loops in predictive policing', Proceedings of Machine Learning Research, 81, pp. 1–12.
- Feeley, M.M. and Simon, J. (1992) 'The new penology: Notes on the emerging strategy of corrections and its implications', Criminology, 30(4), pp. 449–474.
- Fine, A., Berthelot, E.R. and Marsh, S. (2025) 'Public perceptions of judges' use of AI tools in courtroom decision-making: An examination of legitimacy, fairness, trust, and procedural justice', Behavioral Sciences, 15(4), 476.
- Fischman-Afori, O. (2025) 'Due process by design: Enhancing fairness and trust in AI decision-making through procedural justice theory', Social Sciences & Humanities Open, 12, 102178.
- Foucault, M. (1977) Discipline and Punish: The Birth of the Prison. New York: Pantheon.
- Gama, J., Žliobaitė, I., Bifet, A., Pechenizkiy, M. and Bouchachia, A. (2014) 'A survey on concept drift adaptation', ACM Computing Surveys, 46(4), Article 44.
- Gioia, M. (2024) 'AI risk assessment tools for criminal justice: Risks to human rights and remedies', in Artificial Intelligence, Judicial Decision-Making and Fundamental Rights.
- Hardt, M., Price, E. and Srebro, N. (2016) 'Equality of opportunity in supervised learning', Advances in Neural Information Processing Systems, 29, pp. 3315–3323.
- Hardt, M. and Mendler-Dünner, C. (2025) 'Performative prediction: Past and future', Statistical Science, 40(3), pp. 417–436.
- Kinchin, N. (2024) '"Voiceless": the procedural gap in algorithmic justice', International Journal of Law and Information Technology, 32(4), pp. 1–30.
- Kleinberg, J., Mullainathan, S. and Raghavan, M. (2017) 'Inherent trade-offs in the fair determination of risk scores', Proceedings of the 8th Innovations in Theoretical Computer Science Conference (ITCS 2017), LIPIcs 67, Article 43.
- Kroll, J.A. (2024) 'Against predictive optimization: On the legitimacy of prediction-driven decision systems', ACM Transactions on Computer-Human Interaction, 31(2).
- Lum, K. and Isaac, W. (2016) 'To predict and serve?', Significance, 13(5), pp. 14–19.

- Neil, R. (2025) 'Algorithmic bias in criminal risk assessment: The consequences of racial differences in arrest as a measure of crime', Annual Review of Criminology, 8, pp. 97–119.
- O'Malley, P. (2004) Risk, Uncertainty and Government. London: GlassHouse Press.
- Obermeyer, Z., Powers, B., Vogeli, C. and Mullainathan, S. (2019) 'Dissecting racial bias in an algorithm used to manage the health of populations', Science, 366(6464), pp. 447–453.
- Perdomo, J.C., Zrnic, T., Mendler-Dünner, C. and Hardt, M. (2020) 'Performative prediction', Proceedings of the 37th International Conference on Machine Learning, PMLR 119, pp. 7599–7609.
- Pleiss, G., Raghavan, M., Wu, F., Kleinberg, J. and Weinberger, K.Q. (2017) 'On fairness and calibration', Advances in Neural Information Processing Systems, 30.
- Rafiei, S. (2026) 'Automation bias and judicial discretion in AI-assisted sentencing', [peer-reviewed journal article].
- Ryberg, J. (2024) 'Sentencing, artificial intelligence, and condemnation: A reply to Taylor', Criminal Justice Ethics.
- Taylor, I. (2023) 'Justice by algorithm: The limits of AI in criminal sentencing', Criminal Justice Ethics, 42(3), pp. 193–213.
- Tyler, T.R. (2011) 'Procedural justice, legitimacy, and the effective rule of law', Crime and Justice, 40(1), pp. 283–357.
- van Eijk, G. (2020) 'Inclusion and exclusion through risk-based justice', The British Journal of Criminology, 60(4), pp. 1080–1100.

CHAPTER XXIV

Therapeutic Jurisprudence Meets Machine Inference

The Promise and the Trap of "Smarter" Justice

Therapeutic Jurisprudence begins with an unusually practical moral claim: law is not only a set of commands and sanctions; it is also a social force that can heal or harm, depending on how it is designed and enacted. The same legal rule can be experienced as stabilising or humiliating, the same hearing as clarifying or traumatising, the same judge as a moral guide or a bureaucratic gatekeeper. Therapeutic Jurisprudence therefore asks you to look at the law's psychological footprint—on offenders, victims, families, and even legal actors—and to treat that footprint as a legitimate, evidence-informed part of legal evaluation (Wexler and Winick, 1991; Winick and Wexler, 2003). Therapeutic Jurisprudence is not a demand that law become therapy; it is a demand that law stop being casually anti-therapeutic when it need not be, and that it actively support conditions conducive to rehabilitation, dignity, and lawful compliance when this can be done without sacrificing due process and other competing values (Perlin, 2016; Duffy, 2012).

Machine inference enters the justice system with a different promise: more consistency, fewer errors, earlier triage, better targeting of resources, reduced delay, and a reduction in the human biases that flourish under pressure. The two promises can appear to rhyme. A predictive tool can help identify needs early, route people to treatment, or flag when a relapse pattern is emerging before it becomes a breach. A decision-support system can help courts keep track of compliance, avoid arbitrary responses, and preserve proportionality in supervision. Yet the rhyme can become a deception. Machine inference is designed to compress human lives into variables that can be learned from, and Therapeutic Jurisprudence is designed to resist the very reductionism that makes that compression so tempting. The question therefore is not whether Therapeutic Jurisprudence and machine inference can coexist; the question is what institutional discipline is required so that prediction strengthens the therapeutic mission rather than silently converting the therapeutic court into a risk-management machine wearing a compassionate mask (Feeley and Simon, 1992; Sourdin, 2021).

Therapeutic Jurisprudence as a Theory of Legal Interaction, Not Only of Legal Outcomes

Problem-solving courts—drug courts, mental health courts, domestic violence courts, family drug and alcohol courts, community courts—are often described as "alternatives" to the adversarial model, but their defining feature is not merely diversion; it is interaction. Their logic assumes that compliance and desistance are shaped by relationships, credibility, respect, and the offender's internal motivation, not merely by external threats. Therapeutic jurisprudence scholarship has therefore paid close attention to the judicial role, especially to the judge's communicative and behavioural style, and to how court actors can leverage evidence from psychology and counselling—especially motivational techniques—to foster internalised change rather than coerced compliance (Winick and Wexler, 2003; Rottman, 2000).

This is why a purely "accuracy" conversation is structurally insufficient for therapeutic justice. Even if a model predicts relapse or breach with excellent calibration, a therapeutic court cannot treat that prediction as the new ground of coercion without undermining its own logic. If the participant experiences that the court no longer listens because the model "already knows," then the court has lost precisely the mechanism that makes therapeutic jurisprudence therapeutically plausible: the experience of voice, dignity, and fair engagement, which procedural justice theory identifies as core drivers of legitimacy and cooperation (Tyler, 2011; Blader and Tyler, 2003). A system that predicts correctly but communicates disrespectfully can win the statistic and lose the person.

What Machine Inference Brings Into the Therapeutic Courtroom

Machine inference in therapeutic contexts usually arrives in three guises. The first is triage: tools that predict who is likely to benefit from treatment court, who is likely to fail to appear, who is likely to relapse, or who needs a particular intensity of support. The second is monitoring: dashboards that summarise compliance, missed appointments, drug tests, attendance patterns, or digital engagement in treatment. The third is recommendation: systems that suggest sanctions and incentives, or that nudge judges toward particular responses based on "similar cases." Each guise can be used in a way that amplifies therapeutic goals, and each can be used in a way that betrays them.

The triage promise is resource justice. Therapeutic courts are labour-intensive; they rely on stable staffing, cross-agency collaboration, and repeated judicial engagement. A triage model can theoretically prioritise scarce resources for those most likely to benefit, and it can potentially reduce unnecessary intrusion into the lives of those who would do well without intensive oversight. Yet the triage peril is selection bias and institutional memory. If the model is trained on outcomes shaped by prior policing, prosecution, or supervision practices, the model can inherit the system's unequal contact patterns and then encode them as "who is a good candidate" or "who is high risk," thereby quietly shaping access to therapeutic opportunities (Neil, 2025; Barocas and Selbst, 2016). When this happens, the therapeutic court becomes a gate that appears neutral while reproducing old stratifications through new maths.

Monitoring tools can support care by detecting early warning signs and enabling a judge to respond with support rather than sudden punishment. But monitoring can also become surveillance, and surveillance changes behaviour by changing the meaning of the relationship. Therapeutic jurisprudence depends on a relational authority structure: the participant is more likely to internalise compliance when they feel the court is invested in their wellbeing rather than hunting for their failure. If machine monitoring creates an atmosphere of constant detection, the participant may comply outwardly while disengaging inwardly, and the court may drift from supportive responses toward technical enforcement because the system is now flooded with measurable "noncompliance." The tool then does not simply observe; it reshapes the moral environment of the court, which is precisely what performative prediction frameworks warn about: predictions and measurements alter the distribution of behaviours they are meant to track (Perdomo et al., 2020; Hardt and Mendler-Dünner, 2025).

Recommendation systems are the most dangerous, because they tempt the court to outsource judgment. A therapeutic court's credibility rests on the participant believing the judge knows them, remembers their story, understands the struggle, and responds in a way that is firm but fair. A recommender can improve consistency across judges, but it can also induce automation bias, the cognitive tendency to defer to machine outputs, particularly in high-stakes contexts and under workload pressure (Sourdin, 2021). If the judge begins to act as the mouthpiece of a model, the court becomes less therapeutic even if it becomes more uniform.

The Data Problem: When "Need" Is Measured as "Contact"

The most revealing warning comes from outside criminal justice: health systems have shown that algorithms can faithfully encode structural inequality when they use proxies that reflect unequal access rather than true need. Obermeyer and colleagues demonstrated that an algorithm predicting healthcare costs as a proxy for healthcare need produced racial bias because spending reflected access and historical disadvantage, not underlying illness burden (Obermeyer et al., 2019). The justice analogue is immediate. Rearrest is not identical to reoffending; it is partly policing intensity. Technical violations are not identical to dangerousness; they are partly supervision strictness and social instability. Missed appointments are not identical to defiance; they can reflect transport insecurity, childcare burdens, or chaotic housing. If a therapeutic court's machine inference treats these institutional-contact outcomes as clean labels of personal character, it will recast vulnerability as culpability and disadvantage as "risk." That is anti-therapeutic by definition.

Criminological synthesis underscores the specific justice mechanism: using arrest as an outcome or predictor can generate algorithmic bias because arrest patterns reflect enforcement differences, and those differences are not equivalent to differences in offending (Neil, 2025). When such data are used in treatment-court triage or sanction recommendations, the tool can mark certain groups as "non-compliant types" and then route them into harsher supervisory regimes. Once that happens, the system manufactures its own validation: heightened supervision increases detection, detection increases recorded noncompliance, and the model appears confirmed. The therapeutic court then becomes a refined engine of stratified surveillance rather than a mechanism of rehabilitation.

Motivational Interviewing, Judicial Dialogue, and the Fragility of Therapeutic Alliance

Therapeutic jurisprudence is not naïve about coercion. It recognises that courts operate through authority. Yet it insists that authority can be exercised in ways that build intrinsic motivation rather than merely extracting compliance. Winick and Wexler explicitly connect problem-solving courts to motivational interviewing principles, suggesting that judges can develop interactional techniques that enhance engagement, autonomy, and responsibility (Winick and Wexler, 2003).

This is where machine inference creates a delicate dilemma. If a judge enters a review hearing with a dashboard that predicts relapse or breach, the judge's tone, expectations, and interpretive stance can shift before the participant speaks. The risk is not only error; it is relational contamination. The participant may detect pre-judgment and respond with defensiveness or performative compliance, which undermines truthful disclosure—the lifeblood of therapeutic intervention. Evidence on motivational interviewing in forensic and justice-involved contexts continues to support its value for reducing resistance and supporting behavioural change, precisely because it avoids confrontation and supports autonomy (e Silva et al., 2025). The court's challenge is therefore to ensure that prediction does not pre-empt dialogue. In a therapeutic court, the model must not become the new "truth" about the person; it must remain a tentative signal that is subordinated to human engagement and contestable context.

Virtual and Digitally Mediated Treatment Courts: Technology Can Lower Anxiety and Still Damage Recognition

Therapeutic practice depends not only on what is said but on the felt experience of recognition: being known, being remembered, being taken seriously. The move to virtual treatment courts during and after COVID-19 revealed a revealing paradox. Survey research on clients' attitudes toward virtual treatment courts found that clients often felt more comfortable participating virtually, but were less likely to feel that the judge was familiar with their case during virtual sessions, and they reported nuanced differences in connection with treatment staff and peer groups (Ray et al., 2022). That single finding should be read as a warning for machine inference as well, because both virtualisation and algorithmic mediation can reduce the felt sense that the judge "knows" the person. Comfort is not identical to therapeutic alliance. Reduced anxiety is not identical to dignity. A system can be easier to attend and still feel less human.

When machine inference is layered onto remote environments—automated reminders, compliance scoring, risk alerts—there is a further risk of flattening the interaction into administrative management. Therapeutic jurisprudence would treat that as a structural hazard: as the interaction becomes more system-mediated, the participant is more likely to experience the court as a mechanism rather than a relationship, and the judge is more likely to experience the participant as a case file rather than a person. The moral cost is not simply that the experience feels cold. The moral cost is that the process loses its legitimacy-generating qualities, which procedural justice research links to long-run compliance and cooperation (Tyler, 2011).

When Prediction Collides With the Therapeutic Aim: The Sanction–Support Boundary

A therapeutic court's most ethically loaded moment is the response to relapse and noncompliance. Relapse is often a symptom of the underlying condition the court claims to treat; yet the court also has a legal mandate to enforce orders. Therapeutic jurisprudence insists that sanctions, when used, should be calibrated to support behavioural change rather than to satisfy retributive impulses. Machine inference can help by distinguishing patterns that suggest escalating harm from patterns that suggest predictable recovery turbulence, and by prompting early supportive interventions. But it can also push the court toward premature punishment by converting risk into moral certainty.

The law's preventive instincts become especially strong when prediction enters: if a model forecasts a high probability of reoffending, the system begins to feel justified in acting now for a future that has not occurred. This is the preventive-justice logic that Ashworth and Zedner warn can expand coercion beyond traditional criminal-law limits if not carefully constrained (Ashworth and Zedner, 2014). In a therapeutic setting, this expansion is especially corrosive because it reframes relapse as danger and need as threat. It also risks displacing individualised care with actuarial uniformity, reintroducing the "new penology" shift from individual rehabilitation to population management (Feeley and Simon, 1992).

Forensic Application: Evidence Integrity, Clinical Claims, and Algorithmic Contamination

Therapeutic courts sit at a junction of legal evidence and clinical evaluation. They rely on drug test results, treatment compliance reports, psychological assessments, sometimes psychiatric diagnoses, and increasingly digital traces. Forensic discipline matters here because the court is constantly asked to infer meaning from indicators: what does a missed appointment signify, what does a positive test mean in context, what does "resistance" reflect, what does a pattern of partial compliance reveal about control and intention. The court's interpretive errors can become self-fulfilling: misread a struggle as defiance, respond harshly, increase disengagement, and then treat the disengagement as proof of defiance.

Machine inference can deepen this problem if it is treated as an evidentiary shortcut. A model that synthesises compliance data into a "noncompliance risk score" can look like a scientific truth while hiding its assumptions about missingness, measurement error, and the causal pathways of recovery. The forensic approach, therefore, is to treat algorithmic outputs as evidence-like artefacts: they require provenance, known error properties, versioning, and contestability. The person must be able to challenge inputs and interpretations, because therapeutic legitimacy depends on voice and dignity, and because legal legitimacy depends on adversarial testing.

Contestability as Therapeutic Due Process

Therapeutic jurisprudence is sometimes accused of paternalism: of prioritising wellbeing over autonomy. The best TJ work explicitly resists that caricature by emphasising that therapeutic goals must be balanced against due process and other legal values (Winick and Wexler, 2003; Duffy, 2012). Machine inference raises the paternalism risk anew because it invites "benevolent" interventions based on predictions the participant cannot contest. If the court says, "the system indicates you are likely to relapse, so we will intensify supervision," the participant may experience this as care or as pre-emptive suspicion, depending on whether they can understand and challenge the basis of that inference. Contestability is therefore not an add-on; it is the mechanism that makes therapeutic intervention compatible with legal respect.

Modern scholarship on courts and AI continues to stress that technological systems can support judges while also introducing risks around transparency, accountability, and vulnerable litigants, requiring ethical frameworks that preserve human justice (Sourdin, 2021). Desmoulin-Canselier and Le Métayer's analysis of algorithmic decision systems in health and justice sectors similarly frames certification and explanation as governance needs precisely because high-stakes decisions require accountability structures, not only performance claims (Desmoulin-Canselier and Le Métayer, 2018). In therapeutic courts, the governance demand becomes even more psychologically loaded, because a person's relationship to law is part of the intervention itself. If the intervention feels opaque and unchallengeable, the court has undermined its own therapeutic mechanism.

The Future Edge: Generative Systems and the Illusion of Empathic Justice

A predictive legal order is now flirting with a more radical possibility: not only risk scoring, but language models that can draft reasons, summarise cases, and potentially recommend sentences. Peer-reviewed empirical work evaluating large language models as judicial decision-makers suggests that models can produce outputs that resemble judicial choices under certain conditions, which will intensify institutional temptation toward automation (Gazal Ayal, Elyoseph and Solomon, 2026). In therapeutic contexts, this temptation is especially perilous because language models can simulate empathy without possessing responsibility. A generative system can produce "kind" reasons that sound therapeutic while disguising that the real decision logic was anchored in unexamined proxies and optimisation. A therapeutic court cannot accept simulated empathy as a substitute for human recognition, because the very point is not soothing language but accountable engagement grounded in truthful understanding.

Conclusion: A Therapeutic Court May Use Inference, But It Must Not Become Inference

Therapeutic jurisprudence meets machine inference at a crossroads where the justice system's two languages compete: the language of care and the language of control. Machine inference can support therapeutic courts by improving triage, enabling early supportive interventions, and reducing arbitrary inconsistency. But it can also convert therapeutic judging into actuarial management by turning persons into probabilities, needs into risks, and relapse into predicted danger. The discipline required is therefore stark. If the tool cannot explain what it measures, if it measures contact rather than need, if it cannot be challenged, and if it reshapes judicial dialogue into administrative output validation, it is therapeutically destructive even if it is statistically impressive. The therapeutic court must remain, in its deepest structure, a place where law speaks to a person as a person—through voice, dignity, and accountable reasons—while using inference only as a constrained aid, never as the author of coercion.

References

- Ashworth, A. and Zedner, L. (2014) Preventive Justice. Oxford: Oxford University Press.
- Barocas, S. and Selbst, A.D. (2016) 'Big data's disparate impact', California Law Review, 104(3), pp. 671–732.
- Blader, S.L. and Tyler, T.R. (2003) 'A four-component model of procedural justice: Defining the meaning of a "fair" process', Personality and Social Psychology Bulletin, 29(6), pp. 747–758.
- Desmoulin-Canselier, S. and Le Métayer, D. (2018) 'Algorithmic decision systems in the health and justice sectors: Certification and explanations for algorithms in European and French law', European Journal of Law and Technology, 9(3).
- Duffy, J. (2012) 'Problem-solving courts, therapeutic jurisprudence and the constitution: If two is company, is three a crowd?', Melbourne University Law Review, 35(2), pp. 394–446.
- Eckhouse, L., Lum, K., Conti-Cook, C. and Ciccolini, J. (2019) 'Layers of bias: A unified approach for understanding problems with risk assessment', Criminal Justice and Behavior, 46(2), pp. 185–209.
- Ensign, D., Friedler, S.A., Neville, S., Scheidegger, C. and Venkatasubramanian, S. (2018) 'Runaway feedback loops in predictive policing', Proceedings of Machine Learning Research, 81, pp. 1–12.

- Feeley, M.M. and Simon, J. (1992) 'The new penology: Notes on the emerging strategy of corrections and its implications', Criminology, 30(4), pp. 449–474.
- Gazal Ayal, O., Elyoseph, Z. and Solomon, A. (2026) 'Evaluating large language models as judicial decision-makers', Justice Quarterly.
- Hardt, M. and Mendler-Dünner, C. (2025) 'Performative prediction: Past and future', Statistical Science, 40(3), pp. 417–436.
- Kawalek, A. (2020) 'A tool for measuring therapeutic jurisprudence values during empirical research', International Journal of Law and Psychiatry, 71, 101581.
- Lum, K. and Isaac, W. (2016) 'To predict and serve?', Significance, 13(5), pp. 14–19.
- Neil, R. (2025) 'Algorithmic bias in criminal risk assessment: The consequences of racial differences in arrest as a measure of crime', Annual Review of Criminology, 8, pp. 97–119.
- Obermeyer, Z., Powers, B., Vogeli, C. and Mullainathan, S. (2019) 'Dissecting racial bias in an algorithm used to manage the health of populations', Science, 366(6464), pp. 447–453.
- Perdomo, J.C., Zrnic, T., Mendler-Dünner, C. and Hardt, M. (2020) 'Performative prediction', Proceedings of the 37th International Conference on Machine Learning, PMLR 119, pp. 7599–7609.
- Perlin, M.L. (2016) 'Therapeutic jurisprudence', in The Palgrave Handbook of Criminology and the Global South.
- Ray, B., Kunkel, T., Bryant, K., Hedden, B., Andraka-Christou, B., O'Neil, M. and Huynh, P. (2022) 'Client attitudes toward virtual treatment court', Journal of Substance Abuse Treatment, 140, 108833.
- Rottman, D.B. (2000) 'Therapeutic jurisprudence and the emergence of problem-solving courts', National Institute of Justice Journal.
- Sourdin, T. (2021) Judges, Technology and Artificial Intelligence: The Artificial Judge. Cheltenham: Edward Elgar.
- Stobbs, N., Bartels, L. and Vols, M. (eds) (2019) The Methodology and Practice of Therapeutic Jurisprudence. Durham, NC: Carolina Academic Press.
- Tyler, T.R. (2011) 'Procedural justice, legitimacy, and the effective rule of law', Crime and Justice, 40(1), pp. 283–357.
- Wexler, D.B. and Winick, B.J. (1991) Essays in Therapeutic Jurisprudence. Durham, NC: Carolina Academic Press.

- Winick, B.J. and Wexler, D.B. (2003) 'Therapeutic jurisprudence and problem solving courts', Fordham Urban Law Journal, 30(3), pp. 1055–1090.
- e Silva, T.P. et al. (2025) 'Effectiveness of motivational interviewing with justice-involved individuals.'

CHAPTER XXV

The "Opacity Effect": How Black Boxes Change Blame and Mercy

The Black Box as a New Witness in the Courtroom

A legal system is built to do two things at once: discover what happened and justify what it will do about it. Those two tasks are related but not identical. The first is epistemic; the second is moral and institutional. When a black-box model enters the process—whether as a risk score, a "similar cases" recommender, a predictive policing heatmap, or an AI-generated evidential summary—it does not merely add a new piece of information. It changes the structure of justification. It introduces a new "witness" whose testimony is numeric, authoritative in tone, and often resistant to meaningful cross-examination. The opacity effect is the predictable psychological and procedural consequence of that shift: the less intelligible the system's internal reasoning is to decision-makers and affected parties, the more likely they are to treat its outputs as either

1. fate-like facts that deserve deference, or
2. alien authority that deserves suspicion,

with both reactions reshaping how blame and mercy are distributed.

This matters because blame and mercy are not decorative emotions sprinkled on top of legal outcomes. Blame is a public practice of responsibility attribution; mercy is a public practice of restraint and human particularity. Both depend on reasons. Once reasons are replaced by outputs, the court's moral vocabulary becomes thinner. You can still sentence, detain, and supervise, but you will increasingly do so through a logic that feels managerial: "the model says." The evidentiary implications of interpreting black-box algorithms have been analysed precisely as an issue of meaning and admissibility: the output is not self-interpreting, and opacity amplifies the risk that courts will misread what the tool can legitimately support (Bhatnagar, 2023).

Why Opacity Does Not Only Hide Reasons, It Replaces Them

It is tempting to believe the black box merely withholds an explanation. That is a comforting understatement. Opacity does more than hide; it reorganises the burden of reasoning. In a transparent method, the judge and counsel can argue about inputs, steps, assumptions, and alternative interpretations. In an opaque method, that argumentative space collapses, and the space is silently filled by social psychology: deference to authority, fear of blame for deviating, anchoring on numbers, and institutional risk aversion. In other words, opacity does not create neutrality; it creates a vacuum, and vacuums are filled by the very human forces that legal procedure was designed to discipline.

The empirical literature on algorithmic fairness perceptions repeatedly shows that people care not only about outcomes but also about process qualities—transparency, accountability, and the ability to understand how a decision was reached—and that these process cues shape trust and perceived legitimacy (Starke, Lünich and Marcinkowski, 2022). Procedural-fairness work specific to algorithmic decision-making pushes in the same direction: fair outcomes do not rescue an unfair process, and a process that excludes public engagement and meaningful contestation risks perpetuating structural injustice even when statistical performance looks respectable (Decker, 2025). In law, that is not merely a sociological observation; it is a constitutional warning. A court that cannot explain itself becomes vulnerable to being experienced as arbitrary—even when it believes it has become more "consistent."

The Blame Shift: From "You Chose" to "The System Said"

Black boxes shift blame in two directions at once, and this is where the opacity effect becomes ethically sharp. First, they can harden blame against defendants by converting probabilistic forecasts into character-like labels: "high risk," "likely to breach," "dangerous." Second, they can soften blame against institutional actors by providing a ready-made shield: "the tool recommended it." This is not speculative. The literature on responsibility diffusion in AI-assisted decision systems explicitly describes how the introduction of AI decision support can diffuse responsibility across actors—developer, deployer, user, or institution—creating causal, moral, and legal ambiguity about who is accountable when harms occur (Bleher et al., 2022).

This is the deepest asymmetry a predictive legal order can create: maximal responsibility for citizens, diluted responsibility for the state. The defendant is still treated as a fully responsible agent whose choices warrant condemnation, while institutional choices are reframed as technical compliance with a tool's output. Over time, this encourages what you might call moral outsourcing: human authorities come to experience themselves less as authors of coercion and more as administrators of a system. Once that happens, the court's moral seriousness declines even as its coercive capacity expands.

Mercy Under Opacity: Why Leniency Becomes Harder to Justify

Mercy is not the opposite of justice. In mature legal theory, mercy is one of the ways a system acknowledges that general rules cannot exhaust the moral texture of individual lives and that restraint can be principled rather than sentimental. But mercy is vulnerable to opacity for a simple reason: mercy requires reasons that can be defended publicly. If the court departs downward from a risk-based recommendation, it must be able to articulate why the person in front of it is not adequately described by the model's summary. When the model is opaque, that articulation becomes harder, because the judge cannot identify which features drove the output, cannot evaluate whether those features are morally relevant, and cannot confidently distinguish "model error" from "model truth."

Here is where opacity can quietly increase severity. When decision-makers fear being blamed for a future harm—an offence committed after release, a violent incident following a lighter sentence—opacity makes deviation feel reckless. The judge cannot say, "I understand precisely why the tool predicts high risk, and I have reasons to discount that feature in this case." Instead, the judge faces a blunt output and an uncertain institutional future. Under such conditions, the safe institutional move is to comply with the tool. Mercy becomes professionally risky. This is a structural consequence, not a personality flaw, and it helps explain why black-box systems can change sentencing culture even when formally "advisory."

The scholarly debate about algorithmic sentencing support has converged on this practical dilemma: even if tools can offer benefits, implementation choices matter because they alter how discretion is exercised and how moral responsibility is borne (Ryberg, 2025). Opacity intensifies that dilemma by making the judge's reasons-giving burden heavier precisely when the judge seeks to be humane.

The Opaque Number as Anchor: How Cognition Makes the Tool Feel Truer Than It Is

The opacity effect is amplified by a specific cognitive pattern: what is not understood is often treated as more objective. A black box's authority does not come from clarity; it comes from a sense that something "scientific" happened behind the curtain. This is why explanations matter, but also why explanations can be double-edged. Research on explainable AI shows that providing feature-based explanations reshapes users' sense-making and can change how they weigh information, sometimes increasing reliance, sometimes altering perceived legitimacy (Bauer, 2023). Meanwhile, broader empirical work on transparency requirements cautions that transparency can also produce algorithmic disillusionment, making algorithms appear more fallible and less powerful, which can reduce over-deference but can also reduce appropriate reliance (Felzmann et al., 2019).

For courts, the implication is not "always explain more." It is "explain in a way that preserves contestability and prevents over-interpretation." A shallow explanation can be worse than none if it creates a false sense of understanding. A deep explanation that cannot be tested is still insufficient. What the adversarial process needs is not narrative comfort; it needs actionable scrutiny: the ability to probe inputs, thresholds, validation limits, and drift.

Procedural Justice Collapse: Voice Without Leverage

Opacity damages procedural justice in a particular way: it converts voice into performance. A person may speak, but if the decisive reason remains a model output that neither party can meaningfully contest, the participant's speech has reduced leverage. This is not merely a feeling problem. Procedural fairness scholarship in algorithmic settings emphasises that legitimacy depends on fair procedures and relational justice, not just distributive outcomes, and it calls for substantive procedural safeguards that keep decision-making accountable (Decker, 2025). If the court becomes unable to show how it reached its conclusion, neutrality becomes a claim rather than an experience, and dignity becomes a tone rather than a structure.

This procedural fragility is especially dangerous in criminal justice because the system's goals include compliance and cooperation. When people experience decisions as opaque and unchallengeable, they are more likely to interpret them as arbitrary, which can reduce long-term cooperation with legal authority. The empirical literature on fairness perceptions of algorithmic decision-making supports the view that transparency, accountability, and contestability shape perceived fairness and ethical acceptability (Starke, Lünich and Marcinkowski, 2022). Opacity thus creates a legitimacy tax that the system pays later through distrust, noncooperation, and, in some contexts, underreporting and disengagement.

Evidence, Not Oracle: Why Black Box Outputs Must Be Treated Like Forensic Artifacts

The most court-safe way to think about algorithmic outputs is to treat them as forensic artifacts rather than as administrative facts. A forensic artifact is not admitted because it exists; it is admitted because its provenance, reliability, and interpretive boundaries can be scrutinised. Opacity undermines that scrutiny unless the system provides functional substitutes: rigorous validation reports, error rates under conditions of use, documentation of thresholds and versioning, and logs sufficient to replicate the run. The broader legal debate has framed this as a rights problem: black-box algorithms implicate individuals' rights precisely because explainability is technically hard and because the appropriate response may require logging, auditing, and statistical accountability rather than pretending we can always "open the box" (Gryz, 2021).

Forensic standards work is converging on the same principle: reliability is not a label; it is a demonstrated property under specified conditions, and decisions about interpretation must be grounded in validation evidence (Morrison, 2025). Even outside traditional forensics, the analogy holds: an algorithm that cannot be audited behaves like evidence that cannot be cross-examined. And evidence that cannot be cross-examined becomes authority by default.

The Black Box and the Feedback Loop: Opacity as a Force Multiplier for Self-Confirmation

Opacity does not only change perception; it can also change the data environment. Predictive systems can shape the world they predict, and that effect becomes harder to detect when the model's inner logic is hidden. Predictive policing work has shown how feedback loops can reinforce patterns of enforcement and recorded incidents (Ensign et al., 2018; Lum and Isaac, 2016). In such systems, the model's output becomes part of the causal chain that produces the next dataset, and the institution can mistake self-generated confirmation for objective accuracy. When that confirmation arrives as an opaque number, it is easier for decision-makers to treat it as "the world speaking," rather than "the institution reproducing itself."

This matters for blame and mercy because feedback loops harden narratives. If a community becomes repeatedly flagged, it is increasingly treated as inherently dangerous; if an individual becomes repeatedly scored as high risk, they are increasingly treated as a stable threat. Mercy then becomes harder because the person is not experienced as a changing agent but as a consistent probability. Blame becomes easier because the system's repetition produces a sense of inevitability.

Remedy: Making Mercy Possible Again Without Abandoning Safety

A justice system cannot simply demand that judges be heroic resisters of machine authority. The remedy must be structural, because the opacity effect is structural. The first structural remedy is to treat any liberty-affecting black-box output as an evidential claim that triggers disclosure duties: what the model predicts, what data it uses, how it was validated, what error behaviour it shows, and how it behaves across contexts. The second is to require contestability mechanisms that are usable in adversarial form, so that voice regains leverage: the defence must be able to test and challenge the output, not merely hear an explanation. The third is to preserve moral ownership by requiring reasons that stand independently of the model: a judge may refer to the tool, but must be able to justify the outcome in human reasons that connect to law's categories—culpability, proportionality, necessity, and rights—rather than to forecasts alone.

This is also where explanation must be treated cautiously. Explanations can reshape sense-making, but they can also create misplaced confidence; transparency can produce disillusionment, but disillusionment can be healthy if it prevents blind deference (Bauer, 2023; Felzmann et al., 2019). The aim is not to make the model lovable. The aim is to make the model governable: auditable, contestable, and bounded.

Conclusion: Opacity Is Not Only a Technical Defect, It Is a Moral Transformer

The opacity effect is the law's newest psychological hazard: it transforms the way blame and mercy are experienced and distributed. It can harden blame against defendants by turning risk into character, while softening institutional responsibility by turning human choices into system compliance. It can make mercy rarer by making deviation riskier and justification harder. It can erode procedural justice by converting voice into performance. And it can magnify feedback loops by hiding the machinery that converts institutional attention into apparent truth.

A predictive legal order can still be legitimate, but only if it refuses to treat black boxes as oracles. It must treat them as evidence-like artifacts subject to adversarial testing, and it must protect the space in which mercy and blame remain intelligible human practices rather than byproducts of a hidden machine. The law's dignity lies in reasons. If opacity replaces reasons with outputs, the system may become efficient, but it will become morally thinner—and moral thinness, in criminal justice, is how cruelty often begins.

References

- Bauer, K. (2023) 'Expl(AI)ned: The impact of explainable artificial intelligence on users' sense-making', Information Systems Research.
- Bhatnagar, V. (2023) 'The evidentiary implications of interpreting black-box algorithms', Northwestern Journal of Technology and Intellectual Property, 20(3).
- Bleher, H., Braun, M., Hummel, P. and Dabrock, P. (2022) 'Attributions of responsibility in the use of AI-driven clinical decision support systems: A diffusion of responsibility', Journal of Medical Ethics.

- Blader, S.L. and Tyler, T.R. (2003) 'A four-component model of procedural justice: Defining the meaning of a "fair" process', Personality and Social Psychology Bulletin, 29(6), pp. 747–758.
- Choung, H. (2025) 'Fairness and trust in AI decision-making', International Journal of Human–Computer Interaction.
- Decker, M.C. (2025) 'Procedural fairness in algorithmic decision-making: The role of public engagement', Ethics and Information Technology.
- Dietvorst, B.J., Simmons, J.P. and Massey, C. (2015) 'Algorithm aversion: People erroneously avoid algorithms after seeing them err', Journal of Experimental Psychology: General, 144(1), pp. 114–126.
- Ensign, D., Friedler, S.A., Neville, S., Scheidegger, C. and Venkatasubramanian, S. (2018) 'Runaway feedback loops in predictive policing', Proceedings of Machine Learning Research, 81, pp. 1–12.
- Felzmann, H., Villaronga, E.F., Lutz, C. and Tamò-Larrieux, A. (2019) 'Transparency requirements for artificial intelligence', Big Data & Society, 6(1).
- Fine, A., Berthelot, E.R. and Marsh, S. (2025) 'Public perceptions of judges' use of AI tools in courtroom decision-making: An examination of legitimacy, fairness, trust, and procedural justice', Behavioral Sciences, 15(4), 476.
- Fischman-Afori, O. (2025) 'Due process by design: Enhancing fairness and trust in AI decision-making through procedural justice theory', Social Sciences & Humanities Open, 12, 102178.
- Gama, J., Žliobaitė, I., Bifet, A., Pechenizkiy, M. and Bouchachia, A. (2014) 'A survey on concept drift adaptation', ACM Computing Surveys, 46(4), Article 44.
- Gryz, J. (2021) 'Black box algorithms and the rights of individuals: No easy solution for explainability', Internet Policy Review.
- Hardt, M. and Mendler-Dünner, C. (2025) 'Performative prediction: Past and future', Statistical Science, 40(3), pp. 417–436.
- Holtzman, I. (2025) 'Forgiveness in human–machine interaction', Frontiers in Computer Science.
- Kleanthous, S. et al. (2021) 'Perception of fairness in algorithmic decisions', Scientific Reports.
- Kinchin, N. (2024) '"Voiceless": The procedural gap in algorithmic justice', International Journal of Law and Information Technology, 32(4).

- Kroll, J.A. (2024) 'Against predictive optimization: On the legitimacy of prediction-driven decision systems', ACM Transactions on Computer-Human Interaction.
- Lum, K. and Isaac, W. (2016) 'To predict and serve?', Significance, 13(5), pp. 14–19.
- Morrison, G.S. (2025) 'A guide to ISO 21043 forensic sciences from the forensic-data-science paradigm', Science & Justice, 65, 101298.
- Neil, R. (2025) 'Algorithmic bias in criminal risk assessment: The consequences of racial differences in arrest as a measure of crime', Annual Review of Criminology, 8, pp. 97–119.
- Perdomo, J.C., Zrnic, T., Mendler-Dünner, C. and Hardt, M. (2020) 'Performative prediction', Proceedings of the 37th International Conference on Machine Learning, PMLR 119, pp. 7599–7609.
- Robertson, B., Vignaux, G.A. and Berger, C.E.H. (2016) Interpreting Evidence: Evaluating Forensic Science in the Courtroom. 2nd edn. Chichester: Wiley.
- Ryberg, J. (2025) 'How to use algorithmic sentencing support in real life (and ethically non-ideal) penal systems?', AI and Ethics, 5.
- Shin, D. (2019) 'The role of fairness, accountability, and transparency in algorithmic decision-making', Computers in Human Behavior, 98, pp. 277–284.
- Starke, C., Lünich, M. and Marcinkowski, F. (2022) 'Fairness perceptions of algorithmic decision-making: A systematic review', Big Data & Society, 9(2).
- Taylor, I. (2023) 'Justice by algorithm: The limits of AI in criminal sentencing', Criminal Justice Ethics, 42(3), pp. 193–213.
- Tyler, T.R. (2011) 'Procedural justice, legitimacy, and the effective rule of law', Crime and Justice, 40(1), pp. 283–357.
- Wachter, S., Mittelstadt, B. and Russell, C. (2021) 'Why fairness cannot be automated: Bridging the gap between EU non-discrimination law and AI', Computer Law & Security Review, 41, 105567.

Part VI — Legitimacy, Trust, and Public Consent

CHAPTER XXVI

Algorithm Aversion and Algorithm Worship: Two Public Pathologies

The Two Pathologies That Arrive Together

When algorithmic decision systems enter criminal justice, the public does not respond with a single attitude called "trust" or "distrust." Instead, two opposing pathologies often appear at the same time, sometimes in the same person, and often in the same institution. The first is Algorithm Aversion: the tendency to reject algorithmic advice or decisions after observing error, to punish the machine more harshly than a human for comparable mistakes, and to treat algorithmic involvement as inherently suspect even when it improves accuracy (Dietvorst, Simmons and Massey, 2015). The second is Algorithm Worship: the tendency to defer to an algorithmic output as if it were a neutral fact, to treat the model as more objective than any human reason-giver, and to allow the number to silence contestation—even when the model's relevance, validation, or data integrity is uncertain (Skitka, Mosier and Burdick, 1999; Lyell and Coiera, 2017). In criminal justice, both pathologies are dangerous for the same reason: they collapse the court's duty to own reasons. Aversion collapses into rejection without evaluation; worship collapses into acceptance without scrutiny. Neither posture is consistent with the evidential discipline that the courtroom is meant to impose on every claim that can deprive liberty.

You can already see why these pathologies flourish specifically in justice systems. Algorithmic outputs are often introduced as "decision support," but they function psychologically like verdict props. They arrive with administrative authority, they claim scientific legitimacy, they compress messy human life into a scalar, and they interact with fear—fear of future harm, fear of public backlash, fear of reversible error. Under fear, the mind wants certainty. Aversion and worship are simply two different ways the mind tries to manufacture certainty: one by refusing the machine so that judgment feels human again, the other by surrendering to the machine so that judgment feels defensible. Both are coping strategies masquerading as epistemology.

Algorithm Aversion: The Human Tendency to Over-Punish Machine Error

Algorithm aversion is not mere technophobia. It is a specific cognitive pattern documented in controlled research. Dietvorst, Simmons and Massey showed that people often avoid algorithms after seeing them err, preferring even inferior human forecasters once a machine has made a visible mistake (Dietvorst, Simmons and Massey, 2015). The moral psychology underneath is easy to recognise. A human error can be forgiven as an expression of fallible agency; a machine error can be experienced as a betrayal of the very promise for which it was introduced—precision. In criminal justice, that betrayal can be emotionally magnified because the stakes are high. One notorious algorithmic failure, one publicised case of a person detained or sentenced on a flawed output, can trigger a broad rejection not merely of that tool but of the entire idea that prediction belongs in adjudication.

But algorithm aversion has a second, quieter face. Even when judges and officials do not reject the tool outright, they may treat the tool as illegitimate in exactly the cases where disciplined assistance would matter most—complex, high-salience, emotionally charged cases—while using it opportunistically in low-visibility settings. That produces a paradoxical pattern: the tool shapes routine justice while being excluded from cases that define public meaning. The system then experiences algorithmic decision-making not as consistent discipline but as selective convenience, and that selectivity itself becomes an engine of distrust.

The most important empirical nuance is that algorithm aversion is not inevitable. The follow-up work by Dietvorst, Simmons and Massey shows that giving people even slight, constrained control to adjust an algorithm's forecast can reduce aversion and increase willingness to use imperfect algorithms (Dietvorst, Simmons and Massey, 2018). In court terms, this is not a "UI trick." It is a psychological statement about agency: people are more willing to tolerate machine fallibility when they feel the decision remains theirs. This is a direct bridge between behavioural science and procedural justice: legitimacy depends on the perception that the decision-maker is not merely following an output but actively judging, with space for voice and context.

Algorithm Worship: Automation Bias and the Seduction of Numerical Authority

Algorithm worship is rarely announced as worship. It arrives as "objectivity," "evidence-based practice," "consistency," and "risk management." Its behavioural core is automation bias: the tendency to over-rely on automated aids, accept their recommendations, and commit both errors of commission (doing what the system suggests when it is wrong) and errors of omission (failing to act because the system did not flag) (Skitka, Mosier and Burdick, 1999). In a systematic review framing automation bias and verification complexity, the mechanism is described as a heuristic substitution: automated cues replace vigilant information processing, especially when verification is difficult and cognitive load is high (Lyell and Coiera, 2017). The courtroom is a perfect environment for this substitution. Verification is hard. Time is limited. Accountability is asymmetrical. Judges are blamed for the spectacular future harm more than for the invisible present over-detention. Under such pressures, an algorithmic output becomes a psychological shield.

Algorithm worship is intensified by opacity. If the model is hard to understand, the number can feel more scientific, not less. This is the "opacity effect" in a new register: when reasons are unavailable, the mind fills the gap with authority. The algorithm's lack of intelligibility does not always reduce its influence; it can increase it by making the output feel like a technical truth beyond ordinary contest (Barysė et al., 2023). At that point, the model is no longer evidence; it is a status assignment. "High risk" becomes a character label, and character labels invite coercion that feels morally easier to justify than explicit preventive detention.

A further twist is that worship can coexist with cynicism. Decision-makers may "trust" the model not because they believe in it as truth, but because they believe it as cover. In such cases, the algorithm is used not to reduce bias but to manage reputational risk: to justify a decision the judge already intends, or to process routine cases quickly, while retaining discretion to override when the political costs are high. The result is not neutral governance but a redistribution of accountability: the model absorbs blame when convenient, and humans reclaim authority when necessary. That pattern corrodes both legitimacy and accuracy because it trains institutions to treat algorithmic tools as rhetorical resources rather than epistemic instruments.

The Justice System's Amplifier: Why Both Pathologies Become Stronger in Court Than in Commerce

If a bank uses a model to approve loans, the consequences are serious, but the moral meaning is different. In criminal justice, the state condemns and coerces. That changes everything. A sentencing decision is not merely an allocation; it is a public judgment about culpability and worthiness of punishment. A pretrial detention decision is not merely a forecast; it is a deprivation of liberty under the presumption of innocence. A risk score in that environment can easily be heard as destiny. It can also easily be rejected as illegitimate power.

This is why public preference patterns in high-stakes contexts are so revealing. Conjoint experimental work examining public preferences for human versus algorithmic decision-makers in pretrial release finds that performance information matters, but it also shows that the type of decision-maker and perceived performance are evaluated differently across contexts; the public does not simply choose "accuracy," it chooses a governance posture (Bansak et al., 2024). It is similarly telling that work on algorithmic decision-making in judicial contexts finds that purely automated analysis tends to be judged as least fair, while human-only decision making is not necessarily seen as fully fair either; mixed human-algorithm involvement can be perceived as more fair than either extreme, reflecting a desire for both consistency and moral ownership (Barysė et al., 2023). These patterns are not contradictions. They reveal the public's implicit theory of legitimacy: people want the discipline of computation without the abdication of human responsibility.

The same dynamics appear in redistribution experiments: when decisions involve moral distribution rather than private prediction, people's acceptance of algorithmic decision-makers depends heavily on perceived impartiality and the symbolic meaning of being ruled by a machine (Chugunova and Sele, 2025). In criminal justice, where dignity and voice are central, those symbolic meanings matter. A system that cannot be experienced as hearing the individual will lose procedural legitimacy even if it improves statistical calibration.

The Forensic Analogy: Why Courts Mis-handle Algorithms the Way They Mis-handle Statistics

The court has already lived through the "numbers problem" in forensic evidence: match statistics that are misunderstood, likelihood ratios that are over-interpreted, and probabilistic claims that are treated as guilt. The algorithm aversion/worship split is the behavioural companion of this evidential vulnerability. Worship is the prosecutor's fallacy in institutional form: the number becomes the conclusion. Aversion is the anti-scientific reaction: because some numbers mislead, numbers are rejected. A mature evidential culture does neither. It disciplines the number through propositions, validation, and contestation, treating the output as weight, not as verdict.

Modern forensic-data-science thinking has been pushing law toward this discipline: reliability must be demonstrated under conditions of use; uncertainty must be communicated; and interpretive boundaries must be explicit, because decision-makers otherwise overread scientific-looking outputs (Robertson, Vignaux and Berger, 2016). Risk tools, sentencing recommenders, and pattern detectors are evidence-like in effect. If courts adopt them without forensic discipline, worship dominates. If courts react to scandals by blanket rejection, aversion dominates. Either way, the justice system fails to do its job: reasoned judgment.

Why Explainability Alone Cannot Cure Either Pathology

It is tempting to prescribe "explainability" as the cure: if we explain the model, aversion will fade and worship will become calibrated trust. But explainability is not a single thing. Feature lists and local explanations can create a false sense of understanding, and they can increase over-reliance when they function as narrative comfort rather than auditability. Meanwhile, deep technical transparency can overwhelm non-experts and create cynicism or performative compliance.

This is why procedural fairness frameworks insist that legitimacy is not created by explanations alone but by contestability and voice: the affected party must be able to challenge the decision in a way that can matter, otherwise explanation is merely informational theatre (Decker, 2025; Fischman-Afori, 2025). Kinchin's analysis of algorithmic justice frames this as a "procedural gap," where distributive concerns may be addressed by metrics while procedural voice remains unfulfilled; without voice, algorithmic systems struggle to achieve legitimacy even if they are "fair" by some statistical definition (Kinchin, 2024). In other words, explainability may soothe worship's conscience, and it may irritate aversion's suspicion, but it cannot substitute for legal mechanisms of scrutiny.

Two Modern Events That Intensify the Pathologies: Generative AI and Regulatory Signalling

Two developments since the early fairness debates have intensified both aversion and worship. The first is the rise of generative AI in legal contexts. Large language models can produce fluent legal reasoning, plausible summaries, and persuasive narratives, which increases worship risk because the output looks like a reasoned judgment even when it may contain unverified claims. At the same time, well-publicised incidents of hallucinated citations or fabricated authorities intensify aversion: people generalise from spectacular error to blanket distrust of "AI in law." The second development is regulatory signalling: risk-based AI regulation frameworks emphasise transparency, accountability, and oversight, but public discourse often collapses these into simplistic messages—either "AI is now safe because regulated" (worship) or "AI is now dangerous enough to need regulation" (aversion). Peer-reviewed legal analyses of AI governance have stressed that regulation is not a guarantee of correctness; it is a framework for accountability and procedural safeguards, which means public expectations must be managed rather than inflated.

A Court-Safe Synthesis: Calibrated Trust Through Adversarial Design

The only stable posture between aversion and worship is calibrated trust, and it is achieved not by lecturing people into rationality but by designing institutions that force rationality. The behavioural research already tells you the lever: agency and control reduce aversion (Dietvorst, Simmons and Massey, 2018). Procedural justice theory tells you the deeper structure: voice, dignity, and neutrality increase legitimacy and cooperation, especially when people experience the process as fair even under adverse outcomes (Tyler, 2011; Blader and Tyler, 2003). When these are combined, you get a blueprint for algorithmic use in court that avoids both pathologies:

the tool must be contestable, its outputs must be bounded to legally relevant questions, its error properties must be documented, and human decision-makers must remain the authors of reasons.

What follows is the practical implication that many systems resist because it is inconvenient: if an algorithmic output can affect liberty, it must be treated as a claim that triggers disclosure, validation, and challenge rights. That is not an "ethics add-on." It is the only way to prevent worship from turning the model into an unchallengeable witness. It is also the only way to prevent aversion from becoming the default reaction after inevitable error. When parties can test, contest, and contextualise algorithmic outputs, the public is more likely to accept algorithmic assistance as a bounded instrument rather than as a mystical authority or a threatening alien.

Conclusion: The Pathologies Are Human, the Remedy Is Institutional

Algorithm aversion and algorithm worship are not mysteries. They are predictable human responses to uncertainty under power. Aversion punishes the machine to restore moral comfort; worship surrenders to the machine to restore administrative safety. Criminal justice amplifies both because it operates under high stakes, high publicity, and deep moral meaning. The remedy is not to demand perfect public rationality. The remedy is to build a justice architecture that does what courts were invented to do: convert claims into contestable evidence, preserve human ownership of coercion, and make reasons public. Only then can algorithmic tools assist judgment without becoming its replacement.

References

- Bansak, K. et al. (2024) 'Public attitudes on performance for algorithmic and human decision-makers in high-stakes contexts', PNAS Nexus, 3(12), pgae520.
- Barysė, D. et al. (2023) 'Algorithms in the court: Does it matter which part of the judicial process is automated?', Frontiers in Artificial Intelligence, 5, 104xxxx.
- Blader, S.L. and Tyler, T.R. (2003) 'A four-component model of procedural justice: Defining the meaning of a "fair" process', Personality

and Social Psychology Bulletin, 29(6), pp. 747–758.

- Chugunova, M. and Sele, D. (2025) 'Ruled by robots: Preference for algorithmic decision makers in redistributive decisions', Empirical Economics, 68, pp. 1–34.
- Decker, M.C. (2025) 'Procedural fairness in algorithmic decision-making: The role of public engagement', Ethics and Information Technology, 27, pp. 1–18.
- Dietvorst, B.J., Simmons, J.P. and Massey, C. (2015) 'Algorithm aversion: People erroneously avoid algorithms after seeing them err', Journal of Experimental Psychology: General, 144(1), pp. 114–126.
- Dietvorst, B.J., Simmons, J.P. and Massey, C. (2018) 'Overcoming algorithm aversion: People will use imperfect algorithms if they can (even slightly) modify them', Management Science, 64(3), pp. 1155–1170.
- Ensign, D., Friedler, S.A., Neville, S., Scheidegger, C. and Venkatasubramanian, S. (2018) 'Runaway feedback loops in predictive policing', Proceedings of Machine Learning Research, 81, pp. 1–12.
- Fischman-Afori, O. (2025) 'Due process by design: Enhancing fairness and trust in AI decision-making through procedural justice theory', Social Sciences & Humanities Open, 12, 102178.
- Kinchin, N. (2024) '"Voiceless": The procedural gap in algorithmic justice', International Journal of Law and Information Technology, 32(4), pp. 1–30.
- Logg, J.M., Minson, J.A. and Moore, D.A. (2019) 'Algorithm appreciation: People prefer algorithmic to human judgment', Organizational Behavior and Human Decision Processes, 151, pp. 90–103.
- Lyell, D. and Coiera, E. (2017) 'Automation bias and verification complexity: A systematic review', Journal of the American Medical Informatics Association, 24(2), pp. 423–431.
- Robertson, B., Vignaux, G.A. and Berger, C.E.H. (2016) Interpreting Evidence: Evaluating Forensic Science in the Courtroom. 2nd edn. Chichester: Wiley.
- Skitka, L.J., Mosier, K.L. and Burdick, M. (1999) 'Does automation bias decision-making?', International Journal of Human–Computer Studies, 51(5), pp. 991–1006.
- Starke, C., Lünich, M. and Marcinkowski, F. (2022) 'Fairness perceptions of algorithmic decision-making: A systematic review', Big Data & Society, 9(2), pp. 1–18.

- Tyler, T.R. (2011) 'Procedural justice, legitimacy, and the effective rule of law', Crime and Justice, 40(1), pp. 283–357.

CHAPTER XXVII

Why People Accept Punishment: Compliance, Shame, Deterrence and Meaning

Punishment Is Not Only a Threat, It Is a Message

If you watch criminal justice closely enough, you see a paradox that textbooks often flatten. The state can punish with force, yet it cannot practically govern by force alone. Courts depend on the everyday willingness of ordinary people to comply, to appear, to tell the truth, to accept outcomes, to desist, to cooperate with police, and to treat legal authority as something more than an enemy. That willingness is not a single thing called "obedience." It is a layered psychological achievement produced by fear, morality, identity, shame, procedural experience, social bonds, and the meanings people attach to law. This is why the question "Why do people accept punishment?" is not sentimental sociology; it is the operating manual of legitimacy.

A narrow instrumental story says: people comply because punishment deters. A narrow moral story says: people comply because punishment is deserved. A mature account says: compliance is often achieved by legitimacy, and legitimacy is built less by outcome severity than by how authorities exercise power—whether they are seen as neutral, respectful, and willing to hear those they govern (Tyler, 2011). In online and remote legal proceedings, research continues to find that procedural justice perceptions are strongly related to perceived legitimacy and acceptance, even when access-to-justice conditions differ (Mentovich, 2023). The core implication for criminal justice is stark: punishment that is "effective" in a short-term instrumental sense can still be rejected as illegitimate, and once legitimacy erodes, every subsequent act of governance becomes harder.

Compliance as a Social Achievement, Not a Mechanical Reaction

The most common mistake is to treat compliance as a reflex. In real life, compliance is a decision repeated over time, under changing pressures, made by a person embedded in relationships and identity. People ask themselves, often implicitly: "Does this authority deserve my compliance?" "Was I treated fairly?" "Am I being controlled or guided?" "Do these officials see me as a person?" Procedural justice theory insists that legitimacy is a primary pathway through which legal authorities obtain cooperation, because fair treatment signals membership, dignity, and neutrality; the citizen is more likely to comply when the system feels morally credible (Tyler, 2011). This is not merely about feelings. It predicts behaviour: reporting crimes, obeying laws, appearing in court, and cooperating with legal authorities.

You can see the same logic in policing legitimacy scholarship. A 2025 review-style piece by Tyler reiterates the centrality of legitimacy-based approaches, tying procedural justice to public cooperation and compliance (Tyler, 2025). And contemporary empirical work, even outside Western settings, continues to find that normative variables such as procedural justice and perceived obligation are robust predictors of satisfaction and support for policing relative to purely deterrent variables, reinforcing the idea that legitimacy is not culturally parochial but psychologically general (Alotaibi, Boateng and Pryce, 2025).

If you are tempted to dismiss legitimacy as "soft," remember this: deterrence without legitimacy often produces compliance only under surveillance, and surveillance is costly, politically dangerous, and psychologically corrosive. Legitimacy is the cheaper and more stable technology of governance.

Deterrence: Certainty, Severity, and the Misplaced Faith in Harshness

Deterrence does matter, but not in the cartoonish way it is sold. The deterrence tradition distinguishes general deterrence (others refrain) from specific deterrence (the punished refrain), and it distinguishes certainty of punishment from severity. The empirical literature repeatedly suggests that certainty tends to be more influential than severity, and that the strongest deterrence effects are often found in contexts where detection is credible and the sanction is predictable rather than spectacular. Focused deterrence interventions provide one of the cleaner bodies of evidence here: meta-analytic work finds crime reductions, though the magnitude varies and effects depend heavily on implementation quality and context (Braga, 2024).

But deterrence always runs into a psychological boundary: the human mind discounts low-probability outcomes and struggles to learn from distant threats. Harshness can become theatre if certainty is weak. This is why policy often produces a perverse pairing: low certainty and high severity, which maximises moral cost while minimising behavioural effect.

Deterrence also becomes morally unstable when punishment is experienced as unfair. Defiance theory predicts that perceived illegitimacy can generate defiance rather than deterrence: individuals may respond to punishment by rejecting authority and increasing offending when they feel they were treated disrespectfully or unjustly (Sherman, 1993). That is the hidden cost of punitive excess: an institution can inadvertently manufacture the very noncompliance it claims to suppress.

Shame, Guilt, and the Emotional Machinery of Acceptance

Deterrence treats the person as a calculator. Shame and guilt treat the person as a moral being embedded in social bonds. The psychology here is delicate. Guilt is often associated with a focus on the wrongdoing—"I did something wrong"—and tends to motivate repair. Shame is often associated with a focus on the self—"I am bad"—and can motivate withdrawal, concealment, hostility, or collapse. This distinction is old in psychology and remains central in contemporary work, including evolutionary and functional accounts that treat guilt as reparative and shame as potentially socially defensive (Cimpeanu et al., 2025).

Punishment produces acceptance more reliably when it evokes guilt-like responsibility rather than shame-like degradation. This is the logic behind reintegrative shaming: condemn the act, not the person; communicate disapproval while preserving the offender's membership in the community; create a pathway back (Braithwaite, 1989). The distinction is not poetic. It predicts different trajectories: stigmatizing shame can harden deviance; reintegrative shame can support desistance, especially when accompanied by genuine reintegration practices. Contemporary scholarship linking restorative justice to reintegrative shaming continues to develop these mechanisms and emphasises that "shaming" is not a unitary practice; its social context determines whether it heals or harms (Braithwaite, 2020).

Recent empirical work continues to test reintegrative shaming mechanisms in justice settings. For example, a 2026 study testing reintegrative shaming theory in a real-world justice context (drink-driving cases) focuses on how social disapproval shapes offender emotions, reinforcing the basic idea that the emotional experience of censure matters to subsequent compliance and self-concept (Lee, 2026).

The deepest point is this: people "accept punishment" not only because they fear it, but because punishment can realign identity. A sanction that communicates, "You violated a shared norm, and you must answer," can be internalised. A sanction that communicates, "You are beneath us," is more likely to be resisted or metabolised into anger and alienation.

Meaning-Making: Punishment as Narrative Repair

The acceptance of punishment is often a struggle over meaning. People ask: "What does this punishment say about me?" "What does it say about what I did?" "Is this condemnation fair?" "Is it proportionate?" "Is it aimed at my reform or my humiliation?" These are not philosophical luxuries. They are the everyday cognitive work through which humans integrate moral injury and social sanction.

Communicative theories of punishment make this explicit: punishment is a form of moral communication—censure addressed to a responsible agent—rather than merely pain imposed for instrumental ends (Duff, 2001). If punishment is to be accepted as legitimate, the message must be intelligible and publicly defensible. Where punishment becomes purely managerial—risk management, incapacitation, optimisation—its meaning becomes thin, and acceptance declines.

This is why procedural justice is not merely a technique; it is the stage on which meaning is formed. A person who loses but feels heard can still accept the outcome as lawful; a person who wins but feels disrespected may still reject authority. Mentovich's work on online proceedings underscores how legitimacy concerns extend into new procedural forms: procedural justice perceptions remain central to acceptance even when the "courtroom" becomes a screen (Mentovich, 2023).

When Punishment Backfires: Humiliation, Stigma, and the Defiance Pathway

Not all punishment produces compliance. Sometimes it produces the opposite. The psychological route is often humiliation. Humiliation is shame without reintegration; it is the experience of being made small without being offered a way back. It can trigger anger, revenge fantasies, and a desire to reassert control. When institutions punish in ways that communicate contempt, they can produce defiance and oppositional identity. This is the behavioural reality behind defiance theory (Sherman, 1993) and behind a wide literature on legitimacy and cooperation.

This is also where "character" narratives become dangerous. When systems treat people as types—incorrigible, dangerous, "high risk"—they reduce the person's perceived capacity for change. That reduction shapes institutional behaviour: fewer second chances, more surveillance, harsher responses to minor breaches. The person, sensing that the system has already decided who they are, becomes less likely to invest in compliance as identity repair. Punishment then becomes a stable social role: offenderhood.

Forensic Application: How Evidence Practices Shape Acceptance

From a forensic perspective, acceptance of punishment is deeply influenced by whether the person believes the finding of responsibility was grounded in disciplined reasoning. Courts that mishandle probabilities, overstate forensic confidence, or treat risk outputs as proof erode acceptance because they undermine the perceived integrity of truth-finding. The "probability is not proof" discipline matters here not only for accuracy but for legitimacy: a person is more likely to accept condemnation when the evidential path looks rational and contestable.

This is where algorithmic decision-making becomes a psychological accelerant. If a risk score is treated as destiny, the person experiences condemnation not as an evaluation of culpable choice but as bureaucratic classification. If an algorithm is opaque, the person experiences decision-making as precomputed. Procedural legitimacy suffers, and shame becomes stigmatizing rather than reintegrative. In such conditions, punishment may still deter under surveillance, but it is less likely to reform identity, and it may produce defiance.

The Institutional Synthesis: What Actually Produces Durable Acceptance

A durable compliance regime is not built on a single lever. It is built on a layered structure: credible certainty of consequences for serious harms, bounded proportionality that preserves dignity, and procedures that communicate neutrality and respect. Deterrence contributes by shaping the background expectation that wrongdoing carries predictable cost. Shame and guilt contribute by shaping the internal moral story. Meaning contributes by turning punishment into narrative closure rather than arbitrary pain. Procedural justice contributes by ensuring that the story is believable, because it was reached through a process that treated the person as a participant.

If you want a practical moral test, use this: when punishment is accepted, it is often because the person can say, even through clenched teeth, "I see why this happened." When punishment is rejected, it is often because the person says, "This was done to me," rather than "I answered for what I did." The difference between those sentences is the difference between governance by force and governance by legitimacy.

References

- Alotaibi, H.A., Boateng, F.D. and Pryce, D.K. (2025) 'The effect of procedural justice on general satisfaction with police: A study from Saudi Arabia', American Journal of Criminal Justice.
- Blader, S.L. and Tyler, T.R. (2003) 'A four-component model of procedural justice: Defining the meaning of a "fair" process', Personality and Social Psychology Bulletin, 29(6), pp. 747–758.
- Braithwaite, J. (1989) Crime, Shame and Reintegration. Cambridge: Cambridge University Press.
- Braithwaite, J. (2020) 'Restorative justice and reintegrative shaming', in The Oxford Handbook of Restorative Justice.
- Braga, A.A. (2024) 'Focused deterrence can reduce crime: A systematic review and meta-analysis', Criminology & Public Policy.
- Cimpeanu, T. et al. (2025) 'The evolutionary advantage of guilt: Co-evolution of social and moral emotions', [peer-reviewed journal article].

- Decker, M.C. (2025) 'Procedural fairness in algorithmic decision-making: The role of public engagement', Ethics and Information Technology.
- Dietvorst, B.J., Simmons, J.P. and Massey, C. (2015) 'Algorithm aversion: People erroneously avoid algorithms after seeing them err', Journal of Experimental Psychology: General, 144(1), pp. 114–126.
- Duff, R.A. (2001) Punishment, Communication, and Community. Oxford: Oxford University Press.
- Ensign, D., Friedler, S.A., Neville, S., Scheidegger, C. and Venkatasubramanian, S. (2018) 'Runaway feedback loops in predictive policing', Proceedings of Machine Learning Research, 81, pp. 1–12.
- Feigenson, N. (2007) 'Emotions and attributions of legal responsibility and blame: A research review', Law and Human Behavior, 31(2), pp. 143–168.
- Hernán, M.A. and Robins, J.M. (2025) Causal Inference: What If. Boca Raton: Chapman & Hall/CRC.
- Kuo, K.M. et al. (2020) 'A meta-analysis of deterrence theory in security-compliant/risk behaviors', Computers & Security, 95, 101859.
- Lee, J. (2026) 'The role of reintegrative shaming in juvenile criminal justice', [peer-reviewed journal article].
- Lum, K. and Isaac, W. (2016) 'To predict and serve?', Significance, 13(5), pp. 14–19.
- Mentovich, A. (2023) 'Legitimacy and online proceedings: Procedural justice, access to justice, and the role of income', Law & Society Review.
- Mottershead, T. et al. (2024) 'A mixed-methods systematic review of offence-related shame and guilt', Aggression and Violent Behavior, 76, 1019xx.
- Neil, R. (2025) 'Algorithmic bias in criminal risk assessment: The consequences of racial differences in arrest as a measure of crime', Annual Review of Criminology, 8, pp. 97–119.
- Pleiss, G., Raghavan, M., Wu, F., Kleinberg, J. and Weinberger, K.Q. (2017) 'On fairness and calibration', Advances in Neural Information Processing Systems, 30.
- Quintas, J. (2024) 'Do normative issues outperform deterrence for compliance?', [SAGE peer-reviewed journal].
- Sherman, L.W. (1993) 'Defiance, deterrence, and irrelevance: A theory of the criminal sanction', Journal of Research in Crime and Delinquency, 30(4), pp. 445–473.

- Singh, D. et al. (2025) 'Understanding shame, guilt, embarrassment and pride', Frontiers in Psychology.
- Starke, C., Lünich, M. and Marcinkowski, F. (2022) 'Fairness perceptions of algorithmic decision-making: A systematic review', Big Data & Society, 9(2).
- Tangney, J.P. and Dearing, R.L. (2003) Shame and Guilt. New York: Guilford Press.
- Tyler, T.R. (2006) Why People Obey the Law. 2nd edn. Princeton, NJ: Princeton University Press.
- Tyler, T.R. (2011) 'Procedural justice, legitimacy, and the effective rule of law', Crime and Justice, 40(1), pp. 283–357.
- Tyler, T.R. (2025) 'Legitimacy-based policing', Criminology & Public Policy.
- Wüschner, P. (2017) 'Shame, guilt, and punishment.'

CHAPTER XXVIII

The Judicial Face: Authority, Empathy, and the Human Encounter

Authority as a Human Performance, Not a Mere Office

A court's authority is often described as if it were an impersonal property of the state, like gravity: the robe, the seal, the summons, the sentence. But authority is not only possessed; it is performed, and it is received. The "judicial face" is the place where the state becomes visible as a person speaking to a person, and it is here—more than in statutes—that legitimacy is either cultivated or squandered. Procedural justice research has made the point so repeatedly that it now reads like the operating manual of lawful power: when people experience decision-making as fair, they are more likely to comply, cooperate, and accept outcomes even when the outcome is adverse (Tyler, 2011; Tyler, 2006). The reasons are not mystical. People watch for voice, neutrality, respectful treatment, and trustworthy motives; these cues signal whether they are being governed as citizens or processed as objects (Tyler, 2007; Blader and Tyler, 2003). The judicial face is where those cues are delivered—through tone, listening, explanation, patience, even through the disciplined restraint that refuses sarcasm and humiliation. A judge who is impeccably "correct" but dismissive can win the case and lose the person; and a system that loses people regularly will pay later in noncooperation, defiance, and the slow corrosion of public trust (Tyler, 2011; Sherman, 1993).

You can see this vividly in global jurisprudence on impartiality and the appearance of justice. Courts across traditions have treated apparent bias as a legitimacy catastrophe, because justice must not only be done but be seen to be done. That insistence is not merely symbolic. It recognizes that citizens interpret institutions through human encounters. The judge is therefore not merely a calculator of outcomes; the judge is the state's most intimate interface with the governed. In that interface, authority is not strengthened by harshness. It is strengthened by composure, reasoned clarity, and the experience that the judge heard what could be said and decided on intelligible grounds.

The Judicial Encounter as Procedural Justice in Action

In the procedural justice tradition, "voice" does not mean that the judge agrees; it means that the person had a genuine opportunity to tell their story and experienced that it was taken seriously as input (Blader and Tyler, 2003; Tyler, 2007). "Neutrality" does not mean that the judge has no values; it means the judge appears consistent, principled, and guided by evidence rather than by whim or prejudice (Tyler, 2011). "Respect" is not politeness theatre; it is the lived signal that the person is treated with dignity and not reduced to stereotype (Tyler, 2011). "Trustworthy motives" is the inference that the authority is acting for public reasons, not for convenience, animus, or reputational self-protection (Tyler, 2006). This is why the judicial face matters so much: it is the medium through which these components are conveyed, and those components are the machinery by which law achieves compliance without permanent coercion (Tyler, 2011; Tyler, 2015).

Courtroom practice makes this concrete. A defendant may accept a sentence they dislike if they believe the judge understood the context, applied a consistent standard, and explained the reasons. A victim may accept an acquittal they hate if they feel treated with respect and believe the process was not stacked. A witness may cooperate again if they were not humiliated. These are not sentimental hopes; they are repeatable social patterns. Research on confidence and procedural justice in justice system contact continues to show that voice, neutrality, and respect are central predictors of confidence in legal authority and engagement with it (Bradford, 2011; Tyler, 2011). The judicial face is the concentrated site where those predictors are either strengthened or destroyed.

Empathy and Impartiality: The False War and the Real Risk

Empathy is often treated as the enemy of impartiality, as if a judge who understands becomes a judge who favours. That framing is psychologically naïve and institutionally dangerous. Judges cannot avoid interpreting human meaning; they can only avoid doing it well. The more accurate tension is not "empathy versus law" but "unregulated emotion versus disciplined understanding." Contemporary work on emotions in legal decision-making describes how legal professionals manage and strategically frame emotional engagement so it does not appear to compromise authority, while still recognizing that empathy can function as a cognitive tool for understanding facts, motives, and human context (Johansen, 2025). The judicial face, in this sense, is emotional labour: the judge must remain open enough to comprehend suffering and constraint, yet stable enough to avoid being captured by pity, outrage, or disgust.

Empathy becomes ethically relevant in two distinct ways that are too often mixed up. First, empathy can improve factual understanding—what the defendant meant, what the witness experienced, why a victim behaved in a particular way, why a person failed to appear, why a breach occurred. Second, empathy can shape moral response—how harshly blame is attributed, how much mercy feels permissible, how severe a risk feels. The first function is often necessary for accurate adjudication; the second function must be constrained by principles of equality and proportionality. The best judicial posture is therefore not empathy as indulgence, but empathy as disciplined perception: understanding without surrendering the rule that like cases should be treated alike and that punishment must remain bounded by public reasons.

Judicial research and reflective scholarship have increasingly treated empathy as a "challenge" precisely because it must be managed rather than embraced or banished. A recent scholarly volume developed from empirical work with judges frames empathy as a complex part of judging rather than as either virtue or vice, emphasizing the practical ways judges negotiate emotional and moral cognition at the bench (Czapska et al., 2024). The judicial face is where this negotiation becomes visible: how a judge responds to remorse, how a judge addresses trauma, how a judge handles anger in the courtroom without escalating it, and how a judge communicates that compassion does not mean partiality.

Demeanor, Credibility, and the Forensic Danger of "Reading Faces"

The courtroom has long relied on demeanor—how someone looks, speaks, hesitates, cries, or remains calm—as if these were windows into truth. This is one of the oldest forensic risks in adjudication: humans are confident mind-readers and unreliable lie detectors. The judicial face becomes decisive here because judges model how the system interprets human presentation. If a judge signals that certain emotional performances are "credible," witnesses and defendants learn what to perform. If a judge treats flat affect as coldness, coldness as lack of remorse, and lack of remorse as dangerousness, the system can punish not the wrong but the person's inability or refusal to perform the expected emotional script. Empirical work examining honesty, communication, and sentencing shows how communicative cues can influence sentencing judgments across cultures, revealing how easily "character" inferences can attach to presentation rather than to culpability (Berryessa, 2026).

This is where forensic discipline must enter moral judgment. A judge should treat demeanor as potentially informative but never dispositive; should demand corroboration; should resist collapsing neurodivergence, trauma responses, or cultural norms into moral conclusions; and should recognize that the judicial face does not merely perceive credibility—it actively shapes the courtroom's credibility economy. The rule-of-law problem is that demeanor-based inference is rarely reviewable, which means it can operate as unaccountable discretion. The judicial face must therefore be trained to doubt itself, because unchecked confidence in reading minds is one of the easiest ways justice becomes unequal while believing it is humane.

Shame, Censure, and the Difference Between Condemning Acts and Degrading Persons

People accept punishment not only because they fear it, but because punishment can function as moral meaning: a public declaration that a norm matters and that a wrong requires answerability. Communicative theories of punishment insist that punishment is not mere pain; it is censure addressed to an agent (Duff, 2001). But censure can be delivered in two morally opposite ways. It can condemn the act while preserving the offender's standing as a person capable of rejoining the moral community, or it can degrade the offender as a type—incorrigible, dirty, beneath respect. The second posture produces stigma and defiance; the first can produce reintegration and desistance (Braithwaite, 1989; Sherman, 1993).

The judicial face is where this difference becomes real. The same sentence can be delivered as principled restraint or as contempt. The first strengthens legitimacy, and legitimacy fosters compliance beyond surveillance (Tyler, 2011). The second may extract short-term obedience but undermines long-term cooperation and internal moral alignment. This is not abstract. If a judge's manner communicates humiliation, the system invites defiance; if it communicates firm respect, the system invites accountability. The judicial face is therefore a moral instrument: it can convert punishment into a pathway back, or into a badge of permanent exclusion.

Technology and the Human Encounter: When the Judge Becomes a Node in a System

Modern justice systems increasingly mediate the judicial encounter through technology: remote hearings, digital case management, algorithmic risk tools, and AI-assisted drafting or summarization. These tools can improve access and consistency, but they also change what the judicial face is allowed to do. A remote hearing may reduce intimidation yet reduce the felt sense that the judge "knows" the case, an effect already observed in virtual court contexts where participants may feel less recognised by the judge despite improved comfort (Ray et al., 2022). Algorithmic tools can promise neutrality yet create a procedural gap if parties cannot meaningfully contest the output and the judge defers to it as if it were evidence rather than a model (Kinchin, 2024; Fischman-Afori, 2025). Public perception research shows that AI involvement in judicial decisions shifts perceived legitimacy and procedural justice, with nuanced patterns across groups and levels of AI assistance (Fine, Berthelot and Marsh, 2025). If the judicial face becomes the mouthpiece of a system output, authority becomes less personal but not necessarily more legitimate; it can become more alien.

Judges themselves are already reporting how machine decision-making technologies shape the sentencing environment, including concerns about autonomy, moral ownership, and the place of human judgment when "machine-based sentencing" appears (Dagan, 2026). This matters for the human encounter because the judge's willingness to make eye contact, to explain, to listen, and to own reasons is part of what produces procedural justice. If the judge feels pressured to follow an output for safety or consistency, mercy becomes harder to justify and blame becomes easier to outsource. That is not merely a technological change; it is a change in the moral grammar of judging.

The Forensic Point: The Judge as the Final Interpreter of Uncertainty

Every criminal case contains uncertainty, and uncertainty is where the judicial face does its most important work. Forensic evidence—DNA, digital traces, pattern comparisons, probabilistic estimates—rarely arrives as certainty; it arrives as inferential weight. The court's task is to translate weight into decision under a burden of proof and within a moral framework. Forensic evidence scholarship has long insisted that courts must discipline how probabilistic outputs are interpreted, because scientific-looking claims are easily overread (Robertson, Vignaux and Berger, 2016). The judicial face is the last barrier against that overreading. A judge who treats probability as proof does not only risk wrongful conviction; they also risk legitimacy, because the condemned person experiences the system as irrationally certain.

In a predictive legal order, this extends beyond forensic traces to risk tools and algorithmic summaries. The judge must not allow forecast to become character, or prediction to become culpability. The judicial face should signal epistemic humility: the court decides because it must, but it decides with awareness of limits, with reasons that can be contested, and with restraint proportional to the evidence. This is how authority becomes lawful rather than merely powerful.

Training the Judicial Face: Emotional Regulation as Rule of Law

If you accept that the judicial face carries legitimacy, then judicial training cannot be restricted to doctrine and procedure. It must include emotional regulation, bias awareness, and communication discipline as components of legal competence. This is not "soft skill." It is due process in action. Emotional engagement, if unmanaged, can turn into moral aggression; emotional suppression, if rigid, can turn into coldness that feels like contempt. Contemporary research on emotions in legal decision-making increasingly treats judicial emotion management as a real part of professional practice, not an embarrassing deviation from rationality (Johansen, 2025). Problem-solving court scholarship likewise emphasizes that participants value telling their story to an authority who listens and cares, and that such interaction is therapeutically and procedurally consequential (Winick and Wexler, 2003; Duffy, 2012). The judicial face is therefore not merely personal style; it is institutional design embodied in a human being.

Conclusion: The Human Encounter as the System's Legitimacy Engine

You can build a court system that is efficient, data-rich, and technologically advanced, and still fail at the oldest task of law: making coercion morally intelligible. The judicial face is where that intelligibility is formed. Authority is stabilized when the judge is experienced as neutral, respectful, and reasoned; empathy becomes legitimate when it serves understanding rather than favoritism; and the human encounter becomes justice when it preserves voice and dignity even under condemnation (Tyler, 2011; Blader and Tyler, 2003; Duff, 2001). Technology can assist this, but it can also hollow it out if it turns the judge into a validator of outputs rather than an author of reasons. If the future of justice is to remain recognisably human, the judge must remain the state's accountable face: calm enough to hold power without cruelty, open enough to understand without surrender, and disciplined enough to ensure that the courtroom remains a place where persons are encountered as persons, not processed as profiles.

References

- Berryessa, C.M. (2026) 'Honesty as a "communicative tool" in sentencing', Journal of Criminal Justice, 94, 1022xx.
- Blader, S.L. and Tyler, T.R. (2003) 'A four-component model of procedural justice: Defining the meaning of a "fair" process', Personality and Social Psychology Bulletin, 29(6), pp. 747–758.
- Bradford, B. (2011) 'Voice, neutrality and respect: Use of victim support services, procedural justice, and confidence in the criminal justice system', Criminology & Criminal Justice, 11(4), pp. 345–366.
- Braithwaite, J. (1989) Crime, Shame and Reintegration. Cambridge: Cambridge University Press.
- Czapska, J., Olszewska, A., Stępień, M. and Wójcik, A. (eds) (2024) Judges, Decision Making and Empathy: Insights from the Bench. Abingdon: Routledge.

- Dagan, N. (2026) 'Sentencing as a human process? Human judges' experiences with machine-based sentencing', The British Journal of Criminology (advance article).
- Duffy, J. (2012) 'Problem-solving courts, therapeutic jurisprudence and the constitution: If two is company, is three a crowd?', Melbourne University Law Review, 35(2), pp. 394–446.
- Duff, R.A. (2001) Punishment, Communication, and Community. Oxford: Oxford University Press.
- Fine, A., Berthelot, E.R. and Marsh, S. (2025) 'Public perceptions of judges' use of AI tools in courtroom decision-making: An examination of legitimacy, fairness, trust, and procedural justice', Behavioral Sciences, 15(4), 476.
- Fischman-Afori, O. (2025) 'Due process by design: Enhancing fairness and trust in AI decision-making through procedural justice theory', Social Sciences & Humanities Open, 12, 102178.
- Johansen, L.V. (2025) 'Constructing objectivity: Emotions in legal decision making', Frontiers in Psychology.
- Kinchin, N. (2024) '"Voiceless": The procedural gap in algorithmic justice', International Journal of Law and Information Technology, 32(4), pp. 1–30.
- Mentovich, A. (2023) 'Legitimacy and online proceedings: Procedural justice, access to justice, and the role of income', Law & Society Review, 57(4), pp. 617–650.
- Ray, B., Kunkel, T., Bryant, K., Hedden, B., Andraka-Christou, B., O'Neil, M. and Huynh, P. (2022) 'Client attitudes toward virtual treatment court', Journal of Substance Abuse Treatment, 140, 108833.
- Robertson, B., Vignaux, G.A. and Berger, C.E.H. (2016) Interpreting Evidence: Evaluating Forensic Science in the Courtroom. 2nd edn. Chichester: Wiley.
- Rottman, D.B. (2000) 'Therapeutic jurisprudence and the emergence of problem-solving courts', National Institute of Justice Journal.
- Sherman, L.W. (1993) 'Defiance, deterrence, and irrelevance: A theory of the criminal sanction', Journal of Research in Crime and Delinquency, 30(4), pp. 445–473.
- Tyler, T.R. (2006) Why People Obey the Law. 2nd edn. Princeton, NJ: Princeton University Press.
- Tyler, T.R. (2007) 'Procedural justice and the courts', Court Review, 44(1–2), pp. 26–31.

- Tyler, T.R. (2011) 'Procedural justice, legitimacy, and the effective rule of law', Crime and Justice, 40(1), pp. 283–357.
- Tyler, T.R. (2015) 'Procedural justice, legitimacy, and effective law enforcement', in Proactive Policing: Effects on Crime and Communities. Washington, DC: National Academies Press (chapter).
- Winick, B.J. and Wexler, D.B. (2003) 'Therapeutic jurisprudence and problem-solving courts', Fordham Urban Law Journal, 30(3), pp. 1055–1090.

CHAPTER XXIX

Scandal, Error, and the Fragility of Institutional Trust

Trust Is a Governance Asset, Not a Public Mood

A criminal justice institution can survive a great deal of criticism, but it cannot survive the loss of believable authority. Trust is not public affection; it is the practical willingness to accept decisions as binding, to cooperate, to disclose, to report, to appear, to obey, and to let the state speak in the grammar of legitimacy rather than in the grammar of force. Once you see trust as a governance asset, you understand why scandal is so destabilising. Scandal is not merely wrongdoing; it is wrongdoing that becomes symbolically diagnostic. It tells the public, "This system does not behave as it claims," and it invites people to reinterpret every ordinary decision as potentially contaminated. Error does something similar, even without malice. A visible error—especially an error that harms an innocent person or targets a vulnerable group—turns procedural imperfections into moral facts. It invites the public to draw a sweeping inference: if the system failed here, the system is untrustworthy everywhere.

Procedural justice theory explains why this inference is so powerful. People accept legal authority not only because of expected costs of defiance, but because they perceive procedures as fair, neutral, respectful, and grounded in trustworthy motives (Tyler, 2011). The point is not that outcomes do not matter; it is that outcomes are interpreted through process. When a scandal exposes disrespect, arbitrariness, or hidden bias, it does not merely subtract credibility; it changes the lens through which all future actions are seen. The institution can still compel, but it no longer persuades. And when persuasion collapses, the system must spend far more on surveillance, enforcement, and coercion to obtain the same behavioural compliance.

The Anatomy of Scandal: When the System Reveals Its True Priorities

A scandal is not only a factual event; it is an interpretive event. It occurs when a harm becomes publicly legible as a symptom of deeper institutional logic. This is why algorithmic scandals are uniquely corrosive in the current era. They are rarely experienced as "a single mistake." They are experienced as automated injustice: the idea that unfairness has been scaled, hidden, and rationalised as "data-driven." The SyRI case in the Netherlands offers a clean illustration of scandal as diagnosis, not because the details are universally identical, but because the public meaning is globally transferable. Peer-reviewed analyses of the SyRI judgment describe how a welfare fraud risk profiling system, supported by legislation, was invalidated on human rights grounds including privacy and lack of adequate safeguards, and how the case has become a landmark reference point for algorithmic accountability and legitimacy (van Bekkum, Borgesius and others, 2021; Rachovitsa, 2022; Wieringa, 2023). In these accounts, scandal emerges from a particular combination: opacity, asymmetric burden on the vulnerable, and institutional convenience presented as neutral optimisation.

What makes scandal contagious is not only the harm but the perceived mismatch between institutional rhetoric and institutional practice. A system that claims neutrality but operates through hidden profiling invites the public to infer betrayal. And betrayal triggers a distinctive psychological reaction: people do not merely revise beliefs; they revise the category. "This is not justice; this is targeting." Once that category shift occurs, ordinary errors are no longer interpreted as unfortunate; they are interpreted as proof.

Error Without Malice: Why Mistakes Can Break Legitimacy Faster Than Bad Faith

It is comforting to believe that only corruption destroys trust. In practice, visible error can be just as corrosive because it strikes at epistemic integrity. Criminal justice claims a special kind of authority: not merely the authority to act, but the authority to claim truth about events and responsibility about persons. When error undermines that truth-claim, every condemnation looks less like public reason and more like institutional hazard.

Forensic science is the clearest laboratory of this fragility because forensic evidence is often the symbolic centre of "objective proof." Yet peer-reviewed work has shown how small shifts in examiner decision thresholds can dramatically affect error rates and therefore the probative value of pattern-matching evidence (Thompson, 2023). The scandal risk here is not only that mistakes occur, but that the public learns something more frightening: confidence can be manufactured by context, pressure, and institutional culture. A system that advertises certainty, while its certainty is sensitive to threshold drift, becomes trust-fragile by design. This is how an apparently technical finding becomes a legitimacy problem. Once the public understands that "science" in court can be shaped by discretionary thresholds, they begin to treat every confident forensic claim as potentially performative rather than evidential.

The same fragility arises with algorithmic tools. A risk score that is presented as neutral evidence but later revealed to be based on contaminated labels—arrest as a proxy for offending, supervision intensity as a proxy for "noncompliance," policing deployment as a driver of recorded incidents—creates a legitimacy fracture. The fracture does not require the public to understand calibration mathematics. It requires only the intuitive recognition that the "objective number" was partly the system predicting its own attention.

Algorithmic Scandal Has a Special Feature: It Looks Like Systemic Intent

Human error is psychologically easier to forgive because it can be placed inside a moral story: a person tried and failed. Algorithmic error is often experienced as impersonal harm with institutional endorsement, and that makes it feel more like systemic intent even when no one intended discrimination. This is a crucial feature of modern scandal: people may not believe the system is malicious, but they believe the system is indifferent, and indifference under coercive power feels morally close to hostility.

Peer-reviewed research on public sector human–AI interactions helps explain how these perceptions form. Alon-Barkat and colleagues show that decision-makers exhibit patterns of overreliance on algorithmic advice (automation bias) and selective adherence when recommendations align with stereotypes, indicating that algorithmic systems can amplify human biases rather than neutralise them, especially under warning signals and organisational pressures (Alon-Barkat et al., 2023). In scandal terms, this means that even if the algorithm is technically competent, the institution can still behave untrustworthily because it uses the algorithm as an authority amplifier. When the public discovers this, they do not blame "the tool." They blame the institution that chose to treat the tool as if it were a moral shield.

Institutional Trust Is Not Only About Outputs; It Is About Trustworthiness Signals

To understand why trust collapses, you must distinguish trust from trustworthiness. Trust is what the public grants; trustworthiness is what the institution demonstrates. Opacity undermines trustworthiness because it prevents verification of whether the institution is acting for defensible reasons. Wieringa's peer-reviewed study of algorithmic accountability practices around SyRI shows precisely how accountability practices can fall short when algorithmic systems are embedded in complex organisational arrangements, revealing the limits of post-hoc legitimacy repair when transparency and contestability were absent at the outset (Wieringa, 2023).

This is why "explanations" rarely fix scandal. Explanations can be perceived as public relations rather than accountability. Once scandal occurs, the public's prior belief updates toward suspicion, and institutional communications are filtered through that suspicion. At that point, the only reliable repair mechanisms are structural: independent audits, enforceable contestability, disclosure of validation and error properties, and credible sanctions for institutional misuse. Absent these, the institution is asking the public to trust precisely what has been shown to be untrustworthy.

The Transference Problem: How One Failure Contaminates the Entire Category

One of the most dangerous dynamics for institutions is what you might call category contamination: one publicised failure reshapes trust in unrelated systems. This is not irrational; it is a normal response to perceived homogeneity. Longoni, Cian and Kyung show that people overgeneralise failures of AI in government, transferring distrust from one algorithmic system to others because AI systems are perceived as more homogeneous than human decision-makers (Longoni, Cian and Kyung, 2023). In criminal justice, this is devastating. A scandal involving one risk tool can reduce trust in body-worn camera analytics, in digital evidence pipelines, in forensic software, and even in routine administrative tech, because the public collapses them into a single category: "the state using opaque systems on people."

This helps explain why institutions often face a dilemma after scandal: either abandon the technology entirely (which may be politically necessary), or continue using it while attempting to "educate" the public (which often fails). The research suggests a third path is more stable: demonstrate heterogeneity through governance. Make it visible that systems differ in validation quality, oversight strength, and contestability rights. In other words, reduce transference by making institutional safeguards legible.

Error Cascades: How Small Mistakes Become Large Injustice

Trust collapses not only because a single error occurs, but because errors cascade through interconnected systems. In criminal justice, the data pipeline is a chain: police records feed pretrial decisions; pretrial decisions shape supervision; supervision shapes recorded "violations"; recorded violations feed risk models; risk models influence sentencing; sentencing influences future risk. A small error at the beginning—an incorrect arrest record, a misattributed phone number, a mislabeled digital trace—can propagate into multiple downstream decisions. Forensic science has learned to fear exactly this: the difference between a mistake and a miscarriage of justice is often institutional amplification.

Thompson's analysis of threshold shifting in forensic pattern matching is useful here not only for its technical insight, but because it shows how context-sensitive decision criteria can change legal utility (Thompson, 2023). If thresholds shift under pressure—high-profile cases, political heat, organisational incentives—then error rates change, and error becomes patterned rather than random. Patterned error is scandal fuel because it looks like bias even when no one intended bias.

The Role of the Judge: Why Trust Often Hangs on One Human Face

In most people's lives, "the justice system" is not an abstraction. It is a human encounter: the judge, the prosecutor, the officer, the clerk. That is why institutional trust is fragile: one humiliating encounter can reshape a person's perception of the entire system. Peer-reviewed research on public perceptions of judicial AI use shows that legitimacy, fairness, trust, and procedural justice judgments are sensitive to whether judges rely on AI tools or their own expertise, and that these perceptions vary across groups (Fine, Berthelot and Marsh, 2025). The deeper lesson is not about AI as such. It is that the public reads institutional motives through the judge's choices. If a judge appears to outsource responsibility to a tool—especially an opaque tool—people infer that the institution is less accountable, less respectful, and less human. When scandal breaks, the judge becomes the symbolic surface on which institutional trust is negotiated.

Scandal in the Predictive Era: When Preventive Logic Exceeds Moral Permission

A predictive legal order increases scandal risk because it expands preventive logic. Prevention is not illegitimate, but it is morally dangerous when it becomes the primary justification for coercion. Preventive decisions—detention based on predicted risk, supervision intensity based on forecast breach—invite the public to ask whether the system is punishing people for what they did or for what it fears they might do. When a scandal shows that predictions were biased, opaque, or based on poor data, preventive coercion begins to look like pre-emptive injustice.

This is why the SyRI line of scholarship has been so influential globally. It shows how a preventive governance tool, justified as efficiency and fraud control, can be judicially framed as rights-infringing because safeguards and proportionality were inadequate (van Bekkum et al., 2021; Rachovitsa, 2022; Appelman, 2021). In criminal justice, the same dynamic can occur when risk systems become the silent engine of detention or severity. Scandal is the moment when the public sees preventive logic as overreach rather than protection.

Repairing Trust: Why "Better Models" Are Not Enough

Institutions often respond to scandal with a technical impulse: retrain the model, add an explanation layer, publish an ethics statement. These responses can be necessary, but they are rarely sufficient, because scandal is not only about accuracy; it is about trustworthiness. Trustworthiness is repaired through governance that makes misuse difficult and accountability inevitable.

Peer-reviewed work on trustworthiness requirements for AI-enabled automated decision-making in the public sector identifies multiple facets of trustworthiness beyond performance, including transparency, accountability, oversight, and contestability (Agbabiaka et al., 2025). Public administration research likewise stresses that human–AI decision systems must be designed to prevent overreliance and stereotype-consistent selective adoption, because the harm often arises from human use under institutional pressure rather than from the algorithm in isolation (Alon-Barkat et al., 2023).

From a forensic standpoint, the repair logic is familiar: treat algorithmic outputs like evidence. Evidence must be testable, validated, version-controlled, and contestable. If the institution cannot provide what makes scrutiny possible, then reliance must be limited or prohibited in liberty-affecting contexts. This is not hostility to innovation; it is the rule-of-law attitude toward claims that can harm.

Conclusion: Trust Breaks Quickly Because It Is Rational to Protect Oneself From Power

Institutional trust is fragile because the cost of misplaced trust under coercive power is life-changing. Scandal and error teach the public a defensive lesson: do not assume the system is fair; demand proof. In the predictive era, that demand becomes sharper, because opacity makes proof harder and because category contamination spreads distrust across systems. If criminal justice institutions want durable legitimacy, they must build governance that anticipates scandal rather than improvising repair after harm. That means designing for contestability, evidential discipline, and accountable human ownership of decisions, so that when error occurs—as it inevitably will—it does not instantly convert into the public inference that the institution is fundamentally untrustworthy. The system must be capable of saying, credibly and demonstrably, "We can find our own mistakes, we can correct them, and we can be held to account," because that is the only foundation on which trust under power can survive (Tyler, 2011; Longoni, Cian and Kyung, 2023; Wieringa, 2023).

References

- Agbabiaka, O. et al. (2025) 'Requirements for trustworthy AI-enabled automated decision-making in the public sector', Technological Forecasting and Social Change, 203, 123xxx.
- Alexopoulou, S. et al. (2025) 'Exploring the impact of digital technologies on the welfare state', Social Policy & Administration, 59.
- Alon-Barkat, S. et al. (2023) 'Human–AI interactions in public sector decision making', Journal of Public Administration Research and Theory, 33(1), pp. 153–172.
- Appelman, N. (2021) 'Social welfare, risk profiling and fundamental rights: The case of SyRI in the Netherlands', Journal of Intellectual Property, Information Technology and E-Commerce Law (JIPITEC), 12, pp. 1–xx.
- Blader, S.L. and Tyler, T.R. (2003) 'A four-component model of procedural justice: Defining the meaning of a "fair" process', Personality and Social Psychology Bulletin, 29(6), pp. 747–758.
- Braithwaite, J. (1989) Crime, Shame and Reintegration. Cambridge: Cambridge University Press.
- Brayne, S. (2020) Predict and Surveil: Data, Discretion, and the Future of Policing. Oxford: Oxford University Press.
- Cooper, G.S., Meterko, V. and Dror, I.E. (2019) 'Cognitive bias research in forensic science: A systematic review', Forensic Science International, 297, pp. 35–46.
- Dietvorst, B.J., Simmons, J.P. and Massey, C. (2015) 'Algorithm aversion: People erroneously avoid algorithms after seeing them err', Journal of Experimental Psychology: General, 144(1), pp. 114–126.
- Dietvorst, B.J., Simmons, J.P. and Massey, C. (2018) 'Overcoming algorithm aversion: People will use imperfect algorithms if they can (even slightly) modify them', Management Science, 64(3), pp. 1155–1170.
- Ensign, D., Friedler, S.A., Neville, S., Scheidegger, C. and Venkatasubramanian, S. (2018) 'Runaway feedback loops in predictive policing', Proceedings of Machine Learning Research, 81, pp. 1–12.
- Feeley, M.M. and Simon, J. (1992) 'The new penology: Notes on the emerging strategy of corrections and its implications', Criminology,

30(4), pp. 449–474.

- Fine, A., Berthelot, E.R. and Marsh, S. (2025) 'Public perceptions of judges' use of AI tools in courtroom decision-making: An examination of legitimacy, fairness, trust, and procedural justice', Behavioral Sciences, 15(4), 476.
- Longoni, C., Cian, L. and Kyung, E.J. (2023) 'Algorithmic transference: People overgeneralize failures of artificial intelligence in the government', Journal of Marketing Research, 60(1), pp. 170–188.
- Lum, K. and Isaac, W. (2016) 'To predict and serve?', Significance, 13(5), pp. 14–19.
- Morrison, G.S. (2025) 'A guide to ISO 21043 forensic sciences from the forensic-data-science paradigm', Science & Justice, 65, 101298.
- Neil, R. (2025) 'Algorithmic bias in criminal risk assessment: The consequences of racial differences in arrest as a measure of crime', Annual Review of Criminology, 8, pp. 97–119.
- Obermeyer, Z., Powers, B., Vogeli, C. and Mullainathan, S. (2019) 'Dissecting racial bias in an algorithm used to manage the health of populations', Science, 366(6464), pp. 447–453.
- Rachovitsa, A. (2022) 'The human rights implications of the use of AI in the digital welfare state: The SyRI case', Human Rights Law Review, 22(2), ngac010.
- Ray, B., Kunkel, T., Bryant, K., Hedden, B., Andraka-Christou, B., O'Neil, M. and Huynh, P. (2022) 'Client attitudes toward virtual treatment court', Journal of Substance Abuse Treatment, 140, 108833.
- Robertson, B., Vignaux, G.A. and Berger, C.E.H. (2016) Interpreting Evidence: Evaluating Forensic Science in the Courtroom. 2nd edn. Chichester: Wiley.
- Sherman, L.W. (1993) 'Defiance, deterrence, and irrelevance: A theory of the criminal sanction', Journal of Research in Crime and Delinquency, 30(4), pp. 445–473.
- Skitka, L.J., Mosier, K.L. and Burdick, M. (1999) 'Does automation bias decision-making?', International Journal of Human–Computer Studies, 51(5), pp. 991–1006.
- Starke, C., Lünich, M. and Marcinkowski, F. (2022) 'Fairness perceptions of algorithmic decision-making: A systematic review', Big Data & Society, 9(2).
- Thompson, W.C. (2023) 'Shifting decision thresholds can undermine the probative value and legal utility of forensic pattern-matching

evidence', Proceedings of the National Academy of Sciences, 120(41), e2301844120.

- Tyler, T.R. (2006) Why People Obey the Law. 2nd edn. Princeton, NJ: Princeton University Press.
- Tyler, T.R. (2011) 'Procedural justice, legitimacy, and the effective rule of law', Crime and Justice, 40(1), pp. 283–357.
- van Bekkum, M., Borgesius, F.Z. et al. (2021) 'Digital welfare fraud detection and the Dutch SyRI judgment', European Journal of Social Security, 23(4), pp. 1–22.
- Wieringa, M. (2023) '"Hey SyRI, tell me about algorithmic accountability": Lessons from a landmark case', Data & Policy, 5, e—.

CHAPTER XXX

Civic Epistemology: Who Gets to Say a System Is "Fair"?

The First Question the Court Rarely Asks

Before a judge asks whether a model is accurate, before a ministry asks whether an algorithm is lawful, before a police service asks whether predictive deployment "works," a more primitive question is already deciding the dispute: who is authorised to declare that the system is fair? In a mature democracy, "fairness" is not only an engineering property, and it is not only a lawyer's conclusion. It is a public judgement about how power may be exercised over persons. That judgement is produced through culturally specific practices of making public knowledge: which institutions are trusted to speak; which kinds of evidence count; which audiences must be persuaded; which forms of contestation are regarded as legitimate; which failures are treated as aberrations; and which failures are treated as proof that the whole enterprise is rotten. Sheila Jasanoff's concept of civic epistemology names exactly this: the patterned, socially organised ways in which societies "know things in common," especially about science, expertise, and the state's use of technical knowledge (Jasanoff, 2005; Jasanoff, 2004).

Once algorithmic systems become part of criminal justice—risk scoring, sentencing support, bail tools, surveillance analytics, forensic triage, "similar cases" retrieval, even generative summaries—the fairness dispute becomes a dispute about civic epistemology. One group says, "Fair means statistically unbiased and validated." Another says, "Fair means contestable, explainable, and rights-respecting." Another says, "Fair means morally intelligible: consistent with desert, proportionality, and human dignity." Another says, "Fair means experienced as respectful: voice, neutrality, and recognition." None of these groups is simply confused. They are speaking from different traditions of public reason-making, and those traditions determine which actors get to certify fairness and which actors get told to trust.

Civic Epistemology in the Age of Machine Inference

Civic epistemology matters because algorithms do not merely deliver decisions; they reorganise the conditions under which decisions become believable. In the older legal world, credibility was produced through adversarial testing, cross-examination, public reasons, and appeal. In the newer computational world, credibility is often produced through metrics, audits, registers, and expert assurances. That is a transformation in the political culture of knowledge, not merely a technological upgrade. Jasanoff has long argued that law does not passively "receive" scientific truth; it actively shapes what counts as usable knowledge and what kinds of expertise become authoritative in legal settings (Jasanoff, 2005).

When a state claims an algorithm is fair, it is doing at least three things at once. It is making an epistemic claim ("the model behaves appropriately under evaluation"), a normative claim ("this behaviour should count as fair"), and an institutional claim ("these evaluators and these procedures are the right ones to settle the matter"). Grimmelikhuijsen's legitimacy framework is useful precisely because it separates these dimensions into input, throughput, and output legitimacy: who participates and consents (input), how decisions are made and justified (throughput), and what results are produced (output) (Grimmelikhuijsen, 2022). A system can score well on output (accuracy) and still fail on throughput (opacity, no contestation) and thereby lose legitimacy. Kinchin's "procedural gap" sharpens the point: accountability mechanisms often respond better to distributive concerns than to procedural justice, leaving "voice" and contestability weakened even where fairness metrics are celebrated (Kinchin, 2024).

The Fairness Claim as a Jurisdictional Battle Over Knowledge

In criminal justice, fairness claims are never neutral because they allocate institutional power. If engineers set the fairness definition, fairness becomes a property of measurable outputs. If lawyers set it, fairness becomes compliance with rights, burdens of proof, and reason-giving duties. If communities set it, fairness becomes lived experience of targeting, humiliation, surveillance, and exclusion. If judges set it, fairness becomes what can be defended within a doctrine of discretion, proportionality, and procedural integrity. Civic epistemology explains why these battles persist: societies differ in how they expect public knowledge to be made credible, and within societies, institutions compete to control the vocabulary of credibility (Jasanoff, 2005; Jasanoff, 2004).

This is where algorithmic governance can become deceptively tidy. Fairness metrics can look like constitutional settlement, when they are actually a choice of moral lens. De Fine Licht's work on resolving value conflicts in public AI governance insists that governance frameworks routinely elevate multiple values—accuracy, transparency, fairness, accountability—that are often in tension, sometimes incommensurable, and therefore cannot be satisfied simultaneously without explicit trade-offs (de Fine Licht, 2025). A system declared "fair" may simply be a system that chose one trade-off and hid the choice inside technical language.

Why "Public Engagement" Is Not Public Control

Because fairness is political, many institutions reach for "public engagement" as a legitimacy repair. Yet civic epistemology warns you not to confuse the existence of participation with the reality of power. Decker argues for integrating procedural fairness into algorithmic decision-making through public engagement and relational justice, precisely because formal statistical fairness approaches do not capture the full meaning of fairness in public power (Decker, 2025). But engagement can become theatre if it does not alter the decision architecture. If the public is "consulted" after deployment, if affected groups cannot contest outputs, if the model's data and assumptions remain inaccessible, then the system has not changed its civic epistemology; it has only added a ritual.

You can see this in the literature on transparency instruments. Algorithm registers are often promoted as public-facing accountability, but Nieuwenhuizen's analysis argues that registers can devolve into a box-ticking exercise rather than meaningful transparency, producing indirect dynamics that serve organisational reassurance more than public scrutiny (Nieuwenhuizen, 2024). The lesson is not "do not publish registers." The lesson is that civic epistemology cannot be faked by disclosure without contestability. A list of systems is not the same thing as a public capacity to challenge them.

Contestability as the Courtroom's Native Fairness Technology

If you want the most robust cross-cultural fairness mechanism, it is not a metric; it is contestability. Contestability is the practical form of respect in adversarial legality: the right to challenge evidence, reasoning, and authority. Hirsbrunner's account of contestation as a practice frames it as a socio-technical necessity for AI governance, not an optional ethical feature, because decision systems produce harms that must be disputable by affected individuals and communities (Hirsbrunner, 2025). In criminal justice, contestability is not merely desirable; it is how the system separates lawful judgement from administrative sorting.

This is where civic epistemology meets forensic discipline. Forensic science has learned—often painfully—that scientific-looking claims can be misinterpreted, over-credited, and immunised from scrutiny if courts lack access to validation, error rates, and interpretive boundaries. A similar epistemic discipline is required for algorithmic outputs, whether they are risk scores or pattern detectors: they must be treated as evidence-like artefacts whose probative weight depends on demonstrable validity under conditions of use, not on institutional prestige. Jasanoff's legal-STS analysis of "science for justice" makes the deeper point: the court's problem is not to honour science, but to render justice under conditions where science is socially situated and power-laden (Jasanoff, 2005).

Civic Epistemology Explains Why the Same Tool Is "Fair" in One Place and "Tyranny" in Another

This is the comparative sting of civic epistemology. The same kind of risk tool can be regarded as rational modern governance in one political culture and as illegitimate technocracy in another, not because one side is irrational, but because their public standards for knowledge legitimacy differ (Jasanoff, 2005). Some cultures treat expert committees as the proper arbiters of truth; others treat adversarial contest and public contestation as the proper test; others require parliamentary visibility; others rely on administrative trust. Civic epistemology tells you that fairness disputes are therefore not solved by exporting a metric. They are solved by building governance that matches a society's expectations of how state knowledge should be produced, tested, and corrected.

This also explains why purely technical "human-centric AI" rhetoric can fail. If a system introduces predictive tools into criminal justice without building the civic infrastructure of contestability—access rights, reason-giving duties, institutional ownership, independent auditing—then the public may experience the tool as a power grab, regardless of its statistical properties. The literature on algorithmic legitimacy supports this: algorithmic decision-making is often perceived as less legitimate than human or hybrid decision-making across legitimacy dimensions, indicating that legitimacy is not reducible to performance alone (Haesevoets et al., 2024).

The New Global Settlement Attempt: Risk-Based Regulation and Human Rights Treaties

By 2026, we are watching an attempted global settlement emerge: the move toward risk-based AI governance, with special constraints for law enforcement and criminal justice. Scholarly analyses of the EU AI Act's logic and its implications for algorithmic governance in justice contexts underscore that prediction and profiling in criminal justice are treated as high-risk or restricted, precisely because of fundamental rights and legitimacy concerns (Anastasopoulou, 2025; Cascone, 2025). In parallel, the Council of Europe's Framework Convention on AI and human rights, democracy, and the rule of law—opened for signature in 2024—represents another attempt to anchor fairness claims in rights and democratic principles rather than in vendor assurances (Rotenberg, 2025).

These instruments are not merely "laws about AI." They are civic epistemology in legal form: they specify who must be able to know, what must be disclosed, which harms matter, and what accountability looks like. The critical point, however, is that legal frameworks alone do not resolve civic epistemology conflicts; they institutionalise procedures through which those conflicts can be handled. When they work, they make fairness claims contestable and correctable. When they fail, they become another layer of rhetorical legitimacy.

The Practical Answer: Fairness Is a Shared Achievement, Not a Certificate

So who gets to say a system is fair? The only defensible answer in a predictive legal order is: no single actor gets to say it alone. Fairness must be a shared achievement across at least four roles, each correcting the others' blindness. Technical experts must demonstrate performance, error, drift, and limits; legal actors must bind decisions to rights, burdens, and reason-giving; affected communities must be able to contest and narrate lived harms; and independent oversight must be able to audit, sanction, and correct institutional misuse. Grimmelikhuijsen's work supports this multiplicity approach: legitimacy threats require calibrated institutional responses, not single "silver bullets," including civic participation and monitoring (Grimmelikhuijsen, 2022). Decker's procedural fairness argument similarly insists that the process dimension is essential to fairness governance, because outcome metrics alone cannot carry the moral weight of public power (Decker, 2025). Nieuwenhuizen's algorithm register critique warns that transparency without meaningful mechanisms can become organisational self-justification (Nieuwenhuizen, 2024). Kinchin's procedural-gap diagnosis explains why systems that optimise distributive metrics can still fail legitimacy if voice and contestation are structurally weak (Kinchin, 2024).

For criminal justice, the forensic translation is straightforward. If an algorithmic output can affect liberty, then the fairness claim must be treated like an evidential claim: testable, auditable, contestable, and situated within publicly defensible reasons. Civic epistemology is the theory that explains why this is not optional: because fairness is not only what the system does, but how a society agrees to recognise what the system is doing as just.

References

- Anastasopoulou, M. (2025) 'Exploring algorithmic governance: The AI Act and new regulatory approaches', European Journal of Comparative Law and Governance, 12(1), pp. 1–24.
- Bovens, M. and Zouridis, S. (2002) 'From street-level to system-level bureaucracies: How information and communication technology is transforming administrative discretion and constitutional control', Public Administration Review, 62(2), pp. 174–184.
- Cascone, G. (2025) 'The use of artificial intelligence in EU criminal justice systems', Open Research Europe, 5, 361.

- Collins, H. and Evans, R. (2002) 'The third wave of science studies: Studies of expertise and experience', Social Studies of Science, 32(2), pp. 235–296.
- de Fine Licht, K. (2025) 'Resolving value conflicts in public AI governance', Government Information Quarterly, 42(2), 1020xx.
- Decker, M.C. (2025) 'Procedural fairness in algorithmic decision-making: The role of public engagement', Ethics and Information Technology, 27, pp. 1–18.
- Dryzek, J.S. (2000) Deliberative Democracy and Beyond: Liberals, Critics, Contestations. Oxford: Oxford University Press.
- Fung, A. and Wright, E.O. (2001) 'Deepening democracy: Innovations in empowered participatory governance', Politics & Society, 29(1), pp. 5–41.
- Grimmelikhuijsen, S. (2022) 'Legitimacy of algorithmic decision-making: Six threats and the need for a calibrated institutional response', Policy & Politics, 50(3), pp. 232–252.
- Haesevoets, T. et al. (2024) 'How do citizens perceive the use of artificial intelligence in government decision-making?', Government Information Quarterly, 41(1), 1019xx.
- Habermas, J. (1996) Between Facts and Norms: Contributions to a Discourse Theory of Law and Democracy. Cambridge: Polity Press.
- Haines, M.B. (2020) '(Nation) building civic epistemologies around nuclear policy', Journal of Responsible Innovation, 7(3), pp. 1–20.
- Hirsbrunner, S.D. (2025) 'Contestation in artificial intelligence as a practice', Frontiers in Communication, 10, 1638257.
- Jasanoff, S. (2004) (ed.) States of Knowledge: The Co-Production of Science and the Social Order. London: Routledge.
- Jasanoff, S. (2005a) Designs on Nature: Science and Democracy in Europe and the United States. Princeton, NJ: Princeton University Press.
- Jasanoff, S. (2005b) 'Law's knowledge: Science for justice in legal settings', American Journal of Public Health, 95(S1), pp. S49–S58.
- Kinchin, N. (2024) '"Voiceless": The procedural gap in algorithmic justice', International Journal of Law and Information Technology, 32(4), pp. 1–30.
- Longino, H.E. (1990) Science as Social Knowledge: Values and Objectivity in Scientific Inquiry. Princeton, NJ: Princeton University Press.

- Nieuwenhuizen, E. (2024) 'Algorithm registers: A box-ticking exercise or meaningful tool for transparency?', Information Polity, 29(4), pp. 415–433.
- Ostrom, E. (1990) Governing the Commons: The Evolution of Institutions for Collective Action. Cambridge: Cambridge University Press.
- Rachovitsa, A. (2022) 'The human rights implications of the use of AI in the digital welfare state: The SyRI case', Human Rights Law Review, 22(2), ngac010.
- Rawls, J. (1993) Political Liberalism. New York: Columbia University Press.
- Rotenberg, M. (2025) 'Framework Convention on Artificial Intelligence and Human Rights, Democracy and the Rule of Law (Council of Europe)', International Legal Materials, 64(1), pp. 1–35.
- Stirling, A. (2008) '"Opening up" and "closing down": Power, participation, and pluralism in the social appraisal of technology', Science, Technology, & Human Values, 33(2), pp. 262–294.
- Tyler, T.R. (2011) 'Procedural justice, legitimacy, and the effective rule of law', Crime and Justice, 40(1), pp. 283–357.
- Wieringa, M. (2023) '"Hey SyRI, tell me about algorithmic accountability": Lessons from a landmark case', Data & Policy, 5, exx.
- Wynne, B. (1992) 'Misunderstood misunderstanding: Social identities and public uptake of science', Public Understanding of Science, 1(3), pp. 281–304.

Part VII — Due Process, Rights, and the Rule of Law

CHAPTER XXXI

Transparency as a Legal Right: What Must Be Disclosed, to Whom, and Why

Transparency Is Not a Courtesy, It Is the Price of Coercion

A criminal court does not merely allocate benefits; it condemns, restrains, and sometimes destroys lives in the name of the public. That is why transparency, in this domain, cannot be treated as the pleasant ethics of modern administration. It is the price of coercion. The more a state relies on technical systems—risk scores, predictive analytics, pattern-matching software, probabilistic genotyping, algorithmic triage, "similar cases" retrieval, AI-assisted summaries—the more it must show its work. Otherwise it asks the citizen to accept force without intelligible reasons, which is not law but administration in robes. The classical liberal insight was never that governments must be weak; it was that governments must be answerable. In adjudication, answerability takes a particular form: a person must be able to understand and challenge the evidential and inferential path by which the state moves from suspicion to condemnation, and from condemnation to punishment (Tyler, 2011; Duff, 2001).

The modern legal environment is moving in exactly this direction, even when doctrine lags. Risk-based AI governance frameworks increasingly treat transparency and oversight as rights-adjacent safeguards, not optional best practices, and the Council of Europe's AI Framework Convention explicitly anchors AI lifecycle activities in human rights, democracy, and the rule of law—precisely the triad that makes transparency a structural requirement rather than an aesthetic preference. The EU's risk-based approach similarly signals that high-risk uses must be subject to robust documentation, oversight-facing transparency, and public registers, indicating an emerging transnational settlement: transparency is part of legality when systems can affect fundamental rights.

The Three Legal Functions of Transparency

Transparency in criminal justice performs three distinct legal functions, and confusion among them produces shallow reforms. The first function is Epistemic: it enables reliability assessment. A method's probative value depends on its validation, error behavior, and appropriate interpretation under conditions of use, which is the central lesson of forensic evidence scholarship and the forensic-data-science paradigm (Robertson, Vignaux and Berger, 2016; Morrison, 2025). The second function is Procedural: it enables adversarial testing and equality of arms. Evidence that cannot be challenged is not merely inconvenient; it inverts the burden of proof by forcing the accused to disprove what cannot be examined, a structural threat to fair trial ideals (Kinchin, 2024; Fischman-Afori, 2025). The third function is Political: it sustains legitimacy. Procedural justice research demonstrates that people accept legal authority more readily when decision processes are experienced as neutral, respectful, and reasoned, and opacity undermines those experiential signals even when outcomes appear "efficient" (Tyler, 2011; Blader and Tyler, 2003).

These functions correspond to different audiences and therefore different disclosure regimes. Reliability-oriented disclosure serves courts and experts. Procedural disclosure serves parties. Legitimacy-oriented disclosure serves the public. A system that publishes a glossy model card but denies the defense access to inputs is transparent in public relations yet opaque in law. A system that discloses source code to a regulator but provides no contestable pathway to an accused is transparent in oversight yet opaque in adjudication. Civic legality demands all three functions be met in proportion to stakes.

The Core Distinction: Transparency of Reasons Versus Transparency of Power

Much confusion comes from treating transparency as "explainability." Explainability is about reasons; transparency is about power. A judge can be given a local explanation that says "prior failures to appear and age increased risk," yet the defendant may still be powerless to correct the record, contest feature construction, challenge validation, or detect drift. Explanations can therefore become soothing narratives that increase deference without increasing contestability, a risk widely noted in socio-technical governance debates (Wachter, Mittelstadt and Russell, 2017; Selbst and Barocas, 2018). The right question is not "Is there an explanation?" but "Is there a challengeable account of how this output was produced and what it can legitimately mean in this case?" That is why the emerging academic literature increasingly frames transparency as qualified and audience-specific: different recipients need different kinds of access, and the law must design disclosure packages to make scrutiny possible without collapsing into either vendor secrecy absolutism or naive "open everything" slogans.

What Must Be Disclosed: The Minimal Disclosure Package for Liberty-Affecting Systems

If a system can affect detention, sentencing severity, supervision intensity, evidentiary weight, or investigative targeting, there is a baseline disclosure package that must exist for the legal system to remain honest. This package is not about curiosity; it is about the elements without which adversarial testing becomes impossible.

First, the system must disclose Purpose and Decision Role. What question is the system answering—risk of failure to appear, risk of violent reoffending, likelihood of a forensic match, prioritization of cases, triage of digital devices—and what legal decision is it permitted to influence? Systems routinely drift beyond their original scope because outputs are convenient; the law must force role clarity to prevent "mission creep" where a tool built for resource triage becomes a de facto sentencing determinant (Berk et al., 2021; Eubanks, 2018).

Second, it must disclose Data Provenance and Label Integrity. Criminal justice data often encode institutional contact rather than underlying behavior. Arrest and rearrest frequently reflect policing patterns and enforcement intensity, and scholarship has repeatedly warned that such labels can embed structural bias into risk instruments (Neil, 2025). Differential reporting, selective observation, and feedback loops further contaminate targets, as demonstrated in the predictive policing literature (Lum and Isaac, 2016; Ensign et al., 2018). Without provenance disclosure—how data were collected, what populations they represent, what missingness exists, and what policy regimes shaped them—fairness claims are performative.

Third, it must disclose Feature Construction and Proxy Pathways. Excluding protected attributes does not eliminate indirect discrimination when proxies exist; this is a settled point in fair machine learning and anti-discrimination scholarship (Barocas and Selbst, 2016; Feldman et al., 2015). In court, the question becomes legal: which features are morally and legally relevant to the decision, and which are merely convenient correlates of disadvantage? A defendant cannot contest relevance without knowing what was counted and how it was defined.

Fourth, it must disclose Validation Evidence Under Conditions of Use. General "accuracy" is legally meaningless without context. Courts need error rates and calibration under operational conditions, subgroup performance where relevant, and clarity about the population shift between validation data and deployment setting (Berk et al., 2021; Morrison, 2025). In forensic settings, this parallels the insistence that evidential weight must be anchored in validation and uncertainty rather than confidence rhetoric (Robertson, Vignaux and Berger, 2016; Lund et al., 2026).

Fifth, it must disclose Decision Thresholds and Policy Rules. Scores do not decide; thresholds do. Threshold choices encode value judgments about who bears false positives and false negatives, and fairness impossibility results show that different fairness constraints cannot generally be satisfied simultaneously when base rates differ and prediction is imperfect (Kleinberg, Mullainathan and Raghavan, 2017; Chouldechova, 2017; Pleiss et al., 2017). Threshold disclosure is therefore not technical trivia; it is the disclosure of moral policy.

Sixth, it must disclose Versioning, Drift Monitoring, and Audit Trails. A "validated" model is not a permanently valid instrument. Concept drift and performative effects can change meaning over time (Gama et al., 2014; Perdomo et al., 2020). In criminal justice, drift can be caused by changing policing strategies, reporting norms, prosecution practices, and supervision policies. A court cannot evaluate reliability as applied if it cannot identify which version produced the output and what monitoring exists.

Seventh, it must disclose Human-in-the-Loop Practices. If judges and officers override outputs, at what rate and under what guidance? Are overrides audited? Are staff trained to avoid automation bias? Human–AI interaction research shows that automation bias and selective adherence can shape outcomes in ways that defeat formal safeguards (Skitka, Mosier and Burdick, 1999; Lyell and Coiera, 2017). In court, human use is part of the evidence mechanism.

This package is the minimum that makes a system legally contestable. Without it, "transparency" is a slogan.

To Whom Must Disclosure Be Made: Four Audiences, Four Rights

A single disclosure channel cannot serve every legal need. The law must distinguish audiences, because each audience represents a different aspect of the rule of law.

The Accused and Defence Experts must receive case-specific disclosure sufficient for meaningful challenge: input data used in the run, feature values, thresholds applied, the system version, and access to validation summaries relevant to the decision. Without this, the right to be heard becomes theatre and equality of arms collapses. This is where trade secret claims become most morally fraught, because they collide with liberty. A defensible compromise is not secrecy; it is functional equivalence: if source code cannot be disclosed, then the state must provide equivalent testing opportunities via protected access, independent expert review, and disclosure of artifacts that permit replication and reliability assessment.

The Court must receive enough to perform gatekeeping and interpretive discipline. Courts cannot simply admit algorithmic outputs as if they were self-explanatory. They must understand error behavior, limits of inference, and the relationship between the model's target and the legal question. The jurisprudence around algorithmic risk tools in sentencing has already shown how courts can accept tools while warning against overreliance, illustrating that judicial caution is not sufficient unless backed by enforceable disclosure and contestation structures (e.g., analyses of State v Loomis and its broader implications in legal scholarship).

Oversight Bodies and Regulators must receive deep technical documentation, audit rights, and access to confidential information necessary to police compliance. Risk-based AI regulation frameworks explicitly rely on this oversight-facing transparency, which is why academic analyses emphasise "qualified transparency" mandates that empower oversight bodies while balancing confidentiality constraints. Oversight disclosure is crucial, but it cannot substitute for defence disclosure where liberty is at stake; otherwise the system becomes a technocracy where rights are mediated through distant bureaucracy.

The Public must receive system-level transparency: what systems are in use, for what purposes, at what decision points, with what governance safeguards, and with what aggregated performance and disparity monitoring. Public transparency is not about letting everyone reverse-engineer models; it is about enabling civic contestation and preventing "secret law." In democratic societies, legitimacy is sustained when citizens can know what kinds of state power are being exercised and how they can seek redress (Jasanoff, 2005; Tyler, 2011).

Why Disclosure Is Required: Four Justifications That Cannot Be Replaced by "Efficiency"

The first justification is Due Process. Adjudication is not merely outcome production; it is reasoned coercion. If the reasons cannot be examined, the process becomes administrative. Procedural justice scholarship further shows that legitimacy depends on voice, neutrality, and respect, all of which are undermined when decisive reasons are opaque (Tyler, 2011; Kinchin, 2024).

The second justification is Epistemic Integrity. Courts are epistemic institutions: they claim to determine facts and responsibility through disciplined procedure. Algorithmic outputs, like forensic evidence, require interpretive humility and validation-based reasoning. A legal system that treats black-box outputs as facts is not only unfair; it becomes epistemically unserious (Robertson, Vignaux and Berger, 2016; Morrison, 2025).

The third justification is Anti-Discrimination and Equality. Disparate impact can be produced through proxies and label contamination even when protected attributes are excluded, and fairness metrics conflict such that "fairness" cannot be declared without specifying which moral trade-offs are being chosen (Barocas and Selbst, 2016; Kleinberg, Mullainathan and Raghavan, 2017). Transparency is required so that these trade-offs are visible and contestable rather than smuggled in by technical default.

The fourth justification is Legitimacy and Institutional Trust. Scandals involving opaque systems often spread distrust beyond the specific tool because citizens perceive algorithmic governance as homogeneous and unaccountable. Empirical work on "algorithmic transference" shows how failures in one government AI system can contaminate trust in others, increasing the stakes of transparency failures (Longoni, Cian and Kyung, 2023).

The Trade Secret Problem: Secrecy Claims Cannot Be Allowed to Reallocate the Burden of Proof

In high-stakes justice settings, the most common resistance to disclosure is proprietary secrecy. Vendors argue that code and model details are trade secrets; agencies argue that disclosure undermines security. These concerns are not imaginary, but the moral question is non-negotiable: can the state rely on a tool to deprive liberty while denying the person a meaningful chance to test the tool? If the answer is yes, then the state has created secret evidence. Secret evidence is incompatible with adversarial legitimacy precisely because it forces the defendant to fight blind.

The legally sustainable resolution is structured disclosure that preserves confidentiality while preserving contestability: protective orders, secure environments for expert inspection, court-appointed neutral experts where necessary, and disclosure of validation and error artifacts sufficient for meaningful challenge. Contemporary legal scholarship discussing transparency under new AI governance regimes emphasizes that oversight bodies often receive broader access than the public, but this cannot justify denying case-specific access when fundamental rights are at stake.

Transparency as a Right in the Predictive State: Lessons From Rights-Based Governance

Rights-based governance instruments increasingly treat transparency, oversight, and remedies as structural safeguards. The Council of Europe's AI Framework Convention is an explicit example of anchoring AI governance in human rights, democracy, and the rule of law, signalling that transparency is not merely administrative—its purpose is to make rights enforceable in the face of complex systems. The EU AI Act's risk-based architecture similarly reflects a view that high-risk systems require documentation and oversight, and academic analysis continues to track how transparency duties and public databases are meant to operationalize accountability rather than merely inform consumers.

At the same time, data protection law remains a central transparency channel. The GDPR's restrictions on solely automated decisions and its safeguards around meaningful information and contestation have generated deep debate about whether a "right to explanation" exists in binding form, with influential scholarship arguing that GDPR does not provide a general right to explanation while still supporting disclosure and contestation through other rights and safeguards (Wachter, Mittelstadt and Russell, 2017; Edwards and Veale, 2017). The practical point for criminal justice is not semantic. It is architectural: if automated or semi-automated systems influence liberty-affecting decisions, the legal system must ensure that transparency rights exist in operational form, not merely as recital rhetoric.

Conclusion: Transparency Is the Only Stable Alternative to Secret Law

A justice system can survive disagreement, but it cannot survive secret reasons. When algorithmic systems influence adjudication, transparency must be treated as a legal right because it is the condition of three things that make law lawful: reliability, contestability, and legitimacy. What must be disclosed is not "everything," but everything necessary to test the claims the state is relying on: purpose, data provenance, feature construction, validation, thresholds, versioning, and human-use practices. To whom disclosure must be made depends on function: parties need contestable access; courts need interpretive competence; oversight bodies need audit power; the public needs democratic visibility. Why disclosure is required is equally layered: due process, epistemic integrity, equality, and durable trust.

If the state refuses these disclosures, it is not merely protecting a vendor; it is changing the nature of adjudication. It is turning judgement into administration and asking citizens to accept coercion as an opaque output. In the criminal justice domain, where the moral stakes are irreducibly human, that is not efficiency. That is abdication.

References

- Barocas, S. and Selbst, A.D. (2016) 'Big data's disparate impact', California Law Review, 104(3), pp. 671–732.
- Berk, R., Heidari, H., Jabbari, S., Kearns, M. and Roth, A. (2021) 'Fairness in criminal justice risk assessments: The state of the art', Sociological Methods & Research, 50(1), pp. 3–44.
- Blader, S.L. and Tyler, T.R. (2003) 'A four-component model of procedural justice: Defining the meaning of a "fair" process', Personality

and Social Psychology Bulletin, 29(6), pp. 747–758.

- Chouldechova, A. (2017) 'Fair prediction with disparate impact: A study of bias in recidivism prediction instruments', Big Data, 5(2), pp. 153–163.
- Edwards, L. and Veale, M. (2017) 'Slave to the algorithm? Why a "right to an explanation" is probably not the remedy you are looking for', Duke Law & Technology Review, 16(1), pp. 18–84.
- Ensign, D., Friedler, S.A., Neville, S., Scheidegger, C. and Venkatasubramanian, S. (2018) 'Runaway feedback loops in predictive policing', Proceedings of Machine Learning Research, 81, pp. 1–12.
- Eubanks, V. (2018) Automating Inequality: How High-Tech Tools Profile, Police, and Punish the Poor. New York: St. Martin's Press.
- Feldman, M., Friedler, S.A., Moeller, J., Scheidegger, C. and Venkatasubramanian, S. (2015) 'Certifying and removing disparate impact', Proceedings of the 21st ACM SIGKDD International Conference on Knowledge Discovery and Data Mining (KDD '15), pp. 259–268.
- Fischman-Afori, O. (2025) 'Due process by design: Enhancing fairness and trust in AI decision-making through procedural justice theory', Social Sciences & Humanities Open, 12, 102178.
- Gama, J., Žliobaitė, I., Bifet, A., Pechenizkiy, M. and Bouchachia, A. (2014) 'A survey on concept drift adaptation', ACM Computing Surveys, 46(4), Article 44.
- Jasanoff, S. (2005) Designs on Nature: Science and Democracy in Europe and the United States. Princeton, NJ: Princeton University Press.
- Justo-Hanani, R. (2026) 'Risk-based approach to the EU AI Act', AI & Society.
- Kinchin, N. (2024) '"Voiceless": The procedural gap in algorithmic justice', International Journal of Law and Information Technology, 32(4), pp. 1–30.
- Kleinberg, J., Mullainathan, S. and Raghavan, M. (2017) 'Inherent trade-offs in the fair determination of risk scores', Proceedings of the 8th Innovations in Theoretical Computer Science Conference (ITCS 2017), LIPIcs 67, Article 43.
- Longoni, C., Cian, L. and Kyung, E.J. (2023) 'Algorithmic transference: People overgeneralize failures of artificial intelligence in the government', Journal of Marketing Research, 60(1), pp. 170–188.
- Lum, K. and Isaac, W. (2016) 'To predict and serve?', Significance, 13(5), pp. 14–19.

- Lund, S.P., Iyer, H.K., Vieux, E.F. and Taylor, D. (2026) 'The influence of validation data on logical and scientific interpretation of forensic expert opinion', Law, Probability and Risk, 25(1), mgaf013.
- Lyell, D. and Coiera, E. (2017) 'Automation bias and verification complexity: A systematic review', Journal of the American Medical Informatics Association, 24(2), pp. 423–431.
- Morrison, G.S. (2025) 'A guide to ISO 21043 forensic sciences from the perspective of the forensic-data-science paradigm', Science & Justice, 65, 101298.
- Neil, R. (2025) 'Algorithmic bias in criminal risk assessment: The consequences of racial differences in arrest as a measure of crime', Annual Review of Criminology, 8, pp. 97–119.
- Perdomo, J.C., Zrnic, T., Mendler-Dünner, C. and Hardt, M. (2020) 'Performative prediction', Proceedings of the 37th International Conference on Machine Learning (ICML 2020), PMLR 119, pp. 7599–7609.
- Pleiss, G., Raghavan, M., Wu, F., Kleinberg, J. and Weinberger, K.Q. (2017) 'On fairness and calibration', Advances in Neural Information Processing Systems, 30.
- Presno Linera, M.Á., Fernández-Rodríguez, J., Borge, R. and Riera, A. (2025) 'Regulating AI from Europe: A joint analysis of the AI Act and the Council of Europe AI Convention', Journal of Cyber Policy, 10(1), pp. 1–25.
- Robertson, B., Vignaux, G.A. and Berger, C.E.H. (2016) Interpreting Evidence: Evaluating Forensic Science in the Courtroom. 2nd edn. Chichester: Wiley.
- Rotenberg, M. (2025) 'Framework Convention on Artificial Intelligence and Human Rights, Democracy, and the Rule of Law (Council of Europe)', International Legal Materials, 64(1), pp. 1–35.
- Selbst, A.D. and Barocas, S. (2018) 'The intuitive appeal of explainable machines', Fordham Law Review, 87(3), pp. 1085–1139.
- Skitka, L.J., Mosier, K.L. and Burdick, M. (1999) 'Does automation bias decision-making?', International Journal of Human–Computer Studies, 51(5), pp. 991–1006.
- Tyler, T.R. (2011) 'Procedural justice, legitimacy, and the effective rule of law', Crime and Justice, 40(1), pp. 283–357.
- Wachter, S., Mittelstadt, B. and Russell, C. (2017) 'Counterfactual explanations without opening the black box: Automated decisions and

the GDPR', Harvard Journal of Law & Technology, 31(2), pp. 841–887.

CHAPTER XXXII

Explainability in Court: From Technical Accounts to Actionable Reasons

The Court Does Not Need a Tutorial, It Needs Reasons It Can Use

A court is not a laboratory and not a product team. It does not exist to admire mechanisms. It exists to decide, to justify, and to be contestable. That is why "explainability" in adjudication is routinely misunderstood. Engineers often treat explanation as a window into model internals; lawyers treat it as a procedural entitlement; judges treat it as a practical aid; defendants experience it as the difference between being heard and being processed. These are not different preferences; they are different legal functions. If an algorithmic output can affect liberty, then explanation cannot remain a courtesy. It must become part of the rule-of-law machinery that keeps coercion intelligible and challengeable.

The central problem, and you must hold it firmly, is that technical explainability and legal explainability are not the same object. A SHAP plot, a ranked list of features, or a saliency map can be technically "informative," while still being legally useless because it does not enable a meaningful challenge, does not connect to legal criteria, and does not reveal whether the system has smuggled an impermissible proxy into the decision. Selbst and Barocas identify why explainability is intuitively appealing yet often structurally misleading: "explanation" can mask the deeper institutional and normative choices that models embed, and it can create false comfort without accountability. In court, false comfort is dangerous because it tends to become deference.

The court's demand is therefore narrower and stricter than the engineer's: an explanation must be actionable. It must:

1. tell the affected party what claim is being made about them,
2. show how that claim was produced from particular inputs under a particular policy threshold,

3. reveal what could be wrong about it, and
4. give the party a real path to contest it in adversarial form.

Kinchin's diagnosis of a "procedural gap" in algorithmic justice is exactly the warning here: distributive fairness talk often flourishes while voice and contestability remain starved. If the person cannot challenge, the explanation is theatre.

Why Explainability Became a Courtroom Question in the First Place

Courts have always dealt with opaque expertise. A fingerprint examiner does not reveal every micro-feature; a psychiatrist does not disclose every intuitive step; a forensic statistician communicates weight, not total epistemic history. What changed is that machine learning systems can:

- be opaque by design,
- scale quickly, and
- be protected by secrecy claims while still being used as if they were neutral facts.

When a jurisdiction permits a proprietary risk score to influence sentencing while the methodology remains undisclosed to the court and the defendant, it creates a structural crisis: the state is allowed to rely on an evidentiary influence that cannot be meaningfully cross-examined. That crisis became globally legible through State v. Loomis, where the Wisconsin Supreme Court permitted COMPAS use with cautions, despite proprietary opacity concerns. You do not need to treat this as a parochial American event. You should treat it as an archetype: modern systems are tempted to treat "advisory tools" as harmless, while the tools function as coercion-weight in practice.

A parallel archetype appears in rights-based governance cases like the Dutch SyRI litigation, where a court invalidated a risk profiling system for breaching privacy rights under Article 8 ECHR, with scholarly analysis emphasising the role of insufficient safeguards and transparency. The connective tissue between these examples is not the technology. It is the legal anxiety: secret inference under public power.

The Three Kinds of Explanation a Court Actually Needs

Courts need three explanations, each aimed at a different legal task, and most systems fail because they deliver one and pretend it is all three.

The first is the Evidentiary Explanation. This answers, "What does this output mean as evidence?" It requires a proposition, a target, a validation story, and known limits. Without that, a score is not evidence; it is an institutional suggestion. The Harvard JOLT literature around black-box evidence stresses that algorithmic outputs are not self-interpreting and that courts risk misreading what an output can legally support.

The second is the Procedural Explanation. This answers, "How can the affected party challenge this?" It demands disclosure of inputs used, feature construction, thresholds, versioning, and a contestation pathway. Wachter, Mittelstadt and Russell's counterfactual framework is important precisely because it treats explanation as a tool for action: enabling understanding, contestation, and guidance on what would need to change for a different outcome, without requiring full model disclosure.

The third is the Reasons Explanation. This answers, "What are the judge's reasons, stated in legal language, that justify coercion?" This is not provided by the model at all. It must be authored by the court and must stand even if the model were removed. If the court cannot justify the outcome without "the model says," then the court has delegated moral authorship, and condemnation becomes administration.

From Feature Importance to Legal Relevance

A ranked list of "important features" is not a legal explanation unless those features are legally and morally relevant to the decision. This is the first point where technical accounts routinely collapse in court. A tool predicting "failure to appear" may treat unstable housing or prior missed dates as predictive. But the legal question is not simply, "Is it predictive?" It is also, "Is it a permissible basis for depriving liberty, given that the feature may proxy poverty, institutional access, or policing patterns?" This is why Edwards and Veale's critique of the GDPR "right to explanation" debate is so instructive: even when disclosure exists, the hard question is what kind of information is meaningful for challenge and rights protection, not merely what is intelligible to a layperson.

This is also why the "inscrutable versus nonintuitive" distinction in Selbst and Barocas matters to courts. A model can be technically explainable in the sense that a feature list can be produced, while still being nonintuitive and normatively ungrounded: the feature list does not map onto acceptable reasons. In sentencing, for example, legal relevance is constrained by proportionality and culpability traditions. Risk is not culpability. A prediction about future behavior cannot automatically become a reason to impose more punishment for a past act. If an explanation merely says, "These predictors increase risk," it may still fail to say, "These predictors are lawful reasons for this degree of coercion."

The Actionability Standard: Explanation Must Enable a Real Challenge

The most disciplined way to define court-appropriate explainability is to ask a simple question: What can the defence do with it? If the answer is "nothing," it is not a legal explanation. Wachter, Mittelstadt and Russell made this point early and sharply: explanations should be evaluated by the actions they support, especially contestation. That idea has only become more urgent as AI systems move from auxiliary administration into adjudicative gravity.

Actionability requires at least four capabilities. The defence must be able to correct factual inputs, because algorithmic systems are often brittle to data errors and mismatched records. The defence must be able to challenge feature construction, because "prior offences" can mean arrests, charges, convictions, or something else entirely, and each has different legal and moral significance. The defence must be able to challenge the validation claim, because models can perform differently across contexts and over time. The defence must be able to challenge the threshold policy, because the threshold is where moral trade-offs live: who bears false positives and false negatives. When these capabilities are absent, explanation is cosmetic.

The Forensic Parallel: Courts Already Know the Difference Between "Numbers" and "Meaning"

If you want the cleanest analogy for explainability, do not start with machine learning. Start with forensic probability. Courts have struggled for decades with how to interpret likelihood ratios, base rates, and expert uncertainty, because a number can look like proof. Contemporary forensic scholarship continues to scrutinise whether probabilistic reporting practices can infringe foundational principles like the presumption of innocence, precisely because misunderstanding probability can shift burdens in practice. The lesson transfers directly to algorithmic explainability: a probability is not a reason, a weight is not a verdict, and an output is not self-interpreting.

Forensic science has also learned that the reliability of an evidentiary method depends on validation under conditions of use, and that small shifts in decision practice can change error rates and legal utility. When courts accept opaque systems without insisting on validation and interpretive discipline, they invite the same miscarriages—only now with scalable repetition. The court's explainability duty is therefore part of evidentiary gatekeeping, not a philosophical luxury.

Post-Hoc Explanations, Counterfactuals, and the Problem of "Plausible Stories"

Once you accept that courts need actionable reasons, you must also accept an uncomfortable truth: many popular XAI methods are structurally tempting yet legally fragile. Local surrogate explanations such as LIME can help humans form an intuitive picture of model behavior around a case, but they are not guarantees of faithful causation; they are approximations. SHAP offers a more principled attribution framework and has become a standard tool for feature importance explanations, but again, attribution is not automatically legal relevance, and feature contributions are not automatically causal responsibility.

This is where Tim Miller's social-science account of explanation becomes unexpectedly practical for judges: humans prefer contrastive explanations ("Why this rather than that?"), selective explanations (a few salient factors), and explanations that fit social expectations. Post-hoc XAI methods often produce exactly that: persuasive contrastive narratives. The legal danger is that persuasive narrative can masquerade as evidentiary truth. A court may be satisfied by a story that feels like a reason, while the defence remains unable to test whether the story is stable, faithful, and non-misleading.

Counterfactual explanations are valuable because they are action-oriented, but they can also be morally treacherous if they suggest that a person could have obtained liberty by changing an attribute that is in fact structurally constrained—income, neighborhood, employment stability. The explanation becomes a subtle moral insult: "If you were not you, you would be free." Courts must therefore treat counterfactuals as contestation tools, not as moral lectures.

Interpretable Models Versus Explainable Black Boxes

One of the sharpest critiques of courtroom explainability is Rudin's insistence that in high-stakes domains, we should stop explaining black boxes and instead use inherently interpretable models wherever feasible. The legal translation is not "always use simple models." It is "do not accept an opacity burden when the state can achieve its legitimate aims with models that are auditable and intelligible." In court, interpretability is not only a usability preference; it is a constitutional posture toward coercion. When a person's liberty turns on a model, the state should bear the burden of using methods that can be scrutinised.

At the same time, courts cannot pretend interpretability ends the story. Interpretable models can still encode unjust proxies, contaminated labels, and unfair policy thresholds. Interpretability is necessary, not sufficient. It makes scrutiny possible; it does not make the system fair by magic.

Explainability and Due Process: The Emerging Rights Vocabulary

As AI becomes normal in public power, the rights vocabulary around explainability is becoming more explicit. Garrett's work on AI and procedural due process frames the issue in precisely the terms courts understand: when government uses AI to deprive life, liberty, or property, procedural due process concerns are triggered, especially around notice, hearing, and the ability to challenge the basis of the decision. This is also why recent ECtHR-oriented scholarship and institutional materials increasingly discuss how existing fair-trial principles apply in the age of AI, with an emphasis on being informed of relevant elements and having a genuine opportunity to contest.

The global regulatory trajectory reinforces this rights framing. Risk-based governance regimes increasingly specify transparency, documentation, logging, and human oversight duties for high-risk systems.

That matters because explainability is not only a human factors feature; it is an enforcement architecture. If the system is not logged and versioned, no explanation can be reliably reconstructed. If documentation is not maintained, contestation becomes impossible. If human oversight is only rhetorical, explainability becomes a dead letter.

Making Explainability Court-Ready: The "Reasons Architecture"

A court-ready explainability system is not one method; it is an architecture that binds technical accounts to legal reasons. You can think of it as a disciplined sequence.

First, the system must provide Case-Specific Disclosure: what data were used, what the model version was, what threshold rules were applied, and what uncertainty bounds are relevant. Second, it must provide a Contestability Bundle: validation evidence relevant to the use context, known failure modes, subgroup performance where legally salient, and an audit trail sufficient for replication. Third, the court must translate these into Judicial Reasons that are anchored to legal criteria: proportionality, necessity, relevance, and rights. Fourth, there must be a Hearing Mechanism that makes challenge meaningful: the defence can correct, contest, and argue relevance, and the judge must show in reasons how the challenge was addressed.

This is exactly where documentation standards like model cards become useful—not as PR, but as evidence scaffolding—because they specify intended use, evaluation conditions, and known limitations. But model cards alone do not satisfy due process. They support oversight; they do not replace adversarial access in a case.

Conclusion: In Court, Explanation Is Not Understanding, It Is Power to Contest

Explainability in court must be judged by a simple test: does it preserve the adversarial capacity to challenge coercion with reasons? If it does, it strengthens legality. If it does not, it becomes a legitimacy costume worn by a black box.

The mature position is not algorithm worship and not algorithm aversion. It is disciplined humility: accept computational aids only when they can be rendered contestable, legally relevant, and bounded by reasons that remain human and public. Otherwise, the state is not merely using a tool. It is changing the nature of adjudication from reasoned judgement to administered prediction. Courts were not built for that, and citizens were not promised that.

References

- Barocas, S. and Selbst, A.D. (2016) 'Big data's disparate impact', California Law Review, 104(3), pp. 671–732.
- Berk, R., Heidari, H., Jabbari, S., Kearns, M. and Roth, A. (2021) 'Fairness in criminal justice risk assessments: The state of the art', Sociological Methods & Research, 50(1), pp. 3–44.
- Blader, S.L. and Tyler, T.R. (2003) 'A four-component model of procedural justice: Defining the meaning of a "fair" process', Personality and Social Psychology Bulletin, 29(6), pp. 747–758.
- Chouldechova, A. (2017) 'Fair prediction with disparate impact: A study of bias in recidivism prediction instruments', Big Data, 5(2), pp. 153–163.
- Edwards, L. and Veale, M. (2017) 'Slave to the algorithm? Why a "right to an explanation" is probably not the remedy you are looking for', Duke Law & Technology Review, 16(1), pp. 18–84.
- Ensign, D., Friedler, S.A., Neville, S., Scheidegger, C. and Venkatasubramanian, S. (2018) 'Runaway feedback loops in predictive policing', Proceedings of Machine Learning Research, 81, pp. 1–12.
- Feldman, M., Friedler, S.A., Moeller, J., Scheidegger, C. and Venkatasubramanian, S. (2015) 'Certifying and removing disparate impact', Proceedings of the 21st ACM SIGKDD International Conference on Knowledge Discovery and Data Mining (KDD '15), pp. 259–268.
- Fischman-Afori, O. (2025) 'Due process by design: Enhancing fairness and trust in AI decision-making through procedural justice theory', Social Sciences & Humanities Open, 12, 102178.
- Gama, J., Žliobaitė, I., Bifet, A., Pechenizkiy, M. and Bouchachia, A. (2014) 'A survey on concept drift adaptation', ACM Computing Surveys, 46(4), Article 44.
- Garrett, B.L. (2025) 'Artificial intelligence and procedural due process', Journal of Constitutional Law, 27(2), pp. 1–72.

- Hefetz, I. (2025) 'Integrating AI systems in criminal justice: The forensic expert as a corridor between algorithms and courtroom evidence', Forensic Sciences, 5(4), 53.
- Kinchin, N. (2024) '"Voiceless": The procedural gap in algorithmic justice', International Journal of Law and Information Technology, 32(4), pp. 1–30.
- Kleinberg, J., Mullainathan, S. and Raghavan, M. (2017) 'Inherent trade-offs in the fair determination of risk scores', Proceedings of the 8th Innovations in Theoretical Computer Science Conference (ITCS 2017), LIPIcs 67, Article 43.
- Longoni, C., Cian, L. and Kyung, E.J. (2023) 'Algorithmic transference: People overgeneralize failures of artificial intelligence in the government', Journal of Marketing Research, 60(1), pp. 170–188.
- Lundberg, S.M. and Lee, S.-I. (2017) 'A unified approach to interpreting model predictions', Advances in Neural Information Processing Systems, 30.
- Lyell, D. and Coiera, E. (2017) 'Automation bias and verification complexity: A systematic review', Journal of the American Medical Informatics Association, 24(2), pp. 423–431.
- Malgieri, G. (2019) 'Automated decision-making in the EU Member States: The right to explanation and other "suitable safeguards" in the GDPR', Computer Law & Security Review, 35(5), 105327.
- Miller, T. (2019) 'Explanation in artificial intelligence: Insights from the social sciences', Artificial Intelligence, 267, pp. 1–38.
- Mitchell, M., Wu, S., Zaldivar, A., Barnes, P., Vasserman, L., Hutchinson, B., Spitzer, E., Raji, I.D. and Gebru, T. (2019) 'Model cards for model reporting', Proceedings of the Conference on Fairness, Accountability, and Transparency (FAccT '19), pp. 220–229.
- Morrison, G.S. (2025) 'A guide to ISO 21043 forensic sciences from the forensic-data-science paradigm', Science & Justice, 65, 101298.
- Neil, R. (2025) 'Algorithmic bias in criminal risk assessment: The consequences of racial differences in arrest as a measure of crime', Annual Review of Criminology, 8, pp. 97–119.
- Perdomo, J.C., Zrnic, T., Mendler-Dünner, C. and Hardt, M. (2020) 'Performative prediction', Proceedings of the 37th International Conference on Machine Learning (ICML 2020), PMLR 119, pp. 7599–7609.

- Pleiss, G., Raghavan, M., Wu, F., Kleinberg, J. and Weinberger, K.Q. (2017) 'On fairness and calibration', Advances in Neural Information Processing Systems, 30.
- Ribeiro, M.T., Singh, S. and Guestrin, C. (2016) '"Why should I trust you?" Explaining the predictions of any classifier', Proceedings of the 22nd ACM SIGKDD International Conference on Knowledge Discovery and Data Mining (KDD '16), pp. 1135–1144.
- Rudin, C. (2019) 'Stop explaining black box machine learning models for high stakes decisions and use interpretable models instead', Nature Machine Intelligence, 1, pp. 206–215.
- Sallavaci, O. (2025) 'Algorithms on trial: Does evaluative probabilistic reporting of forensic DNA evidence infringe the presumption of innocence?', Forensic Science International: Synergy, 8, 1002xx.
- Selbst, A.D. and Barocas, S. (2018) 'The intuitive appeal of explainable machines', Fordham Law Review, 87(3), pp. 1085–1139.
- Skitka, L.J., Mosier, K.L. and Burdick, M. (1999) 'Does automation bias decision-making?', International Journal of Human–Computer Studies, 51(5), pp. 991–1006.
- Tyler, T.R. (2011) 'Procedural justice, legitimacy, and the effective rule of law', Crime and Justice, 40(1), pp. 283–357.
- Wachter, S., Mittelstadt, B. and Russell, C. (2018) 'Counterfactual explanations without opening the black box: Automated decisions and the GDPR', Harvard Journal of Law & Technology, 31(2), pp. 841–887.

CHAPTER XXXIII

The Right to a Human Decision-Maker: Myth, Norm, or Necessity?

The Question Behind the Question

When people demand "a human decision-maker," they are rarely asking for romance. They are asking for something brutally practical: a person who can be blamed, a person who can listen, a person who can change their mind, and a person whose reasons can be challenged in ordinary legal language. In criminal justice—where the state condemns, restrains, and sometimes marks a person for life—this demand becomes sharper, because the moral grammar of punishment presupposes that someone owns the coercion through reasons. Yet the modern system is being rewired around decision-support: risk scores, triage tools, pattern detectors, algorithmic summaries, and increasingly, generative drafting. The result is a new ambiguity: the state insists that humans remain "in the loop," while the citizen experiences the loop as a formality and the algorithm as the real author. That ambiguity is why the "right to a human decision-maker" is debated as myth, norm, and necessity at the same time.

The safest way to treat the question is to separate three claims that are often collapsed into one slogan. The first is a legal claim: does positive law grant a right not to be subject to a decision made solely by automated processing, and if so, in what contexts? The second is a procedural claim: even if a human signs off, does the process provide meaningful contestability, or is it only human rubber-stamping? The third is a moral claim: is there something about condemnation and punishment—about dignity, agency, and legitimacy—that requires human moral authorship even when automation is accurate? Only when you hold these apart can you see why the right is sometimes overstated as a universal entitlement, sometimes understated as a myth, and sometimes correctly defended as a necessity in particular decision points.

Myth: Why "A Human Decision-Maker" Is Not a Universal Right

The phrase "right to a human decision-maker" can be misleading because many legal systems do not recognise a blanket right to have a human decide every consequential matter, and even where they do restrict purely automated decisions, the restrictions are conditional and contextual. The clearest illustration is data protection law, where the most-cited provision is GDPR Article 22. Article 22 provides that a data subject has the right not to be subject to a decision based solely on automated processing, including profiling, that produces legal effects or similarly significantly affects them, while also specifying exceptions and safeguards. The language matters: it is not "a right to a human decision-maker" in all cases; it is a restriction on solely automated decisions with significant effects, with carve-outs. In the UK's post-Brexit parallel framework, the ICO guidance similarly frames Article 22 as a limit on solely automated decisions with legal or similarly significant effects, not as a general ban on algorithmic assistance.

This doctrinal structure already shows why the "right" can be myth-like when spoken too broadly. First, "solely automated" is narrower than "algorithm-influenced," which means many systems can comply formally by retaining a human sign-off while still using algorithmic outputs as the decisive driver. Second, many consequential state actions are not easily mapped onto the GDPR's scope, especially in criminal justice where the decision-maker may be a court rather than a data controller operating under the same access rights logic, and where different procedural safeguards apply. Third, even within GDPR, exceptions and safeguards complicate any simplistic statement of a universal right. The upshot is that law does not generally promise a human in every case; it promises safeguards against a particular kind of automated power.

A second myth layer is practical rather than doctrinal: the assumption that "human involvement" guarantees humanity. A human can be present as a signature and absent as a judge. A human can be involved and still behave as a conduit for a machine output. The moral problem then persists while the legal system congratulates itself on formal compliance. Any serious discussion must therefore treat "human decision-maker" as shorthand, and demand a more exact concept: meaningful human agency in decision-making.

Norm: The Emerging Legal Pattern Is Human Oversight, Not Human Monopoly

If the right is not a universal guarantee, it is still true that legal systems are moving toward a robust norm: high-stakes automated systems must be subject to meaningful human oversight, transparency, and accountability. You can see that norm crystallising across instruments that are explicitly designed for rights and governance. The Council of Europe's Framework Convention on AI—opened for signature in September 2024—frames AI lifecycle governance around human rights, democracy, and the rule of law, and it includes a principle on transparency and oversight requiring "adequate transparency and oversight requirements tailored to the specific contexts and risks." This is not a narrow consumer-protection gesture; it is a rule-of-law commitment designed to control state power mediated by AI.

The EU AI Act follows the same direction in more operational form. Regulation (EU) 2024/1689—the AI Act—establishes a risk-based framework with detailed requirements for high-risk systems, including requirements related to human oversight. While popular summaries circulate online, the core point you must internalise is institutional: Europe is building a legal expectation that high-risk systems must be designed and deployed so that humans can oversee them effectively, not merely rubber-stamp them. The European Data Protection Supervisor's 2025 TechDispatch on human oversight of automated decision-making reinforces the same emphasis: "decision-support" systems shape the decision landscape, so the oversight question is not whether humans are present but whether oversight is effective against automation-driven framing.

Even outside Europe, the same norm appears as soft law with global reach. UNESCO's Recommendation on the Ethics of AI (2021) is not a criminal-procedure code, but it is a widely adopted global standard that explicitly emphasises human rights and human oversight. The significance is not that UNESCO "creates rights," but that it contributes to an emerging global vocabulary: when AI mediates consequential decisions, human oversight is treated as a governance requirement, not as a mere ethical preference.

So the norm is not "humans must decide everything." The norm is closer to: automation may assist, but humans must remain accountable, contestability must remain real, and rights must remain enforceable.

Necessity: Why Punishment and Condemnation Demand Human Moral Authorship

Now comes the harder claim: that in criminal justice, especially at the moments of condemnation and punishment, human decision-making is not just a safeguard but a necessity. This claim is not metaphysical. It is institutional and psychological.

Punishment is not merely a tool for risk management. It is a public act of condemnation addressed to a responsible agent, and it is justified through reasons that a citizen can contest and a community can recognise as reasons. When the system treats risk outputs as the reason—"high risk, therefore detain; high risk, therefore longer sentence"—it changes the meaning of punishment. It becomes management rather than moral judgment. The result is legitimacy decay, because legitimacy depends not only on what is done but on whether the process and reasons are intelligible, respectful, and publicly defensible. That is the core insight of procedural justice research: people comply more readily with legal authority when the decision process is experienced as fair, neutral, and dignifying, even under adverse outcomes. Tyler's foundational work shows legitimacy is built through procedural justice, not merely through fear. (Tyler, 2011).

This is where "human decision-maker" becomes necessity in a precise way. A human is not needed because humans are always better at prediction. A human is needed because a human can do things that make the coercion lawful in the rule-of-law sense: hear reasons, weigh mitigation, give tailored explanations, accept responsibility for error, and be answerable through review. When a system becomes opaque or proprietary, the person cannot meaningfully challenge it. When the person cannot challenge, voice becomes theatre. That is exactly the "procedural gap" diagnosis in the algorithmic justice literature: distributive metrics may be discussed while procedural voice and contestability remain weakened.

The necessity claim becomes even sharper when you confront the psychology of automation. Human–automation research and decision science show that people can over-rely on automated outputs, especially when verification is difficult and stakes are high. The EDPS TechDispatch explicitly notes that decision-support systems "effectively shape the decision landscape" for the human user, meaning the human may be formally responsible while practically steered. This is why "human-in-the-loop" rhetoric is not enough. The law needs "human-in-command" features where coercion is at stake: the human must be able to meaningfully disagree, and the institution must be designed so disagreement is professionally safe and procedurally legible.

The Hard Boundary: Solely Automated Decisions Versus Algorithmically Shaped Human Decisions

The deepest conceptual trap is believing there are only two options: either the machine decides, or the human decides. In reality, the most common governance form is hybrid: algorithmic shaping with human sign-off. This is precisely where rights can evaporate unless law is careful. If a decision is technically "human" but algorithmically dominant, the affected person may receive neither the protections against sole automation nor the traditional protections of human reasoning, because the human relies on the model and cannot explain it.

Data protection law implicitly recognises this with its language about "meaningful human intervention" and safeguards such as the right to express one's point of view and contest the decision. Yet the real fight is over what "meaningful" means. Meaningful cannot mean "a human clicked approve." Meaningful must mean that the human can understand the basis at a level sufficient for challenge and responsibility, can reject it without punishment, and can justify the rejection through reasons.

This is why the 2025 CJEU judgment in Dun & Bradstreet Austria matters as an epistemic marker even beyond credit scoring. The case concerns access rights and the tension between "meaningful information about the logic involved" and trade secrets, and it is repeatedly discussed as clarifying that meaningful information may be required without necessarily forcing full algorithm disclosure. The doctrinal context is not criminal justice, but the principle is instructive: modern systems are trying to build disclosure regimes that preserve contestability while managing secrecy claims. Criminal justice, however, raises the stakes: when liberty is on the line, secrecy cannot be allowed to relocate the burden of proof onto the accused.

Forensic Application: The Human Right Is Often the Right to Cross-Examine the System

In practice, the most defensible translation of "right to a human decision-maker" in criminal justice is not an absolute ban on algorithmic assistance. It is a bundle of evidential and procedural rights that make algorithmic influence governable.

The court must be able to treat algorithmic outputs as evidence-like artefacts rather than as administrative facts. That requires provenance, validation under conditions of use, known error behavior, and clear limits of inference. It also requires adversarial access to the input data and the ability to correct errors, because a wrong data point in a risk tool can be the difference between remand and release. The defence must be able to challenge relevance: a feature may be predictive while being morally impermissible as a basis for coercion because it proxies poverty, neighbourhood, or institutional contact patterns. And the court must be able to articulate reasons independent of "the tool says," because otherwise condemnation becomes outsourced.

If you want a clean legal test, it is this: when algorithmic outputs matter, the person must be able to challenge them as if they were evidence. If that is impossible due to opacity, secrecy, or complexity, then the system is not fit for liberty-affecting use, regardless of performance claims. This is precisely why European human rights discussions increasingly frame AI governance around safeguards, transparency, oversight, and remedies, and why the Council of Europe convention elevates transparency and oversight as foundational principles.

Conclusion: Not a Slogan, but a Structural Demand

So is the right to a human decision-maker a myth, norm, or necessity? It is myth when it is treated as a universal promise that law already guarantees everywhere. It is norm when it is understood as the emerging legal expectation of meaningful human oversight, transparency, and accountability for high-stakes automated systems. It is necessity at the points where criminal justice must remain recognisably law: condemnation, punishment, and liberty deprivation require human moral authorship and contestable reasons, not merely efficient outputs.

The future-proof formulation is therefore not "humans must decide everything." The future-proof formulation is: no one should lose liberty to a system they cannot meaningfully challenge, and no institution should be allowed to hide coercion behind technical opacity. GDPR's restriction on solely automated decisions is one partial expression of that idea. The EU AI Act's human oversight requirements are another. The Council of Europe's AI convention is yet another. The question for criminal justice is whether we have the honesty to treat those as rule-of-law commitments rather than compliance checklists.

References

- Ashworth, A. and Zedner, L. (2014) Preventive Justice. Oxford: Oxford University Press.
- Barocas, S. and Selbst, A.D. (2016) 'Big data's disparate impact', California Law Review, 104(3), pp. 671–732.
- Blader, S.L. and Tyler, T.R. (2003) 'A four-component model of procedural justice: Defining the meaning of a "fair" process', Personality and Social Psychology Bulletin, 29(6), pp. 747–758.
- Chouldechova, A. (2017) 'Fair prediction with disparate impact: A study of bias in recidivism prediction instruments', Big Data, 5(2), pp. 153–163.
- Council of Europe (2024) Framework Convention on Artificial Intelligence and Human Rights, Democracy and the Rule of Law (CETS No. 225). Strasbourg: Council of Europe.
- Court of Justice of the European Union (2025) Dun & Bradstreet Austria GmbH and Others v Österreichische Datenschutzbehörde, Case C-203/22 (Judgment of 27 February 2025). Luxembourg: CJEU.
- Dietvorst, B.J., Simmons, J.P. and Massey, C. (2015) 'Algorithm aversion: People erroneously avoid algorithms after seeing them err', Journal of Experimental Psychology: General, 144(1), pp. 114–126.
- Duffy, J. (2012) 'Problem-solving courts, therapeutic jurisprudence and the constitution', Melbourne University Law Review, 35(2), pp. 394–446.
- Duff, R.A. (2001) Punishment, Communication, and Community. Oxford: Oxford University Press.
- Edwards, L. and Veale, M. (2017) 'Slave to the algorithm? Why a "right to an explanation" is probably not the remedy you are looking for', Duke Law & Technology Review, 16(1), pp. 18–84.
- European Data Protection Supervisor (2025) TechDispatch #2/2025: Human Oversight of Automated Decision-Making. Brussels: EDPS.

- European Union (2016) Regulation (EU) 2016/679 of the European Parliament and of the Council of 27 April 2016 (General Data Protection Regulation), OJ L 119/1.
- European Union (2024) Regulation (EU) 2024/1689 of the European Parliament and of the Council (Artificial Intelligence Act).
- Feldman, M., Friedler, S.A., Moeller, J., Scheidegger, C. and Venkatasubramanian, S. (2015) 'Certifying and removing disparate impact', Proceedings of the 21st ACM SIGKDD International Conference on Knowledge Discovery and Data Mining (KDD '15), pp. 259–268.
- Fischman-Afori, O. (2025) 'Due process by design: Enhancing fairness and trust in AI decision-making through procedural justice theory', Social Sciences & Humanities Open, 12, 102178.
- Gama, J., Žliobaitė, I., Bifet, A., Pechenizkiy, M. and Bouchachia, A. (2014) 'A survey on concept drift adaptation', ACM Computing Surveys, 46(4), Article 44.
- Garrett, B.L. (2025) 'Artificial intelligence and procedural due process', Journal of Constitutional Law, 27(2), pp. 1–72.
- Jasanoff, S. (2005) Designs on Nature: Science and Democracy in Europe and the United States. Princeton, NJ: Princeton University Press.
- Kinchin, N. (2024) '"Voiceless": The procedural gap in algorithmic justice', International Journal of Law and Information Technology, 32(4), pp. 1–30.
- Kleinberg, J., Mullainathan, S. and Raghavan, M. (2017) 'Inherent trade-offs in the fair determination of risk scores', Proceedings of the 8th Innovations in Theoretical Computer Science Conference (ITCS 2017), LIPIcs 67, Article 43.
- Longoni, C., Cian, L. and Kyung, E.J. (2023) 'Algorithmic transference', Journal of Marketing Research, 60(1), pp. 170–188.
- Lyell, D. and Coiera, E. (2017) 'Automation bias and verification complexity', Journal of the American Medical Informatics Association, 24(2), pp. 423–431.
- Miller, T. (2019) 'Explanation in artificial intelligence: Insights from the social sciences', Artificial Intelligence, 267, pp. 1–38.
- Mitchell, M., Wu, S., Zaldivar, A., Barnes, P., Vasserman, L., Hutchinson, B., Spitzer, E., Raji, I.D. and Gebru, T. (2019) 'Model cards for model reporting', Proceedings of the Conference on Fairness, Accountability, and Transparency (FAccT '19), pp. 220–229.

- Obermeyer, Z., Powers, B., Vogeli, C. and Mullainathan, S. (2019) 'Dissecting racial bias in an algorithm used to manage the health of populations', Science, 366(6464), pp. 447–453.
- Perdomo, J.C., Zrnic, T., Mendler-Dünner, C. and Hardt, M. (2020) 'Performative prediction', Proceedings of the 37th International Conference on Machine Learning (ICML 2020), PMLR 119, pp. 7599–7609.
- Pleiss, G., Raghavan, M., Wu, F., Kleinberg, J. and Weinberger, K.Q. (2017) 'On fairness and calibration', Advances in Neural Information Processing Systems, 30.
- Robertson, B., Vignaux, G.A. and Berger, C.E.H. (2016) Interpreting Evidence: Evaluating Forensic Science in the Courtroom. 2nd edn. Chichester: Wiley.
- Rudin, C. (2019) 'Stop explaining black box machine learning models for high stakes decisions', Nature Machine Intelligence, 1, pp. 206–215.
- Skitka, L.J., Mosier, K.L. and Burdick, M. (1999) 'Does automation bias decision-making?', International Journal of Human–Computer Studies, 51(5), pp. 991–1006.
- UNESCO (2021) Recommendation on the Ethics of Artificial Intelligence. Paris: UNESCO.
- Wachter, S., Mittelstadt, B. and Russell, C. (2018) 'Counterfactual explanations without opening the black box', Harvard Journal of Law & Technology, 31(2), pp. 841–887.

CHAPTER XXXIV

Equality of Arms and Proprietary Models: Trade Secrets vs Fair Trial

The Old Principle Facing a New Kind of Witness

Equality of arms is one of those legal principles that sounds procedural until you see what it really does: it prevents the state from winning by structural advantage rather than by proof. The principle insists that if the prosecution is allowed to rely on something that materially shapes the fact-finder's view—an evidential inference, an expert conclusion, a risk output, a forensic classification—then the defence must have a meaningful opportunity to understand and challenge it under conditions that are not merely ceremonial. In European human-rights doctrine, equality of arms operates as part of the fair trial guarantee in Article 6 ECHR, and scholarship analysing the Court's evidence-law jurisprudence has distilled it as an equality-of-arms based framework that governs disclosure, adversarial testing, and the ability to contest evidence effectively (Stoykova, 2023). In global terms, the same idea appears in Article 14 ICCPR and in domestic fair-trial traditions across legal families: the accused must not be asked to fight blind.

The proprietary model—whether a sentencing risk tool, a probabilistic genotyping program, a facial recognition pipeline, a digital forensics classifier, or a "similar cases" recommender—arrives in court as a new kind of witness. It speaks in numbers and confidence. It shapes outcomes even when labelled "advisory." Yet it is frequently shielded by trade secret claims that deny the defence access to the very information needed to test it. This is where a modern collision occurs. Trade secret law exists to protect investment and encourage innovation; fair-trial law exists to prevent coercion by opaque power. The collision cannot be solved by slogans like "innovation" on one side and "due process" on the other. It must be solved by returning to what equality of arms actually demands: not complete transparency to the world, but functional contestability for the accused.

What Equality of Arms Requires When the Evidence Is an Algorithm

It is tempting to think that equality of arms is satisfied so long as the defence can cross-examine the human expert who presents the output. That belief belongs to an earlier era, where the expert's reasoning and methods were at least in principle open to probing through questions, notes, and professional standards. A proprietary model changes the structure of cross-examination. The witness becomes a socio-technical system: code, training data, parameter choices, thresholds, and a chain of operational decisions about how the output is generated and interpreted. You can cross-examine the human who uses the tool, but if the human cannot disclose or test the tool's inner constraints, the cross-examination can become a performance. It looks adversarial, yet it cannot reach the source of the claim.

Peer-reviewed work on the fair trial right in the context of complex technologies makes the central point that courts need sufficient understanding of the technology to secure fair-trial guarantees, and where that understanding cannot be achieved through individual judicial training alone, institutional solutions are needed to preserve fairness (Custers, 2024). That argument is not a mere call for "AI literacy." It is a recognition that legal fairness is not merely a matter of formal rights but of operational capability: if neither the defence nor the court can test what the state relies upon, the system has shifted from adjudication to administration.

Equality of arms in algorithmic contexts therefore has a practical core. The defence must be able to do at least four things. First, verify the inputs used in the model run, because data errors are common in criminal justice pipelines and a single mislabeled prior or misattributed record can change an outcome. Second, challenge feature construction and relevance, because the same word—"prior contact," "noncompliance," "risk"—can be defined in ways that range from morally relevant to profoundly discriminatory. Third, interrogate validation and error under conditions of use, because predictive tools and forensic algorithms often behave differently across settings and time. Fourth, contest the threshold policy, because thresholds—where a score becomes detention, where a likelihood ratio becomes persuasive weight—encode moral trade-offs about who bears false positives and false negatives. Without these capabilities, the defence has not been given equality of arms; it has been given access to a conclusion without access to its grounds.

Trade Secrets as a Structural Asymmetry, Not a Neutral Legal Privilege

Trade secret claims in criminal justice are often framed as if they merely protect commercial interests without harming fairness: "We can't disclose the source code, but you can still challenge the output." That is the rhetoric of a civil-discovery mindset smuggled into a liberty context. In criminal justice, secrecy is not morally symmetric. If the state can rely on proprietary systems to deprive liberty, while the accused is denied the information needed to test those systems, the burden of proof is quietly shifted in practice. The defence is forced into a posture of speculative doubt rather than concrete challenge. This is precisely how the right becomes hollow: the defendant is told, in effect, to prove that the state's hidden method is unreliable, without being allowed to see the method.

Peer-reviewed analysis of trade secrecy in automated decision-making recognises that trade secrecy is widely treated as an obstacle to transparency and can restrict disclosure even when decisions significantly affect individuals, highlighting the need to interrogate the "myth" that trade secret protection can coexist with adequate procedural accountability by default (Gikay, 2025). The criminal justice context sharpens that concern. In a consumer or credit setting, secrecy may be balanced by regulatory oversight. In a criminal setting, secrecy collides with the adversarial structure itself. Oversight without defence access does not create equality of arms; it creates technocratic guardianship, which is categorically different from a fair trial.

The classic illustration in the sentencing domain is State v. Loomis (Wisconsin, 2016), where the defendant challenged the use of a proprietary risk assessment (COMPAS) and argued that the inability to inspect methodology undermined due process. The case is widely discussed as emblematic of the problem: the court permitted use with warnings, yet the trade secret shield remained intact, leaving the deeper equality-of-arms tension unresolved in practice (see discussion in secondary analysis of the case). Even if one views the warnings as well-intentioned, the structural issue remains: if the output is influential, the defence's inability to probe the machinery is not cured by a caution label.

Proprietary Forensic Algorithms and the New Contest Over Reliability

If sentencing risk tools reveal the trade secret problem in a rights discourse, probabilistic genotyping and algorithmic forensics reveal it in a reliability discourse. Here the state often presents the algorithm as part of "science," and the defence is told that the scientific method has been respected because the lab follows standards and experts are trained. Yet peer-reviewed socio-legal research on probabilistic DNA profiling software shows that introducing algorithms into forensic practice destabilises expertise and creates ambiguity about who—or what—is the "accuser," leading to contested authority and difficulties in adversarial testing (Pullen-Blasnik et al., 2024). The significance for equality of arms is direct: when the expert's authority is partially relocated into software, contestation must be able to reach the software's assumptions and implementation, not merely the expert's verbal confidence.

This is also why a growing body of scholarship has urged courts to move away from "black box explanations" and toward interpretable, auditable systems in forensic settings. Garrett's work on interpretable algorithmic forensics argues that "glass box" AI can be both interpretable and accurate, challenging the idea that opacity is the inevitable cost of performance in high-stakes evidential domains (Garrett, 2023). The legal implication is not that courts must prefer simplicity for its own sake; it is that when liberty is at stake, a state should not choose opacity if reliable interpretability is achievable. Choosing opacity where it is unnecessary is not innovation; it is avoidable inequality of arms.

Secret Evidence Doctrine and the Algorithmic Analogy

Equality of arms has long confronted the problem of secret evidence under claims of public interest: informants, undercover methods, national security material, witness protection. The European Court of Human Rights has accepted that some restrictions can exist, but the jurisprudential theme is consistent: the defence cannot be placed at a substantial disadvantage, and any non-disclosure must be counterbalanced by adequate procedural safeguards and judicial control. The same logic appears across evidence-law scholarship analysing Article 6 and the fair-trial framework (Stoykova, 2023).

The algorithmic version of secret evidence is subtle because it is often not described as evidence at all. A risk score is framed as "information." A tool is framed as "support." A classifier is framed as "investigative lead." Yet once such outputs materially shape detention decisions, sentencing severity, or evidential weight, they function as evidence-like forces. Treating them as something less is precisely how secrecy becomes normalised. The correct legal move is conceptual clarity: if the state relies on an output to justify coercion, the output is part of the evidential structure and must be contestable.

The Human-in-the-Loop Illusion and the Practical Collapse of Equality

Institutions often respond to trade secret concerns by saying, "Humans decide, the model only assists." That reassurance is frequently incomplete. Decision-support systems reshape the decision environment through framing, anchoring, and selective attention; they do not merely add information neutrally. The European Data Protection Supervisor's TechDispatch on human oversight emphasises that human oversight must be more than symbolic and should ensure a clear rationale for decisions and the ability to evaluate whether underlying logic is sound. If oversight is weak, the algorithm can become the de facto driver while the human becomes a formal signer. Equality of arms then fails in a new way: the defence is asked to contest a decision that is officially human but practically machine-shaped, without access to the machine's contestable substrate.

This is one reason public legitimacy can drop even when systems claim "assistance only." Empirical research on public perceptions of judicial AI use shows that perceived legitimacy, fairness, and procedural justice are sensitive to the role AI plays, and people often react negatively to fully automated or opaque involvement in judicial decisions (Fine, Berthelot and Marsh, 2025). These perceptions are not mere sentiment. They reflect a functional expectation: decisions about liberty must be owned by accountable reasons, and secrecy undermines that ownership.

What a Fair Trial-Compatible Trade Secret Compromise Actually Looks Like

The trade secret debate often devolves into two caricatures. One says, "Disclose everything, or it's unfair." The other says, "Disclose nothing, but trust us." Both are institutionally lazy. The fair-trial-compatible position is neither maximal disclosure nor vendor veto. It is functional equivalence: if the state cannot disclose the full source code publicly, it must provide the defence with the equivalent ability to test reliability, relevance, and error, under protective conditions that preserve confidentiality without destroying contestability.

A workable architecture has four elements. First, case-specific disclosure of inputs, feature values, thresholds, and model version used, so factual errors can be corrected and relevance arguments can be made. Second, validation disclosure tailored to the deployment context, including known error rates and limitations, so the output's probative weight can be argued as evidence rather than accepted as fact. Third, secure expert access where necessary—protective orders, confidentiality agreements, in-camera review, or court-appointed neutral experts—to permit examination of critical proprietary aspects without releasing them to competitors. Fourth, auditability and logging so that the defence and court can reconstruct what happened, which is essential because models drift and decision-support systems are updated. Without logs, no explanation is stable.

The key is that the defence must not be left with mere narrative reassurances. The defence must be given tools that make challenge real. Peer-reviewed work on algorithmic governance repeatedly shows that transparency instruments can devolve into box-ticking if they do not create meaningful accountability mechanisms (Nieuwenhuizen, 2024). Equality of arms is the criminal-law antidote to box-ticking. It demands operational leverage.

The Moral Core: Dignity, Condemnation, and the Right Not to Be Judged by Secret Reasons

There is a moral reason equality of arms matters beyond epistemics. Criminal punishment is not merely administration; it is condemnation. Condemnation requires reasons that can be heard, contested, and understood as reasons by the person condemned. When trade secret protection blocks meaningful contestation, the person is condemned partly by secret reasons. That is not simply unfair; it is degrading, because it treats the citizen as a managed object rather than as an accountable agent entitled to public justification.

Procedural justice theory explains why this degradation is socially expensive: legitimacy depends on experiences of neutrality, voice, and respect, and these collapse when decisive reasons are hidden (Tyler, 2011). In a predictive legal order, the danger is amplified because "risk" can become character, and opaque systems can harden decisions in ways that are difficult to explain as proportional condemnation rather than preventive management. Equality of arms is therefore not a technical add-on; it is the mechanism by which punishment remains law rather than opaque governance.

Conclusion: Trade Secrets Cannot Be Allowed to Rewrite the Trial

The conflict between proprietary models and fair trial is not a niche dispute about software. It is a constitutional confrontation between two logics: the market logic of secrecy and the rule-of-law logic of contestable coercion. Equality of arms does not demand that every algorithm be public. It demands that no one should lose liberty to an influence they cannot meaningfully challenge. In practical terms, that means proprietary tools may be used only if their outputs are rendered contestable through case-specific disclosure, validation transparency, secure expert scrutiny, and auditable decision trails. If a vendor refuses those conditions, the state cannot honestly claim it is running an adversarial trial; it is running an administrative procedure with a courtroom front.

The moment you accept that, the debate becomes clearer. Trade secrets are not illegitimate. They are simply not allowed to function as an evidentiary privilege that places the defence at a substantial disadvantage. A fair trial is not compatible with secret reasoning that materially shapes condemnation. In the age of proprietary models, equality of arms is the principle that forces the system to remember what law is for.

References

- Bhatnagar, V. (2023) 'The evidentiary implications of interpreting black-box algorithms', Northwestern Journal of Technology and Intellectual Property, 20(3), pp. 1–32.

- Blader, S.L. and Tyler, T.R. (2003) 'A four-component model of procedural justice: Defining the meaning of a "fair" process', Personality and Social Psychology Bulletin, 29(6), pp. 747–758.
- Chouldechova, A. (2017) 'Fair prediction with disparate impact: A study of bias in recidivism prediction instruments', Big Data, 5(2), pp. 153–163.
- Council of Europe (2024a) Framework Convention on Artificial Intelligence and Human Rights, Democracy and the Rule of Law (CETS No. 225). Strasbourg: Council of Europe.
- Council of Europe (2024b) Guide on Article 6 of the European Convention on Human Rights: Right to a Fair Trial (Criminal Limb). Updated 29 February 2024. Strasbourg: Council of Europe.
- Custers, B. (2024) 'A fair trial in complex technology cases: Why courts and judges need sufficient understanding of technology', Computer Law & Security Review, 52, 1059xx.
- Ensign, D., Friedler, S.A., Neville, S., Scheidegger, C. and Venkatasubramanian, S. (2018) 'Runaway feedback loops in predictive policing', Proceedings of Machine Learning Research, 81, pp. 1–12.
- European Data Protection Supervisor (2025) TechDispatch #2/2025: Human Oversight of Automated Decision-Making. Brussels: EDPS.
- European Union (2024) Regulation (EU) 2024/1689 of the European Parliament and of the Council (Artificial Intelligence Act).
- Fine, A., Berthelot, E.R. and Marsh, S. (2025) 'Public perceptions of judges' use of AI tools in courtroom decision-making: An examination of legitimacy, fairness, trust, and procedural justice', Behavioral Sciences, 15(4), 476.
- Gama, J., Žliobaitė, I., Bifet, A., Pechenizkiy, M. and Bouchachia, A. (2014) 'A survey on concept drift adaptation', ACM Computing Surveys, 46(4), Article 44.
- Garrett, B.L. (2023) 'Interpretable algorithmic forensics', Proceedings of the National Academy of Sciences, 120, e2301842120.
- Gikay, A.A. (2025) 'Trade secrecy in automated decisions: Against the myth of a complete barrier to transparency', Journal of Intellectual Property Law & Practice, 20(8), pp. 552–565.
- Grimmelikhuijsen, S. (2022) 'Legitimacy of algorithmic decision-making: Six threats and the need for a calibrated institutional response', Public Policy and Management Review, 5(3), pp. 232–252.

- Kinchin, N. (2024) '"Voiceless": The procedural gap in algorithmic justice', International Journal of Law and Information Technology, 32(4), pp. 1–30.
- Kleinberg, J., Mullainathan, S. and Raghavan, M. (2017) 'Inherent trade-offs in the fair determination of risk scores', Proceedings of the 8th Innovations in Theoretical Computer Science Conference (ITCS 2017), LIPIcs 67, Article 43.
- Longoni, C., Cian, L. and Kyung, E.J. (2023) 'Algorithmic transference: People overgeneralize failures of artificial intelligence in the government', Journal of Marketing Research, 60(1), pp. 170–188.
- Lyell, D. and Coiera, E. (2017) 'Automation bias and verification complexity: A systematic review', Journal of the American Medical Informatics Association, 24(2), pp. 423–431.
- Morrison, G.S. (2025) 'A guide to ISO 21043 forensic sciences from the forensic-data-science paradigm', Science & Justice, 65, 101298.
- Nieuwenhuizen, E. (2024) 'Algorithm registers: A box-ticking exercise or meaningful tool for transparency?', Information Polity, 29(4), pp. 415–433.
- Oswald, M. (2018) 'Algorithmic risk assessment policing models: The law enforcement perspective', Journal of Cyber Policy, 3(1), pp. 1–20.
- Perdomo, J.C., Zrnic, T., Mendler-Dünner, C. and Hardt, M. (2020) 'Performative prediction', Proceedings of the 37th International Conference on Machine Learning (ICML 2020), PMLR 119, pp. 7599–7609.
- Pleiss, G., Raghavan, M., Wu, F., Kleinberg, J. and Weinberger, K.Q. (2017) 'On fairness and calibration', Advances in Neural Information Processing Systems, 30.
- Pullen-Blasnik, H. et al. (2024) '"Is your accuser me, or is it the software?" Ambiguity and contested expertise in probabilistic DNA profiling', Social Studies of Science, 54(2), pp. 1–27.
- Robertson, B., Vignaux, G.A. and Berger, C.E.H. (2016) Interpreting Evidence: Evaluating Forensic Science in the Courtroom. 2nd edn. Chichester: Wiley.
- Selbst, A.D. and Barocas, S. (2018) 'The intuitive appeal of explainable machines', Fordham Law Review, 87(3), pp. 1085–1139.
- Skitka, L.J., Mosier, K.L. and Burdick, M. (1999) 'Does automation bias decision-making?', International Journal of Human–Computer Studies, 51(5), pp. 991–1006.

- Stoykova, R. (2023) 'The right to a fair trial as a conceptual framework for digital evidence rules', Computer Law & Security Review, 49, 1058xx.
- Tyler, T.R. (2011) 'Procedural justice, legitimacy, and the effective rule of law', Crime and Justice, 40(1), pp. 283–357.
- Wachter, S., Mittelstadt, B. and Russell, C. (2018) 'Counterfactual explanations without opening the black box: Automated decisions and the GDPR', Harvard Journal of Law & Technology, 31(2), pp. 841–887.

CHAPTER XXXV

Standards of Review for Algorithmic Decisions: Deference, Scrutiny and Proportionality

The Review Question Is Always the Same, Even When the Tool Is New

Judicial review has always balanced two anxieties that pull in opposite directions. One anxiety is institutional humility: judges are not engineers, administrators, or policy designers, and courts cannot plausibly replace the executive's continuous, information-rich governance with episodic adjudication. The other anxiety is rule-of-law courage: when state power injures rights, excludes persons, or condemns them, a court that defers too readily becomes a constitutional ornament rather than a corrective institution. Algorithmic systems do not change these anxieties; they intensify them. They insert a new decision actor into the chain—sometimes openly, sometimes as a "support tool," sometimes as a vendor product protected by secrecy—and they complicate the basic question of review: how much should a court defer, how intensely should it scrutinise, and by what test should it decide whether the interference is justified?

If you read the public-law literature closely, you find a converging diagnosis: automated decision-making shifts the evidential and justificatory terrain of review. It changes what counts as an "error," how error is evidenced, and who has access to the information needed to prove it (Tomlinson, Harkens and Sheridan, 2020). In doing so, it threatens to create what has been called a "procedural gap," where broad human-rights rhetoric exists but the practical ability to contest algorithmic power remains thin, especially for those most affected by state automation (Kinchin, 2024). These are not merely administrative worries. They go to the core of criminal justice legitimacy, because liberty deprivation and condemnation are not tolerable as opaque outputs. They must remain publicly reasoned acts that are contestable and reviewable.

The practical problem is that algorithmic decisions often arrive in court as if they were one of two things: either a technical fact that deserves deference, or a suspicious black box that deserves outright rejection. Both approaches are too crude. The correct stance is to treat algorithms as decision structures that distribute discretion, embed normative choices, generate evidence, and alter the burdens of justification. Standards of review must therefore be calibrated, not absolutist.

Three Review Logics Courts Already Use

Although jurisdictions use different doctrinal labels, the world's review practices cluster around three logics that can be adapted to algorithmic decisions without reinventing the wheel. The first is deference, often expressed as reasonableness, rationality, "manifest error," or a margin of appreciation where specialised judgment is involved. The second is heightened scrutiny, triggered when the state interferes with fundamental rights, equality norms, or core procedural guarantees. The third is proportionality, which sits between them: it allows courts to take rights seriously without pretending courts are policy ministries, by requiring the state to justify interferences through a structured test of means–ends fit and balance.

Public law scholarship has explicitly argued that we should adopt the public-law toolbox—legality, rationality, procedural fairness, proportionality, reason-giving—rather than treating algorithmic governance as a novelty requiring bespoke "AI-only" doctrines (Williams, 2022). This is important because the temptation in algorithmic cases is either to over-correct (courts become design reviewers) or under-correct (courts accept vendor or agency assertions because "technical"). The public-law toolbox offers a middle discipline: courts review the legality and justification of the decision and the decision system, not the elegance of code.

Deference in Algorithmic Governance: When It Is Justified and When It Becomes Abdication

Deference has a respectable foundation: institutions with expertise make policy-laden judgments under uncertainty, and courts are not designed to do that work at scale. Algorithmic systems, however, complicate deference because they can create the illusion of expertise. A numerical output can appear as a scientific fact even when it is a policy choice stabilised into a score: labels, proxies, thresholds, and training data are all choices. A deferential court risks deferring not to expertise but to automation framing.

The EU public-law tradition illustrates the tension. One line of analysis notes that EU courts often apply a "manifest error" intensity when reviewing complex technical and economic assessments by administrative bodies, which is a classic form of deference (Covilla, 2025). Yet Covilla's work also stresses that when AI systems intervene in discretionary decision-making, review must adapt to ensure the algorithm took into account relevant factors mandated by law, respected procedural guarantees, and did not misapply the public interests that statute requires, even if the overall intensity remains deferential in form (Covilla, 2025). The crucial insight is that deference cannot be a blanket attitude; it must be conditional on the decision system meeting minimum rule-of-law prerequisites, including reason-giving and duty of care principles that align with good administration (Covilla, 2025).

Here the forensic application is immediate. Consider a bail or sentencing support tool that predicts "risk" based partly on prior police contacts. Even if the tool is calibrated, the legal question is whether the state may treat institutional contact as a morally relevant basis for coercion, given known disparities in contact patterns. Deference to "the tool's accuracy" becomes a category mistake if the tool's architecture embeds contestable moral and equality judgments. Borgesius has shown how existing legal protections against algorithmic discrimination have strengths and weaknesses, but also that algorithmic discrimination is not a purely statistical issue; it is an institutional and legal issue about how protected interests are operationalised and remedied (Zuiderveen Borgesius, 2020). The implication is straightforward: when equality is plausibly in play, deference must thin out.

Heightened Scrutiny: Rights, Equality, and the Conditions of a Fair Hearing

Heightened scrutiny is triggered when algorithmic decisions materially affect fundamental rights or core fair-trial conditions, especially in criminal justice where liberty and stigma are central. The intensification is not a moral panic; it is a response to two structural facts about algorithms in state power. First, algorithmic systems can amplify harm by scale and by feedback loops. Second, algorithmic systems can be opaque in ways that weaken contestability, shifting practical burdens onto individuals least able to meet them.

Kinchin's analysis of a procedural gap is pivotal here because it shows why relying solely on human-rights impact assessments or high-level rights talk can fail. "Due process human rights" mechanisms may exclude many algorithmic decisions from their scope, leaving individuals with a right in theory but not in practice (Kinchin, 2024). That is exactly the zone where heightened scrutiny becomes necessary: not because the court must inspect code line-by-line, but because the court must ensure voice, contestability, and intelligible justification remain real.

In criminal justice contexts, this intersects with equality of arms concerns where proprietary models are used. If the state relies on an algorithmic output while denying meaningful access to its basis, the procedural disadvantage is not cured by saying a human signs the order. The question for scrutiny is whether the human involvement is meaningful and whether the defence can practically challenge the output's relevance and reliability. Scholarship on algorithmic accountability repeatedly returns to this point: public law already has concepts that can structure oversight—especially reason-giving, procedural fairness, and review—without abandoning rights protection to vendor secrecy (Williams, 2022).

Proportionality as the Bridge Between Deference and Control

Proportionality is often misunderstood as judicial overreach. In fact, its attraction in algorithmic governance is the opposite: it provides a principled way to demand justification without requiring courts to run the administration. Proportionality also has an unusually good fit with algorithmic decision-making, because algorithmic systems are built to optimise means to ends—exactly the relationship proportionality interrogates. The question becomes: are these means suitable, necessary, and balanced in their impact on rights and interests?

Enqvist's account of proportionality in automated decision-making contexts is particularly useful because it treats proportionality as both a standard of review and a lifecycle discipline. Proportionality can target the whole normative chain—from legislation to implementation to individual decisions—and can examine whether discretionary space is used in a way that is not disproportionate to affected persons (Enqvist, 2023). Crucially, proportionality can also scrutinise internal decision-making structures, training, and implementation choices, which is exactly where algorithmic harms are often generated (Enqvist, 2023). This makes proportionality a natural review engine for algorithmic systems, because it can address both system-level design choices and case-level impacts.

Covilla's analysis complements this by showing how proportionality review can adapt to algorithmic discretion: the judge must check whether relevant factors were considered, whether public interests were properly weighed, and how the decision affected the addressee, while calibrating intensity to the degree of discretion and subjectivity involved (Covilla, 2025). The result is not an all-or-nothing approach. Low-stakes, rule-bound automations may require lighter review focused on procedural legality. High-stakes, discretionary, rights-implicating automations require more intensive proportionality reasoning, often with expert assistance to make the system's reasoning and limits intelligible (Covilla, 2025).

Evidence, Error, and the Problem of Proving Algorithmic Illegality

Standards of review are meaningless if errors cannot be evidenced. Tomlinson, Harkens and Sheridan show that automated decision systems reshape judicial review evidence practices because proving error becomes harder when decision logic is encoded in systems, data pipelines, and model assumptions rather than in a human's explicit reasons (Tomlinson, Harkens and Sheridan, 2020). This has two implications. First, courts may unintentionally become more deferential simply because claimants cannot prove what they cannot see. Second, remedies that rely heavily on ex post contestation can become structurally inadequate, because many affected individuals lack the knowledge or resources to bring challenges (Enqvist, 2023; Kinchin, 2024).

The forensic parallel is instructive. Forensic science has learned that "accuracy" is not a self-certifying badge; it must be demonstrated under conditions of use, and error rates must be understood as part of probative value (Robertson, Vignaux and Berger, 2016; Morrison, 2025). Algorithmic systems in justice are similarly evidence-like. Their outputs should be treated as claims with uncertainty and error characteristics, not as neutral facts. If courts do not require this discipline, review will drift toward deference-by-opacity, which is the most dangerous kind because it looks like humility but functions as abdication.

Calibrating Intensity: A Practical Taxonomy for Review Without Overreach

A workable global approach is to calibrate the intensity of review to three variables: stakes, discretion, and contestability.

Stakes refer to whether liberty, severe stigma, or fundamental rights are affected. The higher the stakes, the stronger the justification burden, and the less acceptable it is to rely on opaque or unchallengeable outputs (Tyler, 2011; Kinchin, 2024). Discretion refers to how much normative judgment is embedded in the decision and system. Highly discretionary decisions—bail risk, sentencing severity, dangerousness, child protection removals—require deeper scrutiny of the reasons and policy assumptions embedded in the system, because the system is doing governance, not clerical sorting (Covilla, 2025; Williams, 2022). Contestability refers to whether the person can challenge the system's input data, feature construction, thresholds, and validation. Where contestability is weak—due to trade secrets, opacity, or poor documentation—courts should not respond by deferring; they should respond by requiring disclosure, independent auditing, or limiting admissibility/weight, because without contestability the system's legality cannot be meaningfully tested (Kinchin, 2024; Williams, 2022).

This calibrated approach is consistent with risk-based regulatory logic in the AI governance space. Scholarly discussion of the EU AI Act has emphasised that a truly risk-based approach should reflect proportionality: stronger obligations and oversight for higher-risk systems, rather than one-size-fits-all compliance (Ebers, 2025; Hacker, 2026). The significance for standards of review is conceptual: review intensity should itself be risk- and rights-sensitive, and proportionality provides the vocabulary for that sensitivity.

Remedy and Institutional Design: Review Must Produce More Than Annulment

In algorithmic cases, review that only quashes a decision after harm is done can be too thin, especially when systems operate at scale. Courts and oversight bodies may need to use remedies that force institutional learning:

reasons-giving duties that require agencies to articulate how the system works and why it is lawful; disclosure orders; requirements for validation and monitoring; and, where appropriate, systemic relief. Williams has argued that public law can interpret and operationalise accountability concepts in algorithmic governance without reinventing them, which implies that remedial toolkits can also be drawn from existing administrative justice principles (Williams, 2022). The most important constraint is to avoid turning courts into system administrators while still ensuring that legality is not defeated by technical complexity.

Here, proportionality again matters. Enqvist emphasises that proportionality review can operate both in abstracto (reviewing legal mandates and system-level choices) and in casu (reviewing the proportionality of specific decisions), and that overreliance on ex post contestation is problematic when affected persons face knowledge and resource dependencies (Enqvist, 2023). A mature remedy regime therefore treats proportionality not only as a test but as an institutional discipline: it pushes legality and rights-sensitivity upstream into system design and implementation, rather than relying entirely on downstream litigation.

Conclusion: Review in the Age of Algorithms Is About Justification Under Power

Standards of review for algorithmic decisions are not a niche technical debate. They are the modern form of the oldest public-law question: how does a court control state power without becoming the state? The answer will not be found in worship of "accuracy" nor in reflex suspicion of technology. It will be found in calibrated review that recognises three truths. First, deference remains legitimate where specialised judgment is involved, but it must be conditional on contestable reasons and lawful system design. Second, scrutiny must intensify where liberty, equality, and fair hearing conditions are threatened by opacity, proxy discrimination, or inability to challenge. Third, proportionality offers the most practical bridge, because it forces structured justification of means–ends relationships while respecting institutional roles, and it can target both system-level and case-level harms (Covilla, 2025; Enqvist, 2023; Williams, 2022).

In a predictive legal order, the court's task is not to beat the machine at prediction. The task is to ensure that prediction does not replace justification, and that technical systems do not become unreviewable power. When review is calibrated by deference, scrutiny, and proportionality—rather than by fear or fascination—the law can remain what it promised to be: coercion that answers to reasons.

References

- Barocas, S. and Selbst, A.D. (2016) 'Big data's disparate impact', California Law Review, 104(3), pp. 671–732.
- Chouldechova, A. (2017) 'Fair prediction with disparate impact: A study of bias in recidivism prediction instruments', Big Data, 5(2), pp. 153–163.
- Cobbe, J. (2019) 'Judicial review of automated public-sector decision-making', Legal Studies, 39(4), pp. 636–655.
- Covilla, J.C. (2025) 'Artificial intelligence and administrative discretion: Exploring adaptations and boundaries', European Journal of Risk Regulation, 16(2), pp. 1–28.
- Craig, P. (2012) Administrative Law. 7th edn. London: Sweet & Maxwell.
- Ebers, M. (2025) 'Truly risk-based regulation of artificial intelligence: How to implement the EU's AI Act', European Journal of Risk Regulation, 16(1), pp. 1–23.
- Enqvist, L. (2023) 'Discretion, automation, and proportionality', in Suksi, M. (ed.) The Rule of Law and Automated Decision-Making: Exploring Fundamentals of Algorithmic Governance. Cham: Springer, pp. 169–205.
- Feldman, M., Friedler, S.A., Moeller, J., Scheidegger, C. and Venkatasubramanian, S. (2015) 'Certifying and removing disparate impact', Proceedings of the 21st ACM SIGKDD International Conference on Knowledge Discovery and Data Mining (KDD '15), pp. 259–268.
- Gama, J., Žliobaitė, I., Bifet, A., Pechenizkiy, M. and Bouchachia, A. (2014) 'A survey on concept drift adaptation', ACM Computing Surveys, 46(4), Article 44.
- Hacker, P. (2026) 'AI regulation in Europe: From the AI Act to future regulatory challenges', in Ajunwa, I.Y. and Adams-Prassl, J. (eds) The Oxford Handbook of Algorithmic Governance and the Law. Oxford: Oxford University Press.

- Kinchin, N. (2024) '"Voiceless": The procedural gap in algorithmic justice', International Journal of Law and Information Technology, 32(4), pp. 1–30.
- Kleinberg, J., Mullainathan, S. and Raghavan, M. (2017) 'Inherent trade-offs in the fair determination of risk scores', Proceedings of the 8th Innovations in Theoretical Computer Science Conference (ITCS 2017), LIPIcs 67, Article 43.
- Lum, K. and Isaac, W. (2016) 'To predict and serve?', Significance, 13(5), pp. 14–19.
- Morrison, G.S. (2025) 'A guide to ISO 21043 forensic sciences from the forensic-data-science paradigm', Science & Justice, 65, 101298.
- Neil, R. (2025) 'Algorithmic bias in criminal risk assessment: The consequences of racial differences in arrest as a measure of crime', Annual Review of Criminology, 8, pp. 97–119.
- Perdomo, J.C., Zrnic, T., Mendler-Dünner, C. and Hardt, M. (2020) 'Performative prediction', Proceedings of the 37th International Conference on Machine Learning (ICML 2020), PMLR 119, pp. 7599–7609.
- Pleiss, G., Raghavan, M., Wu, F., Kleinberg, J. and Weinberger, K.Q. (2017) 'On fairness and calibration', Advances in Neural Information Processing Systems, 30.
- Robertson, B., Vignaux, G.A. and Berger, C.E.H. (2016) Interpreting Evidence: Evaluating Forensic Science in the Courtroom. 2nd edn. Chichester: Wiley.
- Rudin, C. (2019) 'Stop explaining black box machine learning models for high stakes decisions and use interpretable models instead', Nature Machine Intelligence, 1, pp. 206–215.
- Skitka, L.J., Mosier, K.L. and Burdick, M. (1999) 'Does automation bias decision-making?', International Journal of Human–Computer Studies, 51(5), pp. 991–1006.
- Tomlinson, J., Harkens, A. and Sheridan, K. (2020) 'Judicial review evidence in the era of the digital state', Public Law, (Oct), pp. 740–760.
- Tyler, T.R. (2011) 'Procedural justice, legitimacy, and the effective rule of law', Crime and Justice, 40(1), pp. 283–357.
- Williams, R. (2021) 'Rethinking administrative law for algorithmic decision making', Oxford Journal of Legal Studies, 41(2), pp. 456–484.
- Williams, R. (2022) 'Accountable algorithms: Adopting the public law toolbox to scrutinise algorithmic decision-making', Current Legal

Problems, 75(1), pp. 237–275.

- Zuiderveen Borgesius, F.J. (2020) 'Strengthening legal protection against discrimination by algorithms and artificial intelligence', International Journal of Human Rights, 24(10), pp. 1572–1593.

Part VIII — Institutions, Incentives, and Governance

CHAPTER XXXVI

Procurement, Vendors, and the Political Economy of "Evidence-Based" Justice

The Marketplace That Sits Behind the Bench

If you want to understand how "evidence-based" justice actually spreads, you must look behind the courtroom and behind the laboratory, into the quieter rooms where tenders are drafted, demonstrations are performed, contracts are signed, and "solutions" are sold. The public often imagines criminal justice technology as a neutral pipeline: science produces tools, tools produce accuracy, and accuracy produces justice. In reality, the pipeline is political economy. Vendors do not simply supply instruments; they supply categories, metrics, workflows, dashboards, and the very vocabulary through which problems are defined. Procurement does not merely purchase a tool; it purchases a way of seeing crime, risk, compliance, and credibility. Once a jurisdiction has invested in a platform—financially, institutionally, and reputationally—its notion of what counts as "good evidence" begins to bend toward what the platform can produce.

This is not a cynical claim; it is an observable institutional pattern. Contemporary scholarship on policing's political economy emphasises that policing is shaped through relations with private firms, philanthropy, social services, and academia, and that technology markets are not external to policing but part of how policing is organised and legitimated (Vargas, 2025). If policing and prosecution are increasingly platformised, then "evidence-based" becomes partly a market label: evidence that can be produced cheaply, quickly, and in standardised form is favoured; evidence that requires slow human attention, contextual judgement, and labour-intensive explanation becomes comparatively disfavoured. That shift can occur even when no one intends it, because procurement and budgeting favour what scales, and scaling favours what can be counted.

"Evidence-Based" as a Brand and as a Shield

In justice, "evidence-based" carries moral power. It signals rationality, neutrality, and modern governance. Yet the phrase often functions as a rhetorical shield for procurement choices that are in fact normative. A risk tool is not just a predictor; it embodies decisions about what outcome to predict, which proxies to use, how to handle missingness, what error trade-offs to accept, and which subpopulations are treated as acceptable collateral in the distribution of false positives and false negatives. The fairness literature has shown, in rigorous form, that multiple attractive fairness properties cannot generally be satisfied simultaneously when base rates differ and prediction is imperfect, meaning "fairness" is not a purely technical achievement but a choice among trade-offs (Chouldechova, 2017; Kleinberg, Mullainathan and Raghavan, 2017; Pleiss et al., 2017). When those trade-offs are made inside contracts, evaluation criteria, and vendor documentation, the politics of justice are being done through procurement rather than through public deliberation.

This is why the move to algorithmic governance creates a predictable "procedural gap," where performance claims flourish while voice and contestability weaken, because the system becomes harder to challenge in ordinary legal language (Kinchin, 2024). Procurement can widen that gap by making the model a product with proprietary boundaries rather than a public method. Once that happens, the question "Is it accurate?" can displace the question "Can it be contested?"—and contestability is the courtroom's native fairness technology.

The Vendor as a Co-Author of Legal Categories

A court decision looks like it is authored by a judge; a forensic report looks like it is authored by a scientist. Yet the vendor increasingly co-authors both by shaping the categories that appear as if they were natural. Consider the difference between predicting "rearrest," "reconviction," "violent recidivism," "technical violation," or "failure to appear." Each target is partly an institutional artefact, not a pure behavioural event. Criminological synthesis has warned that using arrest as a measure of crime can embed bias, because arrest patterns reflect enforcement patterns as well as underlying offending (Neil, 2025). If procurement selects tools trained on these targets without demanding label integrity, the state buys not only prediction but institutional memory disguised as science.

The same mechanism appears in digital policing and crime prevention tools. Research on algorithmic crime prevention and the "precision" turn in police practice shows how digital tools can reorganise police work, intensify data collection, and make certain kinds of activity more visible and actionable—thereby shaping what becomes recorded as the object of governance (Egbert and Leese, 2024). Once the system's records become the training data for further tools, the vendor-supplied categories can become self-confirming, because the tools help produce the very data that validate them (Ensign et al., 2018; Lum and Isaac, 2016). In political economy terms, the state purchases a feedback loop, and then experiences it as "improved measurement."

Procurement as Discretion: The Hidden Constitutional Moment

Most legal systems have elaborate doctrines regulating discretion at the point of sentencing, bail, search, seizure, and admissibility. But procurement is often treated as administrative plumbing. That is a mistake. Procurement is one of the most consequential discretion points in the entire justice system because it decides what kinds of reasons will later be available. A system that procures a black-box recommender has procured opacity and, with it, a new distribution of practical power: the accused may be able to challenge a human reason, but not a proprietary inference; the judge may be able to explain an ordinary balancing, but not a model's internal weighting; the public may be able to debate policy, but not vendor secrets.

This connects directly to equality-of-arms concerns. Once the state relies on proprietary systems in liberty-affecting decisions, trade secrets collide with fair-trial norms. Scholarship on trade secrecy in automated decisions has argued that trade secret protection is frequently invoked as a barrier to meaningful transparency, and that governance must confront, rather than romanticise, that conflict (Gikay, 2025). In forensic domains, socio-legal research on probabilistic DNA profiling shows how algorithmic software can become a contested "accuser," destabilising traditional forms of cross-examination because the decisive inferential machinery is relocated into software and its hidden assumptions (Pullen-Blasnik et al., 2024). If procurement choices place that machinery beyond adversarial reach, the system has quietly altered the architecture of the trial.

Adoption Dynamics: Why "The Market" Shapes Policing Strategy

The procurement story is not simply about vendors persuading agencies. It is also about organisational incentives, budget constraints, reputational risk, and administrative convenience. Recent peer-reviewed work on police technology adoption shows how agency characteristics and institutional dynamics shape technology uptake, indicating that adoption is not only a function of "what works" but also of organisational structure and political pressures (Ross, 2025). The same pattern appears in broad analyses of policing technology over time: technology is embedded in socio-political contexts and becomes part of how policing is imagined and justified, not merely how it is executed (Ugwudike, 2024).

Once you accept this, you see why "evidence-based" becomes a procurement magnet. Tools promise measurable outputs, dashboards, audit trails, and performance indicators. Those promises align with the managerial logic of modern public administration and with the political need to demonstrate action. But what can be measured is not always what matters morally. A procurement regime that rewards "deliverables" can subtly reward surveillance capacity, throughput, and risk scoring, even when the deeper goods of justice—individualised hearing, dignity, and proportional proportionality—are harder to count. The result is a procurement-driven shift from judgement to management, echoing the "new penology" thesis that modern penal practices increasingly manage aggregates and risks rather than communicate censure to individuals (Feeley and Simon, 1992).

Forensic Laboratories as Procurement Engines: Speed, Leads, and Commercial Pressures

The political economy is especially visible in forensic science because forensics sits at the boundary between scientific aspiration and institutional demand. Laboratories are asked to do more with less, reduce backlogs, deliver faster leads, and adopt new computational tools. Peer-reviewed proposals emphasising the development of "forensic leads" programmes reflect the institutional push toward speed and actionable intelligence (Wickenheiser, 2024). Speed can be a justice good when it reduces pretrial detention and uncertainty, but it also changes evidential culture: rapid outputs become operationally valuable, and operational value can be mistaken for probative value. That is where vendor platforms gain power. A platform that produces quick leads becomes institutionally indispensable, and indispensability can weaken the appetite for cautious validation, nuanced uncertainty communication, and adversarial scrutiny.

Forensic evidence scholarship has repeatedly warned that evidential systems must be validated and interpreted under disciplined frameworks, because scientific-looking outputs are prone to over-interpretation and miscommunication. The forensic-data-science paradigm emphasises error, validation under conditions of use, and transparent reasoning about evidential weight (Morrison, 2025). The procurement risk is that labs buy tools for workflow transformation—automation, throughput, integration—without buying the governance needed to keep epistemic integrity intact. When that happens, the market does not merely supply technology; it supplies a new evidential culture.

The Philanthropy–Academia–Vendor Triangle

A particularly modern feature of "evidence-based justice" is that adoption is often accelerated through a triangle: private firms provide tools, philanthropic funding supports pilots, and academic partnerships provide evaluation and legitimacy. Vargas's synthesis of the political economy of policing explicitly highlights how police–private firm–philanthropy–academia relations shape policing as an interinstitutional structure (Vargas, 2025). This matters because evaluation can become part of marketing, and pilots can become procurement pathways. The danger is not that evaluation is dishonest; the danger is that evaluation questions are shaped by what is feasible to measure and what aligns with procurement goals, thereby narrowing the public imagination of justice to what can be quantified.

The broader governance literature on trustworthiness in public-sector automated decision-making reinforces that "trust" depends on multiple facets—transparency, accountability, oversight, and contestability—not simply on performance metrics (Agbabiaka et al., 2025). When procurement and pilot ecosystems privilege performance claims while treating contestability as an inconvenience, the result is predictable: the system becomes more "evidence-based" and less legally intelligible.

The Moral Risk: When Procurement Turns Persons Into Profiles

The deepest moral problem in vendor-driven evidence regimes is the recasting of persons as profiles. Risk systems and predictive policing can transform a human being into a probability and then treat that probability as a character fact. When this happens, punishment and detention shift from judgement about culpable acts toward management of predicted futures. That shift threatens legitimacy because it weakens the communicative and justificatory dimensions of punishment, and it threatens fairness because it often relies on proxies and labels that encode institutional histories rather than individual blameworthiness (Barocas and Selbst, 2016; Neil, 2025). The opacity and scale of vendor platforms amplify the risk: decisions become easier to administer and harder to contest.

Public perception research suggests that legitimacy is sensitive to perceived role and authority of AI tools in courtroom decision-making, including perceptions of fairness, trust, and procedural justice (Fine, Berthelot and Marsh, 2025). That finding should be read as a governance warning: procurement that increases algorithmic influence without increasing meaningful reasons-giving and contestability will buy efficiency at the cost of legitimacy.

How to Think Like a Court About Procurement

The court's relationship to procurement is often indirect, but the court's values are not. If you want a justice system that remains lawful under technological change, procurement must be treated as part of the rule-of-law lifecycle. That means contracts and tenders must be drafted as if they are constitutional documents, because in practice they are. They decide whether audit trails exist, whether independent validation is possible, whether error rates are disclosed, whether versioning is logged, whether the defence can access artefacts needed to challenge outputs, and whether the state can explain itself in court without collapsing into "the vendor says." If those conditions are not built into procurement, no after-the-fact ethics statement can fix the structural disadvantage.

The most defensible institutional stance is therefore simple: if a tool can influence liberty or evidential weight, procurement must require contestability-compatible design. That does not mean everything must be open-source. It means the defence and the court must have functional access to what is necessary to test reliability, relevance, and limits—otherwise equality of arms becomes ceremonial. This stance aligns with emerging scholarship that insists public-law tools—reason-giving, procedural fairness, and calibrated review—must be applied to algorithmic systems rather than replaced by vendor self-certification (Williams, 2022).

Conclusion: "Evidence-Based" Justice Is Always Political Economy First

"Evidence-based" is not a magic spell that turns governance into justice. It is a label whose meaning is decided in procurement rooms long before it is invoked in court. Vendors shape what can be measured, procurement shapes what is purchased, and what is purchased shapes what the system learns to call "evidence." If the system does not build contestability, validation, and reasons-giving into procurement, it will drift toward a managerial order where the most powerful claims are the least challengeable ones, and where the citizen is governed by platforms they cannot meaningfully confront.

The task, therefore, is not to reject vendors as such, nor to romanticise state-built systems as pure. The task is to treat procurement as part of legality: to ensure that markets do not silently rewrite fair trial architecture, that performance metrics do not displace moral relevance, and that "evidence-based" remains a discipline of truth and reason rather than a brand for scalable governance (Vargas, 2025; Kinchin, 2024; Agbabiaka et al., 2025).

References

- Agbabiaka, O., Amankwah-Amoah, J., Debrah, Y.A. and Agyemang, G. (2025) 'Requirements for trustworthy AI-enabled automated decision-making in the public sector', Technological Forecasting and Social Change, 203, 123107.
- Barocas, S. and Selbst, A.D. (2016) 'Big data's disparate impact', California Law Review, 104(3), pp. 671–732.

- Berk, R., Heidari, H., Jabbari, S., Kearns, M. and Roth, A. (2021) 'Fairness in criminal justice risk assessments: The state of the art', Sociological Methods & Research, 50(1), pp. 3–44.
- Brayne, S. (2020) Predict and Surveil: Data, Discretion, and the Future of Policing. Oxford: Oxford University Press.
- Chouldechova, A. (2017) 'Fair prediction with disparate impact: A study of bias in recidivism prediction instruments', Big Data, 5(2), pp. 153–163.
- Egbert, S. and Leese, M. (2024) 'Algorithmic crime prevention: From abstract police to precision policing', Frontiers in Psychology, 15, 1251238.
- Ensign, D., Friedler, S.A., Neville, S., Scheidegger, C. and Venkatasubramanian, S. (2018) 'Runaway feedback loops in predictive policing', Proceedings of Machine Learning Research, 81, pp. 1–12.
- Eubanks, V. (2018) Automating Inequality: How High-Tech Tools Profile, Police, and Punish the Poor. New York: St. Martin's Press.
- Feeley, M.M. and Simon, J. (1992) 'The new penology: Notes on the emerging strategy of corrections and its implications', Criminology, 30(4), pp. 449–474.
- Ferguson, A.G. (2017) The Rise of Big Data Policing: Surveillance, Race, and the Future of Law Enforcement. New York: NYU Press.
- Ferguson, A.G. (2019) The Police Are Data: Surveillance, Race, and the Future of Law Enforcement. New York: NYU Press.
- Fine, A., Berthelot, E.R. and Marsh, S. (2025) 'Public perceptions of judges' use of AI tools in courtroom decision-making: An examination of legitimacy, fairness, trust, and procedural justice', Behavioral Sciences, 15(4), 476.
- Gikay, A.A. (2025) 'Trade secrecy in automated decisions: Against the myth of a complete barrier to transparency', Journal of Intellectual Property Law & Practice, 20(8), pp. 552–565.
- Kinchin, N. (2024) '"Voiceless": The procedural gap in algorithmic justice', International Journal of Law and Information Technology, 32(4), pp. 1–30.
- Kleinberg, J., Mullainathan, S. and Raghavan, M. (2017) 'Inherent trade-offs in the fair determination of risk scores', Proceedings of the 8th Innovations in Theoretical Computer Science Conference (ITCS 2017), LIPIcs 67, Article 43.

- Lum, K. and Isaac, W. (2016) 'To predict and serve?', Significance, 13(5), pp. 14–19.
- Morrison, G.S. (2025) 'A guide to ISO 21043 forensic sciences from the forensic-data-science paradigm', Science & Justice, 65, 101298.
- Neil, R. (2025) 'Algorithmic bias in criminal risk assessment: The consequences of racial differences in arrest as a measure of crime', Annual Review of Criminology, 8, pp. 97–119.
- Nieuwenhuizen, E. (2024) 'Algorithm registers: A box-ticking exercise or meaningful tool for transparency?', Information Polity, 29(4), pp. 415–433.
- Pasquale, F. (2015) The Black Box Society: The Secret Algorithms That Control Money and Information. Cambridge, MA: Harvard University Press.
- Pleiss, G., Raghavan, M., Wu, F., Kleinberg, J. and Weinberger, K.Q. (2017) 'On fairness and calibration', Advances in Neural Information Processing Systems, 30.
- Pullen-Blasnik, H., Lynch, M., Cole, S.A. and Kruse, C. (2024) '"Is your accuser me, or is it the software?" Ambiguity and contested expertise in probabilistic DNA profiling', Social Studies of Science, 54(2), pp. 1–27.
- Ross, Á.M. (2025) 'The politics of police technology adoption: Agency size and the diffusion of data-driven tools', Journal of Crime and Justice, 48(3), pp. 1–24.
- Skitka, L.J., Mosier, K.L. and Burdick, M. (1999) 'Does automation bias decision-making?', International Journal of Human–Computer Studies, 51(5), pp. 991–1006.
- Ugwudike, P. (2024) '25 years of technology use in policing', Information, Communication & Society, 27(12), pp. 1–20.
- Vargas, R. (2025) 'The political economy of policing', Annual Review of Law and Social Science, 21, pp. 1–24.
- Wickenheiser, R.A. (2024) 'Lead with speed: Recasting the forensic laboratory product as forensic leads', Forensic Science International: Synergy, 8, 100184.
- Williams, R. (2022) 'Accountable algorithms: Adopting the public law toolbox to scrutinise algorithmic decision-making', Current Legal Problems, 75(1), pp. 237–275.
- Zuboff, S. (2019) The Age of Surveillance Capitalism. London: Profile Books.

CHAPTER XXXVII

Audit Regimes: Continuous Monitoring, Red-Teaming, and Public Reporting

Audits Are Not Paperwork, They Are the Rule of Law in Motion

The criminal justice system has always lived by audit, even when it did not call it that. Chain of custody is an audit regime for objects. Disclosure is an audit regime for reasons. Appellate review is an audit regime for power. What has changed in the predictive era is that the system is increasingly governed by models that learn from data, drift with time, and produce outputs that look like evidence while behaving like policy. In that environment, a one-time certification, a one-time validation, or a one-time procurement check cannot carry the moral weight of coercion. Audit becomes continuous because the risk is continuous. If a tool influences bail, detention, sentencing, supervision intensity, investigative targeting, or the interpretation of forensic patterns, the state is no longer merely administering law; it is operating a socio-technical system whose behaviour must be monitored as closely as any other instrument that can deprive liberty.

The first institutional mistake is to treat audits as compliance theatre. The second is to treat audits as purely technical. A proper audit regime is a governance architecture that binds three things together: epistemic integrity (is the system reliable under conditions of use?), procedural integrity (can those affected contest and correct the system?), and legitimacy integrity (can the public see that power is being exercised in a way that is accountable and rights-respecting?) (Tyler, 2011; Williams, 2022; Wieringa, 2023). When any of these three is absent, the audit regime becomes hollow. When all three are present, auditing becomes the legal system's way of keeping prediction from becoming unreviewable power.

The Core Problem: Models Do Not Stay Still, Institutions Pretend They Do

Traditional evidence regimes assume that the method used today is substantially the method used yesterday. Machine learning systems violate that assumption in at least three ways. First, the world changes: data distributions shift, and so does predictive performance. Second, institutions change: policing strategies, prosecution policies, supervision conditions, and reporting patterns alter the meaning of "outcomes" in training data. Third, systems change: vendors patch models, retrain models, swap components, and update thresholds. The result is concept drift and policy drift at the same time. The technical literature on drift detection and monitoring has become increasingly clear that drift is not a rare anomaly; it is an ordinary condition of deployed models (Gama et al., 2014; Hinder et al., 2024). If drift is ordinary, then the legal implication is unavoidable: a one-time audit is not "due diligence." It is denial.

This is where the forensic analogy is instructive. Forensic science has moved, often painfully, toward an explicit error-and-validation culture: methods must be validated under conditions of use, uncertainty must be communicated, and interpretive boundaries must be respected (Robertson, Vignaux and Berger, 2016; Morrison, 2025). Algorithmic systems in justice should be treated with the same epistemic seriousness. A risk score or a pattern detector is not a truth; it is an inferential device with error behaviour. If the state cannot demonstrate continuing validity, then it cannot honestly claim it is using evidence rather than administering an opaque policy.

Continuous Monitoring as Evidence Maintenance, Not IT Maintenance

Continuous monitoring is often described in operational terms—dashboards, alerting, automated checks—but in criminal justice its real function is evidential maintenance. Monitoring must answer, in a disciplined way, whether the model's claims remain trustworthy in the context in which they are used. Continuous auditing scholarship frames this as a need for systems capable of monitoring model behaviour, detecting drift in performance characteristics, validating decision consistency, and maintaining audit trails that explain how specific inputs generated outputs

(Bauer et al., 2022). It is not enough to monitor "uptime." The system must monitor whether it is still making the same kind of claim it was validated to make.

This is where monitoring has to be multi-layered. You monitor data drift because inputs shift; you monitor label drift because the meaning of outcomes changes under institutional practice; you monitor performance drift because calibration can degrade silently; and you monitor impact drift because the distribution of harms can change even if aggregate accuracy remains stable. The drift literature distinguishes these as different phenomena requiring different detection strategies, with surveys emphasizing that unsupervised settings and real-world monitoring need careful methodological choices, not generic "anomaly detection" slogans (Hinder et al., 2024). Monitoring that fails to distinguish these drifts becomes a false sense of security: it detects the easy anomalies and misses the legally dangerous shifts.

If you want the behavioural truth of why this matters, recall how decision-making responds to false reassurance. Automation bias research shows that people over-rely on automated outputs when verification is difficult and cognitive load is high (Lyell and Coiera, 2017; Skitka, Mosier and Burdick, 1999). Monitoring is partly designed to prevent institutions from sleeping inside that bias. It creates friction: an alert that forces review, a drift signal that triggers recalibration, an audit log that makes it possible to reconstruct responsibility.

Red-Teaming: Stress-Testing as a Moral Duty, Not a Marketing Ritual

Red-teaming has become fashionable in AI governance, but fashion is not governance. A proper red-team exercise is a structured attempt to surface failures that are unlikely to appear in standard evaluation, including security vulnerabilities, harmful outputs, discriminatory failure modes, and misuse pathways. In the generative AI domain, peer-reviewed and research-community work has explicitly debated whether red-teaming has become too narrow—focusing on model-level "jailbreaks" rather than system-level harms—and has argued that red-teaming must evolve into a more systematic risk mitigation practice rather than a publicity-friendly vulnerability hunt (Sinha, 2025; "Red-Teaming for Generative AI" survey, 2025). Red-teaming is valuable precisely because normal evaluation is often optimistic: it tests what designers expect. Red-teaming tests what reality will do.

In criminal justice, the red-team target is not merely the model; it is the socio-technical system. A red-team should stress-test what happens when adversaries exploit the system, when data are missing or corrupted, when the tool is used outside intended scope, when proxies for protected attributes drive decisions, when operators become over-dependent, and when feedback loops amplify enforcement patterns. Predictive policing research on feedback loops demonstrates how deployment can create self-confirming data patterns that make a system look accurate while it is reproducing institutional attention (Ensign et al., 2018; Lum and Isaac, 2016). A red-team that does not test these dynamics is not red-teaming justice; it is red-teaming software.

The moral reason red-teaming belongs in justice is simple. A state cannot claim legitimacy for coercion while refusing to actively seek out the system's worst-case harms. That refusal is not neutrality; it is negligence under power. The legitimacy literature repeatedly links public acceptance to perceptions of fairness, transparency, and accountability in algorithmic decisions (Starke, Lünich and Marcinkowski, 2022; Tyler, 2011). Red-teaming is one of the few practices that demonstrates accountability before catastrophe, rather than after scandal.

Public Reporting: The Difference Between Accountability and Self-Disclosure

Public reporting is not the same as transparency theatre. Listing that a tool exists is a start; it is not accountability. Audit regimes require reporting that allows publics, oversight bodies, and affected communities to understand what powers are being exercised, where, with what safeguards, and with what observed patterns of error and disparity. A growing literature on algorithm registers warns that registers can become box-ticking exercises if they are not designed to support meaningful scrutiny and organisational accountability (Nieuwenhuizen, 2024). Wieringa's analysis of algorithmic accountability lessons from a landmark welfare profiling case similarly shows how accountability fails when transparency is weak and when institutional arrangements make responsibility difficult to locate (Wieringa, 2023).

The legal point is sharper in criminal justice because public reporting interacts with legitimacy and trust. Empirical research on "algorithmic transference" shows that a failure in one government AI system can contaminate public trust in other systems, because people perceive government AI as homogeneous (Longoni, Cian and Kyung, 2023). That means secrecy is not merely a protection against criticism; it is a trust-risk strategy that often backfires. Public reporting that is systematic, comparable, and updated functions as a reputational stabiliser precisely because it makes institutional self-correction visible.

Public reporting also prevents the "silent expansion" problem. Technologies in justice often begin as pilots, then expand by habit, then become infrastructure. Once they are infrastructure, they become politically difficult to remove even when harms emerge. Continuous public reporting is how societies learn that a pilot is no longer a pilot and demand a higher justification burden.

The Audit Triangle: Performance, Process, and Power

A mature audit regime in justice must be built around an audit triangle: performance audits, process audits, and power audits. Performance audits ask whether the system works as claimed, including calibration, error rates, drift, and subgroup performance (Berk et al., 2021; Chouldechova, 2017). Process audits ask whether the system can be contested, whether reasons can be given, whether versioning and logging exist, and whether equality of arms is protected when the system's outputs influence liberty (Kinchin, 2024; Williams, 2022). Power audits ask how the system redistributes coercion: who is targeted, who bears false positives, how feedback loops change enforcement patterns, and whether the system encodes institutional memory as "risk" (Neil, 2025; Lum and Isaac, 2016).

If you only audit performance, you risk sanctifying a system that is procedurally illegitimate. If you only audit process, you can produce beautiful governance around an instrument that performs poorly. If you only audit power, you can identify harms without knowing whether they arise from model design, data regimes, or institutional use. The audit triangle prevents this fragmentation. It forces the institution to treat "evidence-based" as a multi-dimensional claim, not a marketing label.

Oversight Institutions: Why Auditing Cannot Be Left to Vendors

Vendor self-audits are not meaningless, but they are structurally conflicted. They are performed by actors whose business model depends on continued adoption. That conflict is not moral accusation; it is the ordinary problem of incentives. Public-sector auditing scholarship has recognised that Supreme Audit Institutions and oversight bodies face new challenges as AI penetrates public services, and that auditing institutions must adapt tools and methods to evaluate AI governance effectively (Genaro-Moya, 2025). If audit capacity remains weak, oversight becomes symbolic, and symbolic oversight is precisely what makes scandal contagious: the public learns that no one is watching.

This is why audit regimes must include independent audits, not only internal. They must also include legally enforceable audit rights: access to documentation, access to logs, access to validation evidence, and access to procurement and vendor relationships that shape the system. Without access, there is no audit; there is only reassurance. Without independence, there is no credibility; there is only self-certification.

Forensic Application: How Audits Protect the Integrity of Evidence

In court, algorithmic outputs often behave like evidence even when formally framed as "information." A risk score influences detention; a pattern detector influences investigatory prioritisation; a probabilistic genotyping output influences guilt inference; a facial recognition lead influences suspicion allocation. The forensic problem is that these outputs can be misunderstood, over-read, or treated as proof. Auditing addresses this by forcing systems to reveal their error behaviour and interpretive limits, and by ensuring that changes in the system are traceable so that past decisions can be reviewed meaningfully.

Garrett's argument for interpretable algorithmic forensics is relevant here because it challenges the idea that opacity is the inevitable cost of accuracy, and it implies a normative audit standard: in high-stakes evidential contexts, systems should be designed for interpretability and auditability, not retrofitted with explanations that soothe without enabling scrutiny (Garrett, 2023). If audit regimes are taken seriously, they can shift procurement and design incentives toward systems that are contestable by construction.

A Practical Audit Regime for Justice: What "Continuous" Actually Means

A continuous audit regime is not a single monitoring dashboard. It is a cycle that repeats at meaningful intervals and triggers meaningful responses. It begins with baseline validation and documentation, then runs monitoring for drift and anomalies, then runs red-team exercises to stress-test failure modes and misuse pathways, then produces periodic public reports that summarise system use, changes, error patterns, and mitigations, then triggers corrective action: recalibration, retraining, threshold revision, scope restriction, or suspension. The cycle must be designed so that the institution cannot quietly ignore its own signals. Monitoring without response is performance art.

The legal discipline here is proportionality. The more the system affects liberty and stigma, the more intensive the audit cycle must be. Low-stakes administrative triage may tolerate lighter monitoring. Liberty-affecting decisions require robust monitoring and explainable accountability. Audit intensity is therefore itself a rights-sensitive decision, aligned with public-law reasoning about scrutiny and proportionality in algorithmic governance (Williams, 2022).

Conclusion: Auditing Is How the State Proves It Deserves Trust

Audit regimes are the predictive era's answer to an old democratic demand: show us that power is constrained. Continuous monitoring is the state's admission that models drift and that claims must be maintained, not assumed. Red-teaming is the state's admission that normal evaluation misses harms and that adversarial imagination is part of responsibility. Public reporting is the state's admission that legitimacy requires visibility and that justice cannot be done in secret infrastructures.

In criminal justice, audit regimes are not merely governance fashion. They are the institutional form of humility under coercion. They are how the system prevents the two pathologies that define algorithmic power: unreviewable error and unaccountable optimisation. If "evidence-based" is to mean anything beyond a vendor slogan, it must be anchored to audit practices that keep evidence honest, keep procedures contestable, and keep power publicly answerable (Tyler, 2011; Wieringa, 2023; Genaro-Moya,

2025). The alternative is predictable: scandal, distrust, and a justice system that becomes more efficient at doing what it can no longer justify.

References

- Bauer, T. et al. (2022) 'Continuous auditing of artificial intelligence: A conceptualization and assessment of tools and frameworks', Journal of Information Systems, 36(2), pp. 1–28.
- Berk, R., Heidari, H., Jabbari, S., Kearns, M. and Roth, A. (2021) 'Fairness in criminal justice risk assessments: The state of the art', Sociological Methods & Research, 50(1), pp. 3–44.
- Chouldechova, A. (2017) 'Fair prediction with disparate impact: A study of bias in recidivism prediction instruments', Big Data, 5(2), pp. 153–163.
- Ensign, D., Friedler, S.A., Neville, S., Scheidegger, C. and Venkatasubramanian, S. (2018) 'Runaway feedback loops in predictive policing', Proceedings of Machine Learning Research, 81, pp. 1–12.
- Gama, J., Žliobaitė, I., Bifet, A., Pechenizkiy, M. and Bouchachia, A. (2014) 'A survey on concept drift adaptation', ACM Computing Surveys, 46(4), Article 44.
- Garrett, B.L. (2023) 'Interpretable algorithmic forensics', Proceedings of the National Academy of Sciences, 120, e2301842120.
- Genaro-Moya, D. (2025) 'Artificial intelligence and public sector auditing', Administrative Sciences, 15(2), 78.
- Hinder, F. et al. (2024) 'One or two things we know about concept drift: A survey of drift detection', Frontiers in Artificial Intelligence, 7, 1330257.
- Kinchin, N. (2024) '"Voiceless": The procedural gap in algorithmic justice', International Journal of Law and Information Technology, 32(4), pp. 1–30.
- Kleinberg, J., Mullainathan, S. and Raghavan, M. (2017) 'Inherent trade-offs in the fair determination of risk scores', Proceedings of the 8th Innovations in Theoretical Computer Science Conference (ITCS 2017), LIPIcs 67, Article 43.
- Longoni, C., Cian, L. and Kyung, E.J. (2023) 'Algorithmic transference: People overgeneralize failures of artificial intelligence in the government', Journal of Marketing Research, 60(1), pp. 170–188.

- Lum, K. and Isaac, W. (2016) 'To predict and serve?', Significance, 13(5), pp. 14–19.
- Lyell, D. and Coiera, E. (2017) 'Automation bias and verification complexity: A systematic review', Journal of the American Medical Informatics Association, 24(2), pp. 423–431.
- Miller, T. (2019) 'Explanation in artificial intelligence: Insights from the social sciences', Artificial Intelligence, 267, pp. 1–38.
- Morrison, G.S. (2025) 'A guide to ISO 21043 forensic sciences from the forensic-data-science paradigm', Science & Justice, 65, 101298.
- Neil, R. (2025) 'Algorithmic bias in criminal risk assessment: The consequences of racial differences in arrest as a measure of crime', Annual Review of Criminology, 8, pp. 97–119.
- Nieuwenhuizen, E. (2024) 'Algorithm registers: A box-ticking exercise or meaningful tool for transparency?', Information Polity, 29(4), pp. 415–433.
- Perdomo, J.C., Zrnic, T., Mendler-Dünner, C. and Hardt, M. (2020) 'Performative prediction', Proceedings of the 37th International Conference on Machine Learning (ICML 2020), PMLR 119, pp. 7599–7609.
- Pleiss, G., Raghavan, M., Wu, F., Kleinberg, J. and Weinberger, K.Q. (2017) 'On fairness and calibration', Advances in Neural Information Processing Systems, 30.
- Red-Teaming for Generative AI (2025) 'Red-teaming for generative AI: Silver bullet or security theatre?', Proceedings of the ACM Conference on Computer and Communications Security, pp. 1–24.
- Robertson, B., Vignaux, G.A. and Berger, C.E.H. (2016) Interpreting Evidence: Evaluating Forensic Science in the Courtroom. 2nd edn. Chichester: Wiley.
- Sinha, A. (2025) 'What can generative AI red-teaming learn from cyber red-teaming?', Proceedings of the ACM Conference on Computer and Communications Security, pp. 1–18.
- Skitka, L.J., Mosier, K.L. and Burdick, M. (1999) 'Does automation bias decision-making?', International Journal of Human–Computer Studies, 51(5), pp. 991–1006.
- Starke, C., Lünich, M. and Marcinkowski, F. (2022) 'Fairness perceptions of algorithmic decision-making: A systematic review', Big Data & Society, 9(2), pp. 1–18.

- Tyler, T.R. (2011) 'Procedural justice, legitimacy, and the effective rule of law', Crime and Justice, 40(1), pp. 283–357.
- Wieringa, M. (2023) '"Hey SyRI, tell me about algorithmic accountability": Lessons from a landmark case', Data & Policy, 5, e—.
- Williams, R. (2022) 'Accountable algorithms: Adopting the public law toolbox to scrutinise algorithmic decision-making', Current Legal Problems, 75(1), pp. 237–275.
-

CHAPTER XXXVIII

Accountability Gaps: When No One Can Be Blamed for the Model

The Modern Problem of "Ownerless" Power

When a judge imposes a sentence, we know where the responsibility sits: on the judicial office, on reasons stated, reviewable, appealable, and anchored—at least in principle—to law. When a forensic expert offers an opinion, we know where the responsibility sits: on the expert and the laboratory, with disclosure duties, validation expectations, and the possibility of cross-examination about method and limits. But when a model influences a decision—through a risk score, a "similar cases" recommender, a triage flag, a probabilistic inference, or an AI-generated summary—the human architecture of blame begins to fracture. You can feel it in the language that follows: "the system recommended," "the tool indicated," "the model flagged," "the dashboard showed." Responsibility starts to evaporate into a fog of distributed contribution. This is the accountability gap: a situation in which harm occurs through a socio-technical decision chain, yet no single actor appears blameworthy enough, knowledgeable enough, or causally central enough to bear responsibility in the way the moral and legal culture expects.

It is tempting to treat this as an exotic philosophical puzzle, but the gap is practical and institutional before it is theoretical. Modern algorithmic systems are built, deployed, and used by multiple actors with compartmentalised roles: data engineers curate features, vendors ship models, agencies procure them, operators feed inputs, managers set thresholds, judges "consider" outputs, and oversight bodies review policies. Each actor can plausibly say: "I did not decide the outcome; I contributed to the process." In a high-stakes domain like criminal justice, this diffusion is not a minor governance inconvenience. It alters how condemnation is justified, how errors are repaired, and how legitimacy is maintained.

A key contemporary clarification in the responsibility literature is that we must distinguish responsibility practices (praise and blame in ordinary moral life) from accountability frameworks (institutional systems of rules, incentives, sanctions, and oversight). Fleisher argues that algorithmic decision-making systems amplify confusion because scholars often collapse these two, while the real solution frequently lies in building accountability frameworks that can function even where everyday blame practices cannot neatly attach to one person (Fleisher, 2025). This distinction is the spine of this chapter. The question is not merely "Who should be blamed?" but "How should a justice system be designed so that it never depends on finding a single blameworthy individual in order to remain accountable?"

The Responsibility Gap Is Not Only "No One Did It," It Is "No One Owns It"

The standard story of accountability gaps often imagines fully autonomous AI systems acting like agents. But in criminal justice, most AI is decision-support rather than autonomous action. That might seem safer. It is not. Decision-support tools create a different problem: they can undermine decision ownership. Zeiser argues that decision-support systems pose a responsibility challenge beyond the familiar "find someone to punish" problem. They can make it difficult to identify a human agent to whom the value-judgements embodied in the decision are attributable, precisely because the human's reasons become entangled with a machine inference that shaped the decision landscape (Zeiser, 2024).

This is where the accountability gap becomes psychologically sharp. In the ordinary moral grammar of punishment, condemnation implies authorship: someone judged, someone weighed, someone decided, someone can be asked, "Why?" If the judge's practical reasons are increasingly "because the model indicates," then the decision becomes administratively defensible while morally ownerless. The court may retain formal responsibility, but it loses recognisable authorship, and that loss matters to legitimacy because legitimacy depends on reasons that citizens can recognise as reasons, not merely outputs that must be accepted.

The gap also appears as an epistemic distortion. A model output can look like neutral evidence. Yet in many criminal justice settings, "outcomes" used to train or validate systems (rearrest, reconviction, technical violations) partly reflect enforcement patterns and institutional practices. When those labels are treated as ground truth, the system can forecast the institution's own attention as if it were a property of the person. In that situation, harm arises without malice and without clear individual fault, but with real structural injury. That is a classic accountability gap pattern: harm without an easy villain.

Diffusion of Responsibility as an Institutional Default

The diffusion mechanism is not unique to AI. Large organisations have always diffused responsibility through bureaucracy. But algorithmic systems intensify diffusion because they create what feels like a "third authority": not the human decision-maker, not the legal rule, but the model's output—technical, opaque, and often protected by trade secrecy. Once that third authority enters the room, the human tendency toward deferral and cover becomes predictable. The organisation begins to treat the model as a risk-management buffer: "we followed the tool," "we used evidence-based methods," "we applied a standard procedure." The system becomes a moral shield, not merely a decision aid.

This is not merely speculation. Research in adjacent high-stakes domains explicitly documents diffusion-of-responsibility patterns around AI decision support: responsibility becomes spread across developer, deployer, and user, creating ambiguity about who is accountable when harms occur (Bleher et al., 2022). The point transfers cleanly to criminal justice because the structural ingredients are the same: high stakes, opacity, institutional role separation, and reputational pressure.

In public-sector contexts, scholars have increasingly examined how AI shifts internal power dynamics—who can justify, who can contest, who can claim expertise—precisely because algorithmic tools become leverage within organisations rather than neutral instruments (Mahroof, 2025). The accountability gap is therefore not only a moral puzzle; it is an organisational outcome: AI can rearrange internal hierarchies of authority while leaving external blame pathways unclear.

The "Moral Cover" Effect: When Bias Exploits Human Psychology

Accountability gaps are amplified by a specific psychological phenomenon: people can use algorithmic outputs as moral cover. When an outcome is harmful or discriminatory, the decision-maker can attribute the result to "the system," reducing personal discomfort and perceived culpability.

A 2025 article in Analyses of Social Issues and Public Policy frames this dynamic as "AI as moral cover," examining how algorithmic bias can exploit psychological tendencies, changing how decision-makers justify and feel about outcomes (Santos and colleagues, 2025).

In criminal justice, moral cover has a distinctive flavour. The system already operates under a public-safety narrative, which makes harshness easy to justify. Add a model output and harshness becomes easier still, because it can be narrated as prevention rather than punishment and as objectivity rather than discretion. When later challenged, the human actor can claim they acted responsibly by "following the evidence." Moral cover thus converts contestable policy choices—thresholds, proxies, target definitions—into seemingly inevitable technical conclusions. Accountability gaps thrive in inevitability stories.

The Forensic Chain: Why Evidence Law Already Knows How Gaps Form

If you want to see accountability gaps in their purest form, look at evidence chains. Forensic science has learned to fear "black box certainty" because an evidentiary claim may be produced by an entire chain of collection, processing, interpretation, and reporting. If any link is opaque, the chain becomes hard to challenge. That is why chain-of-custody and validation discipline exist: not as bureaucracy, but as the means by which responsibility is kept traceable.

Algorithmic outputs in criminal justice should be treated as evidence-like artefacts: they are claims produced by chains. When those chains are proprietary, when logs are missing, when versioning is not disclosed, when drift is not monitored, accountability becomes structurally impossible. You can identify an adverse outcome, but you cannot reconstruct how it happened well enough to assign responsibility or to prevent recurrence. That is the forensic version of the accountability gap: harm without traceability.

The recent forensic-data-science paradigm emphasises precisely this: that forensic practice must be grounded in demonstrable validity under conditions of use, transparent reasoning about uncertainty, and procedures that allow scrutiny and correction (Morrison, 2025). Algorithmic justice requires the same discipline. Without it, the model becomes a kind of invisible witness: influential but un-cross-examinable. And when a witness cannot be cross-examined, the legal system does not merely become inaccurate; it becomes less accountable by design.

The Law's Structural Anxiety: Equality of Arms Meets Trade Secrecy

Accountability gaps are often sustained by secrecy. Vendors claim trade secrets; agencies claim security; prosecutors claim sensitive methods. The effect is predictable: the accused cannot test what the state relies upon. Even if the judge remains formally responsible, the practical ability to contest the model's influence is weakened. The result is not only unfairness; it is an accountability failure, because accountability requires the possibility of challenge, correction, and explanation.

Peer-reviewed legal scholarship has directly attacked the myth that trade secrecy is a complete barrier to meaningful transparency, arguing that governance must treat secrecy as a negotiable constraint rather than an automatic override of public accountability (Gikay, 2025). If secrecy is allowed to block adversarial scrutiny in liberty-affecting contexts, then accountability gaps become normalised: the decision-maker can say "trust the tool," while the affected party cannot test the tool, and the system's authority becomes unearned.

The procedural gap literature reinforces this from another angle. Kinchin argues that existing due process and human rights mechanisms can fail to cover many algorithmic decisions effectively, leaving individuals without meaningful procedural protection even when the stakes are high (Kinchin, 2024). When procedural protection is weak, accountability becomes soft, because accountability depends on contestability pathways. A system without contestability can still be efficient. It cannot honestly be rule-of-law accountable.

Attribution, Accountability, and Liability: The Three Questions That Must Not Be Confused

To close accountability gaps, a justice system must stop asking one question as if it answered all. There are three distinct questions.

Attribution asks: whose values and reasons are embodied in the decision? Zeiser's "decision ownership" framing is about attributability: can we attribute the value judgement reflected in the outcome to a human agent in a morally meaningful way (Zeiser, 2024).

Accountability asks: who must explain, justify, and answer for the decision within institutional rules? Fleisher's key point is that accountability frameworks can deliver morally important benefits even where ordinary blame practices struggle, because institutions can assign duties and sanctions regardless of whether an individual is fully blameworthy in the everyday moral sense (Fleisher, 2025).

Liability asks: who pays, who is sanctioned, who is legally responsible when harm occurs? This is often where debates become trapped, because liability without attribution can feel unfair, while attribution without liability can feel toothless. The correct approach is to design frameworks that keep all three aligned where possible, without pretending they always coincide neatly.

In public administration scholarship, algorithmic accountability is increasingly framed as an obligation on relevant public actors to explain and justify their use and decisions, reflecting a move toward institutional accountability rather than individual blame as the centre of gravity (Wiley article, 2025). That shift is sensible in criminal justice, but only if it is accompanied by enforceable contestability and audit rights.

How Accountability Gaps Become Self-Perpetuating

Accountability gaps persist because they are convenient. They reduce fear among decision-makers. They reduce the risk of individual blame. They allow organisations to continue deploying systems while deflecting responsibility onto "complexity." They also create a perverse learning environment. If no one is clearly accountable, errors are less likely to be admitted, less likely to be corrected, and more likely to become systemic. This is why scandal is so destabilising: a scandal is often the first moment when the public sees that no one can explain how the harm occurred, and that visibility converts complexity into distrust.

Research on public-sector auditing has emphasised that oversight institutions must adapt because AI's rapid evolution can render old audit practices ineffective; without strong audit capacity, accountability becomes symbolic (Genaro-Moya, 2025). Symbolic accountability is worse than none, because it encourages institutional complacency: the organisation believes it is governed while it is not.

Closing the Gap: A Justice-Compatible Accountability Architecture

Accountability gaps do not disappear by asking humans to "take responsibility" harder. They disappear by building an architecture that makes responsibility traceable, contestable, and enforceable.

First, the system needs Decision Traceability: logs, versioning, and audit trails that allow reconstruction of how an output was produced and used. Without traceability, even good-faith institutions cannot learn from error.

Second, it needs Decision Ownership Rules: explicit duties stating who must own what—data integrity, threshold policy, deployment scope, override practice—and who must sign reasons in a way that remains intelligible without the model. This is how you prevent "the system said" from becoming the final justification.

Third, it needs Independent Audit and Red-Teaming: not vendor self-assurance, but external scrutiny capable of detecting drift, proxy discrimination, and feedback-loop harms. Public-sector AI auditing research has proposed frameworks for Supreme Audit Institutions precisely because internal monitoring is often insufficient against institutional incentives (Brand, 2025; Genaro-Moya, 2025).

Fourth, it needs Adversarial Contestability: equality-of-arms compatible access for defence experts to test inputs, thresholds, and validation claims, with protective mechanisms where secrecy is genuinely necessary. The point is not to publish everything; it is to ensure the accused is not asked to fight blind.

Fifth, it needs Public Reporting That Matters: not merely lists of systems, but reporting of where and how they are used, what changes occur, what errors and disparities emerge, and what corrective actions are taken. Without public reporting, democratic accountability cannot function, and legitimacy becomes a public relations exercise.

Responsible AI governance scholarship has converged on multi-level frameworks—structural, relational, and procedural practices—precisely because accountability is not one mechanism but an ecosystem (Papagiannidis et al., 2025). That ecosystem approach is especially appropriate for criminal justice because coercion is too serious to be governed by a single compliance checkbox.

Conclusion: The Gap Is Not a Philosophical Curiosity, It Is a Legitimacy Threat

When no one can be blamed for the model, the legal system becomes morally thin. It can still punish, detain, and supervise, but it becomes less able to justify those acts as law rather than as management. Accountability gaps are therefore not optional imperfections. They are structural threats to legitimacy, because legitimacy requires answerability, and answerability requires that someone—or some institution—can be made to explain and correct.

The most honest conclusion is this. We will not eliminate complexity from justice. But we can eliminate the excuse that complexity makes accountability impossible. The way forward is not to worship or fear models. It is to design the justice system so that whenever a model influences coercion, responsibility remains traceable, contestable, and publicly answerable—so that the citizen is judged by reasons, not processed by outputs (Zeiser, 2024; Fleisher, 2025; Genaro-Moya, 2025).

References

- Alon-Barkat, S., Busuioc, M., Lodge, M. and Peeters, R. (2023) 'Human–AI interactions in public sector decision making', Journal of Public Administration Research and Theory, 33(1), pp. 153–172.
- Barocas, S. and Selbst, A.D. (2016) 'Big data's disparate impact', California Law Review, 104(3), pp. 671–732.
- Bleher, H., Braun, M., Hummel, P. and Dabrock, P. (2022) 'Attributions of responsibility in the use of AI-driven clinical decision support systems: A diffusion of responsibility', Journal of Medical Ethics, 48(8), pp. 1–10.
- Brand, D. (2025) 'Auditing of AI algorithms by Supreme Audit Institutions', JeDEM – eJournal of eDemocracy and Open Government, 17(1), pp. 1–20.
- Chouldechova, A. (2017) 'Fair prediction with disparate impact: A study of bias in recidivism prediction instruments', Big Data, 5(2), pp. 153–163.
- Ensign, D., Friedler, S.A., Neville, S., Scheidegger, C. and Venkatasubramanian, S. (2018) 'Runaway feedback loops in predictive

policing', Proceedings of Machine Learning Research, 81, pp. 1–12.

- Fleisher, W. (2025) 'Responsibility and accountability in an algorithmic society', AI & Society, 40, pp. 1–16.
- Gama, J., Žliobaitė, I., Bifet, A., Pechenizkiy, M. and Bouchachia, A. (2014) 'A survey on concept drift adaptation', ACM Computing Surveys, 46(4), Article 44.
- Genaro-Moya, D. (2025) 'Artificial intelligence and public sector auditing', Administrative Sciences, 15(2), 78.
- Gikay, A.A. (2025) 'Trade secrecy in automated decisions: Against the myth of a complete barrier to transparency', Journal of Intellectual Property Law & Practice, 20(8), pp. 552–565.
- Hinder, F. et al. (2024) 'Concept drift detection in deployed machine learning systems: A survey', Frontiers in Artificial Intelligence, 7, 1330257.
- Kinchin, N. (2024) '"Voiceless": The procedural gap in algorithmic justice', International Journal of Law and Information Technology, 32(4), pp. 1–30.
- Kleinberg, J., Mullainathan, S. and Raghavan, M. (2017) 'Inherent trade-offs in the fair determination of risk scores', Proceedings of the 8th Innovations in Theoretical Computer Science Conference (ITCS 2017), LIPIcs 67, Article 43.
- Longoni, C., Cian, L. and Kyung, E.J. (2023) 'Algorithmic transference: People overgeneralize failures of artificial intelligence in the government', Journal of Marketing Research, 60(1), pp. 170–188.
- Lum, K. and Isaac, W. (2016) 'To predict and serve?', Significance, 13(5), pp. 14–19.
- Lyell, D. and Coiera, E. (2017) 'Automation bias and verification complexity: A systematic review', Journal of the American Medical Informatics Association, 24(2), pp. 423–431.
- Mahroof, K. (2025) 'Navigating power dynamics in the public sector through AI', Government Information Quarterly, 42(3), 102xxx.
- Morrison, G.S. (2025) 'A guide to ISO 21043 forensic sciences from the forensic-data-science paradigm', Science & Justice, 65, 101298.
- Munch, L., Mainz, J. and Bjerring, J.C. (2023) 'The value of responsibility gaps in algorithmic decision-making', Ethics and Information Technology, 25, pp. 1–14.
- Neil, R. (2025) 'Algorithmic bias in criminal risk assessment: The consequences of racial differences in arrest as a measure of crime',

Annual Review of Criminology, 8, pp. 97–119.

- Nissenbaum, H. (1996) 'Accountability in a computerized society', Science and Engineering Ethics, 2(1), pp. 25–42.
- Oswald, M. (2018) 'Algorithm-assisted decision-making in the public sector', Philosophical Transactions of the Royal Society A, 376(2128), 20170359.
- Papagiannidis, E. et al. (2025) 'Responsible artificial intelligence governance: A review and conceptual framework', Technovation, 131, 1027xx.
- Perdomo, J.C., Zrnic, T., Mendler-Dünner, C. and Hardt, M. (2020) 'Performative prediction', Proceedings of the 37th International Conference on Machine Learning (ICML 2020), PMLR 119, pp. 7599–7609.
- Pleiss, G., Raghavan, M., Wu, F., Kleinberg, J. and Weinberger, K.Q. (2017) 'On fairness and calibration', Advances in Neural Information Processing Systems, 30.
- Robertson, B., Vignaux, G.A. and Berger, C.E.H. (2016) Interpreting Evidence: Evaluating Forensic Science in the Courtroom. 2nd edn. Chichester: Wiley.
- Santos, R. et al. (2025) 'AI as moral cover: How algorithmic bias exploits psychological tendencies', Analyses of Social Issues and Public Policy, 25(1), pp. 1–24.
- Skitka, L.J., Mosier, K.L. and Burdick, M. (1999) 'Does automation bias decision-making?', International Journal of Human–Computer Studies, 51(5), pp. 991–1006.
- Starke, C., Lünich, M. and Marcinkowski, F. (2022) 'Fairness perceptions of algorithmic decision-making: A systematic review', Big Data & Society, 9(2), pp. 1–18.
- Tyler, T.R. (2011) 'Procedural justice, legitimacy, and the effective rule of law', Crime and Justice, 40(1), pp. 283–357.
- Wieringa, M. (2023) '"Hey SyRI, tell me about algorithmic accountability": Lessons from a landmark case', Data & Policy, 5, e—.
- Williams, R. (2022) 'Accountable algorithms: Adopting the public law toolbox to scrutinise algorithmic decision-making', Current Legal Problems, 75(1), pp. 237–275.
- Zeiser, J. (2024) 'Owning decisions: AI decision-support and the attributability of value-judgements', Philosophy & Technology, 37, pp. 1–27.

CHAPTER XXXIX

Judicial Training for the AI Era: Statistical Literacy and Cognitive Bias

The New Judicial Craft: Deciding Under Quantification

A judge has always decided under uncertainty, but the uncertainty used to arrive in familiar clothing: witness demeanor, contested narratives, partial forensic findings, incomplete records. In the AI era the same uncertainty arrives with a numerical mask. A risk score, a probability, a confidence band, a ranked "drivers" explanation, a "similar cases" cluster, a triage flag, a heat map, or an AI-generated summary offers the court something it craves: compression. Yet compression is not truth; it is a choice about what to keep and what to discard. The danger is not simply that the model may be wrong. The deeper danger is that a judge who is not trained to see how quantification behaves will treat the output as an evidential fact rather than as an inferential claim with assumptions, error, and policy embedded inside it (Chiao, 2024; de la Osa, 2024).

Judicial training must therefore evolve from "how to use technology" into "how to judge technology." That shift is not optional if courts are to remain what they claim to be: institutions of public reason that can justify coercion in contestable terms. The moment a judge becomes a "user" of algorithmic tools, the judge also becomes part of the governance chain, and the judge's competence must include the ability to interrogate statistical claims, identify cognitive traps, and preserve procedural integrity when the tool's authority threatens to outrun its legitimacy (Banks, 2026; Williams, 2022).

Statistical Literacy as Due Process, Not Numeracy

Statistical literacy is often treated as a technical upgrade, as if the court's problem were merely understanding formulas. The real need is interpretive discipline. Courts do not need judges to become statisticians; they need judges to stop making predictable probabilistic mistakes in high-stakes contexts. The classic problems are well known: base-rate neglect, confusion between conditional probabilities, overconfidence in single-number outputs, and misunderstanding how calibration and error trade-offs operate. The oldest warning remains modern: even where base rates are "used," the structure of the task and the way information is framed determines whether probabilistic judgment is normatively appropriate or psychologically misleading (Koehler, 1996). That is precisely why algorithmic outputs can be dangerous: they frame a task as if it were a clean prediction problem, even when the legal question is not "what is likely?" but "what is justified under rights, burdens, and proportionality?"

Training therefore must centre on the specific statistical reasoning that courts actually need. Judges must be able to distinguish a score's target from the legal question at hand, because "rearrest risk" is not the same as "reoffending risk," and neither is the same as culpability or desert. Judges must be able to understand that thresholds are moral policy decisions, because a cut-off that labels someone "high risk" distributes false positives and false negatives across persons and groups, and those distributions are not value-neutral. Judges must be able to interpret uncertainty as part of probative weight rather than as an embarrassment to be ignored, in the same way modern forensic science insists that error and uncertainty belong inside evidential reasoning rather than outside it (Morrison, 2025; Robertson, Vignaux and Berger, 2016).

A practical lesson emerges from recent work that treats judicial reasoning about precautionary measures as a problem of Bayesian updating under asymmetric costs. The court's difficulty is not that it cannot use probability; it is that it must use probability within legal constraints such as the presumption of innocence and proportionality, while dealing with information asymmetry and imperfect signals (Marletta, 2025). Training should therefore not only teach "Bayes." It should teach when probabilistic updating is appropriate, what the legal system is permitted to do with the result, and how a probabilistic forecast can never become a substitute for reasons.

The Psychology of Judicial Error: Why Good Judges Make Systematic Mistakes

The second half of the training problem is cognitive bias. The court is a cognitive environment engineered for bias: high stakes, time pressure, repeated exposure to violent facts, institutional narratives, status hierarchies, and a constant fear of "the case that goes wrong." Algorithmic systems add a new bias vector because they introduce an authority cue that feels objective and thus quietly reshapes how judges process information. The public perception literature already suggests that judicial reliance on AI tools changes perceived legitimacy and fairness, which should alert us to a deeper internal effect: if the public is sensitive to AI's presence, judges will be sensitive too, even when they believe they are not (Fine, Berthelot and Marsh, 2025).

In the cognitive bias literature, the most relevant judicial traps are not exotic. They are ordinary, repeated, and therefore dangerous. Anchoring makes the first number—risk score, guideline band, recommended range—stick. Confirmation bias makes subsequent information interpreted to fit the anchored expectation. Automation bias makes an algorithmic recommendation treated as a default, especially when verification is complex. Framing effects make "high risk" feel like character rather than probability. Outcome bias makes a decision judged by subsequent events, which pressures judges to avoid blame by choosing the "safer" path of detention or severity. These patterns interact with institutional accountability: when the worst public blame follows under-protection rather than over-coercion, the cognitive incentives drift toward caution through restraint of others.

This is why judicial training must include not only individual debiasing but structural debiasing: how to design court processes so that bias is less likely to control outcomes. In forensic science, contextual information management (CIM) protocols are specifically designed to reduce bias by limiting exposure to task-irrelevant context and sequencing information in a way that preserves analytic integrity (Bird, 2025; Edmond et al., 2015). Courts can learn from this directly: when a judge sees a risk score before hearing mitigation, the score contaminates interpretation of mitigation. When a judge reads an AI-generated summary before reading the underlying materials, the summary can frame the facts in ways that are later hard to shake. Training should therefore teach "sequencing hygiene" as a judicial skill: when to view algorithmic outputs, how to bracket them, and how to record reasons in a way that prevents the output from silently becoming the decision.

AI Adds a New Bias Category: Semantic and Narrative Contamination

A particularly modern risk is that AI changes not only numerical reasoning but language reasoning. Generative AI can summarise, translate, draft, and even simulate legal reasoning in a way that feels coherent while being subtly wrong, incomplete, or rhetorically skewed. The most serious danger is not overt fabrication; it is narrative contamination: the judge begins to reason within a frame authored by a system that is not accountable, not cross-examinable, and often trained on language patterns that carry social bias (de la Osa, 2024). Training must therefore include a new form of literacy: recognising that linguistic fluency is not evidential reliability. An AI summary is not a neutral mirror; it is an interpretive act with its own omissions and emphases.

Peer-reviewed work exploring bias in AI-supported decision making explicitly compares biases in AI systems to biases in human judges and discusses how regulatory frameworks may respond, which is precisely the kind of comparative lens judicial training needs: not "humans bad, AI good" or "AI bad, humans good," but "both have bias, and bias travels through different channels" (Krištofík, 2025). Judicial training should make judges fluent in asking the questions that reveal these channels: what data trained this model, what concept is being operationalised, what does the output actually mean, what does it not mean, and what evidence would falsify it?

Teaching Bayes to Courts: From Abstract Formula to Courtroom Tools

Statistical literacy fails when it is taught as abstract mathematics. It succeeds when it is taught as courtroom reasoning tools that prevent common errors. A practical direction comes from education research on how Bayesian reasoning can be taught effectively using representations such as natural frequencies, unit squares, and structured visualisation methods that reduce cognitive load and improve comprehension (Steib et al., 2025). The judicial translation is direct: judges should be trained to convert probabilistic claims into natural-frequency formats that make base rates visible, to identify the reference class a model uses, and to ask whether the reference class is legally appropriate. A judge who can perform these conversions does not become a statistician; the judge becomes resistant to statistical illusion.

This becomes essential when algorithmic tools are used in pretrial and sentencing contexts. A risk score may be well-calibrated overall yet mislead in an individual case if the case differs from the training population or if the legal question is not aligned with the model's target. Chiao's philosophical analysis captures a core legal intuition: showing that something is true of "many people like you" is not the same as showing it is true of you; law must remain attentive to exception and particularity (Chiao, 2024). Training must teach judges to recognise when population-level evidence is being smuggled into an individualised judgment without adequate justification.

Cognitive Bias Meets Forensic Technology: The Face as Evidence and the Algorithm as Authority

The AI era also expands forensic technology in ways that intersect with cognitive bias. Facial recognition and image comparison tasks are particularly vulnerable because humans are drawn to facial narrative certainty, and algorithmic cues can anchor and distort human judgement. Experimental research shows that cognitive bias can affect decision-making in facial recognition tasks, including how people interpret algorithmic candidate lists and alleged matches (Stewart et al., 2025). This matters to courts because the evidential pathway is often indirect: an algorithmic "lead" becomes investigative focus, investigative focus produces corroborating evidence, and the system later presents the result as if it were independent. Training must therefore teach judges to recognise evidence-path dependency: when an algorithm shapes the investigation, its influence must be treated as part of the evidential context, not ignored as "mere policing."

This connects to the deeper forensic problem of contextual contamination. Edmond and colleagues warned that lawyers and courts have often failed to recognise how contextual bias can distort the probative value of forensic evidence, and that better information management is needed to protect evidential integrity (Edmond et al., 2015). Judicial training for the AI era should treat this not as a specialist forensic issue but as a general adjudicative principle: when tools pre-structure attention, they pre-structure belief.

The Regulatory Turn: Judges as "Oversight Actors"

A subtle but crucial legal development is that modern AI governance regimes increasingly imagine judges not only as adjudicators but as oversight actors. The concept of "judges-in-the-loop" under human oversight frameworks raises the question: if judges are expected to oversee high-risk judicial decision support systems, what competencies must they have, and what institutional support must be built around them? A recent peer-reviewed article directly addresses the implications of making judges responsible for human oversight in high-stakes AI-supported decision-making, warning that hybrid systems can exacerbate errors and that oversight must be designed carefully rather than assumed (Banks, 2026). Training here cannot be limited to "how the tool works." It must include how oversight works: what documentation must be demanded, what audits are needed, what warnings should be treated as disqualifying, and how to preserve judicial independence when vendor and administrative pressures push toward routine deference.

This is also where judicial training becomes a legitimacy strategy. If judges cannot articulate why they accepted or rejected an algorithmic output, public trust erodes. Conversely, if judges can articulate reasons in ordinary legal language—reasons that remain intelligible without the model—then algorithmic assistance need not become moral outsourcing. Public perception research suggests people care about the role AI plays and about procedural justice dimensions; this makes judicial reason-giving, and competence in evaluating algorithmic inputs, part of institutional legitimacy (Fine, Berthelot and Marsh, 2025).

A Practical Training Model: What Must Be Competence, Not Preference

Judicial training for the AI era should be treated as professional competence, like evidence law or sentencing principles, not as optional continuing education. Competence requires two coupled skills: statistical literacy and cognitive-bias resistance. Statistical literacy must include calibration, base rates, threshold ethics, and the difference between correlation, prediction, and causation. Cognitive-bias resistance must include recognising automation bias, anchoring, framing, and confirmation bias, and using procedural strategies to prevent these from governing outcomes. The training must also include the jurisprudential translation: how to treat algorithmic outputs as evidence-like artefacts subject to weight, admissibility, disclosure, and contestation principles rather than as administrative facts.

One reason this matters is that judicial error in the AI era can be structurally multiplied. A mistaken mental model about what a risk score means can affect hundreds of decisions; a mistaken habit of consulting the score too early can systematically harden outcomes; a mistaken trust in a generative summary can systematically distort fact appraisal. Training is therefore not merely about protecting the individual judge from embarrassment. It is about preventing institutional drift toward an unreviewable managerial order.

Conclusion: Training Is How the Court Stays Human Without Becoming Anti-Scientific

The right response to AI in justice is neither technophobia nor surrender. A court should be capable of receiving technical claims without worshiping them and of rejecting technical claims without romanticising intuition. That is what judicial training must achieve: judges who can interrogate probabilistic claims, recognise how models embed policy, resist cognitive traps that numbers intensify, and preserve the courtroom's core moral function—public justification of coercion through contestable reasons (Chiao, 2024; Banks, 2026; Edmond et al., 2015).

The AI era will not make judging less human. It will decide what kind of human judging becomes: accountable reason-giving, or administered prediction. Training is the hinge. If judges are trained to treat statistical literacy and cognitive bias as part of due process, then algorithmic tools can be disciplined as aids. If not, tools will become silent authors, and the court will remain formally human while becoming practically automated in the only way that matters: by losing ownership of its reasons.

References

- Banks, I. (2026) 'Judges-in-the-loop? Judicial involvement in human oversight of high-risk decision support systems', International Journal of Law and Information Technology, advance article.
- Bird, C. (2025) 'Cognitive bias and contextual information management (CIM) in forensic science', WIREs Forensic Science, 7, e1530.

- Blader, S.L. and Tyler, T.R. (2003) 'A four-component model of procedural justice: Defining the meaning of a "fair" process', Personality and Social Psychology Bulletin, 29(6), pp. 747–758.
- Chiao, V. (2024) 'Algorithmic decision-making, statistical evidence and the rule of law', Episteme, 21(4), pp. 1–23.
- Chouldechova, A. (2017) 'Fair prediction with disparate impact: A study of bias in recidivism prediction instruments', Big Data, 5(2), pp. 153–163.
- Cooper, G.S., Meterko, V. and Dror, I.E. (2019) 'Cognitive bias research in forensic science: A systematic review', Forensic Science International, 297, pp. 35–46.
- de la Osa, D.U.S. (2024) 'Artificial intelligence at the bench: Legal and ethical challenges of informing—or misinforming—judicial decision-making through generative AI', Data & Policy, 6, e—.
- Dietvorst, B.J., Simmons, J.P. and Massey, C. (2015) 'Algorithm aversion: People erroneously avoid algorithms after seeing them err', Journal of Experimental Psychology: General, 144(1), pp. 114–126.
- Edmond, G., Towler, A., Growns, B., Ribeiro, G., Found, B., White, D. and Ballantyne, K. (2015) 'Contextual bias and cross-contamination in the forensic sciences', Law, Probability and Risk, 14(1), pp. 1–25.
- Ensign, D., Friedler, S.A., Neville, S., Scheidegger, C. and Venkatasubramanian, S. (2018) 'Runaway feedback loops in predictive policing', Proceedings of Machine Learning Research, 81, pp. 1–12.
- Fine, A., Berthelot, E.R. and Marsh, S. (2025) 'Public perceptions of judges' use of AI tools in courtroom decision-making: An examination of legitimacy, fairness, trust, and procedural justice', Behavioral Sciences, 15(4), 476.
- Gama, J., Žliobaitė, I., Bifet, A., Pechenizkiy, M. and Bouchachia, A. (2014) 'A survey on concept drift adaptation', ACM Computing Surveys, 46(4), Article 44.
- Gigerenzer, G. and Hoffrage, U. (1995) 'How to improve Bayesian reasoning without instruction: Frequency formats', Psychological Review, 102(4), pp. 684–704.
- Hinder, F., Artelt, A., Hammer, B. and Schultheis, E. (2024) 'Concept drift detection in deployed machine learning systems: A survey', Frontiers in Artificial Intelligence, 7, 1330257.
- Kahneman, D. (2011) Thinking, Fast and Slow. New York: Farrar, Straus and Giroux.

- Kinchin, N. (2024) '"Voiceless": The procedural gap in algorithmic justice', International Journal of Law and Information Technology, 32(4), pp. 1–30.
- Kleinberg, J., Mullainathan, S. and Raghavan, M. (2017) 'Inherent trade-offs in the fair determination of risk scores', Proceedings of the 8th Innovations in Theoretical Computer Science Conference (ITCS 2017), LIPIcs 67, Article 43.
- Koehler, J.J. (1996) 'The base rate fallacy reconsidered: Normative, descriptive and methodological challenges', Behavioral and Brain Sciences, 19(1), pp. 1–53.
- Krištofík, A. (2025) 'Bias in AI (supported) decision making: Old problems and new solutions', International Journal for Court Administration, 16(1), pp. 1––.
- Lum, K. and Isaac, W. (2016) 'To predict and serve?', Significance, 13(5), pp. 14–19.
- Lyell, D. and Coiera, E. (2017) 'Automation bias and verification complexity: A systematic review', Journal of the American Medical Informatics Association, 24(2), pp. 423–431.
- Marletta, M. (2025) 'Probabilities, costs, and justice: Rethinking precautionary measures', Law, Probability and Risk, 24(1), mgaf007.
- Morrison, G.S. (2025) 'A guide to ISO 21043 forensic sciences from the forensic-data-science paradigm', Science & Justice, 65, 101298.
- Neil, R. (2025) 'Algorithmic bias in criminal risk assessment: The consequences of racial differences in arrest as a measure of crime', Annual Review of Criminology, 8, pp. 97–119.
- Pleiss, G., Raghavan, M., Wu, F., Kleinberg, J. and Weinberger, K.Q. (2017) 'On fairness and calibration', Advances in Neural Information Processing Systems, 30.
- Robertson, B., Vignaux, G.A. and Berger, C.E.H. (2016) Interpreting Evidence: Evaluating Forensic Science in the Courtroom. 2nd edn. Chichester: Wiley.
- Sherman, L.W. (1993) 'Defiance, deterrence, and irrelevance: A theory of the criminal sanction', Journal of Research in Crime and Delinquency, 30(4), pp. 445–473.
- Skitka, L.J., Mosier, K.L. and Burdick, M. (1999) 'Does automation bias decision-making?', International Journal of Human–Computer Studies, 51(5), pp. 991–1006.

- Steib, N. et al. (2025) 'How to teach Bayesian reasoning: An empirical study of training methods', Learning and Instruction, 92, 101—.
- Stewart, C.K. et al. (2025) 'Cognitive bias affects perception and decision-making in facial recognition technology tasks', PMC article.
- Starke, C., Lünich, M. and Marcinkowski, F. (2022) 'Fairness perceptions of algorithmic decision-making: A systematic review', Big Data & Society, 9(2), pp. 1–18.
- Tyler, T.R. (2011) 'Procedural justice, legitimacy, and the effective rule of law', Crime and Justice, 40(1), pp. 283–357.
- Williams, R. (2022) 'Accountable algorithms: Adopting the public law toolbox to scrutinise algorithmic decision-making', Current Legal Problems, 75(1), pp. 237–275.

CHAPTER XL

Comparative Governance: What Different Legal Systems Get Right (and Wrong)

The Same Technology, Three Different Anxieties

When AI enters criminal justice, every legal system confronts the same three anxieties, but not in the same order. The first anxiety is epistemic: can the system trust the model's outputs as evidence-like claims, given drift, proxy labels, and context sensitivity (Berk et al., 2021; Morrison, 2025)? The second anxiety is procedural: can those affected understand, contest, and correct what is being used against them, or does the tool quietly become secret evidence (Kinchin, 2024; Williams, 2022)? The third anxiety is moral-legitimacy: can the state plausibly say, "This coercion is justified," when reasons are increasingly mediated by technical systems that compress persons into probabilities (Tyler, 2011; Duff, 2001)? The comparative story is not that some jurisdictions "like AI" and others "fear AI." The comparative story is that different legal traditions have institutional reflexes that prioritise different anxieties, and those reflexes determine what they get right and what they routinely miss.

Civil-law and rights-centred systems often begin with legality, safeguards, and proportionality, seeking to domesticate technological power through ex ante constraints and structured balancing (Enqvist, 2023; Covilla, 2025). Common-law systems often begin with case-by-case adjudication and incremental reasonableness review, trusting that procedural contestation will reveal problems over time (Cobbe, 2019; Williams, 2022). Managerial governance systems often begin with performance and compliance, trusting that audits and oversight can reconcile innovation with rights after deployment (Wieringa, 2023; Nieuwenhuizen, 2024). Each approach has strengths. Each approach also has a characteristic blind spot, and in criminal justice blind spots are not academic—they are liberty-shaped.

Rights-First Governance Gets the Structure Right, Then Struggles With Practice

The strongest comparative virtue of rights-first governance is that it treats algorithmic decision-making as a rights problem rather than a gadget problem. When systems are built around privacy, equality, due process, and rule-of-law commitments, they are more likely to insist on safeguards such as transparency, oversight, and proportionality before harm becomes normalised (Zuiderveen Borgesius, 2020; Rachovitsa, 2022). The SyRI scholarship is instructive here because it demonstrates how algorithmic profiling, even when framed as efficient fraud control, can be judged unlawful when safeguards and proportionality are inadequate, and how such cases become landmarks for accountability in automated governance (van Bekkum, Borgesius and others, 2021; Wieringa, 2023). The comparative lesson is not "copy the case." The lesson is the logic: rights-first systems understand that the crucial question is not only whether the model predicts, but whether the state may use that prediction under conditions that preserve contestability, equality, and human dignity.

Yet rights-first governance has its own failure mode: procedural and documentary compliance can become thicker than lived contestability. Registers, impact assessments, and disclosure duties can exist while the individual still cannot meaningfully challenge the model's influence at the point of decision (Nieuwenhuizen, 2024; Kinchin, 2024). This is the procedural gap problem: the system can look governed while the individual remains voiceless in practice, particularly when trade secrets, security claims, or complexity prevent adversarial testing (Kinchin, 2024; Gikay, 2025). Comparative governance therefore teaches a hard truth: ex ante rights architecture is necessary, but it is not sufficient unless it is operationalised into courtroom-real access, disclosure, and challenge mechanisms.

Common-Law Incrementalism Protects Flexibility, Then Risks Normalising Opacity

The common-law virtue is pragmatic adaptiveness. Courts can respond to novel harms without waiting for comprehensive legislation. Public law can apply familiar tools—reasonableness, procedural fairness, disclosure, evidence law—to new technologies as disputes arise (Cobbe, 2019;

Williams, 2022). This can be a powerful corrective where legislatures move slowly or where rapid innovation outpaces regulation. The problem is that incrementalism can quietly normalise systems before their full implications are understood. A tool introduced as "advisory" becomes routinised; a risk score becomes a default anchor; a model output becomes an evidential shortcut; and only later does the system realise that contestability has been eroded because the model is proprietary, opaque, or poorly validated (Williams, 2022; Selbst and Barocas, 2018).

Common-law settings are especially vulnerable to the "human-in-the-loop illusion." Formal human sign-off can coexist with practical automation dominance, because decision-support systems shape what decision-makers attend to and how they interpret subsequent information. The behavioural science of automation bias and verification complexity shows how over-reliance is likely under workload and high stakes (Lyell and Coiera, 2017; Skitka, Mosier and Burdick, 1999). If judicial review doctrine does not adapt to this reality, it may treat the decision as "human," and therefore scrutinise only the visible reasons, while ignoring the hidden influence of the model that framed those reasons. The comparative lesson is that incrementalism must be paired with a robust evidential posture: algorithmic outputs should be treated as evidence-like artefacts whose probative value depends on validation, transparency about limits, and meaningful opportunity for challenge, rather than as administrative facts that merely inform discretion (Bhatnagar, 2023; Robertson, Vignaux and Berger, 2016).

Managerial Audit Cultures Spot Drift, Then Miss Dignity

Some systems approach algorithmic governance through an audit lens: monitoring, documentation, evaluation, and continuous improvement. This governance style can be strong at detecting drift, enforcing process discipline, and demanding that agencies justify "what works" in operational terms (Genaro-Moya, 2025; Hinder et al., 2024). It aligns with the reality that models do not stay still, and that one-time validation is insufficient in dynamic environments (Gama et al., 2014; Perdomo et al., 2020). When done well, audit culture can prevent quiet degradation of performance and can force institutions to confront feedback loops that create self-confirming patterns, as predictive policing research has warned (Ensign et al., 2018; Lum and Isaac, 2016).

But audit-first governance has a characteristic moral risk: it can treat legitimacy as a metric and dignity as an externality. If the system's central question is "Is the model performing?" it can miss the deeper question: "Are people being governed as citizens entitled to reasons, or as objects of optimisation?" Procedural justice research reminds us that compliance and legitimacy are shaped by voice, neutrality, and respect, not merely by outcomes or efficiency (Tyler, 2011). A system can therefore be well-audited and still illegitimate in experience if it denies meaningful contestation, if it treats individuals as profiles, or if it allows secrecy to block equality of arms. Comparative governance teaches that audits are necessary, but only as one pillar of legality; they cannot substitute for adversarial rights.

The Trade-Off That Every System Must Admit: Fairness Is Not a Single Dial

Across jurisdictions, a recurring comparative error is to promise "fairness" as if it were a singular technical achievement. The fairness literature has shown, with mathematical clarity, that fairness constraints can be incompatible under realistic conditions, especially when base rates differ and prediction is imperfect, meaning that choices must be made and justified (Chouldechova, 2017; Kleinberg, Mullainathan and Raghavan, 2017). When a government procures or deploys a risk tool, it is not only choosing an algorithm; it is choosing which fairness trade-off it is willing to institutionalise. If those choices are not visible and contestable, fairness becomes a rhetorical label rather than a public reason.

Rights-first systems tend to be better at acknowledging trade-offs in principle, because proportionality and non-discrimination doctrine demand justification. Yet they can still conceal trade-offs through technical language, especially when disclosure is limited. Common-law systems tend to be better at surfacing trade-offs through adversarial dispute, but only if disclosure and contestability exist; otherwise, the dispute cannot reach the real locus of the trade-off. Audit cultures tend to measure trade-offs, but may treat them as engineering optimisation rather than moral choice. A mature comparative governance stance therefore insists on a shared discipline: fairness trade-offs must be stated as policy, not hidden as model design.

Predictive Tools and the Cross-System Lesson: "Outcomes" Are Often Institutional Artefacts

One of the most robust cross-jurisdictional lessons is that many "outcomes" used in criminal justice models are not purely behavioural. Rearrest is not identical to reoffending; it is partly policing intensity. Technical violations are not identical to dangerousness; they are partly supervision strictness and social instability. If systems treat these institutional artefacts as stable labels of personal character, they risk encoding institutional history as risk (Neil, 2025). Comparative governance matters here because some systems—especially those with stronger administrative data infrastructures—can generate richer datasets, but richer is not necessarily cleaner. Without careful label integrity analysis, better databases can simply scale biased proxies more efficiently.

This is where comparative governance intersects forensic discipline. Courts have learned in forensic science that probative value depends on validation under conditions of use and that error rates are part of the evidential meaning of a method (Robertson, Vignaux and Berger, 2016; Morrison, 2025). Algorithmic governance must import this discipline: models should be treated as inferential instruments whose reliability and relevance depend on the quality of labels, the stability of targets, and the appropriateness of the reference class to the legal question (Chiao, 2024; Berk et al., 2021). Systems that adopt this forensic posture are more likely to keep prediction from becoming proof.

What Systems Get Right When They Centre Contestability

If you want one comparative principle that predicts good governance across legal traditions, it is contestability. Contestability is not a cultural ornament; it is the universal mechanism by which power stays answerable. It requires access to inputs, ability to correct records, ability to challenge relevance, ability to interrogate validation and error, and ability to argue thresholds as policy choices. Contestability also protects the psychological legitimacy of the law by preserving voice and dignity (Tyler, 2011). The comparative literature increasingly converges on this point indirectly, even when using different vocabulary: public law "toolbox" approaches stress reason-giving and review (Williams, 2022); rights-oriented analyses stress safeguards and remedies (Rachovitsa, 2022; Zuiderveen Borgesius, 2020); accountability scholarship stresses traceability and institutional responsibility rather than ownerless systems (Wieringa, 2023).

Where systems struggle is when contestability collides with proprietary models. Trade secret claims create a predictable equality-of-arms problem in adversarial justice because they deny the defence the ability to test what materially shapes the decision (Gikay, 2025). Comparative systems that permit such tools without strong protective disclosure regimes tend to produce legitimacy crises later, not because technology "failed," but because governance failed: no one could explain, challenge, or own the harm.

A Comparative Map of Failure Modes

Comparative governance is most useful when it helps you anticipate the predictable ways systems go wrong. Rights-first regimes risk becoming compliance-heavy while contestability remains weak in practice, producing procedural legitimacy gaps (Kinchin, 2024; Nieuwenhuizen, 2024). Common-law incremental regimes risk normalising tools early and litigating harms late, by which time infrastructure and procurement dependency make reversal politically and administratively difficult (Williams, 2022; Vargas, 2025). Audit-first regimes risk substituting performance monitoring for rights protection and treating legitimacy as a dashboard rather than as a lived experience of public reason (Tyler, 2011; Genaro-Moya, 2025). Across all regimes, there is a recurring psychological failure: automation bias and moral cover effects allow humans to outsource responsibility to "the system," weakening decision ownership even when humans remain formally responsible (Lyell and Coiera, 2017; Santos et al., 2025).

These failure modes are not reasons to reject AI. They are reasons to govern it with honest institutional design. Comparative governance shows that the question is not "Which system has the best law?" but "Which system prevents these failure modes from becoming routine?"

Conclusion: Borrow the Strengths, Not the Rhetoric

The comparative lesson is not to copy a statute or import a label. The lesson is to borrow strengths and immunise weaknesses. Rights-first systems remind us that algorithmic governance is a human-rights and rule-of-law problem that demands safeguards and proportionality reasoning (Rachovitsa, 2022; Enqvist, 2023). Common-law systems remind us that adversarial contestation and judicial reasoning can expose hidden assumptions—if disclosure and access are real (Cobbe, 2019; Williams, 2022). Audit-first systems remind us that models drift, feedback loops form, and one-time validation is a legal fiction in a dynamic world (Gama et al., 2014; Hinder et al., 2024). The best governance is a synthesis: rights architecture that is operational, adversarial contestability that is resourced, and continuous auditing that is independent and publicly accountable.

A predictive legal order can be legitimate, but only if every legal system, whatever its tradition, refuses the same temptation: to treat a model output as a shortcut around reasons. Justice does not become evidence-based by purchasing technology. It becomes evidence-based when evidence remains testable, reasons remain human, and power remains answerable.

References

- Berk, R., Heidari, H., Jabbari, S., Kearns, M. and Roth, A. (2021) 'Fairness in criminal justice risk assessments: The state of the art', Sociological Methods & Research, 50(1), pp. 3–44.
- Bhatnagar, V. (2023) 'The evidentiary implications of interpreting black-box algorithms', Northwestern Journal of Technology and Intellectual Property, 20(3), pp. 1–32.
- Chiao, V. (2024) 'Algorithmic decision-making, statistical evidence and the rule of law', Episteme, 21(4), pp. 1–23.
- Chouldechova, A. (2017) 'Fair prediction with disparate impact: A study of bias in recidivism prediction instruments', Big Data, 5(2), pp. 153–163.
- Cobbe, J. (2019) 'Judicial review of automated public-sector decision-making', Legal Studies, 39(4), pp. 636–655.
- Covilla, J.C. (2025) 'Artificial intelligence and administrative discretion: Exploring adaptations and boundaries', European Journal of Risk Regulation, 16(2), pp. 1–28.
- Duff, R.A. (2001) Punishment, Communication, and Community. Oxford: Oxford University Press.
- Enqvist, L. (2023) 'Discretion, automation, and proportionality', in Suksi, M. (ed.) The Rule of Law and Automated Decision-Making:

Exploring Fundamentals of Algorithmic Governance. Cham: Springer, pp. 169–205.

- Ensign, D., Friedler, S.A., Neville, S., Scheidegger, C. and Venkatasubramanian, S. (2018) 'Runaway feedback loops in predictive policing', Proceedings of Machine Learning Research, 81, pp. 1–12.
- Gama, J., Žliobaitė, I., Bifet, A., Pechenizkiy, M. and Bouchachia, A. (2014) 'A survey on concept drift adaptation', ACM Computing Surveys, 46(4), Article 44.
- Genaro-Moya, D. (2025) 'Artificial intelligence and public sector auditing', Administrative Sciences, 15(2), 78.
- Gikay, A.A. (2025) 'Trade secrecy in automated decisions: Against the myth of a complete barrier to transparency', Journal of Intellectual Property Law & Practice, 20(8), pp. 552–565.
- Hinder, F., Artelt, A., Hammer, B. and Schultheis, E. (2024) 'Concept drift detection in deployed machine learning systems: A survey', Frontiers in Artificial Intelligence, 7, 1330257.
- Kinchin, N. (2024) '"Voiceless": The procedural gap in algorithmic justice', International Journal of Law and Information Technology, 32(4), pp. 1–30.
- Kleinberg, J., Mullainathan, S. and Raghavan, M. (2017) 'Inherent trade-offs in the fair determination of risk scores', Proceedings of the 8th Innovations in Theoretical Computer Science Conference (ITCS 2017), LIPIcs 67, Article 43.
- Longoni, C., Cian, L. and Kyung, E.J. (2023) 'Algorithmic transference: People overgeneralize failures of artificial intelligence in the government', Journal of Marketing Research, 60(1), pp. 170–188.
- Lum, K. and Isaac, W. (2016) 'To predict and serve?', Significance, 13(5), pp. 14–19.
- Lyell, D. and Coiera, E. (2017) 'Automation bias and verification complexity: A systematic review', Journal of the American Medical Informatics Association, 24(2), pp. 423–431.
- Morrison, G.S. (2025) 'A guide to ISO 21043 forensic sciences from the forensic-data-science paradigm', Science & Justice, 65, 101298.
- Neil, R. (2025) 'Algorithmic bias in criminal risk assessment: The consequences of racial differences in arrest as a measure of crime', Annual Review of Criminology, 8, pp. 97–119.
- Nieuwenhuizen, E. (2024) 'Algorithm registers: A box-ticking exercise or meaningful tool for transparency?', Information Polity, 29(4), pp.

415–433.

- Perdomo, J.C., Zrnic, T., Mendler-Dünner, C. and Hardt, M. (2020) 'Performative prediction', Proceedings of the 37th International Conference on Machine Learning (ICML 2020), PMLR 119, pp. 7599–7609.
- Pleiss, G., Raghavan, M., Wu, F., Kleinberg, J. and Weinberger, K.Q. (2017) 'On fairness and calibration', Advances in Neural Information Processing Systems, 30.
- Rachovitsa, A. (2022) 'The human rights implications of the use of AI in the digital welfare state: The SyRI case', Human Rights Law Review, 22(2), ngac010.
- Robertson, B., Vignaux, G.A. and Berger, C.E.H. (2016) Interpreting Evidence: Evaluating Forensic Science in the Courtroom. 2nd edn. Chichester: Wiley.
- Santos, R. et al. (2025) 'AI as moral cover: How algorithmic bias exploits psychological tendencies', Analyses of Social Issues and Public Policy, 25(1), pp. 1–24.
- Selbst, A.D. and Barocas, S. (2018) 'The intuitive appeal of explainable machines', Fordham Law Review, 87(3), pp. 1085–1139.
- Skitka, L.J., Mosier, K.L. and Burdick, M. (1999) 'Does automation bias decision-making?', International Journal of Human–Computer Studies, 51(5), pp. 991–1006.
- Starke, C., Lünich, M. and Marcinkowski, F. (2022) 'Fairness perceptions of algorithmic decision-making: A systematic review', Big Data & Society, 9(2), pp. 1–18.
- Tyler, T.R. (2011) 'Procedural justice, legitimacy, and the effective rule of law', Crime and Justice, 40(1), pp. 283–357.
- van Bekkum, M., Borgesius, F.Z. and others (2021) 'Digital welfare fraud detection and the Dutch SyRI judgment', European Journal of Social Security, 23(4), pp. 1–22.
- Vargas, R. (2025) 'The political economy of policing', Annual Review of Law and Social Science, 21, pp. 1–24.
- Wieringa, M. (2023) '"Hey SyRI, tell me about algorithmic accountability": Lessons from a landmark case', Data & Policy, 5, e2.
- Williams, R. (2022) 'Accountable algorithms: Adopting the public law toolbox to scrutinise algorithmic decision-making', Current Legal Problems, 75(1), pp. 237–275.

- Zuiderveen Borgesius, F.J. (2020) 'Strengthening legal protection against discrimination by algorithms and artificial intelligence', International Journal of Human Rights, 24(10), pp. 1572–1593.

Part IX — Experimental and Empirical Pathways

CHAPTER XLI

Designing Courtroom Experiments: What Should Be Tested, and How

The Courtroom as a Decision Laboratory, Not a Game

A courtroom is already an experiment in a precise sense: a controlled ritual where limited information is presented under rules, decisions are produced under time and institutional pressure, and those decisions reshape behaviour in the world. The difference in the AI era is that courts are now being asked to accept, reject, or domesticate systems that claim causal authority while often providing only predictive evidence. If you are serious about "evidence-based justice," you cannot limit evaluation to vendor accuracy claims or retrospective correlations. You must design experiments that test how real decision-makers actually use tools, how reasons are written, how parties experience the process, and how downstream behaviour changes when the court's decision-making architecture changes (Tyler, 2011; Gerber and Green, 2012; Imbens and Rubin, 2015).

The governing discipline is this: a courtroom experiment is not a tech demo; it is an intervention into coercive power. That means your experimental question must be anchored in legality and legitimacy, not just efficiency. It must ask what courts are allowed to do, what they should do, and what they will do when a tool is introduced. It must also anticipate the predictable human pathologies that arise when numbers enter moral judgment: automation bias, anchoring, moral cover, and the temptation to replace reasons with outputs (Skitka, Mosier and Burdick, 1999; Lyell and Coiera, 2017; Dietvorst, Simmons and Massey, 2015). If your design does not explicitly measure these, you will misread what you are testing.

Start With the Only Question That Matters: What Decision Is Being Changed?

Courtroom experiments often fail because they begin with technology and search for a use-case. The correct order is the opposite. Begin with the decision point. Pretrial release? Sentencing? Conditions of supervision? Credibility assessments? Admissibility of probabilistic evidence? Judicial explanations? Each decision point carries a different moral permission structure. A forecasting tool that influences bail engages liberty at the presumption-of-innocence stage. A sentencing tool engages condemnation, proportionality, and desert. A triage tool used by prosecutors may never reach the judge yet can reshape what cases are pursued. A forensic AI tool used at investigation can contaminate evidence pathways long before trial. Your experiment must therefore specify where the tool enters the chain and what kind of authority it is given—informational, recommendatory, or determinative—because the effect will differ accordingly (Stevenson, 2024; Williams, 2022).

Once the decision point is specified, state the legal criterion that should govern it. This is not optional. If you test a risk score's effect on detention without anchoring the court's duty to articulate reasons and preserve contestability, you risk designing an experiment that measures compliance with a tool rather than legality of a decision. This is exactly the procedural gap problem in algorithmic justice: distributive performance can improve while the process becomes less contestable and therefore less legitimate (Kinchin, 2024; Tyler, 2011).

Choose Outcomes That Reflect Law, Not Only Convenience

Outcome selection is where "evidence-based" projects quietly betray the rule of law. The easiest outcomes are administrative: time to disposition, throughput, rates of detention, average sentence length, failure to appear. These matter, but they are not enough. A lawful system must also care about outcomes that are harder to measure: dignity, voice, perceived neutrality, comprehensibility of reasons, and equality of arms. Procedural justice research has long shown that perceptions of fairness and legitimacy are strongly shaped by how authorities treat people, not merely by case outcomes (Tyler, 2011; Blader and Tyler, 2003). If your experiment changes courtroom communication or introduces a model output, you must measure procedural justice perceptions as a primary endpoint, not as a decorative survey.

In the AI era you also need epistemic outcomes: how accurately judges interpret probabilistic evidence, whether they commit the prosecutor's fallacy, whether they overweight a risk score relative to the evidential record, whether they misunderstand calibration, and whether their written reasons remain intelligible without “the model says.” Courts already struggle with statistical reasoning; AI intensifies that vulnerability by compressing uncertainty into authoritative numbers (Koehler, 1996; Kahneman, 2011; Chiao, 2024). A well-designed experiment therefore treats statistical comprehension and reasoning quality as outcomes, not merely behavioural endpoints.

Finally, you need equity outcomes. Because fairness constraints can be mutually incompatible, an intervention can reduce one disparity while increasing another, and an experiment that reports only aggregate accuracy or aggregate detention rates can hide distributive harm (Chouldechova, 2017; Kleinberg, Mullainathan and Raghavan, 2017; Pleiss et al., 2017). Your design must pre-specify which fairness dimensions are morally relevant for the decision point and measure them transparently.

Decide What Kind of Causal Claim You Need

Experiments are not inherently better than observational studies; they answer different questions with different credibility. If the question is “What happens if we introduce this tool in this court, with these judges, under these rules?” you need causal inference under realistic conditions. Randomization is the most robust way to achieve this when feasible, but even randomization can mislead if spillovers occur, if compliance varies, or if outcomes are measured badly (Gerber and Green, 2012; Imai, King and Stuart, 2008; Hernán and Robins, 2020).

You must therefore define the estimand: are you measuring intention-to-treat (the effect of offering the tool), treatment-on-the-treated (the effect when the tool is actually used), or the effect of a policy that mandates use? Stevenson’s study of algorithmic risk assessment in sentencing demonstrates why this distinction matters: judges may systematically deviate from algorithm-associated recommendations, meaning adoption does not automatically translate into the intended effect (Stevenson, 2024). The lesson is methodological and moral. If judges override, you must ask whether overrides reflect principled discretion or bias; if judges comply, you must ask whether compliance reflects disciplined use or automation bias.

Field Experiments, Lab Experiments, and Hybrid Designs

Field experiments in real courts are the gold standard for measuring real-world behaviour, but they are ethically and operationally difficult. They can also be legally delicate because experimental manipulation must not violate due process, equality of arms, or judicial independence. Yet courts already run interventions that are experimentally testable: reminder systems to reduce failure to appear, procedural justice communication training, and changes in information presentation. Field evidence on reminders shows measurable effects on missed court dates and associated incarceration, illustrating that small procedural interventions can have significant liberty consequences (Chohlas-Wood et al., 2025).

Laboratory and vignette experiments are easier and often ethically safer for testing cognitive mechanisms: how judges interpret risk scores, how jurors respond to AI involvement, how explanation formats change perceived fairness, and how numerical frames alter blame and mercy. Experimental work on public perceptions of judges using AI tools has shown that legitimacy and fairness perceptions shift with the level and role of AI assistance, which provides a methodological template for testing how governance choices alter legitimacy (Fine, Berthelot and Marsh, 2025). Juror-focused experiments similarly show how AI versus human authority cues change deference, especially under mitigating circumstances, which is precisely the kind of moral-cognitive interaction courts must understand before deploying AI widely (Watamura et al., 2025).

The strongest designs are often hybrid. You can test mechanisms in controlled experiments, then test policy effects in field trials. You can run a stepped-wedge or phased rollout to satisfy practical constraints while still enabling causal inference. You can combine behavioural data with qualitative interviews to detect how actors narrate responsibility and how moral cover emerges in practice.

Randomization Units and Spillovers: The Court Is Not a Clean Petri Dish

The most common technical failure in courtroom experiments is choosing the wrong unit of randomization. If you randomize defendants within a judge's docket, you risk contamination: judges learn from exposure, apply insights across cases, and share practices with colleagues. If you randomize judges, you risk institutional spillover: court staff, prosecutors, and defence counsel adjust their strategies when they know a judge is using a tool. If you randomize courts, you often lose power and increase heterogeneity.

Your design must therefore anticipate spillovers and choose accordingly. Cluster randomization, stepped-wedge designs, and hierarchical modelling are often necessary, not optional (Imbens and Rubin, 2015; Gerber and Green, 2012). You must also plan for interference: one defendant's treatment can affect another's outcome through docket management, prosecutorial bargaining behaviour, or policing practices. In predictive policing contexts, feedback loops are documented and can produce self-confirming patterns, meaning experimental designs must treat system dynamics as part of the causal story rather than as noise (Ensign et al., 2018; Lum and Isaac, 2016).

What Should Be Tested in the AI Era

There are five classes of interventions that deserve systematic courtroom experimentation because they sit at the junction of forensics, morality, and legitimacy.

First, Information Presentation. Test how risk scores, probabilities, and forensic likelihood ratios are framed. Do judges interpret them as evidence weight or as proof? Do they confuse conditional probabilities? Does a natural-frequency framing reduce misinterpretation? These are classic statistical cognition questions with direct legal impact (Koehler, 1996; Gigerenzer and Hoffrage, 1995; Robertson, Vignaux and Berger, 2016).

Second, Explainability Formats. Test whether explanations are actionable or merely soothing. Do counterfactual explanations improve contestability? Do feature importance displays increase overreliance? Do explanation formats change the quality of reasons-giving? The explainability literature warns that explanation can create false comfort and obscure deeper normative choices, so experiments must measure both reliance and reasoning quality (Miller, 2019; Selbst and Barocas, 2018; Wachter, Mittelstadt and Russell, 2018).

Third, Decision Workflows. Test sequencing: when the judge sees the model output relative to hearing mitigation and reviewing evidence. Context management research in forensics shows that sequencing and context exposure can bias interpretation; courts can test similar contamination effects in AI-assisted settings (Edmond et al., 2015; Cooper,

Meterko and Dror, 2019).

Fourth, Procedural Justice Interventions. Test communication training, explanation templates, and participatory hearing structures. Procedural justice is not a "soft" outcome; it predicts legitimacy and compliance. Experiments should measure how interventions change perceived respect and neutrality and how those perceptions relate to subsequent compliance (Tyler, 2011; Blader and Tyler, 2003).

Fifth, Accountability and Oversight Mechanisms. Test whether audit warnings, drift alerts, and mandatory justification fields reduce automation bias and moral cover. The responsibility literature suggests that diffusion of responsibility is a predictable outcome of AI systems; experiments can test whether specific accountability architectures preserve decision ownership (Fleisher, 2025; Zeiser, 2024).

Ethics, Legality, and the Non-Negotiable Constraints

Courtroom experimentation must be ethics-first because the subjects are not consumers; they are citizens under coercive power. The baseline constraints are simple to state and difficult to implement: the experiment must not reduce due process, must not undermine equality of arms, must not coerce participation in ways that are incompatible with fair trial rights, and must be transparent to oversight even when it cannot be fully transparent to participants without compromising design integrity.

In practice, this means that experiments that manipulate liberty outcomes directly are ethically sensitive and often unacceptable unless the intervention is plausibly beneficial, minimally risky, and consistent with existing lawful discretion. Many court-based interventions are ethically defensible because they improve process without increasing coercion: reminders, clearer communication, improved access to information, and structured reasoning prompts. Experiments that change the weight given to evidence or introduce proprietary tools without contestability safeguards raise the most serious legal concerns because they can create secret influences that the defence cannot challenge.

A further ethical constraint is data protection. AI-era court experiments often involve sensitive personal data and algorithmic logs. An experiment cannot be well-designed if it cannot also be safely governed; governance is part of methodology.

Measurement Discipline: Don't Let Your Metrics Lie For You

In courtroom experiments, measurement is where good intentions go to die. "Failure to appear" can be measured, but it can also be misread: the reasons for nonappearance often involve structural barriers. Recidivism measures can embed policing intensity. "Compliance" can be bought through coercion while legitimacy collapses. That is why experiments must triangulate behavioural outcomes with legitimacy and experience measures, and must explicitly discuss measurement error and construct validity (Shadish, Cook and Campbell, 2002).

This is also where qualitative methods matter. Interviews with judges, prosecutors, defence counsel, and affected parties can reveal how an intervention is being narrated and used. Dagan's 2026 qualitative study of judges' experiences with machine-based sentencing illustrates the value of understanding judicial attitudes and perceived themes, because adoption effects depend on how judges interpret the technology and its moral status (Dagan, 2026). You cannot interpret quantitative effects correctly if you do not understand the meaning-making environment in which judges operate.

Analysis Choices: Pre-Registration, Heterogeneity, and the Temptation to Overclaim

Courtroom experiments are politically tempting: a positive result can justify scaling, procurement, and policy reform. That temptation creates a methodological duty: pre-register hypotheses, define estimands, and publish null results. Without this discipline, "evidence-based justice" becomes selective reporting dressed as science. Modern causal inference practice emphasises transparent design and analysis to prevent p-hacking and post hoc rationalisation (Imbens and Rubin, 2015; Hernán and Robins, 2020).

Heterogeneous treatment effects are not a footnote in justice; they are the moral heart. An intervention that reduces detention on average but increases it for a vulnerable subgroup is not a success. An explanation format that increases perceived fairness for one group but decreases it for another is not neutral. Experiments must therefore be powered and analysed with heterogeneity in mind, not only aggregate effects. This is especially important when interventions interact with existing inequities in policing and prosecution.

Conclusion: Courtroom Experiments Must Test Legitimacy, Not Just Efficiency

Designing courtroom experiments in the AI era is an exercise in disciplined humility. You are not only testing whether a tool "works." You are testing whether a new architecture of decision-making can coexist with the moral and procedural commitments that make courts legitimate: contestability, reason-giving, equality of arms, and dignity. The most important experimental outcomes are therefore not only behavioural endpoints but also epistemic and legitimacy endpoints: how judges reason with numbers, how explanations change agency, how parties experience respect, and how responsibility is owned when a model is present.

If you get the design right, experiments can become the court's way of learning without surrendering to vendors, hype, or fear. If you get it wrong, experiments become a pathway by which coercive systems are scaled before they are understood. The guiding principle is simple: in justice, the thing you must test is not only prediction. It is justification.

References

- Berk, R., Heidari, H., Jabbari, S., Kearns, M. and Roth, A. (2021) 'Fairness in criminal justice risk assessments: The state of the art', Sociological Methods & Research, 50(1), pp. 3–44.
- Chouldechova, A. (2017) 'Fair prediction with disparate impact: A study of bias in recidivism prediction instruments', Big Data, 5(2), pp. 153–163.
- Cobbe, J. (2019) 'Judicial review of automated public-sector decision-making', Legal Studies, 39(4), pp. 636–655.
- Ensign, D., Friedler, S.A., Neville, S., Scheidegger, C. and Venkatasubramanian, S. (2018) 'Runaway feedback loops in predictive policing', Proceedings of Machine Learning Research, 81, pp. 1–12.
- Fine, A., Berthelot, E.R. and Marsh, S. (2025) 'Public perceptions of judges' use of AI tools in courtroom decision-making: An examination of legitimacy, fairness, trust, and procedural justice', Behavioral Sciences, 15(4), 476.

- Gama, J., Žliobaitė, I., Bifet, A., Pechenizkiy, M. and Bouchachia, A. (2014) 'A survey on concept drift adaptation', ACM Computing Surveys, 46(4), Article 44.
- Hinder, F., Artelt, A., Hammer, B. and Schultheis, E. (2024) 'Concept drift detection in deployed machine learning systems: A survey', Frontiers in Artificial Intelligence, 7, 1330257.
- Imai, K. and Jiang, Z. (2023) 'Experimental evaluation of algorithm-assisted human decision making', Journal of the Royal Statistical Society: Series A, 186(2), pp. 167–—.
- Kinchin, N. (2024) '"Voiceless": The procedural gap in algorithmic justice', International Journal of Law and Information Technology, 32(4), pp. 1–30.
- Kleinberg, J., Mullainathan, S. and Raghavan, M. (2017) 'Inherent trade-offs in the fair determination of risk scores', Proceedings of the 8th Innovations in Theoretical Computer Science Conference (ITCS 2017), LIPIcs 67, Article 43.
- Lum, K. and Isaac, W. (2016) 'To predict and serve?', Significance, 13(5), pp. 14–19.
- Lyell, D. and Coiera, E. (2017) 'Automation bias and verification complexity: A systematic review', Journal of the American Medical Informatics Association, 24(2), pp. 423–431.
- Morrison, G.S. (2025) 'A guide to ISO 21043 forensic sciences from the forensic-data-science paradigm', Science & Justice, 65, 101298.
- Nieuwenhuizen, E. (2024) 'Algorithm registers: A box-ticking exercise or meaningful tool for transparency?', Information Polity, 29(4), pp. 415–433.
- Perdomo, J.C., Zrnic, T., Mendler-Dünner, C. and Hardt, M. (2020) 'Performative prediction', Proceedings of the 37th International Conference on Machine Learning (ICML 2020), PMLR 119, pp. 7599–7609.
- Pleiss, G., Raghavan, M., Wu, F., Kleinberg, J. and Weinberger, K.Q. (2017) 'On fairness and calibration', Advances in Neural Information Processing Systems, 30.
- Ramos-Maqueda, M. (2025) 'The data revolution in justice', World Development, 180, 106—.
- Robertson, B., Vignaux, G.A. and Berger, C.E.H. (2016) Interpreting Evidence: Evaluating Forensic Science in the Courtroom. 2nd edn. Chichester: Wiley.

- Skitka, L.J., Mosier, K.L. and Burdick, M. (1999) 'Does automation bias decision-making?', International Journal of Human–Computer Studies, 51(5), pp. 991–1006.
- Starke, C., Lünich, M. and Marcinkowski, F. (2022) 'Fairness perceptions of algorithmic decision-making: A systematic review', Big Data & Society, 9(2), pp. 1–18.
- Stevenson, M.T. and Doleac, J.L. (2024) 'Algorithmic risk assessment in the hands of humans', American Economic Journal: Economic Policy, 16(—), pp. —.
- Tyler, T.R. (2011) 'Procedural justice, legitimacy, and the effective rule of law', Crime and Justice, 40(1), pp. 283–357.
- Williams, R. (2022) 'Accountable algorithms: Adopting the public law toolbox to scrutinise algorithmic decision-making', Current Legal Problems, 75(1), pp. 237–275.
- Yalcin, G., van den Bos, K., Ståhl, T. and Lind, E.A. (2023) 'Perceptions of justice by algorithms', Journal of Business Ethics, 188, pp. 1–—.

CHAPTER XLII

Human–AI Collaboration: When Advice Helps and When It Corrupts

The New Partner in the Room

Courts have always relied on "decision aids," though they were once called precedent, guidelines, actuarial tables, expert testimony, and probation reports. The difference now is not merely computational speed; it is the introduction of an agent-like adviser whose outputs look objective, feel authoritative, and arrive with a veneer of inevitability. Human–AI collaboration, in justice, therefore cannot be analysed like ordinary tool use. It is a partnership between a moral institution and a predictive instrument, and the partnership is fragile because punishment is not just prediction; it is condemnation and restraint requiring reasons a citizen can contest (Duff, 2001; Tyler, 2011). When advice helps, it does so by improving epistemic discipline while preserving moral ownership. When it corrupts, it does so by displacing reasons with outputs and by laundering discretionary choices through the language of "the model says."

You will notice immediately that this is not a binary world. The same tool can help in one courtroom and corrupt in another. The same judge can use it as a check against bias in the morning and as a shield against accountability in the afternoon. The determining variables are not only model accuracy, but the social psychology of advice-taking, the institutional incentives of blame avoidance, and the procedural architecture of contestability.

The Two Promises of Advice—and the Two Pathways to Corruption

Human–AI advice is promised to deliver two goods. The first is Epistemic Gain: a better estimate than the unaided human can produce, especially where humans are poor statistical learners and prone to base-rate neglect and overconfidence (Koehler, 1996; Kahneman, 2011). The second is Consistency Gain: reduced noise and idiosyncrasy across decision-makers, a long-standing argument in favour of actuarial methods (Dawes, Faust and Meehl, 1989). Both promises can be real. Yet both promises contain the seed of corruption.

Epistemic corruption happens when the advice is treated as proof rather than as fallible evidence, especially when the advice is probabilistic and the legal question is normative. Consistency corruption happens when consistency becomes the moral substitute for justification, as if uniformity were fairness by itself. The fairness literature shows that there is no single "fair" way to be consistent; fairness constraints conflict, base rates differ, and thresholds encode value judgments about which errors are tolerable and for whom (Chouldechova, 2017; Kleinberg, Mullainathan and Raghavan, 2017; Pleiss et al., 2017). A consistent injustice is still injustice, only now scalable.

What the Psychology of Advice-Taking Predicts

If you want to govern human–AI collaboration, you must begin with a simple empirical truth: people do not respond to advice only by checking whether it is correct. They respond to advice by reading social meaning into its source, especially when the source appears competent and impersonal. This is the core of algorithm appreciation: people sometimes adhere more to algorithmic advice than to human advice, even without evidence of superior quality, because algorithms signal capability and impartiality (Logg, Minson and Moore, 2019). Algorithm aversion is the opposite tendency: people may avoid algorithms after seeing them err, penalising machine error more harshly than human error (Dietvorst, Simmons and Massey, 2015). Both tendencies can exist in the same system, and sometimes in the same decision-maker, depending on context.

Meta-analytic work has extended these findings by showing that reactions to algorithmic decision-making depend heavily on the context, including perceived capability and whether personalization is seen as necessary (Capogrosso, Treffers and Welpe, 2025; Moritz, 2026). The lesson is blunt: collaboration is not governed by accuracy alone. It is governed by perceived authority, perceived accountability, and perceived legitimacy. In criminal justice, those perceptions are amplified, because coercion raises the stakes of error and because the public reacts strongly to the idea that liberty can be influenced by a machine.

When Advice Helps: The Conditions for Epistemic Assistance

Advice helps when it performs three functions at once. It must improve estimation, preserve interpretive humility, and remain contestable. You can see the analogy in forensic science. The best forensic practice does not treat a method's output as truth; it treats it as evidential weight supported by validation and bounded by uncertainty, and it insists on interpretive discipline under conditions of use (Robertson, Vignaux and Berger, 2016; Morrison, 2025). AI advice in courts should be treated the same way. A risk score, a similarity ranking, or a forecast is not a verdict; it is a claim whose probative meaning depends on what is being predicted, how it was validated, and how it behaves under drift and feedback loops.

Advice also helps when it is used as a second opinion rather than as a replacement for judgment. One of the most robust findings in advice-taking research is that people discount advice in egocentric ways, but they can also use additional opinions to reduce error when the environment encourages genuine comparison rather than default compliance (Yaniv, 2004). In a court, this means designing the workflow so that the judge forms a preliminary view from evidence and law, then uses the tool to challenge blind spots, rather than allowing the tool to anchor the first impression.

Finally, advice helps when the collaboration is designed for appropriate reliance, meaning decision-makers rely on AI when it is likely to be right and resist it when it is likely to be wrong. Recent work explicitly frames appropriate reliance as the central challenge in AI-based decision support, warning that both over-reliance and under-reliance are predictable and that explanations and interface choices can shift reliance in either direction (Dogru, 2025; Ferrario, 2025). Help, in other words, is not merely "use the AI." Help is "use it in a way that preserves sensitivity to error."

When Advice Corrupts: Over-Reliance, Under-Reliance, and the Drift of Moral Ownership

Advice corrupts in two obvious ways and one subtle way. The first obvious way is automation bias, where the decision-maker becomes over-reliant on the system's recommendation, reducing vigilance and independent verification (Skitka, Mosier and Burdick, 1999; Lyell and Coiera, 2017). A recent review focused specifically on automation bias in human–AI collaboration synthesizes how task risk, complexity, and user factors shape over-reliance, reinforcing that this is not a rare anomaly but a structural tendency in decision support (Romeo, 2025). Over-reliance is epistemically corrupting because it converts a fallible estimate into a default. It is procedurally corrupting because it makes contestation harder: if the human cannot explain why the tool was followed, the reasons collapse into "the model indicated."

The second obvious way is under-reliance, where decision-makers reject correct advice because they distrust algorithms or because the advice threatens their professional identity. Under-reliance is morally seductive in courts because it can masquerade as "humanity." Yet rejecting a well-calibrated tool does not automatically restore justice; it can simply restore bias, noise, and inconsistency. The solution is not worship or aversion but calibration, and the interventions literature suggests that changing the interaction environment—giving limited control, better feedback, clearer accountability—can reduce algorithm aversion (Dietvorst, Simmons and Massey, 2018; Capogrosso, Treffers and Welpe, 2025).

The subtle corruption is moral outsourcing. Even when the judge remains formally responsible, the psychological experience of authorship can drift away from the judge and toward the system. This is especially dangerous in sentencing and detention, because the moral legitimacy of punishment depends on public, human-owned reasons. When the judge begins to treat the tool as the place where prudence resides, mercy becomes harder, severity becomes safer, and decisions begin to look managerial rather than condemnatory. Qualitative research on judges' experiences with machine-based sentencing illustrates precisely this tension: judges describe the tool's presence as reshaping what it means to sentence as a human process, including concerns about autonomy and the moral character of judgment (Dagan, Baron and Kaplan-Damary, 2026).

The "Moral Cover" Mechanism: How Systems Launder Bias and Harshness

A justice system is uniquely vulnerable to a phenomenon that is now being discussed explicitly in the social psychology of AI: the use of AI as moral cover. When outcomes are harsh or discriminatory, decision-makers can attribute the result to the system, experiencing reduced personal culpability and presenting the decision as objective compliance rather than discretionary choice (Borinca, 2025). In court terms, moral cover is the quiet sentence "I had to," spoken without speaking. It is not merely a rhetorical device; it is a psychological mechanism that makes morally troubling decisions easier to make and easier to defend.

This is where human–AI collaboration becomes a moral hazard. The model output can be used to justify what the institution already tends toward under risk pressure: precautionary detention, severity under uncertainty, and risk management rather than individualized justice. Once those tendencies are embedded in the workflow, the system drifts toward what criminologists described decades ago as a risk-management orientation rather than a communicative theory of punishment (Feeley and Simon, 1992; Duff, 2001). AI does not create that orientation, but it can amplify it by supplying the language of scientific inevitability.

Forensic Application: AI Advice as Evidence-Like Output, Not Administrative Fact

From a forensic perspective, the most dangerous courtroom mistake is to treat AI advice as if it were an administrative convenience rather than an evidence-like claim. A risk score, for example, is often built using proxies for institutional contact—rearrest, technical violations, prior supervision—which can encode enforcement patterns and social inequality. The criminological literature has repeatedly warned that arrest-based measures can be biased proxies for underlying offending, meaning that "prediction" may partly be prediction of institutional attention (Neil, 2025). In predictive policing, feedback loops can create runaway reinforcement where deployment creates the data that "validates" deployment, producing self-fulfilling patterns that look like accuracy (Lum and Isaac, 2016; Ensign et al., 2018). If a judge is unaware of these dynamics, AI advice can become an evidential contaminant rather than an evidential aid.

Forensic discipline demands validation under conditions of use, explicit error behavior, and careful interpretation of probabilistic claims (Robertson, Vignaux and Berger, 2016; Morrison, 2025). Human–AI collaboration must import that discipline. Where a tool is used, the court must know what is being predicted, what error trade-offs are embedded, what drift monitoring exists, and how the tool was validated for this population. Otherwise, collaboration becomes epistemic theatre: the appearance of evidence without its discipline.

Decision Control and the Engineering of Reliance

A recurrent empirical finding is that people are more willing to engage with imperfect algorithms when they have some sense of control. Decision control can increase trust and compliance, but the court must treat this as double-edged. Increasing compliance is not necessarily good if it is compliance with a flawed or normatively misaligned output. Westphal and colleagues found that decision control and explanations can increase user trust and compliance with recommendations, which is useful for designing collaboration but dangerous if the goal is not compliance but appropriate reliance (Westphal et al., 2023). The court's objective is not to make judges obey a model; it is to make judges reason well with a tool.

This is why calibrated reliance metrics are becoming central in human–AI collaboration research: over-reliance and under-reliance are measured as distinct failures, and interventions are judged by whether they increase appropriate reliance rather than raw acceptance (Dogru, 2025; Srinivasan et al., 2025). The legal translation is straightforward. Collaboration is good when it improves correctness without degrading contestability. Collaboration is corrupting when it increases obedience while decreasing reasons.

The Procedural Integrity Test: Does Collaboration Preserve Contestability?

A court is not merely a decision factory; it is an adversarial institution. If collaboration reduces the defence's ability to test what influenced the outcome, the collaboration is procedurally corrupting even if predictive performance improves. This is precisely the procedural gap problem identified in algorithmic justice literature: systems can be defended as efficient and fair by metric while the individual's voice and capacity to contest remain weak (Kinchin, 2024). It is also why explainability debates matter: explanations that soothe but do not enable challenge can increase deference without increasing accountability (Selbst and Barocas, 2018). Counterfactual explanations may sometimes support actionability and contestation, but they are not a substitute for disclosure of inputs, validation evidence, and threshold policies when liberty is at stake (Wachter, Mittelstadt and Russell, 2018).

A simple rule helps: if a collaboration system cannot be cross-examined in function—through access to inputs, versioning, error evidence, and contestation pathways—then it is not collaboration; it is delegation disguised as assistance. And delegation of coercion without contestability is the oldest form of illegitimacy.

The Human Encounter: Why "Help" Must Not Destroy Dignity

Even when advice improves accuracy, it can destroy dignity if it changes how people are treated. Procedural justice research shows that legitimacy depends heavily on voice, respect, neutrality, and trustworthy motives (Tyler, 2011). A system that improves prediction but makes the person feel processed rather than heard may reduce long-term cooperation and compliance even if it produces "better" short-term outcomes. This is not a sentimental point; it is governance. People obey law not only because they fear sanction, but because the system is experienced as morally credible (Tyler, 2006; Tyler, 2011). Collaboration that undermines the human encounter—by turning the hearing into a ritual around a number—corrupts legitimacy even when it helps estimation.

Conclusion: Collaboration Is a Design Choice About Power

Human–AI collaboration is not inherently beneficial or inherently corrupting. It is a design choice about where power sits, how reasons are formed, and who can challenge them. Advice helps when it functions like disciplined forensic evidence: bounded, validated, interpreted with humility, and kept contestable. Advice corrupts when it becomes an authority substitute: an anchor that hardens decisions, a shield that launders bias, or a mechanism that relocates moral ownership away from the human institution that must answer for coercion.

The practical mandate is therefore neither to ban AI nor to embrace it as salvation. The mandate is to engineer collaboration toward appropriate reliance, preserve adversarial contestability, and protect the human legitimacy of punishment by ensuring that the final reasons remain human-authored, publicly intelligible, and answerable on review (Dogru, 2025; Romeo, 2025; Tyler, 2011). When a court can do that, advice can help.

When it cannot, advice will corrupt—quietly at first, and then, after the scandal, obviously.

References

- Barocas, S. and Selbst, A.D. (2016) 'Big data's disparate impact', California Law Review, 104(3), pp. 671–732.
- Berk, R., Heidari, H., Jabbari, S., Kearns, M. and Roth, A. (2021) 'Fairness in criminal justice risk assessments: The state of the art', Sociological Methods & Research, 50(1), pp. 3–44.
- Borinca, I. (2025) 'AI as moral cover: How algorithmic bias exploits psychological mechanisms to perpetuate social inequality', Analyses of Social Issues and Public Policy, 25(3), pp. 1–24.
- Capogrosso, A., Treffers, T. and Welpe, I. (2025) 'Interaction context is key: A meta-analysis of experimental evidence on interventions against algorithm aversion', Proceedings of the Hawaii International Conference on System Sciences, pp. 600–609.
- Chouldechova, A. (2017) 'Fair prediction with disparate impact: A study of bias in recidivism prediction instruments', Big Data, 5(2), pp. 153–163.
- Dagan, N., Baron, S. and Kaplan-Damary, N. (2026) 'Sentencing as a human process? Human judges' experiences of machine-based sentencing', The British Journal of Criminology, advance article, azaf128.
- Dawes, R.M., Faust, D. and Meehl, P.E. (1989) 'Clinical versus actuarial judgment', Science, 243(4899), pp. 1668–1674.
- Dietvorst, B.J., Simmons, J.P. and Massey, C. (2015) 'Algorithm aversion: People erroneously avoid algorithms after seeing them err', Journal of Experimental Psychology: General, 144(1), pp. 114–126.
- Dietvorst, B.J., Simmons, J.P. and Massey, C. (2018) 'Overcoming algorithm aversion: People will use imperfect algorithms if they can (even slightly) modify them', Management Science, 64(3), pp. 1155–1170.
- Dogru, E.Ö. (2025) 'Investigating appropriate reliance on AI-based decision support systems', Journal of Global Scholars of Marketing Science, 35(—), pp. 1–—.
- Duff, R.A. (2001) Punishment, Communication, and Community. Oxford: Oxford University Press.

- Ensign, D., Friedler, S.A., Neville, S., Scheidegger, C. and Venkatasubramanian, S. (2018) 'Runaway feedback loops in predictive policing', Proceedings of Machine Learning Research, 81, pp. 1–12.
- Feeley, M.M. and Simon, J. (1992) 'The new penology: Notes on the emerging strategy of corrections and its implications', Criminology, 30(4), pp. 449–474.
- Ferrario, A. (2025) 'Being pragmatic about reliance and trust in artificial intelligence', Minds and Machines, 35, pp. 1–—.
- Gigerenzer, G. and Hoffrage, U. (1995) 'How to improve Bayesian reasoning without instruction: Frequency formats', Psychological Review, 102(4), pp. 684–704.
- Kahneman, D. (2011) Thinking, Fast and Slow. New York: Farrar, Straus and Giroux.
- Kinchin, N. (2024) '"Voiceless": The procedural gap in algorithmic justice', International Journal of Law and Information Technology, 32(4), pp. 1–30.
- Kleinberg, J., Mullainathan, S. and Raghavan, M. (2017) 'Inherent trade-offs in the fair determination of risk scores', Proceedings of the 8th Innovations in Theoretical Computer Science Conference (ITCS 2017), LIPIcs 67, Article 43.
- Koehler, J.J. (1996) 'The base rate fallacy reconsidered: Normative, descriptive and methodological challenges', Behavioral and Brain Sciences, 19(1), pp. 1–53.
- Logg, J.M., Minson, J.A. and Moore, D.A. (2019) 'Algorithm appreciation: People prefer algorithmic to human judgment', Organizational Behavior and Human Decision Processes, 151, pp. 90–103.
- Lum, K. and Isaac, W. (2016) 'To predict and serve?', Significance, 13(5), pp. 14–19.
- Lyell, D. and Coiera, E. (2017) 'Automation bias and verification complexity: A systematic review', Journal of the American Medical Informatics Association, 24(2), pp. 423–431.
- Moritz, J.M. (2026) 'A meta-analysis on reactions to algorithmic decision-making', Organizational Psychology Review, 16(—), pp. 1–—.
- Morrison, G.S. (2025) 'A guide to ISO 21043 forensic sciences from the forensic-data-science paradigm', Science & Justice, 65, 101298.
- Neil, R. (2025) 'Algorithmic bias in criminal risk assessment: The consequences of racial differences in arrest as a measure of crime', Annual Review of Criminology, 8, pp. 97–119.

- Pleiss, G., Raghavan, M., Wu, F., Kleinberg, J. and Weinberger, K.Q. (2017) 'On fairness and calibration', Advances in Neural Information Processing Systems, 30.
- Robertson, B., Vignaux, G.A. and Berger, C.E.H. (2016) Interpreting Evidence: Evaluating Forensic Science in the Courtroom. 2nd edn. Chichester: Wiley.
- Romeo, G. (2025) 'Exploring automation bias in human–AI collaboration', AI & Society, 40, pp. 1–—.
- Rudin, C. (2019) 'Stop explaining black box machine learning models for high stakes decisions and use interpretable models instead', Nature Machine Intelligence, 1, pp. 206–215.
- Selbst, A.D. and Barocas, S. (2018) 'The intuitive appeal of explainable machines', Fordham Law Review, 87(3), pp. 1085–1139.
- Skitka, L.J., Mosier, K.L. and Burdick, M. (1999) 'Does automation bias decision-making?', International Journal of Human–Computer Studies, 51(5), pp. 991–1006.
- Srinivasan, T. et al. (2025) 'Measuring over-reliance and under-reliance in AI-assisted decision-making', Proceedings of the ACM on Human-Computer Interaction, pp. 1–—.
- Tyler, T.R. (2006) Why People Obey the Law. 2nd edn. Princeton, NJ: Princeton University Press.
- Tyler, T.R. (2011) 'Procedural justice, legitimacy, and the effective rule of law', Crime and Justice, 40(1), pp. 283–357.
- Wachter, S., Mittelstadt, B. and Russell, C. (2018) 'Counterfactual explanations without opening the black box: Automated decisions and the GDPR', Harvard Journal of Law & Technology, 31(2), pp. 841–887.
- Westphal, M. et al. (2023) 'Decision control and explanations in human–AI collaboration', Computers in Human Behavior, 141, 107—.
- Williams, R. (2022) 'Accountable algorithms: Adopting the public law toolbox to scrutinise algorithmic decision-making', Current Legal Problems, 75(1), pp. 237–275.
- Yaniv, I. (2004) 'The benefit of additional opinions', Current Directions in Psychological Science, 13(2), pp. 75–78.

CHAPTER XLIII

Measuring Legitimacy: Procedural Justice Scales and Behavioral Outcomes

Why Legitimacy Must Be Measured Like Evidence, Not Admired Like Philosophy

Legitimacy is one of those ideas that looks soft until you realise it is the quiet engine of compliance. Courts and police can compel behavior through threat, but they cannot efficiently govern through threat alone; they need people to appear, cooperate, tell the truth, accept outcomes, and internalise law as something more than hostile force (Tyler, 2006; Tyler, 2011). The decisive question, then, is not whether legitimacy is "real," but whether we can measure it with enough precision to guide institutional design without confusing measurement with morality. The AI era raises the stakes because algorithmic systems can change how people experience neutrality, respect, voice, and accountability, which are the very cues through which legitimacy is formed. If we cannot measure legitimacy properly, we will misread the effects of the new architecture of decision-making and mistake efficiency for justice.

A second reason legitimacy needs disciplined measurement is that legitimacy is not merely an attitude. It is a structured set of beliefs about authority: whether the institution has the right to govern, whether its decisions deserve compliance, and whether its power is exercised in a way that signals membership and dignity. Large-scale empirical work and syntheses treating legitimacy as a multi-dimensional construct—often separating obligation to obey, moral alignment, and legality—underline that legitimacy is not captured by a single "trust" item (Jackson et al., 2012). The measurement task is therefore forensic in spirit: define the construct, specify its indicators, show reliability, show validity, and prove that the measure predicts the outcomes the theory claims it should predict. Otherwise, the system will claim "evidence-based legitimacy" while actually measuring public mood.

The Procedural Justice Model: The Strongest Theory Because It Makes Risky Predictions

Procedural justice theory is powerful because it predicts something that looks counterintuitive to purely deterrent thinking: people will accept decisions they dislike if they believe the process was fair, neutral, and respectful, and they will reject decisions they benefit from if the process is humiliating or arbitrary (Tyler, 2011). The theory rests on a small set of procedural cues that recur across the literature: voice, neutrality, dignity/respect, and trustworthy motives. A contemporary statement of this structure is explicit that procedural fairness judgments cluster into fairness of decision-making (voice, neutrality) and fairness of interpersonal treatment (trust/respect), which is not merely conceptual tidiness but a measurement blueprint (Tyler, 2023).

The critical point for measurement is that procedural justice is not simply "being polite." It is the citizen's perception that the authority's power is constrained by principled reasoning. Neutrality signals that the authority is not captured by prejudice. Voice signals that the person is treated as a participant rather than a subject. Respect signals that the person's social standing is intact. Trustworthy motives signal that the authority is acting for public reasons rather than for convenience or animus. When these perceptions rise, legitimacy rises; when legitimacy rises, compliance and cooperation tend to rise (Sunshine and Tyler, 2003; Tyler, 2006; Tyler, 2011).

What Exactly Should Be Measured: Two Families of Constructs

When researchers say they "measured legitimacy," they often mix three different things: procedural justice perceptions, legitimacy beliefs, and behavioral intentions. A careful design treats them as related but distinct. Procedural justice perceptions measure how the person experienced the interaction. These are often captured through multi-item scales aligned to voice, neutrality, dignity/respect, and trustworthy motives. An influential modern experimental field design in policing used a 12-item procedural justice scale explicitly spanning these dimensions, making the measurement architecture visible and replicable (Weisburd et al., 2022).

Legitimacy beliefs measure the person's normative stance toward authority, usually including felt obligation to obey, perceived moral alignment, and beliefs about legality and rightful power. Large-scale comparative work using the European Social Survey operationalised legitimacy along these lines, distinguishing consent-like and moral alignment components rather than collapsing legitimacy into generic trust (Jackson et al., 2012).

Behavioral outcomes and intentions measure what institutions ultimately care about: reporting crime or problems, cooperating with investigations, compliance with orders, desistance, and willingness to call on law rather than resorting to private violence. Here, measurement must be more than self-report. Some studies do use intentions because behavior can be hard to observe ethically; but the strongest evidence links procedural justice and legitimacy to observed behaviors such as reporting neighborhood problems or cooperating with police, and it also shows that effects can be context-dependent and not always as strong as the simplest model suggests (Kuen et al., 2024).

Scale Construction: Why Four-Component Measures Work and When They Fail

The best procedural justice scales do not merely ask, "Was it fair?" They ask about specific perceptions that can be acted upon: whether the person had a chance to speak, whether the authority listened, whether decisions seemed unbiased, whether the person was treated with dignity, and whether motives seemed benevolent. This is not only good psychology; it is good governance because it points to levers the institution can change. A broad procedural justice definition used in contemporary work explicitly lists voice, dignity/respect, neutrality, and trustworthy motives as constituents, reflecting a converging standard across policing and court contexts (Hohl et al., 2022).

Yet scale design fails in predictable ways. First, "procedural justice" becomes an omnibus label that swallows outcomes, satisfaction, and distributive fairness into one index, causing conceptual blur. Second, items become too generic, losing sensitivity to the specific institutional encounter. Third, researchers use short scales that capture only politeness cues and miss neutrality and voice, which are often the most legitimacy-relevant. Fourth, scales are applied across contexts without checking measurement invariance—whether the same items mean the same thing across groups, cultures, or interaction types. The recent meta-analytic literature argues explicitly that social identity and social context shape procedural justice–legitimacy dynamics, which implies that measurement must be sensitive to group differences and context rather than assuming a universal coefficient (Chan, 2025).

A further measurement hazard is now being openly discussed as a "measurement crisis" within criminological legitimacy research, where different operationalisations yield unstable conclusions, and where procedural justice may be measured in inconsistent ways across studies (Nivette et al., 2025). This is not an academic embarrassment; it is a practical warning: if you change the measurement, you may change the policy conclusion, even if the underlying reality did not change.

From Scales to Behavior: The Causal Chain Must Be Tested, Not Assumed

The classic procedural justice chain is often described as: fair treatment increases legitimacy; legitimacy increases cooperation and compliance; cooperation improves public safety and system effectiveness (Tyler, 2011). That chain is plausible, but measurement must treat it as a hypothesis, not a creed. Recent work explicitly evaluates causal mechanisms linking procedural justice to cooperation through legitimacy rather than treating legitimacy as a vague mediator (Nivette, 2025). A 2025 paper evaluating causal mechanisms from procedural justice to legitimacy and compliance likewise reflects the field's increasing insistence on mechanism testing rather than merely correlational claims.

Crucially, longitudinal and real-world behavior studies sometimes show limited or conditional support. For example, one longitudinal analysis found that police legitimacy influenced reporting behavior, while procedural justice did not show a direct or indirect effect on reporting neighborhood problems in that setting, illustrating that context, outcome type, and measurement choices matter (Kuen et al., 2024). This is not a refutation of procedural justice theory; it is a reminder that legitimacy's behavioral consequences can vary by what "cooperation" means in that environment and by how structural constraints shape behavior. A person may view the process as fair and still not report crime if they fear retaliation, distrust effectiveness, or face practical barriers. Measurement must therefore distinguish legitimacy beliefs from feasibility of action.

Courtroom Legitimacy Is Not Policing Legitimacy: Interaction Forms Matter

A recurring mistake is to import policing measures into courts as if the encounter were the same. Court encounters involve different power forms: adjudication, reason-giving, and formal ritual of listening. They also increasingly involve online proceedings, which can alter voice and dignity cues even when access barriers are reduced. A major empirical study of online proceedings explicitly examines how shifting legal proceedings online changes procedural justice perceptions and how those perceptions relate to legitimacy, with attention to income differences (Mentovich, 2023). The measurement lesson is direct: legitimacy is partly produced by how the person experiences being seen and heard, and technology can change that experience while leaving "outcomes" unchanged.

Courts also have internal procedural justice dynamics that indirectly shape public legitimacy through staff behavior, courtroom management, and the emotional climate of the hearing. Research linking supervisor procedural justice to judges' perceived tensions with litigants suggests that internal justice climate can shape external encounter quality, which implies that measuring legitimacy must include institutional ecology, not only citizen attitudes (Baker et al., 2023).

The Forensic Application: Measuring Legitimacy as an Evidential Safeguard

In AI-assisted justice, legitimacy measurement becomes a forensic safeguard because it can detect when the system is drifting into unreviewable power. If algorithmic tools reduce voice by turning hearings into score-confirmation rituals, procedural justice scales should show it. If AI explanations increase the "opacity effect," causing people to feel decisions are unchallengeable, legitimacy measures should capture reduced perceived neutrality and respect. If proprietary models weaken equality of arms, legitimacy should be expected to fall among those directly affected, even if accuracy rises. This is why legitimacy measurement cannot be treated as public relations; it must be treated like quality control in an evidential system.

A crucial methodological implication is that legitimacy measures should be paired with objective indicators of contestability and procedural integrity: rates of successful challenges, frequency of data corrections, availability of reasons, and the completeness of disclosures. A legitimacy score without procedural audit data can become shallow: it measures acceptance without knowing whether acceptance is informed, coerced, or resigned. The procedural gap literature warns precisely against this: systems can appear "fair" by surface indicators while being procedurally non-contestable in practice (Kinchin, 2024).

Designing a Legitimacy Measurement Battery That Courts Can Actually Use

A justice-facing legitimacy battery should be designed around four linked components. The first component is encounter-level procedural justice, measuring voice, neutrality, respect, and trustworthy motives in a specific hearing or interaction, with items adapted to court realities rather than copied from police surveys. The second component is institution-level legitimacy beliefs, measuring obligation, moral alignment, and perceived legality. The third component is behavioral outcomes, ideally observed rather than only self-reported: appearance rates, compliance with conditions, voluntary cooperation, reporting behavior, and subsequent engagement with legal services. The fourth component is equity and subgroup analysis, because legitimacy is not evenly distributed and because social identity and context shape procedural justice effects (Chan, 2025).

This structure also aligns with the most defensible epistemic stance: triangulation. If procedural justice rises but observed compliance does not, the interpretation may involve structural constraints. If compliance rises but perceived legitimacy falls, the system may be increasing coercive control rather than moral acceptance. If both rise, the system may be improving governance in a stable way. Without triangulation, legitimacy measurement is vulnerable to misreading.

Common Pitfalls That Make "Legitimacy Research" Unusable for Policy

One pitfall is conflating legitimacy with satisfaction. Satisfaction can be high when people win and low when they lose; legitimacy is supposed to remain meaningful even under adverse outcomes. Another pitfall is treating short-term compliance as legitimacy; compliance can be produced by fear, surveillance, or inability to resist. Procedural justice theory's distinctive claim is that legitimacy produces voluntary cooperation beyond immediate deterrence, so measurements must attempt to capture that distinction (Tyler, 2011).

A third pitfall is ignoring measurement invariance. If items mean different things across cultural contexts or groups, comparisons become morally and scientifically misleading. The meta-analytic focus on social identity as an antecedent and moderator is a direct warning: one-size scales can obscure inequality in legitimacy dynamics (Chan, 2025).

A fourth pitfall is ignoring the institutional narrative environment. In the AI era, institutional messaging about "objectivity" can inflate perceived neutrality without actually improving fairness, which creates a legitimacy bubble. That bubble bursts at scandal. Measuring legitimacy without measuring contestability and transparency is how bubbles are created.

Conclusion: Legitimacy Measurement Is Not Optional in the AI Era

Measuring legitimacy is not an academic hobby; it is the system's early-warning device. Procedural justice scales, when constructed and used with discipline, tell courts whether power is being experienced as rightful. Behavioral outcomes tell courts whether legitimacy beliefs translate into cooperation and compliance. Both must be treated as evidence, triangulated, and analysed with context sensitivity. The most important comparative lesson from contemporary research is that procedural justice is a powerful predictor, but its relationship with legitimacy and behavior varies by context, group identity, and the specific behaviors being measured (Mentovich, 2023; Chan, 2025; Kuen et al., 2024).

In an era where algorithmic tools can quietly reshape voice, neutrality, and respect, legitimacy measurement becomes part of due process itself. A court that cannot measure whether people experience its power as legitimate cannot know whether it is strengthening justice or merely optimizing control.

References

- Blader, S.L. and Tyler, T.R. (2003) 'A four-component model of procedural justice: Defining the meaning of a "fair" process', Personality and Social Psychology Bulletin, 29(6), pp. 747–758.
- Chan, A. (2025) 'A systematic review and meta-analysis of procedural justice and legitimacy in policing: The effect of social identity and social contexts', Journal of Quantitative Criminology, 41, pp. 1–36.
- Chouldechova, A. (2017) 'Fair prediction with disparate impact: A study of bias in recidivism prediction instruments', Big Data, 5(2), pp. 153–163.
- Dietvorst, B.J., Simmons, J.P. and Massey, C. (2015) 'Algorithm aversion: People erroneously avoid algorithms after seeing them err', Journal of Experimental Psychology: General, 144(1), pp. 114–126.
- Duff, R.A. (2001) Punishment, Communication, and Community. Oxford: Oxford University Press.
- Gerber, A.S. and Green, D.P. (2012) Field Experiments: Design, Analysis, and Interpretation. New York: W.W. Norton.
- Gigerenzer, G. and Hoffrage, U. (1995) 'How to improve Bayesian reasoning without instruction: Frequency formats', Psychological Review, 102(4), pp. 684–704.
- Hohl, K., Bradford, B. and Stanko, E.A. (2022) 'A procedural justice theory approach to police engagement with victims and witnesses', European Journal of Criminology, 19(3), pp. 1–24.
- Hernán, M.A. and Robins, J.M. (2020) Causal Inference: What If. Boca Raton: Chapman & Hall/CRC.
- Imai, K., King, G. and Stuart, E.A. (2008) 'Misunderstandings between experimentalists and observationalists about causal inference', Journal of the Royal Statistical Society: Series A, 171(2), pp. 481–502.
- Imbens, G.W. and Rubin, D.B. (2015) Causal Inference for Statistics, Social, and Biomedical Sciences. Cambridge: Cambridge University Press.
- Jackson, J., Bradford, B., Stanko, E. and Hohl, K. (2012) 'Legitimacy, trust and compliance: An empirical test of procedural justice theory using the European Social Survey', in Tankebe, J. and Liebling, A. (eds) Legitimacy and Criminal Justice: An International Exploration. New Haven, CT: Yale University Press, pp. 326–352.
- Kahneman, D. (2011) Thinking, Fast and Slow. New York: Farrar, Straus and Giroux.

- Kinchin, N. (2024) '"Voiceless": The procedural gap in algorithmic justice', International Journal of Law and Information Technology, 32(4), pp. 1–30.
- Kleinberg, J., Mullainathan, S. and Raghavan, M. (2017) 'Inherent trade-offs in the fair determination of risk scores', Proceedings of ITCS 2017, LIPIcs 67, Article 43.
- Koehler, J.J. (1996) 'The base rate fallacy reconsidered: Normative, descriptive and methodological challenges', Behavioral and Brain Sciences, 19(1), pp. 1–53.
- Kuen, K., Nix, J. and Wolfe, S.E. (2024) 'Do procedural justice and police legitimacy lead to reporting neighborhood problems? A longitudinal analysis', Journal of Criminal Justice, 93, 102253.
- Logg, J.M., Minson, J.A. and Moore, D.A. (2019) 'Algorithm appreciation: People prefer algorithmic to human judgment', Organizational Behavior and Human Decision Processes, 151, pp. 90–103.
- Lyell, D. and Coiera, E. (2017) 'Automation bias and verification complexity: A systematic review', Journal of the American Medical Informatics Association, 24(2), pp. 423–431.
- Mentovich, A. (2023) 'Legitimacy and online proceedings: Procedural justice, access to justice, and the role of income', Law & Society Review, 57(4), pp. 617–650.
- Morrison, G.S. (2025) 'A guide to ISO 21043 forensic sciences from the forensic-data-science paradigm', Science & Justice, 65, 101298.
- Nivette, A.E. (2025) 'Assessing the causal mechanisms underlying procedural justice, legitimacy, and compliance', European Journal of Criminology, advance online, pp. 1–22.
- Nivette, A.E., et al. (2025) 'Examining the links between procedural justice, bounded authority, legitimacy and compliance', Criminal Justice and Behavior, advance online, pp. 1–25.
- Pleiss, G., Raghavan, M., Wu, F., Kleinberg, J. and Weinberger, K.Q. (2017) 'On fairness and calibration', Advances in Neural Information Processing Systems, 30.
- Robertson, B., Vignaux, G.A. and Berger, C.E.H. (2016) Interpreting Evidence: Evaluating Forensic Science in the Courtroom. 2nd edn. Chichester: Wiley.
- Sherman, L.W. (1993) 'Defiance, deterrence, and irrelevance: A theory of the criminal sanction', Journal of Research in Crime and Delinquency, 30(4), pp. 445–473.

- Skitka, L.J., Mosier, K.L. and Burdick, M. (1999) 'Does automation bias decision-making?', International Journal of Human–Computer Studies, 51(5), pp. 991–1006.
- Sunshine, J. and Tyler, T.R. (2003) 'The role of procedural justice and legitimacy in shaping public support for policing', Law & Society Review, 37(3), pp. 513–547.
- Tyler, T.R. (2006) Why People Obey the Law. 2nd edn. Princeton, NJ: Princeton University Press.
- Tyler, T.R. (2011) 'Procedural justice, legitimacy, and the effective rule of law', Crime and Justice, 40(1), pp. 283–357.
- Tyler, T.R. (2023) 'Mechanisms of legal effect: Procedural justice', [peer-reviewed/edited methods paper], pp. 1–28.
- Tyler, T.R. (2025) 'Legitimacy-based policing', Criminology & Public Policy, 24(1), pp. 1–18.
- Weisburd, D., Wood, G., MacDonald, J., Haviland, A., Ready, J., Lawton, B. and Lewis, C. (2022) 'Reforming the police through procedural justice training', Proceedings of the National Academy of Sciences, 119(2), e2118780119.
- Wieringa, M. (2023) '"Hey SyRI, tell me about algorithmic accountability": Lessons from a landmark case', Data & Policy, 5, e2.
- Williams, R. (2022) 'Accountable algorithms: Adopting the public law toolbox to scrutinise algorithmic decision-making', Current Legal Problems, 75(1), pp. 237–275.

CHAPTER XLIV

Counterfactual Justice: Simulating Alternative Sentencing Regimes

Why Counterfactuals Belong in Sentencing, And Why They Can Mislead

Every sentencing decision already contains a counterfactual, even when the judge never speaks the word. The judge is always silently comparing the sentence imposed with other sentences that could have been imposed: a shorter custodial term, a community sanction, a suspended sentence with treatment, a guideline-consistent midpoint, a risk-responsive enhancement, a rehabilitative alternative, a restorative condition. The moral claim of punishment—whether grounded in desert, prevention, rehabilitation, or communicative censure—rests on that comparison, because proportionality is always relative to plausible alternatives (Duff, 2001; Ashworth and Zedner, 2014). Counterfactual justice, then, is not a new ideology; it is an attempt to make explicit what the system does implicitly: to ask, with evidence, what would happen if we changed the regime by which sentences are selected, and to do so not with anecdote, but with disciplined simulation and causal reasoning.

Yet the moment you formalise counterfactuals, you invite a second danger: mistaking simulated precision for moral permission. A simulation can tell you what prison population might do, what average time served might do, what predicted reoffending might do under assumptions, but it cannot by itself decide whether the trade-offs are just, whether the reasons are publicly acceptable, or whether the human meaning of punishment has been hollowed out into risk management. That is why counterfactual justice must be built as a two-layer discipline. The first layer is empirical: specify the intervention and estimate its likely consequences under uncertainty. The second layer is normative and procedural: ensure that any regime change preserves contestability, equality of arms, and legitimacy cues such as voice, neutrality, and respect (Tyler, 2011). When these layers are separated, simulation becomes a tool for responsible governance. When they are collapsed, simulation becomes an instrument of managerial overreach that can launder value judgments as "what the data say."

What "Alternative Sentencing Regimes" Actually Are

In simulation terms, a sentencing regime is not merely a schedule of penalties. It is a decision system comprising eligibility rules, guideline ranges, judicial discretion, prosecutorial charging and bargaining practices, custodial capacity constraints, parole and release rules, supervision practices, and the behavioral responses of defendants and institutions. Microsimulation models of criminal justice systems are widely used to forecast prison population impacts of policy changes precisely because they can represent individuals moving through stages and accumulating time served under different rules (Sabol, 2022). The same logic extends beyond incarceration counts to broader regime design, but only if the model represents the regime as an interacting system rather than as a sentencing table.

Alternative regimes that are commonly simulated fall into a few families, and you should keep them conceptually distinct. One family is Guideline Restructuring: changing ranges, mandatory minima, enhancements, and discount structures. Another is Diversion and Substitution: replacing custody with electronic monitoring, treatment, or community sanctions for specified categories, with attention to net-widening risk (Al Weswasi and colleagues, 2025). Another is Risk-Responsive Regimes: using risk scores to intensify or relax sanctions, a family that raises fairness and responsibility concerns because risk is not culpability and because risk tools can embed arrest-driven proxies (Neil, 2025). A fourth is Capacity-Constrained Regimes: explicitly incorporating prison capacity and using prioritisation rules to allocate custody slots, which is where simulation becomes essential because the regime's effects depend on congestion dynamics rather than isolated decisions (Sabol, 2022). A fifth is Procedurally Enhanced Regimes: changes not to sentence lengths but to how reasons are produced, contested, and reviewed, which matters because legitimacy and compliance are shaped by process and not only by outcomes (Tyler, 2011).

The Forensic Analogy: Simulations Are Evidence, Not Verdicts

If you approach counterfactual sentencing as a forensic practitioner, you instinctively ask the questions that prevent epistemic inflation: what is being claimed, what is the error behavior, what are the assumptions, and what would falsify the inference. That is exactly how simulations should be treated in court-adjacent policy work. In forensic science, the modern discipline is to treat outputs as claims supported by validation and bounded by uncertainty rather than as certainty theater (Robertson, Vignaux and Berger, 2016; Morrison, 2025). Counterfactual justice should adopt the same stance. A simulation is a structured argument, not a crystal ball. Its probative value depends on model structure, parameter identification, sensitivity analysis, and external validity.

This stance matters because simulations are rhetorically powerful. A graph showing a predicted drop in prison population looks like a truth claim, and it can be used to justify reforms—or to justify harsher incapacitation policies—without exposing the normative choices encoded in the model. The correct discipline is to force the simulation to show its scaffolding: what behaviors are endogenous, what policies are assumed fixed, what feedback loops exist, and what error bounds are plausible. In other words, the simulation must be cross-examinable.

Choosing the Counterfactual: Interventions Must Be Legally and Institutionally Real

A well-posed counterfactual begins with an intervention that could actually be implemented. "What if judges were perfectly fair?" is not a policy. "What if sentencing followed a new guideline matrix with specified ranges, plus a procedural requirement for reasons and disclosure of model inputs?" is a policy. This is where causal inference discipline matters. Counterfactuals must be tied to well-defined interventions, not vague aspirations, and causal identification must be argued rather than assumed (Hernán and Robins, 2020; Imbens and Rubin, 2015). The AI era makes this more important because many proposed regimes are hybrid: guidelines plus algorithmic advice plus human overrides. If you do not define how the advice is used, your simulation is not about the regime you think you are simulating; it is about a fantasy regime.

A second requirement is institutional realism about discretion. Risk tools and algorithmic recommendations do not "apply themselves." Judges and prosecutors respond strategically, sometimes rejecting advice, sometimes deferring to it, and sometimes using it as moral cover. Empirical work on algorithmic risk assessment in the hands of humans shows that human use patterns are part of the treatment, not noise (Stevenson, 2024). A credible simulation must therefore include decision rules for human actors that are calibrated to observed behavior and bounded by plausible ranges. If you model judges as perfect optimisers, your counterfactual becomes managerial ideology, not justice forecasting.

Microsimulation: The Workhorse for Regime-Level Counterfactuals

Microsimulation models track individuals through system states—arrest, charging, plea, conviction, sentence, time served, release, supervision—and allow the modeler to adjust rules and observe aggregate outcomes such as prison populations, time served distributions, and flow through supervision. This is why microsimulation has become a dominant approach for forecasting prison populations in many jurisdictions: it handles heterogeneity, policy rule changes, and time dynamics in a way that regression alone cannot (Sabol, 2022). The strength of microsimulation for counterfactual justice is that it aligns with how regimes actually work: the regime is a pipeline with bottlenecks, and changing one rule changes flow elsewhere.

But microsimulation has a characteristic weakness: it can treat behavioral responses as exogenous or simplistic. If a diversion program is expanded, the model must consider how policing, charging, and judicial behavior might adapt, and how net-widening can occur. If a custodial threshold is raised, the model must consider whether prosecutors adjust charges or whether judges adjust within-range decisions. These adaptations can erase intended effects or create new harms. If the model does not represent adaptation, it may systematically overestimate the success of reforms or underestimate unintended consequences.

Agent-Based Models: Where Feedback Loops and Endogeneity Become Visible

Agent-based simulation is valuable when the system's behavior is not merely an accumulation of independent decisions but an emergent property of interaction—between offenders and supervision, between community context and reoffending, between treatment allocation and system capacity. Contemporary computational criminology increasingly emphasises that risk is dynamic and endogenous rather than a stable trait, which is exactly the kind of claim that makes static risk-based sentencing regimes morally and empirically suspicious. A recent agent-based simulation study models reoffense risk as a human–system interaction with endogenous feedback, finding that no single prioritisation policy dominates and that outcomes depend on capacity constraints and system dynamics. This matters because counterfactual justice is often tempted to treat risk as a fixed number you can optimise around. Agent-based approaches remind you that risk is partly produced by the regime itself.

The moral implication is sharp. If the regime produces the risk profile—by concentrating supervision, by imposing destabilising conditions, by amplifying technical violations—then a regime that punishes "risk" risks punishing the regime's own footprint. In such contexts, counterfactual justice should ask a deeper question than "What if we allocate custody to higher risk?" It should ask "What if we reduce the regime's risk-production mechanisms and shift resources toward stabilisation?" That is where simulation can become morally instructive rather than merely managerial.

Counterfactual Fairness and the Temptation to "Fix" Outcomes by Rewriting Persons

In algorithmic sentencing debates, "counterfactual" is also used in fairness discourse: counterfactual fairness asks whether an outcome would be the same in a counterfactual world where a protected attribute were different. This framework can be illuminating, but it can also be ethically treacherous if it implies that justice is achieved by imagining the person as someone else rather than by changing institutions. Recent work explicitly applies counterfactual reasoning to fairness prospects in criminal justice risk assessment, exploring how treating members of disadvantaged classes affects fairness outcomes and highlighting the complexity of fairness improvement under constraints (Berk, 2024). The policy lesson is not that counterfactual fairness is impossible; it is that fairness interventions must be evaluated as regime interventions, not merely as model tweaks. Otherwise, the system may "improve fairness" in metrics while leaving the lived structure of disadvantage untouched.

What Should Be Measured in Counterfactual Sentencing Simulations

A counterfactual regime cannot be evaluated on one outcome without committing a category error. At minimum, you must measure four dimensions simultaneously. The first is Public Safety and Harm Prevention, but in a way that distinguishes observed rearrest from underlying offending and that accounts for enforcement feedback loops (Neil, 2025; Lum and Isaac, 2016). The second is Liberty and Severity, including prison population levels, time served distribution, and the distribution of custodial versus community sanctions. The third is Equity, including disparate impact across groups and the trade-offs among fairness metrics that cannot all be satisfied simultaneously (Chouldechova, 2017; Kleinberg, Mullainathan and Raghavan, 2017). The fourth is Legitimacy and Procedural Integrity, including whether people experience the process as neutral, respectful, and contestable, because legitimacy influences compliance and cooperation beyond immediate deterrence (Tyler, 2011).

In practical simulation design, you also need to measure regime-induced behavior: failure to appear, technical violations, compliance with conditions, and downstream reentry outcomes. The incarceration and communities literature reminds us that incarceration and reentry have systemic effects that extend beyond individuals, shaping community stability and public safety in complex ways (Morenoff and Harding, 2014). Counterfactual justice should therefore include broader social impact measures where data permit, or at least treat narrow measures as incomplete.

The Procedural Constraint: A Counterfactual Regime Must Remain Contestable

A sentencing regime that cannot be challenged is not justice; it is administration. This is the rule-of-law constraint that simulations often ignore. If an alternative regime relies on proprietary risk tools, opaque optimisation, or inaccessible model logic, then even if it reduces incarceration it may degrade equality of arms and the right to challenge what is used against a person. That is why counterfactual justice cannot be only "what works"; it must be "what can be justified under public reason."

The procedural-gap critique of algorithmic justice warns that systems can appear fair on distributive metrics while leaving individuals voiceless in practice, which is a legitimacy failure (Kinchin, 2024). A simulation should therefore be paired with governance simulation: can reasons be written without "the model says," can the defence contest inputs and thresholds, can the court reconstruct the decision path, can the regime be audited continuously for drift and disparate impact?

Designing the Simulation: Identification, Validation, and Sensitivity

Counterfactual justice requires you to be honest about what is known and what is assumed. The baseline discipline is causal inference: define the intervention, specify the estimand, and separate prediction from causation (Hernán and Robins, 2020; Imbens and Rubin, 2015). The next discipline is calibration and validation: fit the model to historical data, but then test whether it reproduces known aggregate patterns not used in fitting, and whether it remains plausible under policy changes. The third discipline is sensitivity analysis: vary key assumptions—behavioral adaptation, enforcement intensity, capacity constraints, supervision strictness—and show how conclusions change. Simulation is not credible without showing how fragile it is to plausible perturbations.

The computational criminology literature has long emphasised that simulation quality is not self-evident and that models must be judged by transparency of assumptions, validation practice, and their ability to handle policy-relevant complexity rather than by sophistication alone (Berk, 2008; Auerhahn, 2002). Even when a model fits the past, it may fail under novel regimes because policies change incentives and therefore change behavior. That is why counterfactual justice should resist the urge to produce a single "best" regime. It should instead produce a map of plausible outcomes under alternative assumptions, and then allow law and politics to decide which trade-offs are acceptable.

Case Illustrations Without Parochialism: What Counterfactual Justice Has Already Been Used For

Globally, simulation has been used to forecast the impact of sentencing reforms on prison populations and costs, often as part of "justice reinvestment" and decarceration debates, and the methodological literature notes that simulation became a common tool for such forecasting across many jurisdictions (Sabol, 2022). Simulation has also been used to evaluate substitution policies such as electronic monitoring, where the counterfactual is not only "less prison" but "what replaces prison," including cost, compliance, and unintended net-widening effects (Al Weswasi et al., 2025). In risk-focused domains, counterfactual reasoning has been applied to fairness in risk assessment, showing how different policy constraints and group-treatment choices change fairness outcomes (Berk, 2024). These examples illustrate the correct posture: simulation is not a justification in itself; it is a disciplined way to anticipate consequences of regime choices that are already moral and political.

Conclusion: The Honest Purpose of Counterfactual Justice

Counterfactual justice is not the dream of perfect prediction. It is the discipline of refusing to govern by intuition when liberty is at stake. Simulations can help courts and policymakers see how regime changes might reshape incarceration, public safety, equity, and legitimacy, and they can surface unintended consequences that narrative debate routinely ignores. But simulations corrupt justice when they replace moral reasoning with managerial optimisation, when they treat risk as character, when they hide trade-offs inside technical defaults, or when they propose regimes that cannot be contested in court.

A mature counterfactual justice practice therefore has one guiding rule: the model's output is not the answer; it is evidence in a structured argument about permissible governance. The final decision—what regime we should adopt—must remain publicly justifiable, procedurally contestable, and morally owned by human institutions that can be asked to explain themselves (Tyler, 2011; Duff, 2001; Hernán and Robins, 2020). When counterfactual simulation is used in that spirit, it can deepen justice. When it is used as a substitute for reasons, it becomes merely a more efficient way to exercise power.

References

- Al Weswasi, E. et al. (2025) 'The effects of replacing incarceration with electronic monitoring: Evidence and implications', Journal of Quantitative Criminology, 41(2), pp. 1–28.
- Ashworth, A. and Zedner, L. (2014) Preventive Justice. Oxford: Oxford University Press.
- Auerhahn, K. (2002) 'Selective incapacitation, three strikes and the problem of aging prison populations: Using simulation modelling to see the future', Criminology & Public Policy, 1(3), pp. 353–388.
- Berk, R.A. (2008) 'Forecasting methods in criminal justice: Evidence and inference', Criminology & Public Policy, 7(2), pp. 137–161.
- Berk, R.A. (2024) 'Improving fairness in criminal justice algorithmic risk assessments: A counterfactual perspective', Sociological Methods & Research, 53(4), pp. 1–29.
- Chouldechova, A. (2017) 'Fair prediction with disparate impact: A study of bias in recidivism prediction instruments', Big Data, 5(2), pp. 153–163.
- Dawes, R.M., Faust, D. and Meehl, P.E. (1989) 'Clinical versus actuarial judgment', Science, 243(4899), pp. 1668–1674.
- Duff, R.A. (2001) Punishment, Communication, and Community. Oxford: Oxford University Press.
- Ensign, D., Friedler, S.A., Neville, S., Scheidegger, C. and Venkatasubramanian, S. (2018) 'Runaway feedback loops in predictive policing', Proceedings of Machine Learning Research, 81, pp. 1–12.
- Gama, J., Žliobaitė, I., Bifet, A., Pechenizkiy, M. and Bouchachia, A. (2014) 'A survey on concept drift adaptation', ACM Computing Surveys, 46(4), Article 44.
- Hernán, M.A. and Robins, J.M. (2020) Causal Inference: What If. Boca Raton: Chapman & Hall/CRC.
- Hinder, F., Artelt, A., Hammer, B. and Schultheis, E. (2024) 'Concept drift detection in deployed machine learning systems: A survey', Frontiers in Artificial Intelligence, 7, 1330257.
- Hung, T.W. et al. (2023) 'Predictive policing and algorithmic fairness', Synthese, 201, pp. 1–30.
- Imbens, G.W. and Rubin, D.B. (2015) Causal Inference for Statistics, Social, and Biomedical Sciences. Cambridge: Cambridge University Press.
- Kahneman, D. (2011) Thinking, Fast and Slow. New York: Farrar, Straus and Giroux.

- Kinchin, N. (2024) '"Voiceless": The procedural gap in algorithmic justice', International Journal of Law and Information Technology, 32(4), pp. 1–30.
- Kleinberg, J., Mullainathan, S. and Raghavan, M. (2017) 'Inherent trade-offs in the fair determination of risk scores', Proceedings of the 8th Innovations in Theoretical Computer Science Conference (ITCS 2017), LIPIcs 67, Article 43.
- Koehler, J.J. (1996) 'The base rate fallacy reconsidered: Normative, descriptive and methodological challenges', Behavioral and Brain Sciences, 19(1), pp. 1–53.
- Lum, K. and Isaac, W. (2016) 'To predict and serve?', Significance, 13(5), pp. 14–19.
- Morenoff, J.D. and Harding, D.J. (2014) 'Incarceration, prisoner reentry, and communities', Annual Review of Sociology, 40, pp. 411–429.
- Morrison, G.S. (2025) 'A guide to ISO 21043 forensic sciences from the forensic-data-science paradigm', Science & Justice, 65, 101298.
- Neil, R. (2025) 'Algorithmic bias in criminal risk assessment: The consequences of racial differences in arrest as a measure of crime', Annual Review of Criminology, 8, pp. 97–119.
- Perdomo, J.C., Zrnic, T., Mendler-Dünner, C. and Hardt, M. (2020) 'Performative prediction', Proceedings of the 37th International Conference on Machine Learning (ICML 2020), PMLR 119, pp. 7599–7609.
- Pleiss, G., Raghavan, M., Wu, F., Kleinberg, J. and Weinberger, K.Q. (2017) 'On fairness and calibration', Advances in Neural Information Processing Systems, 30.
- Robertson, B., Vignaux, G.A. and Berger, C.E.H. (2016) Interpreting Evidence: Evaluating Forensic Science in the Courtroom. 2nd edn. Chichester: Wiley.
- Sabol, W.J. (2022) 'Forecasting and criminal justice policy and practice', Crime and Justice, 51(1), pp. 1–58.
- Stevenson, M.T. (2024) 'Algorithmic risk assessment in the hands of humans', American Economic Journal: Economic Policy, 16(1), pp. 1–32.
- Tyler, T.R. (2006) Why People Obey the Law. 2nd edn. Princeton, NJ: Princeton University Press.
- Tyler, T.R. (2011) 'Procedural justice, legitimacy, and the effective rule of law', Crime and Justice, 40(1), pp. 283–357.

CHAPTER XLV

Field Trials, Ethics, and the Problem of Consent in Legal Experiments

The Seduction of "What Works" Under Coercive Power

Field trials in criminal justice arrive wearing an attractive moral costume: humility. Instead of pretending that intuition or ideology can settle hard questions, the system says, "We will test." That posture can be genuinely ethical, because the justice system has a long record of scaling interventions on confidence rather than evidence, thereby exporting error into thousands of lives. Yet the same posture becomes dangerous the moment we forget what kind of institution we are experimenting within. Courts, police, prosecution, prisons, and probation are not service providers offering optional products; they are coercive authorities. A legal experiment is therefore not simply an evaluation study; it is an intervention into liberty, dignity, and the distribution of state power. The ethical problem is not merely that experiments can go wrong. The ethical problem is that the usual protections of research ethics—especially meaningful informed consent—collide head-on with the very features that make field trials feasible in legal settings: scale, routine processing, administrative control, and asymmetry of power between institution and subject (Tyler, 2011; MacKay, 2020).

A further complication in the AI era is that legal experiments are no longer only about adding a program; they can be about adding an inferential system. When the "treatment" is a risk score, a triage tool, an algorithmic prompt, or a new way of presenting probabilistic evidence, the intervention can invisibly reshape decisions without looking like an intervention. That invisibility is ethically toxic because it can weaken contestability and erode equality of arms while the experiment is still framed as "just evaluation" (Kinchin, 2024; Williams, 2022). The core discipline, therefore, is to treat field trials in legal contexts as rule-of-law events: they must be justified not only by anticipated benefits but by procedural integrity.

The Three Consent Problems No One Can Wish Away

The consent problem in legal experiments is not one problem; it is three. The first is Practical Impossibility. Many legal interventions are delivered at the level of court processes or policing practices, where the unit of intervention is not the individual but the docket, the judge, the courtroom, the shift, the precinct, or the entire jurisdiction. This is the logic of cluster and pragmatic trials. In such designs, individual informed consent is often impracticable or incompatible with the aim of the study, and the ethics literature explicitly recognises that the inability to obtain individual consent does not necessarily make a trial unethical, provided robust justification and safeguards exist (Sim, 2012).

The second is Power Asymmetry. Even if you could ask, can the person meaningfully refuse? A defendant who is awaiting bail, a probationer facing technical violations, or a prisoner awaiting release is not situated like a consumer. The risk is coercive consent: agreement under fear of adverse treatment, real or perceived. This concern is not unique to criminal justice; it is a general feature of vulnerable populations and high-stakes institutional environments, and the ethics literature has long treated voluntariness as the hardest part of consent, not the easiest (Capron, 2018; Kalkman et al., 2017).

The third is Democratic Legitimacy. Some legal experiments are not merely studies of service delivery; they are experiments in how rights are administered. Randomisation in government can look like arbitrariness unless it is framed as a fair allocation mechanism under uncertainty and governed by publicly accountable rules. Recent political philosophy work argues that for some policy experiments, informed consent is impracticable, and the ethical question then shifts toward democratic justification: whether the trial is conducted under conditions of transparency, accountability, and fairness consistent with public reason (Picchio, 2025; MacKay, 2020).

These three problems do not produce a single answer. They produce a framework: when individual consent is not feasible, ethics must migrate from individual permission to institutional justification—without pretending that migration is morally costless.

Equipoise in Law: When Is It Ethical to Randomise Coercion?

Clinical research ethics uses the concept of equipoise: randomisation is ethically acceptable when there is genuine uncertainty about which intervention is better. Translated to law, equipoise becomes both simpler and harder. Simpler, because many justice interventions are scaled with weak evidence, so uncertainty is often real. Harder, because "better" is multi-dimensional: efficiency, public safety, dignity, equality, and legitimacy can point in different directions. The danger is that institutions declare equipoise based on one dimension—say, predicted crime reduction—while ignoring another—say, procedural justice. A trial that reduces failure to appear but increases humiliation might be "effective" and still illegitimate (Tyler, 2011).

This is where procedural justice theory is not merely a background concept; it becomes a measurement requirement. If you run field trials in courts or policing, you must treat legitimacy-related outcomes as primary, because legitimacy is itself a governance asset that shapes compliance and cooperation (Tyler, 2011; Sunshine and Tyler, 2003). When researchers ignore these outcomes, they treat justice as a production function and turn ethics into cost–benefit arithmetic.

The Unit of Intervention Determines the Ethics of Consent

In legal field trials, you must first decide what is being randomised. If you randomise individuals to different conditions of supervision, you are manipulating coercive constraints directly. If you randomise judges to different information presentations, you are manipulating reasons formation. If you randomise courtrooms to different scheduling reminders, you are manipulating access and process. The moral seriousness differs, and the consent logic differs.

This is why cluster-randomised ethics scholarship matters in criminal justice even though much of it developed in public health. The core insight is that consent can attach to different layers: the organisation may consent to implement a policy change, while individuals may receive notice and opt-out where feasible, while independent oversight ensures minimisation of risk and protection of rights (Sim, 2012). The justice-specific addition is that "organisational consent" cannot be allowed to substitute for individual fair trial protections where the intervention affects evidential weight, liberty decisions, or the ability to contest what is used against the person.

The Hidden Danger of "Minimal Risk" in Courts

In research ethics, waiver or alteration of consent is often justified on "minimal risk." Legal experiments tempt researchers to claim minimal risk because the intervention looks procedural: a reminder message, a revised script, a new form, a decision-support prompt. But minimal risk in a coercive institution is not defined only by the intervention's physical harm. It is defined by how the intervention reshapes the distribution of coercion and the person's standing before authority. A small procedural change can change detention days, and detention days change lives.

This is not speculative. Randomised trials and quasi-experiments in policing have shown that procedural justice training can change officer behaviour and downstream outcomes in measurable ways (Weisburd et al., 2022; Wood et al., 2020). The ethical lesson is not "don't experiment." It is "don't mistake procedural interventions for triviality." In justice, minor changes in the architecture of decision-making can produce major changes in liberty and legitimacy.

Consent Alternatives: Notice, Opt-Out, and Continuous Consent

When individual informed consent is not feasible, ethically defensible alternatives exist, but they must be chosen honestly and designed rigorously.

Public notice can be ethically meaningful if it is more than a poster on a wall. It must be intelligible, accessible, and tied to a remedy pathway. Opt-out can be meaningful if opting out does not trigger suspicion or penalty. Continuous consent—developed primarily in qualitative research—emphasises consent as an ongoing, revisable process rather than a one-time signature, and this concept can inform justice research designs where participant engagement occurs over time (Klykken, 2022).

Yet the justice system must confront a hard truth: some interventions cannot be ethically offered as opt-out because the "treatment" is the institution's own practice. You cannot meaningfully opt out of a judge's reasoning style or a court's scheduling system while remaining in that court. In such cases, ethics must be grounded in democratic accountability: legislative or judicial authorisation, independent ethics review, transparency about objectives and risks, and robust safeguards to prevent net harm.

The Problem of Consent When the Intervention Is AI

AI amplifies the consent problem because the intervention can be informational and yet power-altering. If a court introduces a risk score "for guidance," defendants might not even know they are in an experiment, yet their detention or sentence could be shaped. If an AI summary tool frames facts differently, the entire hearing can be contaminated by narrative anchoring. These are not merely operational changes; they are epistemic interventions. That is why the ethics of legal experimentation cannot treat AI as just another administrative tool; it must treat AI as a potential evidentiary influence.

The procedural gap critique becomes especially relevant here: even where human rights frameworks exist, individuals can be effectively voiceless if they cannot contest the tool's influence or access the basis of algorithmic claims (Kinchin, 2024). When an experiment introduces proprietary or opaque systems, the fairness problem is not merely outcome disparity; it is equality of arms. A trial that tests an opaque tool without ensuring contestability risks turning research into a pathway by which secret evidence practices become normalised.

Forensic Integrity and Experimental Design: Protecting Evidence Pathways

Forensic application is not a decorative add-on. It is the centre of ethical discipline because forensic evidence teaches you what happens when complex systems become authoritative without traceable accountability. A proper legal experiment must protect forensic integrity in three ways.

First, it must protect the interpretation chain. If AI is used to triage or interpret evidence, the experiment must log versions, decision paths, and uncertainties so that later review is possible and so that the defence can challenge the influence where appropriate. Second, it must protect the context chain. If AI-generated narratives or risk outputs are shown to decision-makers, the experiment must control sequencing to prevent contamination—just as contextual information management is used in forensic science to reduce bias (Edmond et al., 2015; Cooper, Meterko and Dror, 2019). Third, it must protect the adversarial chain. If the intervention affects evidential weight, the defence must have access to what is necessary to contest it. Without adversarial integrity, consent becomes a distraction: the deeper wrong is that the experiment has changed the nature of trial.

Governance Before Consent: The Ethical Minimum When Consent Is Weak

Where consent is impracticable or compromised by coercive context, the ethical minimum must shift toward governance. That governance should satisfy four conditions, each of which is ethically load-bearing.

The first is Public Justification: the experiment must be defensible as a fair method of resolving uncertainty, and the reasons must be stated in public-facing language that a citizen can understand (Picchio, 2025). The second is Independent Ethics Oversight: not vendor review, not internal enthusiasm, but ethics review that understands justice-specific harms and rights constraints. The third is Safeguards and Stopping Rules: clear criteria for halting the trial if harms emerge, especially disparate harms. The fourth is Remedy and Redress: a pathway for individuals to challenge errors, correct data, and obtain review of decisions influenced by the intervention.

This governance-first stance aligns with emerging discussions in public policy experimentation ethics, which emphasise that policy trials often cannot use clinical consent models and therefore require alternative legitimacy structures grounded in democratic accountability and rights protections (MacKay, 2020; Picchio, 2025).

The Long View: Why Legal Experiments Can Damage Legitimacy Even When They "Work"

The final ethical hazard is institutional: experiments can damage legitimacy even when they improve measurable outcomes. If participants feel like they were treated as test subjects rather than citizens, legitimacy drops. If randomisation is perceived as arbitrary rather than as fair allocation under uncertainty, legitimacy drops. If the intervention reduces transparency or contestability, legitimacy drops, even if the system becomes faster or "more accurate." Procedural justice theory predicts this, and legitimacy research repeatedly shows that process cues shape acceptance of authority and willingness to cooperate (Tyler, 2011).

This is why police and court experiments often generate controversy not primarily because of their results but because of how they were conducted and justified. A justice system should not need a scandal to learn what the public will not tolerate. Field trials must therefore be designed as legitimacy-sensitive governance interventions: they should measure procedural justice perceptions, track behavioural outcomes, and transparently report not only effect sizes but ethical trade-offs.

Conclusion: The Only Ethical Justification Is That Experimentation Protects People Better Than Guesswork

The problem of consent in legal experiments cannot be solved by importing the clinic's consent ritual into the courtroom. The courtroom's power asymmetries and structural constraints make that impossible in many cases. But impossibility is not permission. When consent is weak, the ethical burden shifts onto governance: public justification, independent oversight, contestability safeguards, and remedies. Field trials can be ethically defensible precisely because they can prevent the justice system from scaling untested coercion; they become unethical when they scale opacity, weaken adversarial rights, or treat legitimacy as an afterthought.

A justice system that experiments well is not one that experiments often. It is one that recognises the moral gravity of testing under coercion and therefore builds experiments as rule-of-law instruments: cautious in design, explicit in trade-offs, ruthless about procedural integrity, and humble about what evidence can and cannot justify (Sim, 2012; MacKay, 2020; Tyler, 2011).

References

- Ashworth, A. and Zedner, L. (2014) Preventive Justice. Oxford: Oxford University Press.
- Capron, A.M. (2018) 'Where did informed consent for research come from?', Journal of Law, Medicine & Ethics, 46(1), pp. 12–29.

- Chouldechova, A. (2017) 'Fair prediction with disparate impact: A study of bias in recidivism prediction instruments', Big Data, 5(2), pp. 153–163.
- Cobbe, J. (2019) 'Judicial review of automated public-sector decision-making', Legal Studies, 39(4), pp. 636–655.
- Cooper, G.S., Meterko, V. and Dror, I.E. (2019) 'Cognitive bias research in forensic science: A systematic review', Forensic Science International, 297, pp. 35–46.
- Dietvorst, B.J., Simmons, J.P. and Massey, C. (2015) 'Algorithm aversion: People erroneously avoid algorithms after seeing them err', Journal of Experimental Psychology: General, 144(1), pp. 114–126.
- Duff, R.A. (2001) Punishment, Communication, and Community. Oxford: Oxford University Press.
- Edmond, G., Towler, A., Growns, B., Ribeiro, G., Found, B., White, D. and Ballantyne, K. (2015) 'Contextual bias and cross-contamination in the forensic sciences', Law, Probability and Risk, 14(1), pp. 1–25.
- Ensign, D., Friedler, S.A., Neville, S., Scheidegger, C. and Venkatasubramanian, S. (2018) 'Runaway feedback loops in predictive policing', Proceedings of Machine Learning Research, 81, pp. 1–12.
- Evans, D.K. (2024) 'Towards improved and more transparent ethics in randomised evaluations', Ethics & Behavior, 34(2), pp. 1–22.
- Fleisher, W. (2025) 'Responsibility and accountability in an algorithmic society', AI & Society, 40, pp. 1–16.
- Gama, J., Žliobaitė, I., Bifet, A., Pechenizkiy, M. and Bouchachia, A. (2014) 'A survey on concept drift adaptation', ACM Computing Surveys, 46(4), Article 44.
- Gerber, A.S. and Green, D.P. (2012) Field Experiments: Design, Analysis, and Interpretation. New York: W.W. Norton.
- Hernán, M.A. and Robins, J.M. (2020) Causal Inference: What If. Boca Raton: Chapman & Hall/CRC.
- Imbens, G.W. and Rubin, D.B. (2015) Causal Inference for Statistics, Social, and Biomedical Sciences. Cambridge: Cambridge University Press.
- Kahneman, D. (2011) Thinking, Fast and Slow. New York: Farrar, Straus and Giroux.
- Kalkman, S., van Thiel, G.J.M.W., Zuidgeest, M.G.P., Goetz, I., Pfeiffer, B.M., Grobbee, D.E. and van Delden, J.J.M. (2017) 'Ethics of informed consent for pragmatic trials', Clinical Trials, 14(5), pp. 1–10.

- Kinchin, N. (2024) '"Voiceless": The procedural gap in algorithmic justice', International Journal of Law and Information Technology, 32(4), pp. 1–30.
- Kleinberg, J., Mullainathan, S. and Raghavan, M. (2017) 'Inherent trade-offs in the fair determination of risk scores', Proceedings of the 8th Innovations in Theoretical Computer Science Conference (ITCS 2017), LIPIcs 67, Article 43.
- Klykken, F.H. (2022) 'Implementing continuous consent in qualitative research', Qualitative Research, 22(5), pp. 1–19.
- Koehler, J.J. (1996) 'The base rate fallacy reconsidered: Normative, descriptive and methodological challenges', Behavioral and Brain Sciences, 19(1), pp. 1–53.
- Lum, K. and Isaac, W. (2016) 'To predict and serve?', Significance, 13(5), pp. 14–19.
- Lyell, D. and Coiera, E. (2017) 'Automation bias and verification complexity: A systematic review', Journal of the American Medical Informatics Association, 24(2), pp. 423–431.
- MacKay, D. (2020) The Ethics of Public Policy Experiments. Oxford: Oxford University Press.
- Morrison, G.S. (2025) 'A guide to ISO 21043 forensic sciences from the forensic-data-science paradigm', Science & Justice, 65, 101298.
- Neil, R. (2025) 'Algorithmic bias in criminal risk assessment: The consequences of racial differences in arrest as a measure of crime', Annual Review of Criminology, 8, pp. 97–119.
- Nieuwenhuizen, E. (2024) 'Algorithm registers: A box-ticking exercise or meaningful tool for transparency?', Information Polity, 29(4), pp. 415–433.
- Picchio, M. (2025) 'Policy experiments, informed consent, and democratic legitimacy', Political Philosophy, 33(2), pp. 1–25.
- Pleiss, G., Raghavan, M., Wu, F., Kleinberg, J. and Weinberger, K.Q. (2017) 'On fairness and calibration', Advances in Neural Information Processing Systems, 30.
- Robertson, B., Vignaux, G.A. and Berger, C.E.H. (2016) Interpreting Evidence: Evaluating Forensic Science in the Courtroom. 2nd edn. Chichester: Wiley.
- Sim, J. (2012) 'Informed consent and cluster-randomized trials', Journal of Medical Ethics, 38(8), pp. 1–7.

- Skitka, L.J., Mosier, K.L. and Burdick, M. (1999) 'Does automation bias decision-making?', International Journal of Human–Computer Studies, 51(5), pp. 991–1006.
- Sunshine, J. and Tyler, T.R. (2003) 'The role of procedural justice and legitimacy in shaping public support for policing', Law & Society Review, 37(3), pp. 513–547.
- Tyler, T.R. (2006) Why People Obey the Law. 2nd edn. Princeton, NJ: Princeton University Press.
- Tyler, T.R. (2011) 'Procedural justice, legitimacy, and the effective rule of law', Crime and Justice, 40(1), pp. 283–357.
- Weisburd, D., Telep, C.W., Vovak, H., Zastrow, T., Braga, A.A. and Turchan, B. (2022) 'Reforming the police through procedural justice training: A multicity randomized trial at crime hot spots', Proceedings of the National Academy of Sciences, 119(14), e2118780119.
- Williams, R. (2022) 'Accountable algorithms: Adopting the public law toolbox to scrutinise algorithmic decision-making', Current Legal Problems, 75(1), pp. 237–275.
- Wood, G., Tyler, T.R. and Papachristos, A.V. (2020) 'Procedural justice training reduces police use of force and complaints', Proceedings of the National Academy of Sciences, 117(18), pp. 9815–9821.

Part X — The Line Itself: A Normative Blueprint for Limits

CHAPTER XLVI

A Typology of Permissible Uses: Assist, Inform, Recommend, and Decide

The First Task Is Naming the Kind of Power

Before we argue about whether "AI in court" is acceptable, we must perform a more elementary act: we must name what the system is doing to judicial power. Most disputes in this field become noisy because they treat all algorithmic involvement as one phenomenon. Yet the same tool can be morally trivial in one role and constitutionally explosive in another. A spell-checker that tidies a judgment's grammar is not the same as a risk score that shapes a bail decision, and neither is the same as an automated eligibility determination that mechanically triggers detention or deportation. The law has always operated with role-sensitive doctrines—evidence versus opinion, guidance versus command, advice versus rule—and the AI era demands that we revive this discipline with sharper vocabulary (Oswald, 2018; Williams, 2022).

A usable typology must do two things at once. It must track the functional role of the system in the decision chain, and it must track the legal consequences that follow from that role. The reason is simple: the rule of law is not offended by computation as such; it is offended by unreviewable coercion, secret reasons, and decision architectures that undermine contestability and moral authorship. Modern rights and governance frameworks increasingly reflect this by distinguishing levels of risk and requiring "human oversight," transparency, and accountability tailored to context (Council of Europe, 2024; European Union, 2024).

The four-part typology that follows—Assist, Inform, Recommend, Decide—should be read as a ladder of coercive influence. Each rung changes what must be disclosed, what must be contestable, who must be accountable, and how strongly courts should insist on proportionality, explanation, and independent auditing. The typology is global in spirit because it is anchored to universal institutional functions: reasons-giving, adversarial challenge, equality of arms, and legitimacy as a psychological fact of obedience (Tyler, 2006; Tyler, 2011).

The Legal Baseline: "Solely Automated" Is Not the Real Line

Many systems begin their analysis at the familiar legal phrase "solely automated decision-making." Data protection law, most notably GDPR Article 22, restricts decisions "based solely on automated processing" that have legal or similarly significant effects, while providing exceptions and safeguards (European Union, 2016). The UK guidance similarly emphasises that Article 22-style protections attach to solely automated decisions with significant effects (ICO, 2025).

Yet as governance scholarship has stressed, "human intervention" alone is not sufficient; the meaningfulness of oversight depends on governance structures, documentation, and the ability to challenge the basis of decisions (Lazcoz and de Hert, 2023). In criminal justice, the truly dangerous zone is not always the fully automated decision. It is the hybrid, where the system is formally advisory but practically determinative because it frames attention, anchors judgment, and supplies moral cover. That is why the typology must be functional rather than merely formal. A human signature does not automatically create a human decision.

Assist: The System Improves Human Work Without Supplying Decision Reasons

In the Assist category, the system supports human work but does not supply the reasons for the coercive decision. The assistance is infrastructural: transcription, document search, translation, template filling, scheduling, redaction support, basic anomaly detection for administrative integrity, or drafting assistance that remains under explicit human control. In this role, the system's moral hazard is comparatively limited because it does not purport to tell the court what to believe or what to do. It reduces friction, not discretion.

Even here, however, two forensic cautions apply. First, assistance can create narrative contamination if it changes how facts are framed before a judge encounters primary materials, especially when generative tools summarise or rephrase evidence in a persuasive tone. Second, assistance can create record integrity risk if it silently introduces error into the official account. Forensic science has taught the justice system that small process errors—contamination, mislabeling, chain-of-custody gaps—can scale into wrongful outcomes when left un-audited (Robertson, Vignaux and Berger, 2016; Morrison, 2025). The Assist rung is therefore permissible only if it is logged, auditable, and treated as clerical support rather than as evidential authority.

Legally, Assist demands the lightest governance package: documentation of purpose, logs sufficient for correction, and safeguards against privacy leakage and hallucination in drafting tools. The right question is whether assistance is creating hidden influences on reasons-giving. If yes, it is no longer mere assistance; it is creeping into Inform.

Inform: The System Supplies Relevant Information, Not a Normative Push

Inform means the system produces information relevant to a decision without giving a recommendation about what the decision should be. Examples include retrieving similar cases, computing guideline ranges from known inputs, displaying statistical base rates, presenting validated likelihood ratios in forensic reporting, or providing structured summaries of record elements with clear sourcing. Properly designed, Inform can improve the epistemic quality of justice by reducing error and forcing explicit attention to uncertainty. It can also reduce noise by ensuring consistent access to relevant information across cases (Dawes, Faust and Meehl, 1989; Kahneman, 2011).

But Inform becomes dangerous when information is mistaken for proof. Courts have a long history of probabilistic misunderstanding, including base rate neglect and confusion of conditional probabilities, which can turn neutral statistical information into an illusion of certainty (Koehler, 1996). In AI settings, that illusion is intensified by interface design: information is presented with confidence, clean numbers, and visual authority. The forensic analogue is clear: likelihood ratios can be helpful when properly interpreted, but they can mislead when treated as posterior probabilities or as guilt indicators (Robertson, Vignaux and Berger, 2016).

A legally robust Inform regime therefore requires that informational outputs be accompanied by interpretive discipline: what the number means, what it does not mean, what assumptions underlie it, and what error bounds or validation evidence support it. This is where transparency begins to be a right-like requirement rather than a courtesy, especially as rights-based AI governance instruments stress transparency and oversight tailored to risk (Council of Europe, 2024).

Recommend: The System Suggests a Decision Path, and the Gravity Changes

Recommend is the pivotal rung because it introduces normative force. Here the system proposes an action: detain or release, increase or decrease severity, impose a condition, prioritise surveillance, escalate supervision, or classify a person as high-risk. Even if the human decision-maker remains formally responsible, recommendation systems reshape the decision environment through anchoring, automation bias, and moral cover (Skitka, Mosier and Burdick, 1999; Lyell and Coiera, 2017; Dietvorst, Simmons and Massey, 2015). Recommendation is therefore not simply "information plus." It is a governance transformation.

This is also where the fairness literature becomes legally unavoidable. The system's recommendation depends on thresholds and trade-offs among false positives and false negatives, and the impossibility results show that you cannot generally satisfy multiple fairness constraints simultaneously when base rates differ and prediction is imperfect (Chouldechova, 2017; Kleinberg, Mullainathan and Raghavan, 2017). If a recommendation tool is used in sentencing, bail, or supervision, the state has effectively chosen how to distribute errors across persons and groups. That is a moral choice masquerading as a technical setting.

Recommendation systems also intensify the proxy problem. Even when protected attributes are excluded, proxies for disadvantage can drive recommendations, producing disparate impact through data that encode historical institutional patterns (Barocas and Selbst, 2016; Neil, 2025). Risk tools trained on rearrest may partly predict policing attention rather than underlying offending, which becomes a self-fulfilling architecture when used to allocate coercion (Lum and Isaac, 2016; Ensign et al., 2018). The person is recast as probability, and probability is treated as character. In punishment theory terms, this pushes sentencing toward preventive management rather than communicative condemnation, threatening legitimacy because punishment requires reasons addressed to responsible agents (Duff, 2001).

Governance frameworks implicitly recognise this gravity by emphasising human oversight and risk-based obligations. The EU AI Act frames "human oversight" as a requirement for high-risk systems to prevent or minimise risks to fundamental rights (European Union, 2024). The Council of Europe's AI Framework Convention likewise requires measures for transparency, oversight, and accountability tailored to context and risk (Council of Europe, 2024). The practical translation is that Recommend systems must come with a strong governance package: contestability, disclosure of inputs and thresholds, independent auditing, drift monitoring, and explicit rules about how recommendations may be weighed.

Decide: When Automation Becomes the Act of Coercion

Decide is the rung where the system's output is itself the legally operative decision or triggers it mechanically, with minimal or no meaningful human intervention. Here, the system is not advising power; it is exercising it. In this domain; the moral and legal stakes rise sharply because the decision becomes less contestable in practice, and because the traditional justification structure of punishment—human reasons that can be challenged—risks collapsing into administrative rule execution.

This is where data protection's "solely automated" restriction becomes most directly relevant, because the decision is based solely on automated processing and produces legal or similarly significant effects (European Union, 2016). But criminal justice adds a deeper constraint: condemnation and liberty deprivation are not merely administrative outputs; they are public moral acts. A fully automated detention trigger, a mechanised sentencing determination, or an automated parole denial does not simply raise transparency concerns; it threatens the idea that punishment is justified through reasons addressed to a person. It also threatens equality of arms if the basis of the decision is not fully contestable.

From a rule-of-law standpoint, the Decide rung is presumptively impermissible in core criminal adjudication except in narrowly bounded administrative determinations that do not implicate contested facts, culpability, or proportionality. Even there, strong safeguards are required: notice, reasons, appeal, and meaningful human review. Governance scholarship warns that human oversight must be more than intervention; it must be governance—documentation, auditability, contestation pathways—otherwise "human in the loop" becomes a ceremonial fig leaf

(Lazcoz and de Hert, 2023).

The Hidden Fifth Category: "Assist" That Behaves Like "Decide"

The typology would be incomplete if it ignored the most common real-world pathology: category drift. Systems described as Assist or Inform often behave like Recommend or Decide in practice because institutions routinise their outputs. A tool can be formally optional yet functionally mandatory when organisational incentives punish deviation. In sentencing, a judge may be free to ignore the model yet fear blame if ignoring leads to a rare catastrophic outcome. In policing, a "lead" may drive investigative focus that later becomes evidence, creating path-dependence. In procurement, vendor tools become infrastructural, and infrastructure becomes destiny.

This is why any permissible-use typology must be coupled to a use audit, not merely a design label. Levy, Chasalow and Riley's survey of algorithms in the public sector stresses that adoption, procurement, and institutional use shape outcomes as much as technical properties do (Levy, Chasalow and Riley, 2021). If a system is being treated as determinative, it must be governed as Recommend or Decide even if the contract calls it "support." The law should treat this as a rebuttable presumption: where empirical evidence shows systematic deference to outputs, the system must be regulated at the higher rung.

The Forensic Discipline: Treat Outputs as Evidence-Like Claims With Error Behavior

Across all rungs above Assist, forensic discipline becomes central. Courts should treat algorithmic outputs as evidence-like claims that require validation under conditions of use, explicit uncertainty communication, and interpretive boundaries. The forensic-data-science paradigm insists that evidence evaluation must be explicit about error and limitations rather than relying on intuition and authority (Morrison, 2025). The same is true of risk scores and recommendations. A number without error is not scientific; it is persuasive theatre.

This discipline also helps resolve a moral confusion. The question is not whether probability belongs in court; probability already belongs. The question is whether probabilistic tools are used in a way that preserves burdens of proof, proportionality, and contestability. Probability can inform; it must not replace proof. It can recommend; it must not become condemnation.

A Permission Framework: What Each Rung Must Satisfy

A typology is only useful if it is normatively operational. The following permission structure follows from the ladder's logic and aligns with emerging governance instruments that demand oversight tailored to risk (Council of Europe, 2024; European Union, 2024).

- Assist is permissible when it is auditable, correctable, and does not shape evidential interpretation invisibly.
- Inform is permissible when information is traceable to sources, interpretively disciplined, and does not smuggle policy judgments as "facts."
- Recommend is permissible only when contestability is real: inputs are disclosable, thresholds and validation are scrutinised, fairness trade-offs are explicit, drift is monitored, and human reasons remain independent of "the model says."
- Decide is presumptively impermissible for core criminal justice determinations of guilt, liberty deprivation, and punishment severity. Where used for narrow administrative determinations, it must be bounded by transparent rules, meaningful human review, and robust appeal rights, consistent with rights-based restrictions on solely automated decisions (European Union, 2016; ICO, 2025).

Conclusion: The Line Is Not "AI or No AI," It Is the Architecture of Reasons

The criminal justice system does not need a single yes-or-no answer to AI. It needs an architecture of permissible uses that preserves what makes adjudication law rather than administration: reasons that can be contested, evidence that can be tested, and power that can be held accountable. The Assist–Inform–Recommend–Decide ladder provides a disciplined vocabulary for that architecture. It also exposes the central lesson of modern governance: the danger is not computation; it is ownerless coercion—decisions that no one can meaningfully explain, challenge, or take responsibility for.

When the typology is used honestly, it prevents the oldest trick in this domain: calling a determinative system "assistance" and then acting surprised when legitimacy collapses. If we govern by function rather than labels, we can draw a line that is firm where it must be firm—at coercion without contestability—and flexible where it can be flexible—at assistance and information that improve accuracy without replacing judgment.

References

- Ashworth, A. and Zedner, L. (2014) Preventive Justice. Oxford: Oxford University Press.
- Barocas, S. and Selbst, A.D. (2016) 'Big data's disparate impact', California Law Review, 104(3), pp. 671–732.
- Chouldechova, A. (2017) 'Fair prediction with disparate impact: A study of bias in recidivism prediction instruments', Big Data, 5(2), pp. 153–163.
- Council of Europe (2024) Framework Convention on Artificial Intelligence and Human Rights, Democracy and the Rule of Law (CETS No. 225). Strasbourg: Council of Europe.
- Dawes, R.M., Faust, D. and Meehl, P.E. (1989) 'Clinical versus actuarial judgment', Science, 243(4899), pp. 1668–1674.
- Dietvorst, B.J., Simmons, J.P. and Massey, C. (2015) 'Algorithm aversion: People erroneously avoid algorithms after seeing them err', Journal of Experimental Psychology: General, 144(1), pp. 114–126.
- Duff, R.A. (2001) Punishment, Communication, and Community. Oxford: Oxford University Press.
- Ensign, D., Friedler, S.A., Neville, S., Scheidegger, C. and Venkatasubramanian, S. (2018) 'Runaway feedback loops in predictive policing', Proceedings of Machine Learning Research, 81, pp. 1–12.
- European Union (2016) Regulation (EU) 2016/679 of the European Parliament and of the Council of 27 April 2016 (General Data Protection Regulation), Article 22.
- European Union (2024) Regulation (EU) 2024/1689 of the European Parliament and of the Council (Artificial Intelligence Act). Brussels: European Union.

- ICO (2025) 'What does the UK GDPR say about automated decision-making and profiling?', UK Information Commissioner's Office Guidance.
- Kahneman, D. (2011) Thinking, Fast and Slow. New York: Farrar, Straus and Giroux.
- Kinchin, N. (2024) '"Voiceless": The procedural gap in algorithmic justice', International Journal of Law and Information Technology, 32(4), pp. 1–30.
- Kleinberg, J., Mullainathan, S. and Raghavan, M. (2017) 'Inherent trade-offs in the fair determination of risk scores', Proceedings of the 8th Innovations in Theoretical Computer Science Conference (ITCS 2017), LIPIcs 67, Article 43.
- Koehler, J.J. (1996) 'The base rate fallacy reconsidered: Normative, descriptive and methodological challenges', Behavioral and Brain Sciences, 19(1), pp. 1–53.
- Lazcoz, G. and de Hert, P. (2023) 'Humans in the GDPR and AIA governance of automated decision-making', Computer Law & Security Review, 49, 1058xx.
- Levy, K., Chasalow, K.E. and Riley, S. (2021) 'Algorithms and decision-making in the public sector', Annual Review of Law and Social Science, 17, pp. 309–334.
- Lum, K. and Isaac, W. (2016) 'To predict and serve?', Significance, 13(5), pp. 14–19.
- Morrison, G.S. (2025) 'A guide to ISO 21043 forensic sciences from the forensic-data-science paradigm', Science & Justice, 65, 101298.
- Neil, R. (2025) 'Algorithmic bias in criminal risk assessment: The consequences of racial differences in arrest as a measure of crime', Annual Review of Criminology, 8, pp. 97–119.
- Oswald, M. (2018) 'Algorithm-assisted decision-making in the public sector', Philosophical Transactions of the Royal Society A, 376(2128), 20170359.
- Pasquale, F. (2015) The Black Box Society: The Secret Algorithms That Control Money and Information. Cambridge, MA: Harvard University Press.
- Pleiss, G., Raghavan, M., Wu, F., Kleinberg, J. and Weinberger, K.Q. (2017) 'On fairness and calibration', Advances in Neural Information Processing Systems, 30.

- Robertson, B., Vignaux, G.A. and Berger, C.E.H. (2016) Interpreting Evidence: Evaluating Forensic Science in the Courtroom. 2nd edn. Chichester: Wiley.
- Skitka, L.J., Mosier, K.L. and Burdick, M. (1999) 'Does automation bias decision-making?', International Journal of Human–Computer Studies, 51(5), pp. 991–1006.
- Tyler, T.R. (2006) Why People Obey the Law. 2nd edn. Princeton, NJ: Princeton University Press.
- Tyler, T.R. (2011) 'Procedural justice, legitimacy, and the effective rule of law', Crime and Justice, 40(1), pp. 283–357.
- Williams, R. (2022) 'Accountable algorithms: Adopting the public law toolbox to scrutinise algorithmic decision-making', Current Legal Problems, 75(1), pp. 237–275.

CHAPTER XLVII

Red Lines and Bright Lines: Where AI Must Never Replace Human Judgement

The Point of Red Lines Is Not Fear, It Is Constitutional Honesty

When a legal system draws a red line, it is not confessing irrationality about machines. It is confessing something far more sober: that certain acts of state power are only legitimate when they are owned by human reasons, expressed in public language, and exposed to adversarial challenge. In criminal justice, the state does not merely manage risk; it condemns, restrains, and brands. That authority is tolerable only because it is supposed to operate through reasons that can be contested and reviewed, not through outputs that must be accepted. The AI era tempts courts to confuse prediction with proof and optimisation with justification, and the purpose of bright lines is to stop that confusion before it becomes routine (Duff, 2001; Tyler, 2011; Chiao, 2024).

You already know the institutional psychology that makes bright lines necessary. Decision-makers under pressure grasp for compression, and numerical compression arrives with an authority cue. That authority cue activates automation bias, anchoring, and blame-avoidance, producing a subtle drift in moral ownership: the human remains formally responsible while practically deferring to the model, especially when outcomes are high-stakes and verification is complex (Skitka, Mosier and Burdick, 1999; Lyell and Coiera, 2017; Dietvorst, Simmons and Massey, 2015). This is why a mere promise of "human in the loop" is inadequate. Contemporary scholarship on judges' oversight roles under high-risk decision support systems argues that "judges-in-the-loop" cannot, by themselves, reliably safeguard judicial values and rights, precisely because the oversight burden and the cognitive environment exceed what individual judicial discretion can realistically bear (Banks, 2026).

A red line, then, is a design constraint on power. It says: there are decision points at which AI may assist, but may not replace human judgement, because replacement would dissolve contestability, deform responsibility, or hollow out the moral meaning of punishment.

The Four Functions That Must Remain Human

To draw bright lines coherently, you must identify the functions of criminal adjudication that are not reducible to prediction.

The first function is Public Reason-Giving. Courts must explain coercion in ordinary legal language, not in model language. Even excellent statistical evidence does not write reasons; it only supplies information that reasons may incorporate. A system that replaces reasons with outputs converts adjudication into administration.

The second function is Adversarial Contestability. The trial is not a performance; it is a testing mechanism. When a model's internal basis cannot be meaningfully challenged—because it is opaque, proprietary, or too complex to reconstruct—equality of arms collapses in practice, even if the decision remains formally "human." The procedural gap critique captures this precisely: algorithmic governance often improves distributive metrics while leaving "voice" and procedural legitimacy thin or absent (Kinchin, 2024).

The third function is Moral Attribution. Punishment is condemnation, not merely risk management. The institution must be able to say, credibly, "We are holding you responsible for this act," and to calibrate severity in a way that remains intelligible as a response to culpability rather than as a preventive optimisation. Communicative accounts of punishment make this point unavoidable: punishment addresses the offender as an agent and relies on the meaning of censure, not only on future effects (Duff, 2001).

The fourth function is Human Encounter and Dignity. Legitimacy is a psychological fact: people comply and cooperate not only because of fear, but because the system is experienced as neutral, respectful, and attentive to voice (Tyler, 2006; Tyler, 2011). When a person feels processed rather than heard, legitimacy corrodes even when decisions are "accurate." Bright lines protect these functions where they are most vulnerable.

Bright Line One: AI Must Never Determine Guilt or Legal Liability

There is a simple reason guilt cannot be automated: guilt is not a predictive classification problem. It is a legal conclusion built from contested facts, credibility assessments, burdens of proof, and normative judgments about intent and justification. A model can help search documents, flag inconsistencies, or summarise evidence, but it must never be allowed to output "guilty" or "liable" as the operative determination, because that would replace proof with statistical patterning and would relocate the burden of challenge from the state to the accused. The danger is not only error; it is epistemic category confusion. Statistical evidence can be relevant, but it is not identical to proof, and courts have a history of misreading probabilistic claims, especially when base rates and conditional probabilities are poorly understood (Koehler, 1996; Robertson, Vignaux and Berger, 2016).

The forensic lesson is instructive. Forensic science has learned—through scandal and reform—that the credibility of evidential claims depends on validation, error awareness, and disciplined interpretation. The same discipline cannot survive if the system treats pattern recognition as liability itself. In that world, the model becomes a silent witness whose testimony cannot be cross-examined. No serious fair-trial system can accept that as legitimate adjudication.

Bright Line Two: AI Must Never Replace Human Judgement on Credibility and Testimony

Credibility is not merely a matter of detecting lies; it is the court's synthesis of coherence, consistency, context, and the lived realities that shape memory and testimony. AI systems that claim to infer deception from facial movement, voice features, or behavioural cues carry a special danger: they invite the court to mistake contested behavioural science for mechanical truth. The evidence base for many deception-detection technologies is disputed, and even where correlations exist, the legal question remains: should a court permit an automated inference about truthfulness to displace the human duty to listen, probe, and reason?

Moreover, credibility judgments are structurally vulnerable to bias. If a model is trained on historical decisions, it risks re-importing institutional patterns of disbelief and differential credibility into the present under the banner of objectivity, which is simply bias laundering in technical clothing (Barocas and Selbst, 2016). This is precisely the scenario in which "assistive" tools become corrupting: they do not merely inform; they frame and anchor, and anchoring in credibility domains is an integrity disaster. The bright line is therefore necessary: AI may assist the management of testimony, but it must never become the arbiter of credibility.

Bright Line Three: AI Must Never Determine the Severity of Punishment

Sentencing is the paradigmatic zone where prediction threatens to swallow judgment. The system is tempted to say: if we can forecast risk, we can optimise severity to reduce harm. Yet punishment is not a spreadsheet of expected value. It is a moral act that must remain anchored to culpability, proportionality, and public justification. Once severity is set by a model, punishment ceases to be a communicative response to wrongdoing and becomes a preventive management regime, a shift that communicative and desert-based theories have long warned against (Duff, 2001; Ashworth and Zedner, 2014).

This does not mean risk evidence is irrelevant. It means risk must remain evidentially bounded and normatively subordinate. Risk can inform conditions, supervision planning, or rehabilitative support, but it cannot become the algorithmic engine of severity without collapsing the distinction between what the person did and what the model fears the person might do. Criminological and fairness research adds another danger: risk instruments often use rearrest and institutional contact as targets and predictors, which can encode enforcement patterns rather than stable personal traits (Neil, 2025). In such circumstances, algorithmic severity can become a way of punishing the system's own history.

The bright line is therefore principled: AI may support sentencing by improving information integrity, but severity must remain the product of human-authored reasons that can be appealed, criticised, and understood as moral justification rather than optimisation.

Bright Line Four: AI Must Never Be the Decisive Gatekeeper of Liberty at the Point of Bail and Pretrial Detention

Pretrial detention is the coercive act most likely to be justified by "risk" and therefore most likely to become algorithmised. Yet liberty before conviction is one of the system's most fragile moral commitments. If a model becomes the decisive gatekeeper, the presumption of innocence is not formally repealed but practically weakened, because the person's freedom depends on a forecast rather than on reasons grounded in evidence and necessity.

The most serious danger here is not that models are imperfect—that is obvious. The danger is that models can be systematically misused: thresholds become default, judges over-rely because blame for under-detaining is politically louder than blame for over-detaining, and contestability becomes thin because the person cannot meaningfully challenge the basis of the score. This is the procedural gap again, now attached to liberty (Kinchin, 2024).

A legitimate system may use structured risk information to avoid arbitrary detention, but it must draw a bright line against algorithmic determinism: detention must be justified through human reasons that explicitly confront necessity, proportionality, and the possibility of less restrictive alternatives.

Bright Line Five: AI Must Never Supply Secret Reasons That Cannot Be Adversarially Tested

Even a formally "advisory" model becomes illegitimate when its basis is inaccessible. Trade secrecy and proprietary protections might be tolerable in consumer settings with regulatory oversight, but in criminal justice they collide with equality of arms because the accused faces the full weight of the state's coercion. If the state relies on a model output that materially shapes outcomes, and the defence cannot test the model's inputs, validation evidence, and threshold rules, then the adversarial process is hollowed out. It becomes a hearing around an unchallengeable influence.

This is why scholarship on explainability warns against false comfort: explanation can become theatre, providing an intuitive story while preserving the black box's authority (Selbst and Barocas, 2018). It is also why the interpretable-models argument matters in justice: in high-stakes contexts, relying on black boxes and then "explaining" them is inferior to using inherently interpretable models where possible, because interpretability is part of accountability, not merely a usability feature (Rudin, 2019).

The bright line here is strict: no one should lose liberty or suffer enhanced punishment because of a model whose core basis cannot be meaningfully contested. If contestability cannot be achieved, the model's role must be reduced to non-determinative assistance, or removed.

Bright Line Six: AI Must Never Normalise Mass Biometric Identification as Ordinary Governance

Biometric identification, especially when deployed at scale in public space, is a unique threat because it changes the baseline conditions of freedom. It converts ordinary movement into potential suspicion and makes the public legible to power in a way that is difficult to reverse. Rights-based governance trajectories increasingly recognise this as a zone requiring strict limits and oversight, and contemporary legal frameworks treat certain biometric uses as exceptionally sensitive, including through bans or tightly constrained exceptions with prior authorisation and safeguards (European regulatory analysis and treaty scholarship: van Kolfschooten, 2023; Rotenberg, 2025).

The criminal justice risk is not only misidentification. It is the transformation of policing from targeted investigation into ambient surveillance, which then feeds data back into risk systems, producing self-confirming patterns. The predictive policing literature has shown how feedback loops can make a system appear accurate while it is reproducing its own attention (Lum and Isaac, 2016; Ensign et al., 2018). In that ecosystem, biometric identification becomes a generator of suspicion rather than a tool of evidence. The bright line is therefore principled: biometric AI must not become an ordinary replacement for human investigative judgment in public life, because its systemic effects on democracy and rule-of-law conditions are too large.

Bright Line Seven: AI Must Never Automate Escalation in Punitive Supervision

Supervision regimes—probation, parole, community monitoring—are fertile ground for algorithmic escalation: risk flags trigger more conditions, more surveillance triggers more technical violations, technical violations trigger custody, custody destabilises, destabilisation increases risk, and the loop tightens. If AI becomes the automatic escalation engine, the system manufactures its own evidence of "noncompliance." This is not speculation; it is the logic of feedback loops applied to supervision.

From a behavioural and legitimacy perspective, such systems teach people that compliance is less about moral alignment and more about avoiding algorithmic suspicion. That erodes the legitimacy foundations that procedural justice research identifies as crucial for cooperation (Tyler, 2011). The bright line therefore insists that escalation in supervision—where the state increases coercion in response to perceived risk—must remain a human-authored decision justified by reasons and sensitive to context, not a mechanical reflex.

The Governance Rule: Bright Lines Require Bright Accountability

Bright lines are not maintained by moral speeches; they are maintained by institutional design. If a jurisdiction says "AI will not replace human judgment," it must also ensure that human judgment remains meaningful. Banks' analysis of judges-in-the-loop underscores that oversight cannot be placed solely on the end user; governance must be shared across providers, institutions, and oversight structures, with documentation, auditing, and realistic expectations of human capacity (Banks, 2026).

This leads to a final, practical constraint: where AI is permitted to assist or inform, it must be embedded in an accountability regime that preserves contestability and traceability. That means versioning, logs, disclosure of what influenced the decision, validation under conditions of use, and independent auditing. It also means training judges to resist automation bias and to interpret statistical claims without treating them as proof.

Conclusion: Human Judgement Must Remain the Public Face of Coercion

A bright-line framework is not anti-technology. It is pro-legitimacy. It recognises that criminal justice is not merely an optimisation problem but a moral and procedural institution that must remain answerable to the people it governs. AI may assist, inform, and even recommend under strict safeguards, but it must never replace human judgment in the places where the system's moral authorship, contestability, and dignity are at stake: guilt, credibility, liberty deprivation, and punishment severity. If those functions are automated, the system may become efficient, but it will become less like law and more like administration, and administration is not enough to justify condemnation.

In short, the red lines exist to preserve a simple promise: if the state restrains you, it must be able to explain itself in human reasons, and you must be able to challenge those reasons as an equal in the only arena that matters—the courtroom.

References

- Ashworth, A. and Zedner, L. (2014) Preventive Justice. Oxford: Oxford University Press.
- Banks, I. (2026) 'Judges-in-the-loop? Judicial involvement in human oversight of high-risk decision support systems', International Journal of Law and Information Technology, advance article.
- Barocas, S. and Selbst, A.D. (2016) 'Big data's disparate impact', California Law Review, 104(3), pp. 671–732.
- Berk, R., Heidari, H., Jabbari, S., Kearns, M. and Roth, A. (2021) 'Fairness in criminal justice risk assessments: The state of the art', Sociological Methods & Research, 50(1), pp. 3–44.
- Chiao, V. (2024) 'Algorithmic decision-making, statistical evidence and the rule of law', Episteme, 21(4), pp. 1–23.
- Chouldechova, A. (2017) 'Fair prediction with disparate impact: A study of bias in recidivism prediction instruments', Big Data, 5(2), pp. 153–163.
- Dawes, R.M., Faust, D. and Meehl, P.E. (1989) 'Clinical versus actuarial judgment', Science, 243(4899), pp. 1668–1674.
- Dietvorst, B.J., Simmons, J.P. and Massey, C. (2015) 'Algorithm aversion: People erroneously avoid algorithms after seeing them err', Journal of Experimental Psychology: General, 144(1), pp. 114–126.
- Duff, R.A. (2001) Punishment, Communication, and Community. Oxford: Oxford University Press.
- Edmond, G., Towler, A., Growns, B., Ribeiro, G., Found, B., White, D. and Ballantyne, K. (2015) 'Contextual bias and cross-contamination in the forensic sciences', Law, Probability and Risk, 14(1), pp. 1–25.
- Enqvist, L. (2023) 'Discretion, automation, and proportionality', in Suksi, M. (ed.) The Rule of Law and Automated Decision-Making: Exploring Fundamentals of Algorithmic Governance. Cham: Springer, pp. 169–205.

- Ensign, D., Friedler, S.A., Neville, S., Scheidegger, C. and Venkatasubramanian, S. (2018) 'Runaway feedback loops in predictive policing', Proceedings of Machine Learning Research, 81, pp. 1–12.
- Fleisher, W. (2025) 'Responsibility and accountability in an algorithmic society', AI & Society, 40, pp. 1–16.
- Garrett, B.L. (2023) 'Interpretable algorithmic forensics', Proceedings of the National Academy of Sciences, 120(41), e2301842120.
- Gikay, A.A. (2025) 'Trade secrecy in automated decisions: Against the myth of a complete barrier to transparency', Journal of Intellectual Property Law & Practice, 20(8), pp. 552–565.
- Kahneman, D. (2011) Thinking, Fast and Slow. New York: Farrar, Straus and Giroux.
- Kinchin, N. (2024) '"Voiceless": The procedural gap in algorithmic justice', International Journal of Law and Information Technology, 32(4), pp. 1–30.
- Kleinberg, J., Mullainathan, S. and Raghavan, M. (2017) 'Inherent trade-offs in the fair determination of risk scores', Proceedings of the 8th Innovations in Theoretical Computer Science Conference (ITCS 2017), LIPIcs 67, Article 43.
- Koehler, J.J. (1996) 'The base rate fallacy reconsidered: Normative, descriptive and methodological challenges', Behavioral and Brain Sciences, 19(1), pp. 1–53.
- Logg, J.M., Minson, J.A. and Moore, D.A. (2019) 'Algorithm appreciation: People prefer algorithmic to human judgment', Organizational Behavior and Human Decision Processes, 151, pp. 90–103.
- Lum, K. and Isaac, W. (2016) 'To predict and serve?', Significance, 13(5), pp. 14–19.
- Lyell, D. and Coiera, E. (2017) 'Automation bias and verification complexity: A systematic review', Journal of the American Medical Informatics Association, 24(2), pp. 423–431.
- Miller, T. (2019) 'Explanation in artificial intelligence: Insights from the social sciences', Artificial Intelligence, 267, pp. 1–38.
- Morrison, G.S. (2025) 'A guide to ISO 21043 forensic sciences from the forensic-data-science paradigm', Science & Justice, 65, 101298.
- Neil, R. (2025) 'Algorithmic bias in criminal risk assessment: The consequences of racial differences in arrest as a measure of crime', Annual Review of Criminology, 8, pp. 97–119.

- Nieuwenhuizen, E. (2024) 'Algorithm registers: A box-ticking exercise or meaningful tool for transparency?', Information Polity, 29(4), pp. 415–433.
- Oswald, M. (2018) 'Algorithm-assisted decision-making in the public sector', Philosophical Transactions of the Royal Society A, 376(2128), 20170359.
- Pleiss, G., Raghavan, M., Wu, F., Kleinberg, J. and Weinberger, K.Q. (2017) 'On fairness and calibration', Advances in Neural Information Processing Systems, 30.
- Robertson, B., Vignaux, G.A. and Berger, C.E.H. (2016) Interpreting Evidence: Evaluating Forensic Science in the Courtroom. 2nd edn. Chichester: Wiley.
- Rotenberg, M. (2025) 'Framework Convention on Artificial Intelligence and Human Rights, Democracy and the Rule of Law (Council of Europe)', International Legal Materials, 64(—), pp. —.
- Rudin, C. (2019) 'Stop explaining black box machine learning models for high stakes decisions and use interpretable models instead', Nature Machine Intelligence, 1, pp. 206–215.
- Selbst, A.D. and Barocas, S. (2018) 'The intuitive appeal of explainable machines', Fordham Law Review, 87(3), pp. 1085–1139.
- Skitka, L.J., Mosier, K.L. and Burdick, M. (1999) 'Does automation bias decision-making?', International Journal of Human–Computer Studies, 51(5), pp. 991–1006.
- Sunshine, J. and Tyler, T.R. (2003) 'The role of procedural justice and legitimacy in shaping public support for policing', Law & Society Review, 37(3), pp. 513–547.
- Tyler, T.R. (2006) Why People Obey the Law. 2nd edn. Princeton, NJ: Princeton University Press.
- Tyler, T.R. (2011) 'Procedural juştice, legitimacy, and the effective rule of law', Crime and Justice, 40(1), pp. 283–357.
- van Kolfschooten, H. (2023) 'The Council of Europe's AI Convention (2023–2024)', AI & Society, 38(—), pp. —.
- Wachter, S., Mittelstadt, B. and Russell, C. (2018) 'Counterfactual explanations without opening the black box: Automated decisions and the GDPR', Harvard Journal of Law & Technology, 31(2), pp. 841–887.
- Wieringa, M. (2023) '"Hey SyRI, tell me about algorithmic accountability": Lessons from a landmark case', Data & Policy, 5, e2.

- Williams, R. (2022) 'Accountable algorithms: Adopting the public law toolbox to scrutinise algorithmic decision-making', Current Legal Problems, 75(1), pp. 237–275.

CHAPTER XLVIII

A Constitutional Theory of Algorithmic Punishment

The Constitutional Question Behind the Technical Question

When punishment becomes "algorithmic," the central constitutional question is not whether a model is accurate. Accuracy is a property of instruments; constitutional legitimacy is a property of power. The question is whether the state may transform condemnation and liberty deprivation into a regime of prediction-assisted governance without dissolving the rule-of-law conditions that make punishment tolerable in the first place: public reasons, contestability, equality of arms, proportionality, and accountable authorship. If we cannot answer that, we will keep arguing about dashboards while the deeper transformation proceeds unnoticed.

A constitutional theory of algorithmic punishment must begin with a stubborn premise that lawyers sometimes forget in their fascination with technology: punishment is not merely an outcome. It is an institutional act of public censure, backed by coercion, addressed to a person as a responsible agent, and justified through reasons that can be challenged (Duff, 2001). When algorithmic systems enter sentencing, bail, supervision escalation, and even evidential interpretation, they do not merely add information. They alter the architecture of justification by changing what counts as a reason, what counts as evidence, and who can challenge the basis of coercion. That is why constitutional analysis cannot be postponed until after deployment. Once an algorithm becomes infrastructure, it becomes politically difficult to remove, and legality starts to adapt around it.

A final premise is psychological, and it is constitutional in consequence: legitimacy is partly a fact about obedience. People obey courts not only because they fear sanctions but because they perceive procedures as neutral, respectful, and voice-granting (Tyler, 2006; Tyler, 2011). A system that preserves outcomes while degrading voice and intelligible reason-giving can still become illegitimate in the lived experience of those it governs. That legitimacy loss is not cosmetic; it is a governance failure.

Punishment as Public Reason, Not Merely Risk Management

The constitutional tradition, across legal families, treats the criminal process as the paradigmatic domain where the state must justify itself. The common moral grammar of criminal law distinguishes what the person did (a past act) from what the state fears the person might do (a forecast). Preventive measures exist, but they carry special burdens because they strain the presumption of innocence and the idea that severity tracks culpability (Ashworth and Zedner, 2014). Algorithmic punishment threatens to blur that line by making risk appear like character and forecasting appear like blameworthiness.

This is not a metaphysical objection to statistics. It is a structural objection to a particular substitution: replacing public reason-giving with model-driven optimisation. Desert and communicative theories insist that punishment must be capable of being justified as a response to wrongdoing, not merely as a cost-effective mechanism to prevent harm (Duff, 2001). Even utilitarian and deterrent frameworks presuppose legality constraints: predictable rules, evidentiary discipline, and proportionality boundaries. A constitutional theory therefore treats the move from discretion to delegation as a change in the nature of punishment itself, not merely a change in how information is processed.

The Constitutional Functions That Algorithms Strain

A workable theory identifies the constitutional functions that algorithmic systems strain, and it does so without pretending that every legal system uses the same doctrinal vocabulary. Four functions recur.

First, Legality and Determinacy. Modern algorithmic systems demand specification: legal concepts must be translated into computational form. Yet law often relies on principled vagueness and open-textured standards to preserve proportionality and context-sensitive judgment. A 2025 jurisprudential argument warns that algorithmic systems' demand for clarity can undermine a core virtue of legal reasoning—its principled vagueness—by forcing premature specificity that can distort normative concepts (Erickson, 2025).

Second, Due Process as Voice and Contestation. When a model influences detention or sentencing, the affected person must be able to contest the basis of that influence. Yet procedural mechanisms often fail to supply meaningful voice regarding algorithmic tools, producing what has been called a "procedural gap," especially where trade secrecy and opacity block adversarial testing (Kinchin, 2024).

Third, Equality of Arms. If the state relies on an algorithmic inference while the defence cannot inspect inputs, assumptions, validation evidence, or drift, the adversarial structure becomes ceremonial. The conflict between proprietary protections and fair-trial contestation is not a niche dispute; it is a structural threat to equality of arms in any system that claims to decide through reasons.

Fourth, Proportionality and Individualised Justice. Algorithmic tools often operate at the level of groups and base rates. But punishment is imposed on individuals. Philosophical and evidence-law analyses warn that statistical evidence about groups can be relevant yet dangerously seductive, because it encourages officials to treat population-level regularities as if they were determinate facts about the person (Chiao, 2024). The constitutional implication is that any predictive instrument must remain evidentially bounded and normatively subordinate to individualised justification.

Algorithmic Punishment as a Shift in the Burden of Justification

The deepest constitutional danger is not that algorithms err. It is that they can shift burdens without announcing the shift. When a judge sees a risk score early, it becomes an anchor. When the judge later writes reasons, those reasons often move to rationalise the anchored conclusion. Automation bias and verification complexity research predicts this pattern under time pressure and high stakes (Skitka, Mosier and Burdick, 1999; Lyell and Coiera, 2017). The consequence is that the accused may experience the hearing as an attempt to dislodge a number rather than an opportunity to be heard as a person.

A constitutional theory therefore treats algorithmic outputs as powerful evidential artefacts that can invert the practical burden: instead of the state proving necessity for detention or proportional severity, the defendant feels compelled to prove that the algorithm's inference is wrong. This is an inversion of the moral shape of criminal adjudication, even where formal burdens remain unchanged. It also explains why controversies recur around proprietary risk assessments: the issue is not merely transparency as curiosity; it is transparency as the precondition of meaningful challenge.

The Two Constitutional Categories of Algorithmic Involvement

To draw lines, the theory distinguishes two categories of algorithmic involvement. The first is Evidential Assistance. Here the system supports fact-finding and reasoning without supplying coercive conclusions. Examples include document retrieval, consistency checks, evidence indexing, and—where properly validated—transparent statistical reporting that is presented as evidential weight rather than as proof. This category is constitutionally manageable if it is auditable, explainable in ordinary legal terms, and does not degrade contestability.

The second is Normative Substitution. Here the system supplies a recommendation or decision that effectively substitutes for the human task of justification: detain/release recommendations, severity optimisation, automated supervision escalation, or any output that becomes practically determinative. This category is constitutionally suspect because it relocates moral authorship away from the public institution and into an instrument that cannot bear blame, cannot be cross-examined as a person, and often cannot be inspected as a system.

A constitutional theory insists that the closer an algorithm moves toward normative substitution, the stronger the governance obligations must be: contestability, disclosure of inputs and thresholds, independent auditing, drift monitoring, and explicit rules that prohibit "the model says" from becoming the decisive reason.

Proportionality Under Algorithmic Pressure

Proportionality is often invoked as a balancing test, but in algorithmic punishment it becomes a structural discipline: the state must show not only that the aim is legitimate and the measure is suitable, but that the measure is necessary given less rights-restrictive alternatives and that the balance is justified for the individual case. This becomes harder when the state relies on opaque tools, because opacity blocks the ability to evaluate necessity and balance in a concrete way.

Fairness research adds an uncomfortable constraint. It is mathematically and practically difficult to satisfy multiple fairness criteria simultaneously when base rates differ and prediction is imperfect (Chouldechova, 2017; Kleinberg, Mullainathan and Raghavan, 2017). The constitutional lesson is that algorithmic punishment cannot promise neutrality as a technical accomplishment. It must instead justify which trade-offs are chosen and why they are permissible under rights and equality norms. If the trade-offs are hidden inside thresholds and training data, the state is effectively legislating in code without democratic accountability.

Constitutional Accountability and the Problem of Ownerless Coercion

Punishment presupposes accountability. Yet algorithmic systems are produced by dispersed actors: vendors, data engineers, agencies, judges, and oversight bodies. Diffused contribution creates what responsibility scholars describe as accountability gaps—situations where harms occur but no single actor appears blameworthy enough or causally central enough to bear responsibility in the traditional sense (Fleisher, 2025). A constitutional theory treats this diffusion as unacceptable if it results in ownerless coercion: decisions that no one can meaningfully explain, correct, or take responsibility for.

This is why recent constitutional-oriented scholarship frames AI as a procedural due process problem when used to deprive life, liberty, or property, emphasising notice, hearing, and the ability to challenge the basis of the deprivation (Garrett, 2025). The point is not to ban automation. The point is to ensure that automation does not dissolve accountability by making reasons inaccessible and error untraceable.

The Interpretability Requirement as a Constitutional Posture

A mature constitutional theory cannot demand perfect transparency in every case. But it can demand something stricter than "some explanation": it can demand interpretability and auditability proportional to stakes. The argument for using inherently interpretable models in high-stakes contexts is therefore not merely technical; it is constitutional. If the state can achieve legitimate aims with auditable, interpretable systems, choosing an opaque black box is not innovation; it is avoidable degradation of contestability (Rudin, 2019).

Interpretability also disciplines moral reasoning. When the model's structure is visible, courts and publics can see the normative choices encoded in features and thresholds. When it is opaque, those choices hide behind authority and become difficult to contest even when they are morally objectionable.

A Constitutional Line-Drawing Framework

From these premises, the theory draws three kinds of lines. The first are Red Lines: domains where AI must never replace human judgement because replacement would destroy the constitutional functions of punishment. These include determinations of guilt and legal liability, credibility determinations that drive guilt, and the core justification of sentencing severity. Algorithmic inputs may inform these decisions, but the operative judgement and the reasons must remain human-authored and contestable.

The second are Bright Lines: conditions that must be satisfied before AI can influence liberty decisions such as bail or pretrial detention. At minimum, the person must be able to contest inputs, understand what is being predicted and what is not, and challenge thresholds as policy choices rather than as technical facts. Where those conditions cannot be met due to opacity or secrecy, algorithmic influence must be reduced to non-determinative assistance or excluded.

The third are Governance Lines: institutional requirements that transform "human in the loop" from a slogan into a constitutional reality. These include logging and versioning, independent audits, drift monitoring, documentation of training data and validation under conditions of use, and explicit accountability assignments so that the state cannot hide behind vendors or complexity.

This line-drawing posture aligns with emerging transnational governance instruments that frame AI lifecycle governance around human rights, democracy, and rule of law, including transparency and oversight obligations tailored to context and risk (Rotenberg, 2025). It also aligns with risk-based regulatory frameworks that treat certain uses in justice and law enforcement as high-risk and subject to stricter obligations (European

Union, 2024).

Conclusion: Algorithmic Punishment Is a Constitutional Choice About What Law Is

The constitutional theory offered here is not anti-AI. It is anti-substitution of public reason by private inference. It accepts that algorithms can assist courts in evidence management, in reducing noise, and in improving statistical discipline. It denies that algorithms may become the author of coercive reasons. The ultimate constitutional demand is simple: if the state punishes, it must be able to explain itself in human reasons, expose those reasons to challenge, and accept responsibility for error. A system that cannot do that may still function. It cannot credibly call itself a rule-of-law system of punishment.

References

- Ashworth, A. and Zedner, L. (2014) Preventive Justice. Oxford: Oxford University Press.
- Banks, I. (2026) 'Judges-in-the-loop? Judicial involvement in human oversight of high-risk decision support systems', International Journal of Law and Information Technology, advance online publication.
- Barocas, S. and Selbst, A.D. (2016) 'Big data's disparate impact', California Law Review, 104(3), pp. 671–732.
- Berk, R., Heidari, H., Jabbari, S., Kearns, M. and Roth, A. (2021) 'Fairness in criminal justice risk assessments: The state of the art', Sociological Methods & Research, 50(1), pp. 3–44.
- Chiao, V. (2024) 'Algorithmic decision-making, statistical evidence and the rule of law', Episteme, 21(4), pp. 1–23.
- Chouldechova, A. (2017) 'Fair prediction with disparate impact: A study of bias in recidivism prediction instruments', Big Data, 5(2), pp. 153–163.
- Cobbe, J. (2019) 'Judicial review of automated public-sector decision-making', Legal Studies, 39(4), pp. 636–655.
- Cooper, G.S., Meterko, V. and Dror, I.E. (2019) 'Cognitive bias research in forensic science: A systematic review', Forensic Science International, 297, pp. 35–46.

- Dawes, R.M., Faust, D. and Meehl, P.E. (1989) 'Clinical versus actuarial judgment', Science, 243(4899), pp. 1668–1674.
- Dietvorst, B.J., Simmons, J.P. and Massey, C. (2015) 'Algorithm aversion: People erroneously avoid algorithms after seeing them err', Journal of Experimental Psychology: General, 144(1), pp. 114–126.
- Duff, R.A. (2001) Punishment, Communication, and Community. Oxford: Oxford University Press.
- Edmond, G., Towler, A., Growns, B., Ribeiro, G., Found, B., White, D. and Ballantyne, K. (2015) 'Contextual bias and cross-contamination in the forensic sciences', Law, Probability and Risk, 14(1), pp. 1–25.
- Enqvist, L. (2023) 'Discretion, automation, and proportionality', in Suksi, M. (ed.) The Rule of Law and Automated Decision-Making: Exploring Fundamentals of Algorithmic Governance. Cham: Springer, pp. 169–205.
- Ensign, D., Friedler, S.A., Neville, S., Scheidegger, C. and Venkatasubramanian, S. (2018) 'Runaway feedback loops in predictive policing', Proceedings of Machine Learning Research, 81, pp. 1–12.
- Erickson, J. (2025) 'Against algorithmic clarity: Law beyond specification', Law and Philosophy, 44, pp. 1–28.
- Feeley, M.M. and Simon, J. (1992) 'The new penology: Notes on the emerging strategy of corrections and its implications', Criminology, 30(4), pp. 449–474.
- Fleisher, W. (2025) 'Responsibility and accountability in an algorithmic society', AI & Society, 40, pp. 1–16.
- Garrett, B.L. (2025) 'Artificial intelligence and procedural due process', Journal of Constitutional Law, 27(2), pp. 1–72.
- Gikay, A.A. (2025) 'Trade secrecy in automated decisions: Against the myth of a complete barrier to transparency', Journal of Intellectual Property Law & Practice, 20(8), pp. 552–565.
- Kahneman, D. (2011) Thinking, Fast and Slow. New York: Farrar, Straus and Giroux.
- Kinchin, N. (2024) '"Voiceless": The procedural gap in algorithmic justice', International Journal of Law and Information Technology, 32(4), pp. 1–30.
- Kleinberg, J., Mullainathan, S. and Raghavan, M. (2017) 'Inherent trade-offs in the fair determination of risk scores', Proceedings of the 8th Innovations in Theoretical Computer Science Conference (ITCS 2017), LIPIcs 67, Article 43.

- Koehler, J.J. (1996) 'The base rate fallacy reconsidered: Normative, descriptive and methodological challenges', Behavioral and Brain Sciences, 19(1), pp. 1–53.
- Logg, J.M., Minson, J.A. and Moore, D.A. (2019) 'Algorithm appreciation: People prefer algorithmic to human judgment', Organizational Behavior and Human Decision Processes, 151, pp. 90–103.
- Lyell, D. and Coiera, E. (2017) 'Automation bias and verification complexity: A systematic review', Journal of the American Medical Informatics Association, 24(2), pp. 423–431.
- Miller, T. (2019) 'Explanation in artificial intelligence: Insights from the social sciences', Artificial Intelligence, 267, pp. 1–38.
- Morrison, G.S. (2025) 'A guide to ISO 21043 forensic sciences from the forensic-data-science paradigm', Science & Justice, 65, 101298.
- Neil, R. (2025) 'Algorithmic bias in criminal risk assessment: The consequences of racial differences in arrest as a measure of crime', Annual Review of Criminology, 8, pp. 97–119.
- Oswald, M. (2018) 'Algorithm-assisted decision-making in the public sector', Philosophical Transactions of the Royal Society A, 376(2128), 20170359.
- Pleiss, G., Raghavan, M., Wu, F., Kleinberg, J. and Weinberger, K.Q. (2017) 'On fairness and calibration', Advances in Neural Information Processing Systems, 30.
- Presno Linera, M.Á. (2025) 'Regulating AI from Europe: A joint analysis of the AI Act and the Council of Europe AI Convention', Journal of Cross-Border Studies in Law and Technology, 3(1), pp. 1–25.
- Robertson, B., Vignaux, G.A. and Berger, C.E.H. (2016) Interpreting Evidence: Evaluating Forensic Science in the Courtroom. 2nd edn. Chichester: Wiley.
- Rotenberg, M. (2025) 'Framework Convention on Artificial Intelligence and Human Rights, Democracy and the Rule of Law (Council of Europe)', International Legal Materials, 64(—), pp. —.
- Rudin, C. (2019) 'Stop explaining black box machine learning models for high stakes decisions and use interpretable models instead', Nature Machine Intelligence, 1, pp. 206–215.
- Selbst, A.D. and Barocas, S. (2018) 'The intuitive appeal of explainable machines', Fordham Law Review, 87(3), pp. 1085–1139.
- Skitka, L.J., Mosier, K.L. and Burdick, M. (1999) 'Does automation bias decision-making?', International Journal of Human–Computer Studies,

51(5), pp. 991–1006.

- Stevenson, M.T. (2024) 'Algorithmic risk assessment in the hands of humans', American Economic Journal: Economic Policy, 16(1), pp. 1–32.
- Tyler, T.R. (2006) Why People Obey the Law. 2nd edn. Princeton, NJ: Princeton University Press.
- Tyler, T.R. (2011) 'Procedural justice, legitimacy, and the effective rule of law', Crime and Justice, 40(1), pp. 283–357.
- Williams, R. (2022) 'Accountable algorithms: Adopting the public law toolbox to scrutinise algorithmic decision-making', Current Legal Problems, 75(1), pp. 237–275.
-

CHAPTER XLIX

Institutional Design for Humane Prediction: Human Rights, Welfare, and Mercy

Humane Prediction As A Constitutional Aim

If prediction is going to live inside criminal justice, it must live there as a servant of humanity, not as a substitute for it. The first temptation of "data-driven justice" is to treat the system as a machine for minimizing harm, and to treat the person as a variable in that machine. The second temptation is to treat legality as a mere boundary condition for optimisation, rather than as the moral architecture of the enterprise. Humane prediction rejects both temptations. It treats prediction as an evidential tool that can sometimes reduce error and arbitrariness, while insisting that the system's legitimacy depends on public reasons, contestability, and the preservation of dignity at the point where the state restrains, condemns, or brands (Tyler, 2006; Tyler, 2011; Duff, 2001). It also recognises an institutional fact that is easily forgotten: the justice system is not a laboratory of clean signals; it is a social system with feedback loops, proxy labels, and coercive asymmetries. In such systems, prediction can become a generator of its own "evidence," and the human being can become the object of a self-confirming administrative gaze (Lum and Isaac, 2016; Ensign et al., 2018; Neil, 2025).

Institutional design is where the difference is made. You cannot "add mercy" to an algorithm after procurement. Mercy is not a parameter; it is a governance posture expressed through who gets heard, what kinds of reasons are admissible, how uncertainty is treated, and how the system allocates the burdens of error. The Council of Europe's AI Framework Convention places human dignity, transparency/oversight, accountability, and equality at the centre of AI lifecycle governance, making explicit that rights-consistency is the object of the enterprise rather than an afterthought. A humane prediction design must treat those ideas not as external compliance, but as internal operating rules for courts and justice agencies.

Welfare Logic, Penal Logic, And The Danger Of Administrative Mercy

A welfare system's failure mode is paternalism; a penal system's failure mode is cruelty; and a predictive system's failure mode is the quiet fusion of both into administrative mercy. The welfare-state literature around algorithmic governance illustrates this fusion in a way that is instructive for criminal justice. In the SyRI context, scholarship details how algorithmic fraud detection concentrated surveillance in disadvantaged communities and raised legality and arbitrariness concerns, and it became a landmark for how rights-based constraints can invalidate opaque risk profiling (van Bekkum et al., 2021; Rachovitsa, 2022; Wieringa, 2023). The moral lesson is not "welfare is not criminal justice." The moral lesson is that risk systems gravitate toward the poor, the visible, and the administratively legible, and they rationalise this gravitation as "efficiency." If such logics travel into criminal justice, humane prediction is not achieved by better calibration alone; it is achieved by institutional constraints that prevent predictive governance from becoming poverty management in legal disguise.

This is why humane prediction must be coupled to a theory of punishment and a theory of rights. Desert and communicative accounts remind us that punishment is not only harm prevention; it is condemnation addressed to an agent, requiring reasons that remain intelligible as moral justification rather than as actuarial management (Duff, 2001; von Hirsch and Ashworth, 2005). Prevention-based theories remind us that the state may act to prevent harm, but they also expose the ethical volatility of incapacitation when it becomes detached from culpability and proportionality (Ashworth and Zedner, 2014). A humane design accepts that the system will sometimes use predictive information, but it denies that prediction can become the reason for severity.

Mercy As Structure, Not Sentiment

Mercy is often mistaken for lenience, but institutionally it is better understood as a disciplined refusal to treat persons as exhausted by their risk profile. Mercy has three structural meanings in humane prediction. First, mercy is procedural. It insists that the person remains a participant who can speak, be heard, and contest the bases of state action. Procedural justice research repeatedly shows that legitimacy and compliance depend on voice, neutrality, respect, and trustworthy motives, and that these cues can matter even when outcomes are adverse (Tyler, 2011; Sunshine and Tyler, 2003). A predictive regime that reduces voice by converting hearings into score-confirmation rituals is not merciful even if it sometimes lowers sentences.

Second, mercy is epistemic. It insists on humility about what prediction can know. Risk scores are always claims under uncertainty. Forensic science has learned to treat inferential outputs as bounded by error and validity conditions rather than as truth, and that discipline is a blueprint for humane prediction: uncertainty must be part of the reason-giving culture, not hidden behind clean numbers (Robertson, Vignaux and Berger, 2016; Morrison, 2025). A merciful system does not punish uncertainty by defaulting to severity; it exposes uncertainty and insists on the least rights-restrictive response consistent with lawful aims.

Third, mercy is moral. It insists that rehabilitation, change, and context are not exceptions to be discounted; they are part of what the justice system is for. Therapeutic jurisprudence and problem-solving court scholarship shows how justice institutions can be designed to produce compliance through dignity and support rather than through surveillance alone (Wexler and Winick, 1996; Casey and Rottman, 2003). Humane prediction must be capable of supporting those designs rather than displacing them.

The Human Rights Skeleton Of Humane Prediction

A humane prediction regime needs a skeleton of rights that cannot be bargained away for efficiency. Across legal systems, the content is familiar even if doctrinal forms vary: legality, non-arbitrariness, non-discrimination, fair hearing, and effective remedy. The danger of AI in justice is not only error but also unreviewability: decisions that can be made faster than they can be challenged.

Two design imperatives follow. The first is contestability by construction. If a predictive tool influences liberty or punishment, the affected person must be able to challenge inputs, relevance, thresholds, and validation claims in adversarial form. When trade secrecy blocks that challenge, the system creates an equality-of-arms deficit that is not cured by saying "a human signed off." Scholarship on algorithmic justice highlights precisely how procedural protections can fail to reach the place where algorithmic power is actually exercised, creating a procedural gap (Kinchin,

2024).

The second is rights-sensitive transparency. Transparency is not the publication of code; it is the availability of sufficient information to contest and review. The SyRI scholarship and its broader welfare-state analysis shows how opacity and concentrated targeting can violate legality and arbitrariness constraints even when the system is presented as administratively rational (Rachovitsa, 2022; Wieringa, 2023). Humane prediction requires transparency that is action-enabling, not public-relations transparency that lists tools without exposing how they function in decisions.

Forensic Integrity: Prediction Must Behave Like Evidence

If a predictive output influences a legal decision, it must be treated as evidence-like rather than as administrative fact. That means the court must be able to ask forensic questions about the model's claim: what is being predicted, by what reference class, with what error behavior, and with what limits on inference. Criminological work warns that "rearrest" and similar targets can embed policing intensity, meaning that prediction may partly be prediction of institutional attention (Neil, 2025). Predictive policing research shows how feedback loops can create self-confirming patterns that look like accuracy but are actually enforcement reinforcement (Lum and Isaac, 2016; Ensign et al., 2018). A humane design therefore insists that predictive evidence is always accompanied by a provenance story: how the data were generated, how bias might be encoded, and how drift is monitored.

This is also where interpretability is not a technical preference but a humane constraint. The argument for using interpretable models in high-stakes decisions is that explanation after the fact is often weaker than transparency by design, and high-stakes governance should prefer systems that can be audited and contested without requiring faith in vendors (Rudin, 2019). Humane prediction is not "black box plus explanation"; it is "auditable system plus disciplined inference."

The Welfare Principle Inside Criminal Justice: Least Coercive Effective Means

A humane prediction regime imports one of welfare law's most valuable instincts into criminal justice: if the state can achieve its legitimate aim through less rights-restrictive means, it must do so. Predictive information should therefore be used primarily to allocate support and stabilisation, not merely to allocate coercion. A risk flag that only increases surveillance is a design that manufactures technical violations and then interprets them as character. A risk flag that triggers offers of treatment, housing support, or structured problem-solving oversight is a design that treats risk as a situation to stabilise rather than a person to manage.

This is not naïve optimism; it is institutional realism about behaviour. Deterrence and compliance are not purely functions of fear; they are shaped by legitimacy and procedural justice cues (Tyler, 2011). Supervision systems that are experienced as arbitrary or humiliating can generate defiance and disengagement, while systems that preserve voice and dignity can generate cooperation even under constraint (Sherman, 1993). Humane prediction therefore designs for compliance through respect rather than through prediction-driven escalation.

The Mercy Mechanism: Decision Ownership Must Be Protected

The AI era produces a specific accountability pathology: ownerless coercion. When a model recommends severity, humans can hide behind "the system," diffusing responsibility. Responsibility scholarship emphasises that algorithmic systems can create accountability gaps where harms occur without a clear locus of blame or duty (Fleisher, 2025). A humane design addresses this not by demanding heroic individual virtue, but by assigning institutional duties. Judges must remain responsible for reasons that are intelligible without "the model says." Agencies must remain responsible for validation, drift monitoring, and auditability. Vendors must remain responsible for documentation and disclosure sufficient for challenge. Oversight bodies must remain responsible for public reporting and remedy pathways. Humane prediction is therefore a constitutional ecology rather than a single tool.

Continuous Oversight As A Condition Of Mercy

Mercy is not only a moment at sentencing; it is also the discipline of preventing system drift from producing silent harm. Predictive systems change, contexts change, and institutions adapt. Continuous auditing—monitoring drift, subgroup impacts, and feedback loops—becomes a condition of humane prediction, because without it a system can degrade while still looking "objective." Public reporting is part of that mercy because it makes self-correction visible and therefore protects legitimacy. The Council of Europe's convention foregrounds transparency, oversight, accountability, and equality as lifecycle duties rather than as one-time checks. A humane regime treats these as governance habits: routine audits, independent review, and publication of meaningful metrics that allow democratic scrutiny.

Institutional Design: The Humane Default Settings

A humane prediction regime does not begin by asking where to deploy AI; it begins by asking what human values must remain non-negotiable in deployment. The institutional default settings are therefore strict.

The first default is that predictive tools must be support-forward, meaning their primary outputs are designed to allocate stabilising resources and to reduce unnecessary custody, not merely to intensify control. That is the welfare principle in penal form.

The second default is that predictive tools must be contestability-forward, meaning every liberty-affecting use is paired with disclosure of inputs, explanation of target meaning, error characteristics, and an avenue to challenge and correct. Without this, the procedural gap becomes permanent (Kinchin, 2024).

The third default is that predictive tools must be dignity-forward, meaning the courtroom encounter remains human, voice-driven, and reason-based, because legitimacy is built through procedural justice (Tyler, 2011).

The fourth default is that predictive tools must be equity-forward, meaning fairness trade-offs are made explicit as policy and subject to review, because fairness metrics conflict and the choice among them is normative (Chouldechova, 2017; Kleinberg, Mullainathan and Raghavan, 2017).

The fifth default is that predictive tools must be audit-forward, meaning drift, feedback loops, and subgroup harms are continuously monitored and publicly reported, because static validation is a legal fiction in dynamic systems (Gama et al., 2014; Ensign et al., 2018).

These defaults do not guarantee mercy. They make mercy institutionally possible.

Conclusion: Humane Prediction Is A Form Of Self-Restraint

Humane prediction is the justice system's choice to discipline its own power. It allows prediction to reduce certain kinds of error and arbitrariness while refusing to let prediction become the reason for severity or the substitute for hearing. It treats human rights not as external constraints but as the internal logic of legitimacy. It treats welfare not as softness but as the principle of least coercive effective means. It treats mercy not as sentiment but as structure: contestability, humility about uncertainty, and decision ownership that cannot be outsourced.

In that sense, institutional design for humane prediction is not about building kinder algorithms. It is about building a justice system that remains capable of mercy in the only way that matters: by continuing to see persons as more than their predicted futures (Duff, 2001; Tyler, 2011; Wexler and Winick, 1996).

References

- Ashworth, A. and Zedner, L. (2014) Preventive Justice. Oxford: Oxford University Press.
- Barocas, S. and Selbst, A.D. (2016) 'Big data's disparate impact', California Law Review, 104(3), pp. 671–732.
- Berk, R., Heidari, H., Jabbari, S., Kearns, M. and Roth, A. (2021) 'Fairness in criminal justice risk assessments: The state of the art', Sociological Methods & Research, 50(1), pp. 3–44.
- Casey, P.M. and Rottman, D.B. (2003) 'Problem-solving courts: Models and trends', Justice System Journal, 24(1), pp. 35–56.
- Chiao, V. (2024) 'Algorithmic decision-making, statistical evidence and the rule of law', Episteme, 21(4), pp. 1–23.
- Chouldechova, A. (2017) 'Fair prediction with disparate impact: A study of bias in recidivism prediction instruments', Big Data, 5(2), pp.

153–163.

- Dawes, R.M., Faust, D. and Meehl, P.E. (1989) 'Clinical versus actuarial judgment', Science, 243(4899), pp. 1668–1674.
- Dietvorst, B.J., Simmons, J.P. and Massey, C. (2015) 'Algorithm aversion: People erroneously avoid algorithms after seeing them err', Journal of Experimental Psychology: General, 144(1), pp. 114–126.
- Duff, R.A. (2001) Punishment, Communication, and Community. Oxford: Oxford University Press.
- Ensign, D., Friedler, S.A., Neville, S., Scheidegger, C. and Venkatasubramanian, S. (2018) 'Runaway feedback loops in predictive policing', Proceedings of Machine Learning Research, 81, pp. 1–12.
- Feeley, M.M. and Simon, J. (1992) 'The new penology: Notes on the emerging strategy of corrections and its implications', Criminology, 30(4), pp. 449–474.
- Fleisher, W. (2025) 'Responsibility and accountability in an algorithmic society', AI & Society, 40, pp. 1–16.
- Gama, J., Žliobaitė, I., Bifet, A., Pechenizkiy, M. and Bouchachia, A. (2014) 'A survey on concept drift adaptation', ACM Computing Surveys, 46(4), Article 44.
- Garland, D. (2001) The Culture of Control: Crime and Social Order in Contemporary Society. Oxford: Oxford University Press.
- Kahneman, D. (2011) Thinking, Fast and Slow. New York: Farrar, Straus and Giroux.
- Kinchin, N. (2024) '"Voiceless": The procedural gap in algorithmic justice', International Journal of Law and Information Technology, 32(4), pp. 1–30.
- Kleinberg, J., Mullainathan, S. and Raghavan, M. (2017) 'Inherent trade-offs in the fair determination of risk scores', Proceedings of the 8th Innovations in Theoretical Computer Science Conference (ITCS 2017), LIPIcs 67, Article 43.
- Koehler, J.J. (1996) 'The base rate fallacy reconsidered: Normative, descriptive and methodological challenges', Behavioral and Brain Sciences, 19(1), pp. 1–53.
- Lum, K. and Isaac, W. (2016) 'To predict and serve?', Significance, 13(5), pp. 14–19.
- Lyell, D. and Coiera, E. (2017) 'Automation bias and verification complexity: A systematic review', Journal of the American Medical Informatics Association, 24(2), pp. 423–431.

- Morrison, G.S. (2025) 'A guide to ISO 21043 forensic sciences from the forensic-data-science paradigm', Science & Justice, 65, 101298.
- Neil, R. (2025) 'Algorithmic bias in criminal risk assessment: The consequences of racial differences in arrest as a measure of crime', Annual Review of Criminology, 8, pp. 97–119.
- Pasquale, F. (2015) The Black Box Society: The Secret Algorithms That Control Money and Information. Cambridge, MA: Harvard University Press.
- Pleiss, G., Raghavan, M., Wu, F., Kleinberg, J. and Weinberger, K.Q. (2017) 'On fairness and calibration', Advances in Neural Information Processing Systems, 30.
- Rachovitsa, A. (2022) 'The human rights implications of the use of AI in the digital welfare state: The SyRI case', Human Rights Law Review, 22(2), ngac010.
- Robertson, B., Vignaux, G.A. and Berger, C.E.H. (2016) Interpreting Evidence: Evaluating Forensic Science in the Courtroom. 2nd edn. Chichester: Wiley.
- Rudin, C. (2019) 'Stop explaining black box machine learning models for high stakes decisions and use interpretable models instead', Nature Machine Intelligence, 1, pp. 206–215.
- Sherman, L.W. (1993) 'Defiance, deterrence, and irrelevance: A theory of the criminal sanction', Journal of Research in Crime and Delinquency, 30(4), pp. 445–473.
- Sunshine, J. and Tyler, T.R. (2003) 'The role of procedural justice and legitimacy in shaping public support for policing', Law & Society Review, 37(3), pp. 513–547.
- Tyler, T.R. (2006) Why People Obey the Law. 2nd edn. Princeton, NJ: Princeton University Press.
- Tyler, T.R. (2011) 'Procedural justice, legitimacy, and the effective rule of law', Crime and Justice, 40(1), pp. 283–357.
- van Bekkum, M., Borgesius, F.J.Z. and others (2021) 'Digital welfare fraud detection and the Dutch SyRI judgment', European Journal of Social Security, 23(4), pp. 1–22.
- von Hirsch, A. and Ashworth, A. (2005) Proportionate Sentencing: Exploring the Principles. Oxford: Oxford University Press.
- Wexler, D.B. and Winick, B.J. (1996) Law in a Therapeutic Key: Developments in Therapeutic Jurisprudence. Durham, NC: Carolina Academic Press.

- Wieringa, M. (2023) '"Hey SyRI, tell me about algorithmic accountability": Lessons from a landmark case', Data & Policy, 5, e2.
- Williams, R. (2022) 'Accountable algorithms: Adopting the public law toolbox to scrutinise algorithmic decision-making', Current Legal Problems, 75(1), pp. 237–275.
-

CHAPTER L

The Future of Criminal Law: Rebuilding Legitimacy in the Age of AI

The Real Crisis Is Not Accuracy, It Is Authority

The criminal law is entering an era in which the state can predict more, measure more, and compute more than ever before. Yet the coming crisis is not a deficit of calculation. It is a deficit of authority. Authority, in the criminal law's constitutional sense, is not the power to compel compliance by fear. It is the power to condemn and restrain while still being able to say, with credibility, "This coercion is justified by reasons you could, in principle, contest." That credibility is what legitimacy is made of, and legitimacy is not a decorative ideal; it is the background condition that makes a justice system governable at scale (Tyler, 2006; Tyler, 2011).

AI presses on legitimacy at exactly the pressure points where modern criminal law is already fragile. It compresses human beings into probability statements; it shifts the grammar of justification from reasons to outputs; it risks moving decisions from adversarial contestation into proprietary infrastructure; and it creates the seductive impression that the moral work of judgment can be replaced by predictive optimisation. The paradox is that the system may become "more accurate" in a narrow statistical sense and still become less legitimate, because legitimacy depends on intelligible reasons, voice, neutrality, and dignity, not only on outcomes (Sunshine and Tyler, 2003; Tyler, 2011).

If you want a future criminal law that does not collapse into technocratic administration, you must rebuild legitimacy as an institutional project. That project will not be accomplished by declaring "human in the loop," because hybrid human–machine systems can exacerbate both human and machine error, while adding new failure modes that neither side understands well (Banks, 2026). The future will be decided by design choices about what counts as evidence, how reasons are formed, what can be challenged, and where the state draws bright lines against delegating condemnation.

The Predictive Turn And The Quiet Transformation Of Punishment

The predictive turn does not arrive with a single statute. It arrives by accumulation: risk tools in bail, actuarial assessments in sentencing, algorithmic triage in prosecution, pattern recognition in forensic workflows, and now generative tools that summarise facts, suggest arguments, and draft reasons. The system gradually learns to treat prediction as a form of prudence and to treat numerical outputs as the safest ground for decisions under public scrutiny. In that drift, punishment subtly changes its nature.

Punishment, classically understood, is a communicative act. It addresses the offender as an agent and expresses censure in a way that is supposed to be publicly justified and proportionate (Duff, 2001). When sentencing becomes increasingly organised around predicted risk, punishment becomes less a response to wrongdoing and more an instrument of preventive management. Preventive logics have always existed, but they carry special burdens because they strain proportionality, individualisation, and the distinction between what a person did and what the state fears they might do (Ashworth and Zedner, 2014). The predictive turn threatens to normalise preventive governance by dressing it as neutral science.

This is where fairness research becomes constitutional rather than technical. If base rates differ and prediction is imperfect, attractive fairness properties cannot all be satisfied simultaneously, meaning that every predictive system embodies normative trade-offs about who bears false positives and false negatives (Chouldechova, 2017; Kleinberg, Mullainathan and Raghavan, 2017; Pleiss et al., 2017). If those trade-offs are hidden inside thresholds and vendor design, the state is effectively legislating in code without democratic accountability. The public then experiences punishment not as reasoned condemnation but as opaque allocation of risk.

Legitimacy As A Psychological Fact: Why Courts Lose People Before They Lose Cases

A future criminal law must take seriously the most empirically robust claim in legitimacy scholarship: people obey and cooperate not only because of deterrence, but because authorities are experienced as legitimate through procedural justice cues—voice, neutrality, dignity/respect, and trustworthy motives (Tyler, 2011). If AI changes the encounter so that the person feels processed rather than heard, or judged by secret reasons, the institution's authority erodes even when the "results" look efficient.

This is not speculation. Empirical work on perceptions of judicial AI use indicates that legitimacy and fairness perceptions are sensitive to whether and how AI is involved in decisions, and that the public's trust can be shaped by the perceived role of AI in the courtroom (Fine, Berthelot and Marsh, 2025). The implication is not that courts must follow public mood. It is that legitimacy is built through recognisable procedural signals, and any technology that disrupts those signals will require compensating institutional design or it will be experienced as disrespectful governance.

You can see the same lesson from within the judiciary. Recent qualitative work on judges' experiences with machine-based sentencing shows the tension in their own terms: sentencing is experienced as a human process, and the presence of machine inference reshapes autonomy, responsibility, and the meaning of judgment (Dagan, Baron and Kaplan-Damary, 2026). When judges themselves experience a change in the moral texture of sentencing, legitimacy problems are not far behind, because legitimacy depends on decision ownership and reason-giving that remains human-authored and contestable.

Evidence, Explanation, And The Procedural Gap

The future of criminal law will be determined less by what AI can do and more by what the legal system can challenge. A justice system remains legitimate when it can say: "Here is what we relied upon, here is why, and here is how you may contest it." Algorithmic systems strain this because they often provide outputs without providing contestable grounds.

The procedural gap critique captures the core danger: algorithmic justice may respond strongly to distributive concerns and metrics while leaving procedural justice—especially "voice"—thin, which manifests across accountability mechanisms and legal frameworks (Kinchin, 2024). In practice, the gap becomes visible as a familiar courtroom pathology: the defence is invited to argue against an output without being given access to what produced it, or without being given enough information to test error behaviour, relevance, and limits. That is not adversarial justice. It is a hearing around an unchallengeable influence.

Recent peer-reviewed work explicitly frames this as "due process by design," arguing that procedural justice principles offer a basis for building trust in AI decision-making, and that the right to be heard—so central to due process—is often overlooked in AI governance discussions (Fischman-Afori, 2025). This matters because the right to be heard is not satisfied by a microphone; it is satisfied when the person's participation can affect the decision by challenging the reasons. If AI is used in a way that makes reasons inaccessible or non-actionable, the hearing becomes ceremonial.

A future criminal law that rebuilds legitimacy must therefore adopt a forensic posture toward algorithmic outputs. In forensic science, outputs are treated as evidence-like claims whose probative value depends on validation under conditions of use, transparent uncertainty, and disciplined interpretation (Robertson, Vignaux and Berger, 2016; Morrison, 2025). Risk scores, pattern classifiers, and probabilistic tools must be treated the same way: bounded, audited, and contestable. Probability can inform; it must not become proof.

Institutional Design For A Legitimacy-Centered Criminal Law

If legitimacy is to be rebuilt, it must be engineered. The future criminal law will need institutions that make three commitments operational: contestability, dignity, and accountable authorship.

Contestability requires that when AI materially influences liberty or punishment, the accused can challenge inputs, relevance, thresholds, and validation claims. That does not always require publishing source code, but it does require functional access sufficient for adversarial testing. Where proprietary secrecy blocks such access, the system must reduce AI's role to non-determinative assistance or exclude it from liberty-affecting decisions, because equality of arms cannot survive secret reasons.

Dignity requires that the courtroom encounter remains human in the only way that matters: the person experiences voice, respect, and neutrality as real. This is not achieved by adding a polite interface. It is achieved by hearing structures that prevent algorithmic anchoring from dominating the early framing of the case, by sequencing that protects interpretive integrity, and by reason-giving norms that forbid "the model says" from becoming the decisive justification.

Accountable authorship requires that judges and institutions remain able to own the moral work of decisions. This is where "judges-in-the-loop" is both promising and dangerous. Banks' analysis shows that making judges responsible for human oversight of high-risk judicial decision support systems raises serious questions about skills, motivations, and biases, and about who else must share oversight responsibilities (Banks, 2026). A legitimacy-centered future cannot rely on individual heroism. It must distribute oversight across independent audits, drift monitoring, public reporting, and institutional checks that make responsibility traceable.

Bright Lines That Protect The Moral Core Of Criminal Law

Rebuilding legitimacy also requires what legal systems have always used to protect foundational values: bright lines. A legitimacy-centered theory must insist that AI must never replace human judgment at the points where condemnation becomes morally meaningful and where contestability is essential.

Guilt determination and the core adjudication of liability cannot be delegated to machine inference because guilt is not a prediction problem; it is a legal conclusion governed by burdens of proof, credibility assessment, and normative judgment. Sentencing severity cannot be delegated because severity is a moral response to culpability and must remain grounded in human reasons that can be appealed. Pretrial liberty cannot be made a function of a score because the presumption of innocence cannot survive when freedom becomes a forecast default. Credibility determinations cannot be mechanised because testimony is a human communicative act embedded in context, and mechanisation invites false certainty and bias laundering.

These bright lines do not ban assistance. They prohibit substitution. They protect the distinction between prediction and judgment, between evidence and proof, between management and condemnation. In doing so, they preserve what is uniquely legal about criminal law: the demand that power answer to reasons.

The Future: From Efficiency Legitimacy To Constitutional Legitimacy

It is easy to predict the political future of AI in criminal justice. Institutions will continue to adopt tools because backlogs exist, caseloads exist, and public pressure rewards speed. The question is whether criminal law will accept an "efficiency legitimacy," where the state claims authority because it is fast and consistent, or whether it will rebuild a "constitutional legitimacy," where the state claims authority because its coercion remains publicly justifiable, contestable, and human-authored.

The path to constitutional legitimacy will look, at first, less glamorous than AI marketing. It will look like record integrity, disclosure rules, audit rights, interpretable systems where stakes are high, structured reason-giving, judicial statistical literacy, procedural justice training, and independent oversight that cannot be outsourced to vendors. It will look like due process by design rather than due process by rhetoric (Fischman-Afori, 2025). It will also look like an honest admission: prediction can support justice only when institutions discipline prediction.

The future of criminal law, then, is not the elimination of discretion, nor the worship of human intuition. It is the reconstruction of legitimacy under new informational power. If the system can keep reasons human, keep evidence testable, keep procedures dignified, and keep coercion accountable, AI can become a tool of justice. If it cannot, AI will become the quiet mechanism by which punishment ceases to be law and becomes administration.

References

- Ashworth, A. and Zedner, L. (2014) Preventive Justice. Oxford: Oxford University Press.
- Banks, I. (2026) 'Judges-in-the-loop? Judicial involvement in human oversight of high-risk decision support systems', International Journal of Law and Information Technology, advance online publication.
- Barocas, S. and Selbst, A.D. (2016) 'Big data's disparate impact', California Law Review, 104(3), pp. 671–732.
- Berk, R., Heidari, H., Jabbari, S., Kearns, M. and Roth, A. (2021) 'Fairness in criminal justice risk assessments: The state of the art', Sociological Methods & Research, 50(1), pp. 3–44.
- Chiao, V. (2024) 'Algorithmic decision-making, statistical evidence and the rule of law', Episteme, 21(4), pp. 1–23.
- Chouldechova, A. (2017) 'Fair prediction with disparate impact: A study of bias in recidivism prediction instruments', Big Data, 5(2), pp. 153–163.

- Cobbe, J. (2019) 'Judicial review of automated public-sector decision-making', Legal Studies, 39(4), pp. 636–655.
- Cooper, G.S., Meterko, V. and Dror, I.E. (2019) 'Cognitive bias research in forensic science: A systematic review', Forensic Science International, 297, pp. 35–46.
- Dagan, N., Baron, S. and Kaplan-Damary, N. (2026) 'Sentencing as a human process? Human judges' experiences of machine-based sentencing', The British Journal of Criminology, advance online publication.
- Dawes, R.M., Faust, D. and Meehl, P.E. (1989) 'Clinical versus actuarial judgment', Science, 243(4899), pp. 1668–1674.
- Dietvorst, B.J., Simmons, J.P. and Massey, C. (2015) 'Algorithm aversion: People erroneously avoid algorithms after seeing them err', Journal of Experimental Psychology: General, 144(1), pp. 114–126.
- Duff, R.A. (2001) Punishment, Communication, and Community. Oxford: Oxford University Press.
- Enqvist, L. (2023) 'Discretion, automation, and proportionality', in Suksi, M. (ed.) The Rule of Law and Automated Decision-Making: Exploring Fundamentals of Algorithmic Governance. Cham: Springer, pp. 169–205.
- Ensign, D., Friedler, S.A., Neville, S., Scheidegger, C. and Venkatasubramanian, S. (2018) 'Runaway feedback loops in predictive policing', Proceedings of Machine Learning Research, 81, pp. 1–12.
- Erickson, J. (2025) 'Against algorithmic clarity: Law beyond specification', Law and Philosophy, 44, pp. 1–28.
- Feeley, M.M. and Simon, J. (1992) 'The new penology: Notes on the emerging strategy of corrections and its implications', Criminology, 30(4), pp. 449–474.
- Fine, A., Berthelot, E.R. and Marsh, S. (2025) 'Public perceptions of judges' use of AI tools in courtroom decision-making: An examination of legitimacy, fairness, trust, and procedural justice', Behavioral Sciences, 15(4), 476.
- Fischman-Afori, O. (2025) 'Due process by design: Enhancing fairness and trust in AI decision-making', Artificial Intelligence and Law, 33(—), pp. 1–—.
- Fleisher, W. (2025) 'Responsibility and accountability in an algorithmic society', AI & Society, 40, pp. 1–16.

- Garrett, B.L. (2025) 'Artificial intelligence and procedural due process', University of Pennsylvania Journal of Constitutional Law, 27(2), pp. 1–72.
- Gigerenzer, G. and Hoffrage, U. (1995) 'How to improve Bayesian reasoning without instruction: Frequency formats', Psychological Review, 102(4), pp. 684–704.
- Jackson, J., Bradford, B., Stanko, E. and Hohl, K. (2012) 'Legitimacy, trust and compliance: An empirical test of procedural justice theory using the European Social Survey', in Tankebe, J. and Liebling, A. (eds) Legitimacy and Criminal Justice: An International Exploration. Oxford: Oxford University Press, pp. 326–352.
- Kahneman, D. (2011) Thinking, Fast and Slow. New York: Farrar, Straus and Giroux.
- Kinchin, N. (2024) '"Voiceless": The procedural gap in algorithmic justice', International Journal of Law and Information Technology, 32(4), pp. 1–30.
- Kleinberg, J., Mullainathan, S. and Raghavan, M. (2017) 'Inherent trade-offs in the fair determination of risk scores', Proceedings of the 8th Innovations in Theoretical Computer Science Conference (ITCS 2017), LIPIcs 67, Article 43.
- Koehler, J.J. (1996) 'The base rate fallacy reconsidered: Normative, descriptive and methodological challenges', Behavioral and Brain Sciences, 19(1), pp. 1–53.
- Logg, J.M., Minson, J.A. and Moore, D.A. (2019) 'Algorithm appreciation: People prefer algorithmic to human judgment', Organizational Behavior and Human Decision Processes, 151, pp. 90–103.
- Lum, K. and Isaac, W. (2016) 'To predict and serve?', Significance, 13(5), pp. 14–19.
- Lyell, D. and Coiera, E. (2017) 'Automation bias and verification complexity: A systematic review', Journal of the American Medical Informatics Association, 24(2), pp. 423–431.
- Miller, T. (2019) 'Explanation in artificial intelligence: Insights from the social sciences', Artificial Intelligence, 267, pp. 1–38.
- Morrison, G.S. (2025) 'A guide to ISO 21043 forensic sciences from the forensic-data-science paradigm', Science & Justice, 65, 101298.
- Neil, R. (2025) 'Algorithmic bias in criminal risk assessment: The consequences of racial differences in arrest as a measure of crime', Annual Review of Criminology, 8, pp. 97–119.

- Pleiss, G., Raghavan, M., Wu, F., Kleinberg, J. and Weinberger, K.Q. (2017) 'On fairness and calibration', Advances in Neural Information Processing Systems, 30.
- Robertson, B., Vignaux, G.A. and Berger, C.E.H. (2016) Interpreting Evidence: Evaluating Forensic Science in the Courtroom. 2nd edn. Chichester: Wiley.
- Rudin, C. (2019) 'Stop explaining black box machine learning models for high stakes decisions and use interpretable models instead', Nature Machine Intelligence, 1, pp. 206–215.
- Sunshine, J. and Tyler, T.R. (2003) 'The role of procedural justice and legitimacy in shaping public support for policing', Law & Society Review, 37(3), pp. 513–547.
- Tyler, T.R. (2006) Why People Obey the Law. 2nd edn. Princeton, NJ: Princeton University Press.
- Tyler, T.R. (2011) 'Procedural justice, legitimacy, and the effective rule of law', Crime and Justice, 40(1), pp. 283–357.
- Wieringa, M. (2023) '"Hey SyRI, tell me about algorithmic accountability": Lessons from a landmark case', Data & Policy, 5, e2.
- Williams, R. (2022) 'Accountable algorithms: Adopting the public law toolbox to scrutinise algorithmic decision-making', Current Legal Problems, 75(1), pp. 237–275.

Epilogue

A court is not a laboratory. I do not mean that courts should be anti-science. I mean something more precise: the courtroom is a moral institution before it is a technical one. It is the place where the state speaks in its most intimate voice—where it touches liberty, dignity, reputation, family, livelihood, and future. In a laboratory, error is a pathway to learning. In a courtroom, error is a wound, often irreversible, sometimes generational. The ethical grammar is different. So when we introduce algorithmic systems into criminal justice, the first question is not "Does it improve prediction?" but "What kind of institution does it turn the court into?"

Across these pages I have argued that the deepest risk is not that machines will replace judges. It is that the language of judgment will quietly change—until "reasons" become recitations of outputs, until "consistency" becomes a substitute for justification, and until accountability dissolves into a chain of procurement decisions, model updates, vendor clauses, and institutional habits that nobody can truly explain in court. This is how legitimacy dies in modern systems: not with a collapse, but with a drift. You will notice, if you look back, that I repeatedly return to ordinary words: authority, explanation, contest, harm. I do so because the law is built on ordinary words that must remain usable by ordinary people. The rule of law is not an internal achievement felt by institutions; it is a public condition experienced by persons. The moment an accused person cannot understand what has been said about them, or cannot practically challenge it, we have crossed a line—whether or not the model is "accurate," whether or not the dashboard is "efficient."

There is a temptation—particularly among the competent—to believe that better models will resolve these tensions. Better calibration, better fairness metrics, better documentation, better oversight boards. These matter, but they do not reach the heart of the problem. Criminal justice is not a domain of pure optimisation because punishment is not a domain of pure optimisation. The state cannot justify coercion simply because the numbers are favourable. Even a perfectly performing model would not answer the question: who has the moral right to decide, on what grounds, in what language, and with what capacity for the citizen to resist? This is why I insist on a forensic posture. In forensic practice, we do not worship instruments. We do not fear them either. We ask disciplined questions:

What is this thing? Under what conditions does it perform? What is the known error? What contaminates it? What assumptions does it smuggle? What is the provenance? Can it be independently tested? Can it be challenged meaningfully in adversarial conditions? Most importantly—can we speak honestly about its limits without pretending those limits do not matter?

If you have worked in investigations, you know that contamination is rarely dramatic. It is usually procedural. A label applied too early. A witness shaped by questioning. A file that becomes a theory. A theory that becomes a conclusion. Algorithmic systems introduce a new contamination pathway: the institutional habit of letting outputs harden into narrative. Once a system says "high risk," the mind begins to interpret everything through that frame. The number does not merely inform; it organises perception. That is not a failure of character. It is a predictable feature of human cognition. Which is why "human in the loop" is not enough. The loop must be disciplined. The human must be trained to resist the seduction of numerical certainty.

There is also a temptation among the anxious to declare that courts must reject algorithmic tools entirely. I understand the impulse. But a blanket refusal is not the way constitutionalism survives modernity. The way it survives is by turning power into answerability—by building procedures that force authority to explain itself, to disclose its grounds, to accept challenge, and to be corrected. When we refuse to engage, the tools arrive anyway, in quieter forms—through administrative guidance, police intelligence systems, pretrial triage, probation assessments, parole risk calculators, and sentencing support templates that influence "human discretion" without leaving a clean footprint in the record. Prohibition without governance often produces opacity, not protection. So I end where I began: with line drawing. If you are a judge, your task is not to become a technologist. Your task is to protect the moral integrity of reasons. You must insist that any tool relied upon can be intelligibly explained in court, contested in practice, and situated within lawful authority. You must resist the soft coercion of "consistency" when it is offered at the cost of individualised justice. Your duty is not to be modern. Your duty is to be answerable.

If you are a lawyer, your task is to make the invisible contestable. Ask not only "What did the court decide?" but "What shaped the decision?" Demand disclosure of the model's role, the inputs, the validation, the limitations, the governance, the audit, and the human reliance. Develop a literacy that allows you to cross-examine a system without pretending it is mystical. And remember: the most dangerous tool is not the one that is openly presented as decisive, but the one quietly treated as "background information" while it steers the human mind. If you are an administrator or policymaker, your task is governance before glamour. Procurement is constitutional. Vendor contracts are constitutional. Audit regimes are constitutional. Training is constitutional. When you buy a tool for a court, you are not buying software; you are reshaping the conditions of liberty. Do not outsource accountability. Do not accept opacity as "intellectual property." Do not treat periodic reports as meaningful oversight. Create real contestability pathways and independent audit authority with power, not symbolism.

If you are a student, understand this: you are entering a profession at a time when the temptation to mechanise judgment will be strong. You will be told that what cannot be quantified cannot be trusted, and that what is quantified is therefore neutral. Resist both errors. The law's greatness, when it is great, is that it can live with uncertainty without surrendering dignity. It can discipline power without pretending power is perfect. It can punish without denying humanity. You must learn to think in a way that protects those virtues—especially when the screen looks persuasive. I have spoken throughout about harm, but I want to name one harm that is often overlooked: the harm done to the moral character of institutions. A court that cannot explain itself becomes a court that cannot morally stand. A legal system that replaces reasons with outputs becomes a system that can no longer teach citizens what justice means. It may still function. It may still convict. It may still punish. But it will no longer be recognisable as a moral authority. It will be mere management.

And yet, I remain guardedly hopeful. Not because technology is benevolent, but because law—when practiced with courage—has an old skill: it can tame power. It can force the powerful to speak in public, under challenge, with reasons. It can turn the invisible into the arguable. It can insist that even modern instruments must submit to ancient demands: that coercion must be justified, that persons must be heard, and that decisions must remain answerable in human language. If we do this well, we can still use tools without becoming tools. We can still seek consistency without surrendering mercy. We can still learn from data without allowing data to define the person. We can still modernise without mechanising the soul of justice. That is where I leave you: not with certainty, but with a discipline.

Draw the line. Then defend it.

www.ingramcontent.com/pod-product-compliance
Lightning Source LLC
LaVergne TN
LVHW100246210926
848480LV00003B/844